THE CRIMINAL LAW OF GENOCIDE

INTERNATIONAL AND COMPARATIVE CRIMINAL JUSTICE

Series Editors:

Mark Findlay, *Institute of Criminology, University of Sydney*
Ralph Henham, *Nottingham Law School, Nottingham Trent University*

This series explores the new and rapidly developing field of international and comparative criminal justice and engages with its most important emerging themes and debates. It focuses on three interrelated aspects of scholarship which go to the root of understanding the nature and significance of international criminal justice in the broader context of globalization and global governance. These include: the theoretical and methodological problems posed by the development of international and comparative criminal justice; comparative contextual analysis; the reciprocal relationship between comparative and international criminal justice and contributions which endeavor to build understandings of global justice on foundations of comparative contextual analysis.

Other titles in the series:

Restorative Justice: Ideals and Realities
Margarita Zernova
ISBN 978 0 7546 7032 2

The Crime of Destruction and the Law of Genocide
Their Impact on Collective Memory
Caroline Fournet
ISBN 978 0 7546 7001 8

The Genocide Convention: An International Law Analysis
John Quigley
ISBN 978 0 7546 4730 0

A World View of Criminal Justice
Richard Vogler
ISBN 978 0 7546 2467 7

Punishment and Process in International Criminal Trials
Ralph Henham
ISBN 978 0 7546 2437 0

The Criminal Law of Genocide
International, Comparative and Contextual Aspects

Edited by

RALPH HENHAM
Nottingham Law School, UK

and

PAUL BEHRENS
University of Leicester, UK

ASHGATE

Published by
Ashgate Publishing Limited
Wey Court East
Union Street
Farnham
Surrey GU9 7PT
England

Ashgate Publishing Company
Suite 420
101 Cherry Street
Burlington, VT 05401-4405
USA

Ashgate website: http://www.ashgate.com

British Library Cataloguing in Publication Data
The criminal law of genocide : inernational, comparative
   and contextual aspects. - (International and comparative
   criminal justice)
   1. Genocide 2. Trials (Genocide) 3. International offenses
   I. Henham, Ralph J., 1949- II. Behrens, Paul
   345'.0251

Library of Congress Cataloging-in-Publication Data
The criminal law of genocide : international, comparative, and contextual aspects / edited by
Ralph Henham and Paul Behrens.
     p. cm. -- (International and comparative criminal justice)
   Includes index.
   ISBN 978-0-7546-4898-7
   1. Genocide. 2. International criminal courts. I. Henham, Ralph J.,
1949- II. Behrens, Paul.

   K5302.C75 2007
   345'.0251--dc22

2006039320

ISBN 978 0 7546 4949 7

Reprinted 2009

Mixed Sources
Product group from well-managed
forests and other controlled sources
www.fsc.org Cert no. SA-COC-1565
© 1996 Forest Stewardship Council
FSC

Printed and bound in Great Britain by
MPG Books Ltd, Bodmin, Cornwall.

Contents

Notes on Contributors

Alex Bates is a criminal barrister with 10 years experience of major criminal prosecution and defence cases. In 2002, he was appointed Junior Counsel to the Crown, Attorney General's Panel of Prosecution Advocates. In May 2003, he became the youngest ever International Prosecutor at the United Nations Interim Administration Mission in Kosovo (UNMIK). In 2005, he completed an LLM in International Human Rights and Humanitarian Law at Lancaster University, researching the challenges of prosecuting genocide. Mr Bates is currently Senior Assistant Co-Prosecutor to the United Nations Assistance Mission to the Khmer Rouge Tribunal, based in Phnom Penh, Cambodia.

Paul Behrens is a Lecturer at the University of Leicester. He studied law and history in Germany and England and has worked in the past, *inter alia*, for the European Communities Committee of the House of Lords, London. In 2001, he was awarded an LLM. for a thesis on diplomatic law by the University of Birmingham. Mr Behrens has published articles on international criminal law and international humanitarian law and is currently completing a PhD thesis on diplomatic law.

Shivon Byamukama completed her LLB at Makerere University, Uganda and her Bar Course at the Law Development Centre, Kampala, Uganda in 2003. She then worked with the Ministry of Commerce and the National Bureau of Standards in Rwanda where her main duties concerned legislative drafting. In 2004, she won a research scholarship from Glasgow Caledonian University to pursue PhD research on 'The legal aspects of Gacaca tribunal jurisdiction and the Reconciliation process in Rwanda'. Ms Byamukama is a member of the Ugandan Bar.

Sadi Cayci, Associate Professor, Colonel, Military Judge (Retired), is currently International Law Advisor at the Centre for Eurasian Strategic Studies (ASAM), Ankara, Turkey. He retired from the Turkish Armed Forces, when he was the legal adviser to the Chief of the Turkish General staff. His special areas of interest are national security, law of the armed conflict, countering terrorism, and international criminal law. As a Lecturer, he continues his activities both in Turkey and abroad, which will include being a Course Director for the International Military courses on the Law of Armed Conflict, held at the International Institute of Humanitarian Law, Sanremo, Italy.

Roméo Dallaire, Lieutenant-General, can look back on a career of 35 years in the military. During this time, he occupied a variety of commands at national and international levels, and became one of Canada's most respected soldiers. In 1994, he led the UN mission in Rwanda. His book, *Shake Hands With the Devil*, an account of his experiences during the 1994 genocide, has received the prestigious Governor

General's Literary Award for Non-Fiction for 2004. He was summoned to the Senate of Canada on 24 March 2005.

Shahram Dana is an Assistant Professor of Law at Maastricht University (Netherlands) and was previously a legal officer at the UN International Criminal Tribunal for the Former Yugoslavia (ICTY). He teaches human rights, international criminal law, international humanitarian law, European and comparative criminal law, and international dispute settlement. His research interests include international prosecutions in the context of international politics and power, ethics and justice in international decision-making, and normative foundations of international legal order. Currently, he focuses on the philosophy, legality, and methodology of international punishment by international criminal courts with a view towards developing an integrative theory that reinforces the values of humankind and the aims of international prosecutions. He has written and lectured extensively on these topics.

Fiona de Londras is a graduate of University College Cork, Ireland (BCL (hons), LLM (hons)). She is currently reading for a PhD in the capacity of international human rights law to be a controlling force in domestic counter-terrorism legislation, and is an NUI travelling PhD Student (2005–2008) and President's Research Scholar (2005–2008). She is a part-time Lecturer in Griffith College Dublin and has held visiting positions in University of Peshawar (Pakistan) and the Feminism and Legal Theory Project (Emory University).

Caroline Fournet obtained a Master of International Law with distinction from the Raoul Wallenberg Institute of Human Rights and Humanitarian Law in Lund, Sweden for a thesis entitled 'Nuremberg and its Aftermath: Accountability for Crimes Against Humanity – Case Study: France'. In 2003, she obtained her PhD at the University of Leicester on a thesis entitled: 'Crimes Against Humanity: The Accumulated Evil of the Whole'. After an internship at the Association for the Prevention of Torture, a non-governmental organization based in Geneva, she was appointed as a Lecturer at Exeter University's School of Law.

Chris Gallavin (LLB First hons cant, PhD Hull) is a Lecturer of Law at the School of Law, University of Canterbury, New Zealand where he is also Director of the LLM in International Law and Politics. Dr Gallavin is a former Lecturer of the University of Hull. He currently teaches criminal law and evidence at Canterbury. His PhD focused on Prosecutor Discretion in the International Criminal Court.

Ralph Henham is the leader of the British Academy project on the Criminal Law of Genocide. He is also one of the founders of the International and Comparative Criminal Trial Project, in whose framework the research initiative 'The Criminal Law of Genocide' was conducted. He has worked for the Nottingham Law School since 1979. In 1998, he was appointed Professor of Criminal Justice at Nottingham Trent University. Professor Henham was recently awarded a visiting Fellowship at the Centre for Criminology, University of Oxford to pursue research on sentencing in international criminal trials.

John A. Kapranos Huntley is a Professor of Law at Glasgow Caledonian University, Scotland.

Michael G. Karnavas is a Criminal Defence Lawyer with over 20 years of experience. He has worked as State and Federal Public defender in Alaska, USA. Before the ICTY, Karnavas was Lead Counsel during the trial phase for Vidoje Blagojević. He is currently Lead Counsel for Dr. Jadranko Prlić at the ICTY, while also serving as President of the Association of Defence Counsel-ICTY.

Zachary D. Kaufman (BA Yale, M. Phil. Oxford) is a Juris Doctorate (JD) candidate at Yale Law School while he is also completing his DPhil (PhD) in International Relations at the University of Oxford, where he is a Marshall Scholar. Mr Kaufman has worked on transitional justice issues while serving at the US Departments of State and Justice, the UN International Criminal Tribunals for Rwanda and the former Yugoslavia, and the International Criminal Court. Mr Kaufman founded and leads two non-profit organizations that are helping to build Rwanda's first public library. He is also a Board Member and Senior Fellow of Humanity in Action. During 2005–2006, Mr Kaufman was a Fellow at Stanford University's Center on Democracy, Development, and the Rule of Law.

Henry T. King, Jr., was a Prosecutor at the Nuremberg Trials, and a Chairman of the Section on International Law and Practice of the American Bar Association. He served as a member of the ABA Task Force on War Crimes in the Former Yugoslavia. He has published over 70 articles on international legal subjects and a book on one of the Nuremberg defendants, entitled *The Two Worlds of Albert Speer*. On 4 June 2002, Professor King was awarded an honorary degree of Doctor of Civil Laws by The University of Western Ontario. In 2003, he was made an honorary member for life of the Canadian Bar Association. Henry King is Professor of Law at the Case Western University.

Kishan Manocha studied medicine and subsequently trained in psychiatry, working for a year as a Research Fellow in Forensic Psychiatry at the University of London; he is also Member of the Royal College of Psychiatrists of the UK. In 1999, he switched to law and obtained a BA and an LLM (specializing in international law and with First Class Honours) from Cambridge University. In 2003, he worked for a spell at the Special Court for Sierra Leone, and between January and March 2005, he was General Roméo Dallaire's Research Assistant at the Carr Centre for Human Rights at Harvard. Kishan Manocha was called to the Bar in 2004 and commenced pupillage at 25 Bedford Row, a leading criminal chambers in London, in October 2006.

Juan E. Méndez is the first United Nations Special Adviser on the Prevention of Genocide. As a result of his involvement in representing political prisoners in

Argentina, he was arrested by the military dictatorship of that country and adopted by Amnesty International as a 'Prisoner of Conscience'. He was General Counsel of Human Rights Watch from 1994 and President of the Inter-American Commission on Human Rights from 2002. Mr Méndez is currently president of the International Center for Transitional Justice. Juan Méndez is the recipient of several human rights awards, a member of the bar of Mar del Plata and Buenos Aires, Argentina, and the District of Columbia, US.

Paul Ng'arua is a Senior Trial Attorney at the International Criminal Tribunal for Rwanda. Mr Ng'arua was called to the bar in Kenya in 1990. From 1998 to 2002, he was Director of Prosecutions of the Kingdom of Swaziland. Ng'arua is currently in charge of the prosecution of the Interim Government of Rwanda in a case which received the name 'Government II'. In 2004, he received the Special Achievement award for Prosecutors by the International Association of Prosecutors.

Tonja Salomon was called to the Berlin Bar in 2006. She is currently working as a criminal defence lawyer in Berlin. She studied law in Potsdam and Barcelona. In 2005, she worked for the Appeals Section of the Prosecution at the International Criminal Tribunal for Rwanda.

Raffi Sarkissian is Chairman of the Campaign for Recognition of the Armenian Genocide, a UK-based single-issue pressure group established in 1994 (www.crag. org.uk), involved in public speaking and author of several articles on Current Affairs and the Armenian Genocide. Mr Sarkissian served as Chairman of the Armenian Community and Church Council in the UK (1997–2002) and was a founding member of The Forum of Armenian Associations of Europe (Geneva, 1999). Raffi Sarkissian obtained BSc in Electrical & Electronic Engineering and MSc in Digital Systems and Instrumentation in the UK. He is the head of Manufacturing Operations at Learning Technology PLC (Viglen Limited).

William A. Schabas is Professor of Human Rights Law at the National University of Ireland, Galway, where he is also Director of the Irish Centre for Human Rights. He is the author of one of the principal texts (*Genocide in International Law: The Crime of Crimes*) on the subject of genocide, and his writings have been frequently cited by the Trial and Appeals Chambers of the International Criminal Tribunal for the Former Yugoslavia. He served as one of the international members on the Sierra Leone Truth and Reconciliation Commission.

Tuiloma Neroni Slade was the Presiding Judge of Pre-Trial Chamber II of the International Criminal Court from 2003 to 2006. He was formerly Attorney-General of Samoa. From 1993 until 2003, he was Ambassador to the USA and Samoa's Permanent Representative at the United Nations in New York. Judge Slade was closely involved with the processes for the development of the International Criminal Court, as head of the Samoan delegations to the negotiations, a Vice-President of the Rome Conference in 1998 and Coordinator for the Preamble and Final Clauses of the draft Statute of the Court.

Larissa van den Herik is Lecturer in international law at Leiden University. Her PhD Thesis, for which she received the Bulthuis van Oosternielandprize, is titled *The Contribution of the International Criminal Tribunal for Rwanda to the Development of International Law* (Martinus-Nijhoff). She is the editor-in-chief of the *Leiden Journal of International Law*. Until 2005, Dr van den Herik was a Researcher and Lecturer at the Free University, Amsterdam.

Sten Verhoeven obtained a Candidate in Law degree from the Katholieke Universiteit Brussels with distinction in 1999. He continued his legal studies at the Katholieke Universiteit Leuven, where he received his law degree with distinction in 2002. During 2002–2003, he studied International Relations and Conflict Prevention at the same university. He participated twice in the Jessup International Law Moot Competition for the Katholieke Universiteit Leuven. From October 2003, he has been Assistant at the Institute for International Law at the KU Leuven. Sten Verhoeven is currently working on a PhD thesis on the sources of international law.

Jan Wouters was Legal Adviser to the Belgian Minister of Finance in 1989 and Law Clerk at the Court of Justice of the European Communities from 1991 to 1994. From 1997 to 2003, he was Professor of European Banking and Securities Law at Maastricht University. From October 1998, he has been Professor of International Law and the Law of International Organisations, Director of the Institute for International Law and Chairman of the International Relations Council at the Katholieke Universiteit Leuven.

Preface

When knowledge of the atrocities of the National Socialist regime spread, there was a feeling among contemporary observers that they were faced with a phenomenon that was poorly addressed by the existing rules of international law. In those days, Winston Churchill felt that the world was in the presence of a 'crime without a name'. And in those days, Raphael Lemkin, a Polish lawyer who had lost 49 members of his family in the Holocaust, gave a name to the crime. It was in his seminal book *Axis Rule in Occupied Europe* (1943/1944) that the term 'genocide' made its first appearance; the root of a concept on which this current collection of scholarly writings is based.

Lemkin was convinced that the appearance of this crime predated the Holocaust. Today, it is necessary to acknowledge that the crime did not disappear when the gates of Auschwitz were opened. The criminal tribunals which deal with genocide today investigate its occurrence in the Cambodia of Pol Pot, in the Rwanda of 1994, in the territory of the Former Yugoslavia, in East Timor and in Iraq under Saddam Hussein. The question of genocide in Darfur has given rise to a variety of conflicting assessments. The legal evaluation of the crimes and the ways which are open to the international community to prevent and to counteract it, are topics which remain, unfortunately, of burning relevance.

In 2004, the Nottingham Law School started a research initiative, which endeavoured to investigate the crime of genocide. The project, entitled 'The Criminal Law of Genocide – International, Comparative and Contextual Aspects' intended to analyse the phenomenon of genocide not only from the perspective of international criminal law. Its aim was the adoption of a contextual view, which would embrace an examination of the historical, political and social conditions and influences on the crime and the repercussions of its commission in these fields.

In the framework of this initiative, an International Conference on Genocide was convened in September 2005 which brought together some of the foremost authorities on international criminal law, including judges and practitioners from all three international criminal tribunals. Over the course of two days, a variety of aspects of the crime were debated, and scholarly papers on selected problems were presented. Most of the chapters in this book are based on these contributions, which have been carefully revised and edited to present a topical work which fulfils high standards of academic quality.

The Criminal Law of Genocide is presented in five sections. The first part deals with the evolution of the crime and its codifiction and includes two very different perspectives of the Armenian events in 1915 as well as a chapter by a former Prosecutor at the Nuremberg Trials, who had met Raphael Lemkin in the course of his work. In the second part, a variety of case studies are presented – the particular focus here is on Darfur, but this section also includes a contribution on Rwanda, co-written by the former Head of the UN Mission to that country. The third part deals with particular elements of genocide, which allows a better understanding of the concept of the crime. The fourth part, entitled 'International and Domestic Prosecution of Genocide' contains a review of the ways in which various tribunals have approached genocide, written by academics and practitioners in the field (including a former Judge of the International Criminal Court). The fifth part deals with the prevention of genocide, alternative justice resolutions and sentencing and includes a contribution by the first UN Special Adviser on the Prevention of Genocide.

Our thanks go to all authors who have contributed to this unique collection of writings on genocide. We would also like to thank the British Academy whose funding has made the project on the Criminal Law of Genocide possible.

Ralph Henham
Paul Behrens
Nottingham, October 2007

PART I

HISTORICAL PERSPECTIVES

Chapter 1

The Armenian Genocide: A Contextual View of the Crime and Politics of Denial

'Dedicated to the 90th Anniversary of
the Armenian Genocide'

Raffi Sarkissian

From Genocide to Holocaust

The Armenian Genocide of 1915 occurred less than 30 years before the Jewish Holocaust. Adolf Hitler knew very well of how the world quickly forgot the Armenians. Hitler drew comparisons between the Armenian Genocide and what he was planning, using it as a means to encourage his followers. He said, 'I have given the command – and I shall shoot everyone who utters one word of criticism, for the goal to be obtained in the war is not that of reaching certain lines but of physically demolishing the opponent. Accordingly, I have put my death-head formations in place with the command for them to send to death relentlessly and without compassion, many men, women and children of Polish origin and language. Only thus shall we gain the living space that we need. Who after all is today speaking of the destruction of the Armenians?' (Adolf Hitler, 1939).[1]

Twenty-five years earlier on 29 September 1915, Turkish minister of the interior, Talat Pasha conveyed to the Governor of Aleppo '... all of the Armenians living in Turkey are to be destroyed and annihilated ... Without taking into consideration the fact that they are women and children and disabled, their very existence will be ended, regardless of how terrible the means of destruction may be, and without being moved by feeling of compassion.'

Before World War I and after Turkish military officers of Union and Progress (Ittihad ve Taraghy) took power in Turkey, they established an alliance with Germany. They were widely referred to as 'Young Turks' who proved to be capable of using violence in order to achieve their goals.

---

1 Modern History Sourcebook: Adolf Hitler, the Obersalzberg Speech. www.fordham.edu/halsall/mud/hitler-obersalzberg.html/

At the beginning of WWI the Young Turks devised a plan that on the surface aimed to modernize Turkey whereas in reality the intention was to cleanse Turkey of Armenians, Greeks, and other minorities. The nation was mobilized to exterminate the Armenian population of Eastern Anatolia through systematic, premeditated and coordinated efforts that began in 1914 and were accelerated over the following years. Through secret orders Armenian men were rounded up and sent into forced labour for the building of the Trans-Turkish railways. The government then ordered the mass execution of Armenian political leaders and intellectuals of Constantinople in April 1915. Women and children were also uprooted and driven into the desert under the guise of resettlement and often without food or shelter.

In discussing the doom of 'two million or more Armenians' slated for wholesale 'deportation', Ambassador Morgenthau observed, 'As a matter of fact, the Turks never had the slightest idea of re-establishing the Armenians … When the Turkish authorities gave the order for these deportations, they were merely giving the death warrant to a whole race; they understood this well, and, in their conversation with me, they made no particular attempt to conceal the fact'[2]. In other words, from the very outset the genocidal intent was there; the respective decision was firm and implacable. The German state archives, containing a vast amount of wartime confidential and secret reports from German ambassadorial, consular, and military officials stationed in Turkey during the war as that country's allies, amply and unmistakably attest to this fact.[3]

The process of humiliation and dehumanization of Armenians throughout the campaign was reported through several western foreign officials and missionaries. They contributed towards the extensive evidence based upon which the Armenian genocide was acknowledged at the time as 'crime against humanity' and more recently recognized by several countries and parliaments.[4]

The first attempt to establish an international criminal court was made on 24 May 1915, accompanied by the suggestion that massacres of ethnic minorities within a State's own borders might give rise to both State and individual responsibility. The joint declaration by governments of Great Britain, France and Russia, asserting that 'in the presence of these new crimes of Turkey against humanity and civilisation, the allied Governments publicly inform the Sublime Porte that they will hold personally responsible for the said crimes all members of the Ottoman Government as well as those of its agents who are found to be involved in such massacres'.

After the fall of the Ittihadist government and as the First World War came to an end, most of the senior Ittihad leaders found refuge in Germany. The new Turkish Government arrested several of Ittihad party leaders who were suspected of direct involvement in the deportations and annihilation of Armenians, preparing cases

---

2   Morgenthau, and Ambassador, 'The Murder of A Nation', Chapter XXIV; http://www. lib.byu.edu/~rdh/wwi/comment/morgenthau/Morgen24.htm.

3   Dadrian, V.N. (1994), 'Documentation of the Armenian Genocide in German and Austrian Sources', in *Widening Circle of Genocide: A Critical Bibliographic Review*, 3 Charny, I. (ed.) (New Brunswick, NJ: Translation), pp. 104–107.

4   Dadrian, V.N. (2004), 'Patterns of Twentieth Century Genocides: The Armenian, Jewish, and Rwandan cases' 6(4) *Journal of Genocide Research* 487.

against them for criminal offences under Turkish law. A series of trials followed during the 1918–1920 Armistice period resulting in an important catalogue of confessions, secret party orders and papers providing evidence of the tactics and of means employed by the Ittihadist leaders in their campaign for annihilation of the Armenians.

During the trials, Yözgat Deputy Sakir personally testified to the fourth sitting of the Yözgat trial series (11 February 1919) that the orders for 'massacre' were relayed 'secretly'. Secret wire evidence was introduced at the ninth (22 February 1919) and twelfth (6 March 1919) sittings of the same trial series to substantiate the charge of the secret intent of massacre underlying the entire system of deportations. During a debate in the Chamber of Deputies on the Armenian massacres, Trabzon Deputy Hafiz Mehmet declared that he and other deputies had known for a long time that the government had ordained the program of extermination of Armenians, relying chiefly on the Special Organisation for its implementation (Teshkilate Mahsuse).[5]

The aforesaid trials were strongly contested by the Turkish nationalist movement, who opposed the prosecutions, symbolizing them as foreign efforts aimed at dismembering Turkey. What followed under the leadership of Mustapha Kemal resulted in delays and obstructions of Turkey's criminal prosecutions, providing opportunities for destruction of evidence, the escape of those on trial, as well as wide spread demonstrations and public unrest. Furthermore, due to the rivalry of Britain, France and USA for the potential that Turkey offered of opportunities in oil and other valuable resources as well as Kemal's ability to exploit this opportunity, the international treaties that followed, particularly the conditions set forth by treaty of Serves of 1920, did not result in justice for the Armenians. In the mid-1920, a political officer at the British High Commission in Istanbul cautioned London of practical difficulties involved in prosecuting Turks for the Armenian massacres, including obtaining evidence. By late 1921, the British had negotiated a prison exchange agreement with the Turks resulting in the release of and the genocide suspects held in Malta.[6] This failure went on to have substantial effect on the course of history and the developments towards World War II, Nazis and the Holocaust.

Attempts by Turkish jurists to press for trial before the national courts of those responsible for the atrocities were slightly more successful. Prosecuted on the basis of the domestic penal code, several ministers in the wartime cabinet and leaders of the Ittihad party were found guilty by a court martial, on 5 July 1919, of 'the organisation and execution of crime of massacre' against the Armenian minority. The guilty, main architects of the genocide Talaat Pasha, Minister of the Interior and Enver Pasha, Minister of War were sentenced, *in absentia*, to capital punishment. Further trials were conducted before other Ottoman courts, partly on the basis of Article 171 of the Ottoman military code concerning the offence of plunder of goods, and invoking 'the sublime precept of Islam' as well as 'humanity and civilisation' to condemn 'the crimes of massacre, pillage and plunder'. These trials resulted in the conviction

---

5   Dadrian, V.N. (1991), *Documentation of the Armenian Genocide in Turkish Sources*, (New York: State University of New York at Geneseo), pp. 96–100.

6   Schabas, W.A. (2000), *Genocide in International Law*, (Cambridge: Cambridge University Press).

and execution of three of the perpetrators, Mehmed Kemal (county executive of Bogazhya), Abdullah Avni (of the Erzincan gendarmerie), and Behramzade Nusret (Bayburt county executive and District Commissioner Ergani and Urfa (Edessa)).[7]

The Armenian genocide could have easily been extended to include the Ottoman Jews. The Jewish population of Yishu were well aware they were next in line for a Turkish genocide. Indeed, during the spring of 1916, the order for their expulsion from Jaffa was a distinct possibility. Due to the intervention of the US and German consuls with the Turkish Government in Jerusalem the plan was halted thus avoiding the same fate that befell the Armenians.[8]

In drawing parallels and similarities between the Armenian genocide and the Holocaust, the most significant reason appears to be that both Armenians and Jews were despised minorities undergoing rapid social mobilization and adaptation to the modern world, under the regimes of the Ottoman Empire and Imperial Germany respectively. In addition both imperial regimes were swept away by revolution and war, as well as being succeeded by revolutionary vanguards who became the perpetrators of the two genocides; finally, both genocides occurred in the middle of major wars.[9]

The fact that the Armenian Genocide had been so readily forgotten contributed to the failure of the European Jewish Community to notice the early activities leading to Hitler's final solution. More importantly, perhaps, the close alliance of Ottoman Turkey and Germany at the time, as well as the propagation of ideologies based on the belief of racial supremacy in the former and in its more extreme sense fascism in the latter, are further reminders that at the time of war, or whenever the opportunity may be considered favourable, the threat imposed by the ruling majority may culminate in the extermination of national minorities.

Recognition of the Armenian Genocide and Politics of Denial

The ample existence of documentary evidence on the genocide of Armenians and the research material published later in the twentieth century, as well as the effort of international scholars, Armenian institutions and individuals, the responsibility of recognizing the crime became the subject of discussion at various international forums. Since April 1965, several parliaments, legislative bodies and assemblies have recognized the Armenian Genocide. In the case of France (2001) denial of the Armenian Genocide is considered a crime and therefore protected by law. On 18 January 2001 the French National Assembly – resisting intense pressure from the Turkish Government – adopted a measure publicly recognizing the Armenian Genocide. According to National Assembly Representative Francois Rochebloine,

---

7   de Zayas, A. (2004), *The Genocide against the Armenians 1915–1923*.

8   Auron, Y. (2000), *The Banality of Indifference: Zionism and the Armenian Genocide*, (Place: Transaction Books).

9   Melson, R. (1988), 'Revolutionary Genocide: On the Causes of the Armenian Genocide of 1915 and The Holocaust', Purdue University, Remembering for the Future, The impact of the Holocaust on the Contemporary World, Theme II, papers presented at the International Scholars' Conference Oxford, 10–13 July.

recognition of the Armenian Genocide opens the door to 'respect for human rights and the establishment of trust' between Turkey and its neighbours.

In the days leading up to the vote, Turkish Government officials applied heavy pressure to the Administration of the French President Jacques Chirac and members of the French Assembly, threatening those Franco-Turkish relations would suffer if the Armenian Genocide resolution was approved. Following the adoption of the measure, the Turkish Government condemned the vote, stating that a 'serious and lasting' blow had been dealt to bilateral relations. The Turkish Ambassador to France was immediately recalled for 'consultations'. According to Agence France Presse, the head of the Turkish trade chamber called for a boycott of French goods in retaliation to the Armenian Genocide vote. However, the Turkish co-chairman of the Turco-French Business Council denounced moves of immediate economic retaliation. 'We should not act hastily. It is easy to spoil relations, but rebuilding them is difficult', he noted.

In addition an assembly of over 20 international historians acknowledged the truth of the Armenian Genocide in 2001. Polish, German and Lithuanian Parliaments are the most recent in joining the ranks of progressive governments who acknowledge historical truth without diverting their attention and becoming entangled in politics of Denial. Furthermore, in June 2005, The International Association of Genocide Scholars wrote to the Prime Minister of Turkey, R.T. Erdogan, stating that ... 'We note that there may be differing interpretation of genocide – how and why the Armenian Genocide happened, but to deny its factual and moral reality as genocide is not to engage in scholarship but in propaganda and efforts to absolve the perpetrator, blame the victim, and erase the ethical meaning of this history' ... .

In the UK, the City of Edinburgh Council officially recognized the Armenian Genocide on 17 November 2005, this followed a lengthy debate with presentations made by deputations from Turkish organizations with arguments against the motion and an Armenian deputation headed by Campaign for Recognition of the Armenian Genocide (Edinburgh and London chapters), which consisted of personal family testimonies, historical, legal and political arguments in favour of the motion, presented by Dr Hagop Bessos, Dr Donald Bloxham and Dr Harry Hagopian respectively.

Despite an intensive campaign and attempts by Turkish organizations and its embassy in London to block the motion, after a few postponements the council continued with its agenda resulting in a clear majority vote in favour of the motion. The motion states:

> This Council notes that a number of Parliaments around the world have recognized, as genocide, events that began in Anatolia in 1915, including, most recently, an 82% vote in favour of recognition in the European Parliament on 28 September 2005. Council also notes that recognition was acknowledged when Edinburgh hosted the UK's Annual Holocaust Memorial Day in 2003.

> Council recognizes that atrocities and tragedies occurred on all sides in the conflicts which began in 1915, but supports the view that the Ottoman actions against the Armenian community did constitute genocide.

Council welcomes Turkey's application for membership of the European Union and supports dialogue and reconciliation between the Turkish and Armenian peoples. Council does not support the view that genocide recognition should be made a condition for membership of the European Union.

Given the recent successes and the progress made in Recognition of Armenian Genocide, and during 2005, the 90th Anniversary, the Turkish Government (following the steps of its predecessors) has intensified its efforts in denying the reality of the genocide. Having exhausted its resources for denial, it is beginning to take contradictory actions by undermining its integrity and credibility.

In May 2005, the first all-Turkish Conference on 'The Armenian Issue' due to take place at Bogazici University from 25 to 27 May was 'postponed' after justice minister Cemil Çiçek accused the organizers of treason. This unique conference jointly organized by history departments of Bogazici and Sabanci as well as Comparative Literature department of Bilgi universities under the title of 'Ottoman Armenians during the decline of the Empire: Issues of Scientific Responsibility and Democracy' had created a vast interest with 26 distinguished academics on the organizing and consulting committees from Turkey, Germany, USA and France.

'The emergence of different and critical opinions will be to Turkey's benefit, because it will show how rich in pluralist thinking Turkish society actually is.' The press release stated, 'Today, 90 years after the tragic 1915 incidents, it's time for Turkey's people of science and thought to jointly raise their voices differing from the official thesis' on the Armenian killings.

It was precisely this aspect of the conference that appeared to arouse the suspicion of what Turks call the 'deep state' – the entrenched statist-nationalist establishment comprising conservative members of Turkey's state bureaucracy, judiciary and military. Such an open manifestation of intellectual dissent prompted an immediate and forceful response from leading representatives of 'deep state' thinking.[10]

Çiçek condemned the initiative as a blow to government efforts to counter a growing Armenian campaign to have the killings recognized internationally as genocide, which many fear may cloud Turkey's bid to join the European Union. 'This is a stab in the back of the Turkish nation … this is irresponsibility', Anatolia quoted Çiçek as saying at a parliament debate.

Critical opinions do exist in Turkey. Some 110 academics and the respected Turkish Economic and Social Studies Foundation have already voiced their opposition to the official policy of genocide denial. But the government is trying to silence this real opposition by creating myths of treason and of being stabbed in the back. Further, two local NGOs – the Izmir Contemporary Attorneys' Association and Izmir Human Rights Association – filed charges with the Supreme Court of Appeals against Justice Minister Çiçek, claiming he had violated several articles of the Turkish Constitution. Çiçek's remarks were truly outrageous but unfortunately the pressure exerted resulted in postponement of the conference. The postponement resulted in a wave of criticism within Turkey as well as the EU and the USA. Turkish Government once again realized that restricting freedom of thought and expression

---

10 Torbakov, I. (2005), 'Postponement of History Conference Sparks Controversy in Turkey'. Eurasianet.org, 14 June.

may have detrimental effect on their application for EU accession, and after several articles and criticisms the conference was given the green light.

The policy of denial and misrepresenting historical documents clearly manifests itself in a recent publication by The Turkish Historical Society (*Türk Tarih Kurumu, THS*) the Armenians: Expulsion and Migration (*Ermeniler: Sürgün ve Göc*) (Ankara, 2004), by Hikmet Özdemir, Kemal Çiçek, Ömer Turan, Ramazan Çalik and Yusuf Halaçoglu. According to Taner Akçam (University of Minnesota, USA), the contents as well as the meaning of some of the German and American documents have been obviously distorted to conform to the thesis of the book. This distortion takes six different forms:

1. Glaringly incorrect translations;
2. Alteration of information, including numbers;
3. Omission of words or sentences which would weaken or refute their claims;
4. Summarising or paraphrasing of certain documents for which complete, accurate, and literal translation was claimed;
5. Summarising and paraphrasing in such a way as to invert the ideas and opinions of the person cited; and
6. Selective quotation of diplomats whose statements, in their proper context, had the opposite import … the THS and these five writers have distorted and misrepresented original foreign archival documents. It is critical that the English-speaking public and the academic community be aware of the lengths to which the Turkish State and 'official state employees' will go to manipulate public opinion.[11]

It is therefore not surprising to note that a close association exists between the denialist camp, the Turkish military and government agencies. The military exerts enormous influence on political developments and is opposed to a public discussion of sensitive historical issues.

A single example of this is offered as evidence: the report by Walter Rössler, German Consul in Aleppo, dated December 20, 1915.

The Turkish authors have put words in the mouth of the German Consul in Aleppo, Walter Rössler, altogether misrepresenting his point of view. Here is a lengthy section from the Turkish authors (pp. 105–106):

> Throughout the course of the First World War approximately 500,000 Armenians were deported to areas, currently located in Syria and Iraq, which were not war zones at the time. During this same period somewhere between 350,000 and 500,000 Armenians went, for a variety of reasons, from the regions of Eastern Anatolia and the Black Sea to the Caucuses. If we take into account that in the course of the events of World War I a total of around 200,000 Armenians lost their lives and that somewhere between 400,000 and 500,000 Armenians remained within the borders of the Ottoman Empire, and if we keep in mind that the total Armenian Population within the empire at the outset of the war was around 1.5 million, then our figures would appear to provide a complete accounting. At

---

11 Akçam, T., (2005), 'Anatomy of a crime: the Turkish Historical Society's manipulation of archival documents' 7(2) *Journal of Genocide Research*, 255.

the end of 1915, the German Consul Rössler confirmed our above account when he wrote, 'that nearly 500,000 Armenians were exempted from deportation, and 500,000 [others] were brought to Mesopotamia and Syria' (Emphasis by Taner Akçam.)

What is understood by reading the previous paragraph? The authors claim that Rössler shares their estimates and confirms their figures. Now let's read Rössler's own account:

> The Loss of human life is greater or less according to the region from which those who have been dispatched have come. In eastern Asia Minor [the loss] is by large much greater than in the western [portion]. In the East countless convoys have been at least 75% decimated, unless the women and girls have been carried off to Muslim Harems or, in the best case, they have found refuge among Muslim families. Those who did arrive in Mesopotamia (for instance, Ras ul-Ain or Tel Abiad) were so exhausted that a great portion of them also subsequently succumbed. Under these circumstances, from the outset one would not venture to dispute the number of 800,000 Armenians killed that was published by the English side.[12]

Rössler also supplies a passage taken from the *Frankfurter Zeitung* stating that:

> No one who is familiar with the circumstances in Turkey will believe this figure. If one accepts this figure [it would mean that] more than 30% of all of those Armenians living in Turkey – women and children included – would have been killed. That is entirely out of the question.[13]

To which he responds, 'Unfortunately, it is not out of the question. I have over the past months again and again reported on this most gruesome state of affairs and dreadful conditions, which either brought about or accompanied the massacre. It is [therefore] reasonable to conclude that after such events the number of those who have perished must be extraordinarily high.'[14] Later on in his report Rössler provides his own figures:

---

12 PA-AA, / R14089/MF7136/98-71371/11.
'Je nach den Gegenden, aus denen die Verschickten kommen, ist der Verlust an Menschenleben grosser oder geringer gewesen. Im östlichen Kleinasien im grossen und ganzen seht viel grosser als im weslichen. Im Osten warden von zahlreichen Zügen 75% umgekommen sein, soweit nicht Frauen und Mädchen in muhammedanische Haremsverschleppt worden sind oder in günstigeren Fällen in muhammedanischen Familien Schutz gefunden haben. Die in Mesopotamien (z.B. Ras ul Ain oder Tell Abiad)angekommen Reste waren derart erschöpft, dass ein sehr grosser Teil von ihnen auch noch erlegen ist. Unter diesen Umständen erscheint es gewagt, die von englischer Seite veröffentlichte Zahl von 800,000 gotötetn Armenier als von vornherein unmöglich zu bekämpfen.'
13 'Niemand wird an diese Zahl glauben, der die Verhältnisse in der Türkei kennt. Mit dieser Zahl wären über 30% aller in der Türkei lebeden Armenier einschliesslich Frauen und Kinder getötet. Das ist ganz ausgeschlossen.'
14 '... leider is es nicht ausgeschlossen. Über die Vorkommnisse und Zustände der grauenhaftesten Art, die Vernichtung herbeigeührt order begleitet haben, habe ich in den letzten Monaten wieder und immer wieder berichtet. Der Schluss ist zulässig, dass nach solchen Vorkommnissen die Zahl der Umgekommenen ausserordentlich hoch sein muss.'

The total number of Armenians in Turkey, 2½ million ... The number of those in all of Asia Minor [who have been] exempted from the deportations is ½ million at the very most ... no more than ½ million have arrived in Syria and Mesopotamia ... The mortality rate among those who have arrived in Syria and Mesopotamia is extraordinarily high and will remain so for quite some time, as a direct consequence of the deportation, whose end is still nowhere in sight. Under these circumstances, it would seem that the total number of 800,000 deaths, which is [given] by those circles who can be taken seriously and who may be better informed than others, is to be deemed as authentic, and it is not beyond the realm of possibility that the [actual] figure is much higher.[15]

Considering the evidence, can anyone really claim that Rössler's account 'confirms' that of Çiçek and company?

Taner Akçam provides several examples to substantiate the above, concluding that the book contains numerous intentional distortions of data-tactics, which are very difficult to reconcile with the idea of academic honesty. In light of the numerous deliberate alterations of data presented in the review article Dr Akçam firmly asserts – using the most polite expression possible – that the Turkish Historical Society and its authors have violated the 'sense of trust' that is the necessary basis for relations among scholars. By systematically 'doctoring' the data of many of the documents they have used, the authors of *Ermeniler: Sürgün ve Göc* have violated the rule of academic honesty and in the process have completely obliterated their own credibility and that of the Turkish Historical Society. Dr Akçam concludes by stating '*Ermeniler: Sürgün ve Göc* is an intellectual crime, not only against the Turkish academic community, but also against the international community of scholars.'

We also note an alarming article in the Turkish Penal code (Article 301) – one that has remained on the Turkish statute book despite many pressures against it – criminalizing any mention of the Armenian Genocide which renders any statement about this genocide punishable under Turkish law. This clampdown on the fundamental freedom of expression and movement is being manifested in other nefarious ways too, by an oppressive judicial discrimination and public vilification against Turkish historians, writers and publishers (the likes of Taner Akçam, Orhan Pamuk, Ragip Zarakolu and Halil Berketay) who have dared to refer to the Armenian Genocide. Reports such as Baskin Oran (commissioned in October 2004 by the government on 'Human Rights' in Turkey), have shown a systematic violation of human rights in Turkey today that cannot be ignored by EU legislators or by our own politicians in the UK.

---

15 'Gesamtzahl der Armenier in der Türkei 2½ Millionen ... Im gesamten Kleinasien ist hoch gerechnet ½ Million von der Verchickung verschont gelieben ... in Syrien und Mesopotamien ist hoch gerechnet eine halbe Million angekommen ... Die Sterblichkeit unter den in Syrien und Mesopotamien angekommenen ist ausserordentlich hoch und wird noch lange als unmittelbare Folge der Verschickeung, deren Ende noch keineswegs herbeigekommen ist, hoch bleiben. Unter diesen Umständen wird, so ergibt sich, eine Gasamtzahl von 800,000 Umgekommenen von Ernst zu nehmenden Kreisen, die besser unterrichtet sein können, als andere, für wahrscheinlich erachtet, ja es gilt sogar für möglich, dass die Zahl noch höher ist'.

The conflict within the social and political structures in Turkey, namely the progressive movement towards democracy and European values and the traditionalist policy of Pan-Turkism, has placed a critical task on the government to enhance its communication with Turkish intellectual society. This in effect is the only means to overcome Turkey's current dilemma and allow it to move ahead towards developing a true democratic and multicultural vision for Turkey.

In the international arena, the governments of the USA and the UK give their total support to Turkish denialist policies. It is therefore not surprising to note that neither of these countries has officially recognized the historical truth of the Armenian Genocide.

In January 2005, the Royal Academy exhibited 'Turks: A Journey of a Thousand Years, 600–1600.' It was certainly a unique and a major exhibition worth visiting. However, some of the reviews and articles that followed conveniently ignored important portions of Ottoman and Turkish history. *Sunday Times* (Comments 21 January 2005 Turkish Treasure), stated, '[the Turks came] to absorb, embellish and unify the cultures of the Greek and Romans, Christians and Jews, Byzantium and Balkans.' A more truthful reporting should have mentioned that the incoming Turkic tribes conquered the territories belonging to other peoples and established a vast ruthless empire, where the non-Muslim were subjected to extra taxation, in addition to being periodically chastised by kidnappings, massacres and lootings. It is true that many forms of art flourished during the Ottoman rule, but these were mainly the Islamic ones.

How could the Turks 'absorb, embellish and unify' the local cultures? How is it that in a land, where over 2.5 million Armenians and millions of Greeks lived at the beginning of the twentieth century, there are only about 60,000 left? Is this called 'unifying cultures' or, more truthfully, 'ethnic cleansing on a massive scale' or genocide?

Is it not ironic that in the arts world we have adopted the adjective 'young Turks' to refer to the young and upcoming artists, the *avant-garde*? I wonder if this would have been the case had the International Criminal Court prosecuted perpetrators of the Armenians Genocide – the Young Turks early in twentieth century [had the ICC existed at the time].

Paul Owen from *The Guardian* on the other hand wrote:[16]

> It seems suspicious, your friends say, that the Royal Academy's Turks: A Journey of a Thousand Years, 600–1600 exhibition has opened just as the EU prepares to open accession talks with Ankara. Quickly scanning Philip Hensher's piece in the *Independent*, you admit that if the EU question "were not in the air … it seems unlikely … that we would be seeing such an exhibition … It is pretty clear that the Topkapi Museum [in Istanbul] has been told firmly to send half its best things to London in the Turkish national interest."

Europe is about to outline its action plan with regard to the European Neighbourhood Policy and Armenia. Further, Turkey, facing growing international pressure, has resorted to an increasingly costly campaign to export its genocide denial campaign beyond its borders.

---

16 Owen, P. (2005), 'Turks at the RA', *The Guardian*, Tuesday 25 January.

In the USA the American Foreign Service Association recently announced that John M. Evans, the US ambassador to Armenia, was to receive a prestigious award for 'constructive dissent' for characterizing as genocide the deaths of 1.5 million Armenians in the waning days of the Ottoman Empire in 1915. His comments stirred such a diplomatic tempest that ambassador Evans not only had to retract his remarks but also had to later clarify his retraction.

The selection committee met again at the beginning of June 2005, and decided to withdraw the honour, known as the Christian A. Herter Award. They decided not to offer any award in the category, reserved for a senior Foreign Service officer.[17]

The timing of the association's decision appeared curious, given it came just before the Turkish Prime Minister Recep Tayyip Erdogan arrived in Washington for a meeting with President Bush to bolster strained US-Turkish relations. John W. Limbert, president of the association, said that no one at the organization could remember an award being withdrawn after it had been announced. 'It is not something we do easily', he said.

Speaking at public event in California, Evans referred to the 'Armenian genocide' and said that the US Government owes 'you, our fellow citizens, a more frank and honest way of discussing the problem'. He added that 'there is no doubt in my mind what happened' and it was 'unbecoming of us, as Americans, to play word games here'.

A similar political alliance in the denialist sense also exists between Turkey and Israel. It would be fair to suggest that Israel should feel the moral responsibility to recognize the Armenian Genocide, but in reality due to its few allies in the region Israel has to make compromises to avoid damaging its relations with Turkey.

According to Israel Charny, 'We have an absolute moral responsibility to recognise the Armenian Genocide... Respecting and honouring the memory and history of each and every genocide is the first essential step towards creating new means of preventing genocide to all people in future.'[18]

Some of the ways in which denial of genocide causes 'violence to others' have been identified by Israel W. Charny in his essay on 'The Psychology of Denial of Known Genocides.' Charny emphasizes that denial conceals the horror of the crimes and exonerates those responsible for it. This point is echoed by historian Deborah Lipstadt, who in her book on denial of the Holocaust, writes, 'Denial aims to reshape history in order to rehabilitate the perpetrators and demonise the victim.'[19]

Conclusion

Given the recurrence of genocides in recent history and the continuation of the crime being committed by the authorities of countries against their people,

---

17 Kessler, G. (2005), *Washington Post* staff writer, *Washington Post*, DC. June 9, p. A19. http://www.washingtonpost.com/wp-dyn/content/article/2005/06/08/AR2005060802253_pf.html.

18 Charny, I.W. (2005), 'Israel Hasbara Committee', New York, May 2005.

19 Lipstadt, D.E. (1993), *Denying the Holocaust: The Growing Assault on Truth and Memory*, (New York: The Free Press and Toronto: Maxwell MacMillan), 217.

it would be fair to suggest that due to advances in science and technology and weapons of mass destruction, perpetration of genocides may occur without prior or clear early warnings. Similarly, it would be equally fair to note that twenty-first century civilization with its elaborate network of news agencies, satellite and broadcasting technology, is fully equipped for dissemination of information and where necessary the capability to deploy preventative measures based on international law and supported by diplomatic, humanitarian and military means. It also has the comprehensive ability to bring to a halt any possible attempts at genocides, conducted thorough investigation as well as employing mechanisms for prevention and suppression of genocide and in extreme cases for escalation to the UN and the International Criminal Court for direct intervention in accordance with Articles 43–47 of the UN Charter and legitimate backing for the arrest, indictment and trial of perpetrators of genocide at the ICC.[20]

We have witnessed several genocides and crimes against humanity throughout the twentieth century. Indeed, the number of victims claimed in the process exceeds that of all the wars and human conflicts over the same period. Yet we have responded better in dealing with aftermath of wars, or even natural disasters. Through systematic approach and analysis appropriate early warning systems are devised and implemented across the globe providing us with adequate time to save lives. Yet through political expediency we fail to prevent genocides.

There has been considerable progress against denial, with number of parliaments recognizing the Armenian Genocide growing rapidly, despite Turkey's consistent efforts in falsification and misrepresentation of facts. There is a need for politicians and government officials to take a stance against denial of the Armenian Genocide by participating in memorial events and remembering all genocides. Parliaments and governments should work hand-in-hand in this respect.

While invasion of Iraq and removal of a despotic regime from power at the cost of billions of dollars may be considered justifiable by politicians and while billions of dollars are spent on space projects, the reality of genocide in Darfur continues. Is this because Iraqi lives and democracy are considered to be more valuable, or perhaps its oil!

Declaring that genocide has taken place in Sudan's Darfur region by Colin Powell, the US Secretary of State is not a solution. Action must be taken to stop it, investigate the crime and punish the perpetrators. Crimes of Genocide must be taken seriously and dealt with decisively. Denial of genocide should no longer be tolerated. The United Nations and the International Criminal Court must be given the overriding authority to scrutinize crimes of genocide.

In the aftermath of the World War II, the Germans not only stood before the ruins of their fragmented country. They also, in the light of the crimes committed under National Socialist rule, stood before moral ruin and the question of guilt, which after a relatively short phase of repression, led to unprecedented historical scrutiny. Perhaps the government in Turkey can learn from history by having the courage to explore its darkest pages and submit to its past.

---

20 Hagopian, H. (2005) 'Lessons of Genocide: 1915, 1994 & 2004', 25 May, available at: http://www.crag.org.uk/articles/article22.html.

Zafer Senocak, a widely published poet and journalist of Turkish origin living in Germany on the subject of Turkey's EU accession writes, 'In the 21st century, Turkish society will no longer be able to afford this rotten foundation of repression and crude historical falsification if it wants to be invited into the circle of Europeans. The Turks cannot demand that others come to terms with their histories when they themselves are only willing to believe in a version they invented.'

Throughout this chapter, examples have shown how Turkish authorities intentionally falsify history and export their policy of denial of the Armenian Genocide. In doing so Turkish denialists try to shift the burden of proof to Armenians by accusing Armenians of atrocities against the Turkish population during and immediately after the World War I. These are political tactics employed for abrogating themselves of legal responsibility.

Trying to impute the burden of intent upon Armenians! Doesn't this imply that Turkish authorities are trying to relieve themselves of the burden of genocide?

Chapter 2

Armenian Genocide Claims:
A Contextual Version of the
1915 Incidents

Sadi Cayci

Introduction

The 'Armenian genocide' claims pose an important challenge in Turkey's foreign relations. Some members of the international community appear to harbour a view on the events in 1915 which is lacking in context. Recent examples include a statement by the *Los Angeles Times* according to which:

> [w]hat happened in Armenia in 1915 is well known. The Ottoman Empire attempted to exterminate the Armenian population through slaughter and mass deportation. It finished half the job, killing about 1.2 million people.[1]

In an 'Open Letter to the Turkish Prime Minister', the International Association of Genocide Scholars noted that:

> [t]here may be differing interpretations of genocide – how and why the Armenian Genocide happened, but to deny its factual and moral reality as genocide is not to engage in scholarship but in propaganda and efforts to absolve the perpetrator, blame the victims, and erase the ethical meaning of this history.[2]

Tessa Hofmann is of the opinion that:

> [u]nder the guise of WWI more than half of the estimated two and a half million Ottoman Armenians perished, most men during massacres, and most women, children and

---

1 'It Was Genocide', *The Los Angeles Times Online* (published 22 March 2006), http://www.latimes.com/news/opinion/commentary/la-ed-armenia22mar22,0,79681175. story?coll=la-home-commentary.

2 'Open Letter to Turkish Prime Minister', International Association of Genocide Scholars, *AZG Armenian Daily Online* (published 28 June 2005), http://www.azg.am/ ?lang=EN&num=2005062801.

aged people from starvation and exhaustion during death marches and the subsequent liquidation of concentration camps.[3]

According to some authors, this general view of the international community is part of a greater strategy in a long-term political campaign whose aims include the recognition by Turkey of the existence of an Armenian Genocide, but also restitution and return of the population.[4]

This chapter will attempt to provide its readers with the somewhat neglected context of the Armenian claims and enable them to evaluate relevant questions with regard to Turkish counter-claims as well.

The Importance of a Free Discussion

With a Resolution dated 15 June 2005, the German Parliament expressed its concern about the fact that a comprehensive discussion of the incidents concerning the Ottoman era is impossible in Turkey.[5] To some, it appears that:

> Turkey's self-destructive obsession with denying the Armenian genocide seems to have no limits […] [A] Leading Turkish novelist, Orhan Pamuk, was charged with "insulting Turkish identity" for referring to the genocide (the charges were dropped after an international outcry) […] [the] Turkish government considers even discussion of the issue to be a grave national insult and reacts to it with hysteria.[6]

In the opinion of the *Los Angeles Times*:

> [in spite] of a plethora of evidence gathered by Henry Morgenthau, the U.S. ambassador in Constantinople from 1913 to 1916, that detailed how the Turkish government engaged in the systematic annihilation of Armenians, the Turks still refuse to admit culpability […] … Prime Minister Recep Tayyip Erdogan should order a halt to Pamuk's prosecution, and his government needs to foster more freedom of expression and thought in Turkey …[7].

Pamuk, a Turkish novelist, had stated that one million Armenians were killed during the 1915 massacres.[8]

---

3   Hofmann, T. (2005) 'Europe, Turkey and the Armenian Genocide', Lecture at the University College London, (published 20 January), http://www.crag.org.uk/articles/article17.html.

4   'Tamer Acikalin's statement in Sami Kohen' (1998), 'Ermenilerin "4T" stratejisi', *Milliyet*: 18, 2 June.

5   'Almanya Federal Parlamentosu, Ermeni Soykirimi Iddialarini Kabul Etti' (2005), *ABHaber Online* (published 16 June), http://www.abhaber.com/haber_sayfasi.asp?id=5808.

6   'Turkey, Armenia and Denial', *International Herald Tribune Online* (published 15 May 2006), http://www.iht.com/articles/2006/05/15/opinion/edturkey.php.

7   'Turkey's War with History', *The Los Angeles Times Online* (published 8 September 2005), < http://www.latimes.com/news/opinion/la-ed-turk8sep08,04558858.story?coll=la-home-oped.

8   Vick K. (2005), 'Turkey Charges Acclaimed Author', *The Washington Post*: A24, September 1.

While – perhaps rightly – criticizing the judicial prosecution which this statement triggered, many observers may have missed an essential point. For the Turkish public, the real issue probably was not established by Pamuk's statement, but by a general failure of the West, to critically evaluate the Armenian claims, while sometimes according too much weight to the opinions of persons who may not have the necessary expertise on the subject matter.

This problem does not appear to be confined to the exercise of the freedom of expression in Turkey. One may recall that the Chairman of the Turkish History Society, Professor Yusuf Halacoglu, had to face prosecution for denying the Armenian Genocide in a lecture in Bern, Switzerland, while Turhan Comez, a Turkish Member of Parliament, did not face similar problems when arguing the same point in Yerevan, Armenia, during his visit to that country.[9]

Rule of Law – Rule of Politics?

Several national parliaments, including those of the US, the United Kingdom, Germany, and Switzerland, have by now recognized the genocide of the Armenians by the Ottoman empire. The question may be asked whether these acts of recognition, in themselves, carry any particular significance in the legal sphere. However, some parliaments went further and made it illegal to counter the Armenian claims.[10] Recently, a supplementary piece of legislation, envisioning punishment of up to five

---

9   Sevinc (2005), 'Bern'den Erivan'a Soykirim Celiskisi', *Hurriyet*: 23, 12 June. Other examples of relevance include the removal of the Turkish perspective from the discussion of genocide and Human Rights in the school curriculum in Massachusetts high schools in 2000. Elizabeth Mehren, 'Genocide as History: legal flashpoint', *The Los Angeles Times Online* (published 25 April 2006), http://www.latimes.com/news/nationworld/nation/la-na-armenians25apr25,0,119923.story?coll=la=home-nation. Several CDs and DVDs were confiscated by the British police when Amb. (Ret.) Gunduz Aktan and Prof. Norman Stone entered the United Kindom in order to attend a symposium on Armenian issues in Edinburgh, Scotland. Hilal Yilmaz, 'Turklerin Duzenledigi Ermeni Sempozyumuna Ingiliz Engeli', *Hurriyet Online* (published 23 October 2005), http://www.hurriyet.com.tr/dunya/3425089-p.asp. It was also reported that legal action is taken in Germany against a Turkish group for their statements denying the Armenian Genocide, under Article 130 of the German Penal Code and Article 189 of the German Civil Code. Anahit Hovsepian, 'Those Denying the Genocide to Face Trial', *Armenian Club Forum Online* (published 7 July 2005), http://groong.usc.edu/news/msg116738.html.

10   Law No. 2001-70 of 29 January 2001: 'France publicly recognizes the Armenian Genocide of 1915.' In a more general context, the first law to outlaw holocaust denial – understandably – was enacted in Germany, in 1985. Its aim was to prevent insult to the honour of the Jews living in the country. In France, there is a criminal law in effect, punishing refusal of genocide committed against Jews, during World War II. Art. 9, Law No. 90-615 of 13 July 1990, known as 'Loi Gayssot' (The Gayssot Law) which makes it an offence to question in public, existence of the crimes tried at Nuremberg International Military Tribunal. Austria, Belgium, Spain, Switzerland and Israel have similar legislation. See: 'Combating Holocaust denial through law in the United Kingdom', *Institute for Jewish Policy Research Online*, (Report, No. 3, published in 2000), http://www.jpr.org.uk.

years in prison and a fine of up to 45,000 Euros for denial of the Armenian Genocide was shelved in France because of lack of time for Parliamentary discussion.[11]

At this juncture, it is worth mentioning a joint declaration by a group of prominent French historians which does not support the above mentioned bill. According to the joint declaration, there should be no dogma, no taboo in history. A historian does not appraise nor condemn events; historians only seek explanations. History thus is not a servant to current events and does not judge past events based on today's sensitivities.[12]

As a principle, the same should apply to the interpretation of history by the courts. As the *Washington Post* stated, '[C]ourts are a capricious venue for arguments about history'.[13] The judicial venue, it appears, fails to contribute positively to the search for facts. Nor should history be written through legislative acts. Such behaviour makes law and justice vulnerable to politics and is therefore an inherently problematic approach.

A Summary of Facts

The author is not a historian. The information presented below should therefore be considered as a reflection of the common perception in Turkish academia and the general public. Although these opinions are *prima facie* convincing and substantiated by supporting documentation, they need to be authenticated and evaluated in all aspects by impartial and neutral experts on nineteenth century Ottoman history.

The 1877–1878 Ottoman Russian War, the Ottoman defeat, the 1878 Treaty of Yesilkoy (San Stefano) and the conclusion of the Berlin Agreement to replace the previous agreement between Russia and the Ottoman State establish the general historical framework for the events under discussion.[14] The requirement of reform on behalf of non-Muslim peoples living in Eastern Anatolia, and the delegation of authority to States Parties to the agreement to control the relevant process, gave an impetus to the Armenian national initiative. However, it must be stated that the Berlin Agreement did not envision self-government for the Armenians. The disappointment over this development may be considered as one of the factors shaping the development of the Armenian situation.[15]

Before the First World War, Armenian insurgents had taken up arms against the Ottoman empire, believing in the support of the major powers of the time. The

---

11 French Foreign Minister Philippe Douste-Blazy stated that Armenian cause is correct and it should be respected. Turkey is to be blamed: '… For its part, Ankara denies the genocide charges ….' See: Teresa Küchler, 'Brussels Shies Away From Turkey: armenian genocide dispute', *Euobserver Online* (published 19 May 2006), http://euobserver.com/9/21647.

12 Elveren (2005), '19 Cesur Tarihciden Ozgurluk Bildirisi', *Hurriyet*: 22, 16 December.

13 'The Courts and History' (2001), *The Washington Post:* B06, 4 February.

14 Article 16, Yesilkoy Agreement; Article 61, Berlin Agreement. See *Gecmisten Bugune Turk-Ermeni İliskileri* (1989), Ankara: Genelkurmay Basimevi, pp. 21–22.

15 See also the Report prepared by Paul Cambon, the French Ambassador to Istanbul, dated 20 February 1894.

Yenikoy Agreement of 8 February 1914, between Russia (representing the major powers) and the Ottoman Government, had envisaged the appointment of two general inspectors to two regions in Eastern Anatolia. However, because of the outbreak of the First World War, a proper implementation of this provision was not possible.

The Dashnak conference held in Erzurum, in autumn 1914 laid the groundwork which conditioned the campaign of Armenian separatists against the Ottoman empire. The Young Turk Government of the time, in order to assure Armenian support for the Ottoman State, offered the Armenians autonomy.[16] Some Armenian volunteer units however did collaborate during the war with the Russians, against the Ottoman empire.[17] The attacks on certain Muslim villages near the border areas can be traced back to actions by Armenian separatists.

In the winter of 1914/1915, the region between Erzurum and Van became an area of conflict between Turks, Kurds, and Armenians.[18]

Recently, discovered correspondence has made it possible to identify Western influence on the readiness of Ottoman Armenians to resort to armed uprising in the hope of establishing an independent Armenia in parts of Ottoman territory.[19]

Insurgency

The basic political and military objective of some parts of the Armenian population during the Armenian uprising seemed to follow the same strategy that had previously been successfully pursued by other ethnic groups which had gained their independence from Ottoman rule, especially in the Balkans region. The 1876 Bulgarian insurgency, the 1877–1878 Ottoman-Russian War, and the 1878 decisions of the Congress of Berlin on the need for reforms in the Eastern provinces gave strength to the idea that a strategy similar to that of the Bulgarians could be employed in this context as well.

However, as Armenians did not constitute the majority of the population in the region, it was essential to rely on help from the outside.[20] Some organized Armenian armed groups had hoped to be able to present their case of oppression by the Ottoman empire to the the First World War Allies – the 'Triple Entente Powers' (Russia, France and Britain) – as persecution; the objective being to provide the Allies with

---

16 Gurun, K. (1985), *The Armenian File: the myth of innocence exposed*, London–Nicosia–Istanbul: K. Rustem & Bro. and Weidenfeld & Nicolson Ltd., pp. 188–89.

17 Forming four battalions, consisting of volunteers, Armenians preceded and opened the way for the main Russian forces, to invade Ottoman territory. See Timur (2001), *1915 ve sonrasi Turkler ve Ermeniler*, Ankara: Imge Kitabevi, 2nd edition, pp. 41–45.

18 Yerasimos, S. (2002), *Birinci Dunya Savasi ve Ermeni Sorunu*, Ankara: Turkiye Bilimler Akademisi, p. 13.

19 For a summary of findings by Assistant Prof. Ergunoz Akcora of the Firat University, see: 'Ermenilerin Turk Katliami Mektuplarda', *Zaman Online* (published 7 April 2006), http://www.zaman.com.tr/?bl=sondakika&alt=haberler&hn=273742.

20 See McCarthy, J. (1998), *Muslumanlar ve Azinliklar*, Istanbul: Inkilap Kitabevi, pp.45–89; Ali Guler (1996), *XX. Yuzyil Baslarinin Askeri ve Stratejik Dengeleri İcinde Turkiye'deki Gayri Muslimler: sosyo-ekonomik durum analizi*, Ankara: Genelkurmay Basim Evi, pp. 75–82, 94–96.

political and especially humanitarian grounds for a justified intervention in affairs of the Ottoman empire.[21]

Before the 1915 incidents, the first Armenian uprising had started in the Zeytun (Maras) region, and from 30 August 1914 to September 1915, several clashes and violence had taken place in the region. A second uprising had taken place in the Bitlis region. It had lasted from January 1915 to 26 February 1915. When Armenian volunteer battalions accompanying Russians attacked on the Ottoman borders, local Armenians changed their strategy. Van had been used as a staging area. There had been several Armenian uprisings, including Bitlis and Mus, and the victims included parts of the Muslim population. From November 1914, Armenians had formed armed units in North Eastern Anatolia and another 200,000 men had volunteered to join Russian armed forces. It can be argued that uprisings in different parts of Anatolia put the Ottoman empire into a vulnerable security situation. Following the events of 15 April 1915, in which many Mahmudiye Muslims lost their lives, the Armenian forces launched a new offensive in and around Van, Catak and Bitlis.[22]

Countering Insurgency

In countering the insurgency, the Ottoman Minister of the Interior, Talat Bey first issued a warning to Erzurum deputy Vartkes Efendi, which included instructions on the implementation of a mass relocation as a result of the 'conspiracy against the State'. After a deterioration of the security situation was perceived, the Office of the Ottoman Commander-in-Chief, on 25 February 1915, issued a circular to all troops, ordering the disarmament of Armenians in the Ottoman Army. But it also called on the troops to be alert, and not to start any prosecution, unless a clear and imminent danger of actual attack existed. It also instructed them not to harm obedient nationals.[23]

It is worth noting that the conflict between the Armenians and the Ottoman empire and the casualties that resulted was not limited to people living in the region. More than 180,000 individuals had come from many other parts of the world. By February 1915, 12,446 Armenians had joined the French Occupation Forces.[24]

The Ottoman Ministry of the Interior, on 1 April 1915, sent a letter to the provinces, ordering the relocation of Armenian police officers and public servants who were no longer trusted and had taken a direct or active part in the hostilities.

The Ottoman Third Army Command, in a message to the governor of Bitlis, asked for the protection of innocent civilians and other citizens loyal to the government. The capture of an Armenian teacher, named Osep, who had carried an inventory of weapons issued in the vicinity, triggered the main Armenian uprising in the area. The

---

21 Stefanos Yerasimos, supra. No. 26, p. 10.

22 Not all uprisings resulted in such tragedies. For details, see: *Ermeni Komitelerinin Amaclari ve İhtilal Hareketleri* (2003) (Ankara: Genelkurmay Askeri Tarih ve Stratejik Etut Baskanligi Yayinlari), pp. 141–195.

23 *Belgelerle Ermeni Sorunu* (1992), (Ankara: Basbakanlik Basimevi), pp. 182–183.

24 Ozdemir et al. (2004), *Ermeniler: Surgun ve Goc* (Ankara: Turk Tarih Kurumu Basimevi.), p. 66.

Ottoman army then resorted to military measures to counter the insurgency. In the end, however, the Ottoman army had to leave the city of Van. The conflict in the Van region had also resulted in many Muslim casualties. By 15 April 1915, Armenian insurgents, under the command of Aram, had succeeded in the establishment of *de facto* control in Van area.[25]

When the insurgency in the Van region started, and Armenians announced the establishment of a state in the region, the arrest of leaders of the Armenian Committees in Istanbul was ordered on 24 April 1915. At first, the Ottoman Ministry of Interior decided to detain the leading figures only, and to shut down all organizations that were aiding and abetting the insurgency.[26] On 24 April 1915 two hundred and thirty-five leaders of the insurgency were detained. Of these, 155 individuals had been subject to enforced residence in Cankiri province, North of Ankara. One of them, Vartabet Komidas – in whose name a monument was erected in Paris – was allegedly killed during the mass relocation; but evidence has emerged showing that he was in fact pardoned at an early stage of the proceedings, together with his brother, on a petition submitted by them.[27]

On 9 May 1915, Talat Pasha issued instructions to the governors of Erzurum, Bitlis and Van, ordering the relocation of Armenians living in the South of Erzurum, Van and Bitlis, to the South.[28]

On 17 May 1915, the Ottoman Forces had to withdraw from the city and Van was surrendered to the Russians.[29] The almost total extinction of the Ottoman Third Army due to the harsh winter conditions of 1915 during the Sarikamis operation against Russian Armies again renewed Armenian hopes that a Western intervention in Ottoman affairs might take place. The Ottoman army tried to suppress the activities of insurgents in the region.

On 27 May 1915, the Mass Relocation Act, as a complementary – administrative and security – measure had been the put into effect. It authorized the regional commanders, in time of mobilization, to take all necessary means to disrupt any activity directed against the defence of the country.[30] This measure concerned 702,000 Armenians, who were to be moved to the Mousul and Aleppo regions which, at the time, belonged to the Ottoman empire. Official records suggest that at least 50,000 casualties occurred, as a result of inadequate security measures, attacks by bandits, and illness. Additionally, many Armenians became trapped between the Russian and the Ottoman armies when the 66th Russian Division was defeated.

---

25 Meanwhile, on several occasions, complaints and appeals by the Armenian Patriarch in Istanbul had been investigated and had apparently proved to be incorrect: *Belgelerle Ermeni Sorunu* (1992), supra No. 32, pp. 202–222.

26 *Belgelerle Ermeni Sorunu* (1992), pp. 223–230.

27 While living in Istanbul, in September 1917, Komidas was permitted to travel to Vienna, Austria, for medical treatment. Then he went to Paris, and passed away there during the 1920s. By April 1915, the total Armenian population in Istanbul had numbered 77,765. See: 'Sozde Ermeni Iddialarini Curuten Belgeler' *Zaman Online* (published 20 April 2006), http://www.zaman.com.tr/?bl=sondakika&alt=haberler&hn=277900.

28 Ozdemir, H. et al. (2004), pp. 61–63.

29 Ozdemir, H. et al. (2004), pp. 53–60.

30 *Ermeni Komitelerinin Amaclari* ve *İhtilal Hareketleri* (2003), footnote on p. 201.

Counter-measures: Security Aspects

The Government's decision to relocate Armenians to other parts of the Ottoman empire has by some authors been understood as a wartime measure, which was not uncommon in this period. The key Government Decree stated that, 'when those Armenians resident in the aforementioned towns and villages who have to be moved are transferred to their places of settlement and are on the road, their comfort must be assured and their lives and property protected; after their arrival their food should be paid for out of refugees' appropriations until they are definitively settled in their new homes. Property and land should be distributed to them in accordance with their previous financial situation as well as current needs; and for those among them needing further help, the Government should build houses, provide cultivators and artisans with seed, tools, and equipment [...] This order is entirely intended against the extension of the Armenian Revolutionary Committees; therefore do not execute it in such a manner that might cause the mutual massacre of Muslims and Armenians.'[31]

As the Ottomans had been engaged in a deadly fight in the Canakkale region, and uprisings could not be contained as desired, the Government decided to relocate Armenians living in Eastern Anatolia, to another province of the Ottoman empire, in the Southern region. Meanwhile, the engagements of the Ottoman Army at several fronts during the war put the Armenians that were being relocated in a rather vulnerable position against Kurdish attacks. Given the poor military capacity available for internal security operations, the suppression of such attacks had proved to be rather difficult. On the other hand, the victims of the insurgency – including many members of the Muslim population – should likewise not be forgotten.[32]

Talat Pasha's instruction to the Governors of Erzurum, Diyarbakir, Elazig and Bitlis, dated 14 June 1915, stated that every feasible precaution had to be taken for the physical safety of the population in the process of mass relocation. On 12 July 1915, Talat Pasha issued a second instruction to the Governor of Diyarbakir, dated 12 July 1915, emphasizing the importance given to the protection of the lives of the Armenian and Christian populations.[33]

A contextual view will have to include in the consideration of the relocation of the population the perceived threat to national security as formed by the insurgency and the evidence (on which the Ottoman government relied) of the joining of foreign forces by some Armenian volunteers.[34]

---

31 '1915 Mayis Tarihli Bakanlar Kurulu Talimati', Basbakanlik Arsivi, Istanbul, Meclis-i Vukela Mazbatalari: cilt 198, karar no. 1331/163 in Hasan Pulur , 'Ermeni Tehciri...', *Milliyet* (published (12 October 2000); http://www.milliyet.com.tr/2000/10/12/yazar/pulur.html.

32 Oztuna, Y. (2005), 'Ermeniler Kullanildi', *Turkiye*: 1, 5 January.

33 Elekdag, S., 'Soykirimi iddiasini curuten belgeler', *Milliyet* (published 16 October 2000) http://www.milliyet.com.tr/2000/10/16/yazar/elekdag.html.

34 See Fein, B., 'An Armenian and Muslim Tragedy?, Yes! Genocide? No!' (published 1 April 2001 with the permission of ATAA – Assembly of Turkish American Associations) http://azerbaycan.hypermart.net/tragedy.htm.

Counter-measures: Legal Aspects

The examination of the relocation of the Armenians from Eastern Anatolia to cities in Iraq and Syria must also be considered against the background of contemporary State practice. As the target locations were situated within the Ottoman empire, it would be technically incorrect to speak of deportations, although the relocation might qualify as 'forcible transfer' in today's terminology. The view can be expressed that the relocations were not aimed at reprisal, revenge, punishment or persecution of Armenians. It is an often neglected fact that the Act on Mass Relocation made no specific reference to Armenians. Given the difficult conditions existent at the time, this author believes that the relocation may have been justified by reference to the security of the State.[35]

Counter-measures: Humanitarian Aspects

The tragic events of 1915 had not been started by Muslims; but many Muslims were among the victims of the Ottoman-Armenian conflict.[36] According to documents of the Turkish State Archive, between 1910 and 1922, 523,000 Muslims (Turks) were among the casualties.[37] It is arguable that they were also among the first victims of this conflict.

Investigation and Prosecution of Alleged Crimes

There is evidence that the prosecution of certain Ottoman officials with regard to their personal involvement in the implementation of the mass relocations, did take place.[38]

---

35 For the activities of Armenians during the First World War, Ottoman Government's policies, linguistic analysis of the term 'tehcir' (relocation), texts of the Ottoman laws and regulations, instructions to all units by the Ottoman Supreme Military Command, Ottoman Ministry of Interior circulars, on the implementation of the mass relocation, see Gurun (1985), *The Armenian File: the myth of innocence exposed* (London–Nicosia and Istanbul: K. Rustem & Bro. and Weidenfeld & Nicolson Ltd.), pp. 186–214; *Gecmisten Bugüne Türk-Ermeni İliskileri*, pp. 51–67.

36 One should keep in mind that this was the period of the First World War. All male persons eligible for military service had already been mobilized and left their places of residence, excluding non-Muslim minorities.

37 Based on officially documented figures, for the first time made public by Yusuf Sarinay, the Director General of the Turkish Prime Ministry's State Archive, during a panel meeting at Baskent University, *Massacres Against Turks in History*, Ankara, 25 February 2005. (For a detailed list, see: 'Ermeni Ceteleri 523 Bin Turk'u Katletmis' (2005), *Hurriyet*: 19, 18 April. The complete list includes the figures of a total of 523,955 Turkish casualties, covering the period from 1906 to 1922.) There have been discoveries of several mass graves, where Turkish victims had been buried. See: *Ermeni Komitelerinin Amaclari ve İhtilal Hareketleri*, Annexed documents; 'Kilic yarigi – Cocuklari bile sungulemisler' (2003), *Hurriyet*: 22, 28 May; Fikri Nazif Ayyildiz (2000), 'Ermeniler ihtilale nasil hazirlanmisti?', *Nokta*, 15–21 October 2000, Year 19, No. 2000/42, p. 12.

38 In late 1915, Ottoman Government set up investigation committees, and 1,397 individuals, of which the majority were public officials, were prosecuted. Some received jail

However, the existence of fair trial procedures in this context is subject to some doubt. The prosecution itself has been seen as having been politically motivated, and the trials were held *in absentia* and under the influence of the occupying powers.[39] The new Ottoman Government had not hesitated to align itself with the occupying powers and to exert their best efforts to please them. The victims of the insurgency had not formed the focus of the criminal charges.[40]

During the occupation of Istanbul, the occupying powers attempted to bring charges against Ottoman officials. To intern the suspects until the completion of the investigation, some were sent to exile on the island of Malta. It appears however that no conclusive evidence was produced to support any official charge against those suspects.

The 1915 Incidents: A Legal Assessment on Responsibility

As the Ottoman State no longer exists and neither government agents nor private individuals who may have been involved in the events are still alive, it appears that any discussion of individual criminal responsibility in this regard is irrelevant.

Who might then respond to Armenian claims and the counter-claims? In this regard, it seems necessary to examine international law with regard to the 1915 incidents, as it applies to all the relevant parties. The view can be supported that all political, military, legal, humanitarian and other questions were in fact settled by the *Friendship and Brotherhood Treaty Between Turkey and Soviet Russia* (Moscow, 16 March 1921)[41] and the *Friendship Treaty Between Turkey, Armenia, Azerbaijan and Georgia* (Kars, 13 October 1921).[42] These treaties, which are still in effect, have as *leges speciales* precedence over general treaty law. This is the reason why the Armenian issue had not been considered at the Lausanne Peace Conference, at the conclusion of which all remaining political, military, humanitarian and legal questions were dealt with and settled by the *Lausanne Peace Treaty* of 24 July 1923.[43] Therefore, contrary to the opinion of Richard Hovannisian, the Turks did not go through a long period of amnesia, but considered *pacta sunt servanda* as

---

terms for dereliction of duty; others were executed. (See: Yusuf Sarinay, in Tarik Isik (2004), 'Soykirima tek kanit yok', *Radikal*: 8 December.)

39 For a detailed account of the trials of the leadership of Union and Progress Party, see: Osman Selim Kocahanoglu (1998), *Ittihat – Terakki'nin Sorgulanmasi ve Yargilanmasi* (Istanbul: Temel Yayinlari) pp. 36–45.

40 See Taner Timur (2001), *1915 ve sonrasi Turkler ve Ermeniler* (Ankara: Imge Kitabevi, 2nd edition), pp. 77–78. However, a trial took place against Soghomon Tehlirian, who on 15 March 1921 was charged in Berlin with the assassination of Talat Pasha in Berlin, but was then acquitted by the court.

41 Art. 1, 13.

42 Art. 2, 4, 15.

43 Preamble, Art. 58, and Annex No. VIII – Declaration and Protocol on General Amnesty. (See also: Ataov (2001), 'The Genocide deceit', *Turkish News*: 9, 1 February.)

a basic tenet of Western legal values, hoping for the start of a new and friendly relationship.[44]

Conclusion

It would be certainly wrong to claim that no massacre, no tragedy concerning the Armenians had taken place in 1915. But a comprehensive contextual view has to consider not only the considerable numbers of Armenian victims, but also the Muslim casualties of insurgencies against the Ottoman empire.[45]

Even in a simple case of criticizing, for example, a one hour movie, the risk of manipulation of the target audience exists if the basis of the criticism is a scene of selected three minutes. It is likewise wrong to make a selection from among a series of events, to accept them as mere facts, and to take them as the basis for a negative assessment. In this author's view, the Armenian allegations are lacking in context.

Last year the Turkish Prime Minister Erdogan, in a letter to Armenian President Kocharian proposed the establishment of a fact-finding committee, consisting of Turkish and Armenian historians. But the offer was rejected.[46]

Another initiative, by a group of retired Turkish ambassadors to give a lecture on Turkish Armenian relations and Armenian claims at the School of the Public Diplomacy at University of South California was cancelled by the University administration, on the ground that the subject matter was irrelevant to public diplomacy.[47]

A dialogue of the deaf is not the correct method to settle this issue. What is necessary, in this respect is an exchange of documents, expert opinion, and any other information available, including any oral history material.[48] Only through a series of comprehensive expert meetings can some meaningful conclusions hopefully be reached. To this end, an ad hoc academic working group, consisting of political, legal and military historians, public international lawyers and diplomats might be a good start.

---

44 Elizabeth Mehren, supra No. 11.

45 See the statement by Robert Mantran (1998), in 'Ermeniler soykirima ugramadi', *Hurriyet*: 18, 29 June.

46 'Armenians Push Prison Time for "Genocide" Deniers in France', *The New Anatolian* (published 19 April 2006), http://www.thenewanatolian.com/priny-4991.html.

47 'Dusunce Ozgurlugu ABD', *Radikal* (published 26 March 2006), http://www.radikal.com.tr/haber.php?haberno=182469.

48 Ottoman archives in Turkey, archives in the Russian Federation, Germany, Austria, France, Armenia, the Zoryan Institute of Boston are only some examples.

Chapter 3

Genocide and Nuremberg

Henry T. King Jr.

I first saw Rafael Lemkin, the man who identified genocide as an international crime and who in fact coined the word 'genocide,' at the Grand Hotel in Nuremberg in 1946.[1] At that time he was unshaven, his clothing was in tatters and he looked dishevelled. When I saw him at Nuremberg Lemkin was very upset. He was concerned that the decision of the International Military Tribunal (IMT) – the Nuremberg Court – did not go far enough in dealing with genocidal actions. This was because the IMT limited its judgment to wartime genocide and did not include peacetime genocide. At that time Lemkin was very focused on pushing his points. After he had buttonholed me several times I had to tell him that I was powerless to do anything about the limitation in the Court's judgment.

To sum up, at the time I thought that Lemkin was a 'crank' and I gave him short shrift. But Lemkin, despite his appearance, was to have a vital role in pushing genocide as an international crime and in the development of the United Nations Convention on Genocide.

Rafael Lemkin was a Polish Jewish lawyer whose family was decimated by the Nazis. His interest in what was to be known as genocide starts with concern over the unpunished Turkish massacre of hundreds of thousands of Armenians. The Turkish official who ordered the massacre was not brought to trial but the young man who allegedly assassinated him was. Lemkin saw a great anomaly between the situation of an individual who had allegedly committed a single murder being put on trial for his life while the instigator of the massacre of thousands of people went scot free. He wanted to correct this injustice, so in the 1930s Lemkin prepared a draft of a law that would punish those who committed the destruction of people for racial, religious or national origin reasons. He wanted the concept of Universal Jurisdiction to apply to the law's enforcement so that those who committed these crimes could be tried whenever they were caught, regardless of where the crime was committed and regardless of the defendant's nationality or official status. Lemkin worked for years to get this law adopted and he was at Nuremberg to pursue this objective when I met him in 1946.

By 'genocide' we generally mean the destruction of a national or racial or religious group. The definition comes from the Greek word 'genos' (race, tribe) and the Latin 'cide' (killing).

---

1   See Notes on Contributors.

The importance of abolishing genocide is about learning to value diversity. As Rafael Lemkin wrote in 1944:

> Our whole cultural heritage is a product of the contributions of all nations. We can best understand when we realize how impoverished our culture would be if the peoples doomed by Germany, such as the Jews, had not been permitted to create the Bible or to give birth to an Einstein, a Spinoza; if the Poles had not had the opportunity to give to the world a Copernicus, a Chopin, a Curie, the Czechs a Huss, and a Dvorak; the Greeks a Plato and a Socrates; the Russians, a Tolstoy and a Shostakovich.

Hitler's concept of a 'master race;' namely the Germans, brought the Nazis into direct conflict with those who favoured diversity. Hitler wanted to dignify genocide as a sacred purpose of the German people. National Socialism was, in his mind, the doctrine of the biological superiority of the German people.

A hierarchy of racial values determined the ultimate fate of the many peoples that fell under German domination. Jews and Gypsies were to be completely annihilated. The Poles, the Slovenes, the Czechs, the Russians and all other inferior Slav peoples were to be kept on the lowest social level. Those felt to be related by blood – the Dutch, the Norwegians, the Alsatians – were to have the alternative of espousing Germanism or sharing the fate of 'inferior' people.

Raphael Lemkin coined the word 'genocide' in 1944 and in 1945 Robert Jackson, the architect of Nuremberg, was charged by President Harry S. Truman with the trial of the major Nazi war criminals. At the time of Justice Jackson's appointment enough was known of the genocide activities of the Nazis to recognize that this would be one of the points of focus at the trial.

Jackson was appointed on 2 May 1945, and he reported back to President Truman on 6 June 1945, with a plan for the conduct of the trials. Included in that report as crimes which the trials should deal with were 'atrocities and persecutions on racial and religious grounds committed since 1933.' These genocidal activities were to be included in the crimes with which the Nazis were to be charged. Jackson's recognition of genocidal activity as a crime was the first of its kind in an international criminal proceeding. Jackson also recognized that genocidal activity could take place in peacetime as well as wartime when, in his report to President Truman, he specified that the trial should cover genocidal crimes occurring 'since 1933.'

Jackson had been charged by President Truman to negotiate with the Allies (UK, France, USSR) a procedure for the trial of the major Nazi war criminals. These negotiations took place in London in the early summer of 1945. The negotiations were difficult at times, particularly with the USSR, but were eventually successful. The result was the London Charter of 8 August, 1945.

Genocidal activity was specified as a crime under the London Charter but was on its face limited to wartime genocide and implicitly did not include peacetime genocide.

The Crimes Against Humanity reference is as follows:

> Article 6(c) Crimes Against Humanity; namely, murder, extermination, enslavement, deportation and other inhumane acts committed against any civilian populations before or during the war, or persecutions on political, racial or religious grounds in execution of or in connection with any crime within the jurisdiction of the Tribunal whether or not in violation of the domestic law of the country where perpetrated.

This definition was hurtful and helpful to the development of a definition of the crime of genocide activity. As a matter of first instance it said that 'Persecution on political, racial or religious grounds' was actionable only when committed in the execution of or in connection with any crime within the jurisdiction of the Tribunal. This meant such activity was condemned only when related to Crimes Against Peace or War Crimes. Thus, in the opinion of the International Military Tribunal (the Nuremberg Court) only wartime genocide was deemed actionable. But the definition was helpful in another respect when it held such persecution to be a crime 'whether or not in violation of the domestic law of the country where perpetrated.' In other words, German law was to be of no relevance with regard to punishment for these crimes. And, more specifically, German law could not authorize such crimes. The test in adjudging these crimes was implicitly to be international law and not local law. Read in the abstract, this was, indeed, an important limitation on sovereignty and one that was to prove helpful in dealing with such crimes subsequently.

Genocide activity was recognized as a crime in the indictment against the top Nazis on 6 October 1945, when in accusing them it stated:

> They [the defendants] conducted deliberate and systematic genocide viz the extermination of racial and national groups, against the civilian population of certain occupied territories in order to destroy particular races and classes of people and national, racial or religious groups, particularly Jews, Poles and Gypsies and others.

The trial began 20 November 1945 and for almost a year the Court and the world heard of the genocidal activities of the Nazis with such evidence coming primarily from documents of the Nazis' own making.

The evidence produced at Nuremberg did indeed give full support to the charge of genocide. Rafael Lemkin was particularly impressed with the statements by Sir Hartley Shawcross and Sir David Maxwell-Fyfe for the British prosecution and Auguste Champetier de Ribes and Charles Dubost for the French prosecution, who elaborated at length and with great eloquence on the Crime of Genocide in the course of the Nuremberg proceedings. Lemkin also commented favourably on the work of Brigadier General Telford Taylor in the subsequent proceedings who used the concept of genocide to good effect, for example in the case of the Nazi doctors who experimented on captive human beings. Here the defendants performed experiments to develop techniques for outright killings and abortions on the one hand and castration and sterilization on the other. Certainly, the commission of these crimes against Jews, Poles and others fit the Nazi genocidal ambitions.

The United Nations' General Assembly on 11 December, 1946 broadly endorsed the Nuremberg principles as reflected in the IMT judgment, and by separate resolution affirmed the principle of genocide as a crime, the adoption of the resolution relating to genocide was followed by a push towards the drafting and adoption of a UN convention relating to genocide. This was accomplished in October 1948 and with sufficient ratifications the convention went into effect in 1951. Even the USA has now ratified the convention after 40 years of scrutiny and with significant reservations:

> The first reservation of the USA related to Article IX of the Convention. Article IX of the Convention provides that disputes concerning the application of the Convention,

including those relating to the responsibility of a state for genocide, shall be submitted to the International Court of Justice. The US reservation to the Convention states that with respect to any disputes involving the USA such disputes may only be submitted to the International Court of Justice with the specific consent of the USA. That consent is required in each case.

The second reservation of the USA was to the effect that nothing in the Convention requires or authorizes legislation or other action by the USA prohibited by the US Constitution as interpreted by the USA.

These reservations are crippling. They mean that no case regarding the enforcement of the Convention involving the USA is to be brought before the International Court of Justice without the consent of the USA. Further, the USA shall be the sole judge as to whether actions required under the Convention are prohibited by the Constitution of the USA.

In light of the above, one might conclude that the adherence of the USA to the Convention was more symbolic than binding in actuality.

Most of the countries in the world have now ratified the Genocide Convention.

Genocide was the basis for the conviction of Adolf Eichmann by Israel in 1962. In the 1990s, the UN Security Council, by resolution, established Tribunals at The Hague and Tanzania to cover, among other crimes, genocide in the former Yugoslavia and Rwanda. The International Criminal Court, which went into effect in 2002, includes the crime of genocide as a separate offense within its purview, in addition to crimes against humanity and war crimes (and aggression when defined).

Genocide as Defined in the Rome Statute:

'means any of the following acts committed with intent to destroy in whole or in part a national ethnic, racial or religious group as such:

a. killing members of the group
b. causing serious bodily or mental harm to a member of the group
c. deliberately inflicting on the group conditions of life calculated to bring about its destruction in whole or in part
d. imposing measures to prevent birth within the group
e. forcibly transferring children of the group to another group'

(This definition is a replica of the definition of genocide set forth in the Genocide Convention.)

Genocide provisions as implemented in all these fora are direct descendants of genocide as charged at Nuremberg, although the latter have more particularity. Genocide as set forth in the Rome Statute establishing the International Criminal Court encompasses peace time genocide as well as war time genocide.

Nuremberg was largely the creation of Supreme Court Justice Robert H. Jackson. In his report to President Harry S. Truman of 6 June 1945, which outlined a blueprint for Nuremberg, Jackson proposed the elimination of the defenses of sovereign immunity (acts of state) and superior orders. This recommendation became a part of the London Charter of 8 August, 1945 upon which the trial was based. These two features became very significant to the recognition of genocide as a crime against humanity. For when asked why he carried out the extermination of 2,500,000 individuals at Auschwitz, Rudolf Hoess, the Auschwitz commandant, said he was carrying out orders. But because of Jackson's foresight in drafting the London Charter, this was to be no excuse for Hoess' misdeeds. Similarly, Otto Ohlendorff, when questioned why he ordered the extermination of 90,000 Jews, gypsies and Russian commissars in southern Russia, answered that he was ordered to do so. Both Hoess and Ohlendorff were sentenced to death by hanging for their crimes. Moreover, the elimination of the defense of sovereign immunity by Jackson in his plan for Nuremberg, which was also included in subsequent structures for war crimes trials, is the reason Slobodan Milosevic is before the bar of justice at The Hague today.

The other area in which Jackson played a role was in holding those who carried out genocidal acts responsible for those acts, was his advocacy of the principle of universal jurisdiction. The concept of universal jurisdiction is of long standing in international law stemming from its application from the seventeenth century onwards to pirates, so long as the nation trying them had physical possession of the individuals. In his opening statement at Nuremberg Jackson said: 'the real complaining party at your bar is civilization.' This was paralleled by his statement 'to pass these defendants a poisoned chalice is to put it to our lips as well.'

The Nuremberg Court (the International Military Tribunal) went along with the concept of Universal Jurisdiction when it said in its judgment that the four plaintiff nations at Nuremberg were doing collectively what each could have done individually. Richard Goldstone, the first prosecutor at The Hague proceedings, said that Universal Jurisdiction was the most important principle derived from Nuremberg. The principle of Universal Jurisdiction is particularly applicable to extreme international crimes such as genocide. In 1962, Adolf Eichmann was charged in Israel with genocide. His defense was that Israel was not a state at the time the crimes were committed, so that he could not be charged with a violation of Israeli law. The Israeli Court brushed aside this defense and held that Eichmann's crimes were so terrible that the doctrine of Universal Jurisdiction applied and he could be tried for them in any court in any country, regardless of where they had been committed. Thus, Eichmann was sentenced to hang based on the Israeli Court's adoption of the principle of universal jurisdiction.

There was also another significant way in which Nuremberg aided the development of the recognition of genocide as an international crime. This was in the draft of the Crimes Against Humanity provision in the London Charter.

In this provision it was stated in effect that the law of Germany provided no cover for those charged with such crimes. In other words, Hitler's order to implement the final solution could not be used as a defense by those carrying it out. This was truly an invasion of sovereignty as it had previously been understood. But it gave genocide status as a crime over and above national boundaries. Specifically, local law or the orders of local officialdom could no longer justify criminal activity such as genocide. A higher law – international law – which included genocide as a crime, was to be the order of the day.

The conviction and hanging of individuals at Nuremberg for genocidal activity was also important to the acceptance of genocide as a crime. The conviction of Julius

Streicher, the 'Jew-baiter of Nuremberg,' is a case in point. In finding Streicher guilty the International Military Tribunal stated:

> Streicher's indictment for murder and extermination at the time when Jews in the east were being killed under most horrible conditions clearly constitutes persecution on political and racial grounds in connection with War Crimes as defined by the Charter and constitutes a Crime Against Humanity.

Nuremberg indeed made an important contribution to the recognition of genocidal activity as criminal when it included, among the crimes charged, 'persecution on political, racial and religious grounds' and when it excluded domestic law as justification for such crimes. The International Military Tribunal judgment's limitation to cover only wartime genocide was not followed in Control Council Law #10 of 20 December 1945, which governed the Nuremberg subsequent proceedings. This law covered peacetime genocide, as well as wartime genocide. Twelve subsequent proceedings trials were conducted under this law. However, in the Ministries Case the Court dismissed a count dealing with peace time genocide for lack of jurisdiction.

Conclusion

There is an old adage that goes 'You shouldn't judge a book by its cover.' This certainly applied in the case of Rafael Lemkin as I knew him at Nuremberg. He was dishevelled and rough cut as he appeared to me, but he possessed a soul which had a steely determination to correct a national and international wrong and the world is better for it today. For it was Lemkin's determination to identify and codify genocide that made genocide a front-burner crime at Nuremberg. Our world today is much better for his efforts. The Genocide Convention and the structures of the *ad hoc* tribunals of The Hague and Tanzania, as well as that of the International Criminal Court, are all very explicit in identifying genocide as an international crime of the greatest magnitude.

It was one of the great coincidences of history that Robert Jackson's emergence as a leader in the international legal community at Nuremberg almost coincided with Lemkin's definition of genocide and the publication of his critical book *Axis Rule in Occupied Europe* outlining the particulars of the genocidal activities by the Nazi regime in Europe.

Jackson, in his report to President Truman of 6 June 1945, stated that 'persecution on racial or religious grounds "should be one of the bases for the trial of the Nazis."' This approach was followed in the London Charter of 8 August, 1945, which provided the basis for the Nuremberg trial. Jackson followed up his focus on genocide in the indictment of the Nazi leaders on 6 October 1945, when in the indictment he references genocide as one of the crimes with which the Nazis were charged.

Genocide conducted on the scale on which the Nazis conducted it requires participation by considerable numbers of people acting under the leadership of key officials. By eliminating the defenses of Sovereign Immunity and Superior Orders, Jackson wanted to call to account those who carried out genocide and other crimes and to punish them accordingly. This gave bite to the Crime of Genocide. Moreover,

Jackson's approach in eliminating these two defenses was replicated in the structure of the two *ad hoc* tribunals at The Hague and Tanzania and in the Rome Statue establishing the International Criminal Court.

Finally, implicit in Jackson's approach – as reflected by his opening and closing statements at Nuremberg – is the principle that, like genocide, some international crimes are so heinous that they can be the subject of trials in any court that is willing to take jurisdiction over them. This approach removes technical jurisdictional obstacles to such trials. The principle of Universal Jurisdiction certainly provided the basis for the trial of Adolf Eichmann in the Israeli Courts for his monstrously genocidal activities. Moreover, the principle of Universal Jurisdiction is incorporated in the Torture Convention of the UN and it was used by the US Circuit Court of Appeals to convict John Demjanjuk. It is also incorporated into the Restatement of the Foreign Relations Law of the USA.

We should close with an acknowledgement of respect and gratitude for Rafael Lemkin and Robert Jackson as recognition of their activities in creating a better world for all of us. Genocide remains a crime in today's world, but those who commit it are now being tried and punished for their acts. Hopefully, this will dissuade others from the commission of the Crime of Genocide.

At war's end Rafael Lemkin said that we needed diversity for the world to progress. What he said was true then and it is emphatically more true today in the highly mechanized and technologically orientated world in which we live. As our world grows 'smaller' our appreciation for diversity must grow larger.

With regard to Robert Jackson and his contribution to the recognition and punishment of genocide as a crime at Nuremberg, I can say emphatically that there would have been no Nuremberg without Robert Jackson. It was his creation! As he put it so well:

> This is the first case I have ever tried where I had to persuade others that a court should be established, help negotiate its establishment, and when that was done, not only to prepare my case, but find a court room in which to try it.

PART II

CASE STUDIES

Chapter 4

Has Genocide Been Committed in Darfur? The State Plan or Policy Element in the Crime of Genocide

William A. Schabas

'The Commission concludes that the Government of Sudan has not pursued a policy of genocide.'[1] This is perhaps, as Claus Kress has written, 'probably the key sentence'[2] in the January 2005 report of the International Commission of Inquiry established by the United Nations Security Council.[3] The Council was responding to a request from the government of the USA, which said it was acting in accordance with Article VIII of the 1948 *Convention for the Prevention and Punishment of the Crime of Genocide*, apparently the first such application of the provision since its adoption.[4] The Commission worked efficiently, and presented its report within three months.[5]

Many human rights activists were disappointed by the conclusion that genocide had not been committed, and some went so far as to treat the Commission report as some kind of whitewash or even betrayal. Yet the Commission said that although it would not use the stigma of genocide, terrible atrocities suitably described as crimes against humanity had certainly been committed:

> The above conclusion that no genocidal policy has been pursued and implemented in Darfur by the Government authorities, directly or though the militias under their control, should not be taken as in any way detracting from, or belittling, the gravity of the crimes perpetrated in that region. As stated above genocide is not necessarily the most serious international crime. Depending upon the circumstances, *such international offences as crimes against humanity or large scale war crimes may be no less serious and heinous*

---

1   'Report of the International Commission of Inquiry on violations of international humanitarian law and human rights law in Darfur', UN Doc. S/2005/60, para. 518.

2   Kress, C. (2005), 'The Darfur Report and Genocidal Intent', 3 *Journal of the International Criminal Justice*, p. 562, p. 563.

3   UN Doc. S/RES/1564 (2004), para. 12.

4   Secretary Colin L. Powell, Testimony Before the Senate Foreign Relations Committee, Washington, 9 September 2004.

5   See, particularly, Alston, P. (2005), 'The Darfur Commission as a Model for Future Responses to Crisis Situations', 3 *Journal of International Criminal Justice*, p. 600.

than genocide. This is exactly what happened in Darfur, where massive atrocities were perpetrated on a very large scale, and have so far gone unpunished.[6]

The Commission blamed Sudan for the same category of crimes that was the basis of the conviction of Nazi war criminals at Nuremberg, and that was first used, in 1915, to describe the persecution of the Armenians by the Ottoman regime. Indeed, the Commission's analysis very helpfully reminds us that genocide and crimes against humanity are cognates, and that a finding that there was no genocide, in a technical sense, in no way absolves tyrants of their responsibility for atrocities.

The Commission called for prosecution of crimes against humanity by the International Criminal Court.[7] Because Sudan is not a party to the *Rome Statute*, Security Council referral, in accordance with Article 13(b) of the *Rome Statute of the International Criminal Court*,[8] is the appropriate mechanism to trigger the jurisdiction of the Court. Several weeks after the Darfur Commission issued its report, the United Nations Security Council responded to the report by referring 'the situation in Darfur since 1 July 2002' to the International Criminal Court.[9] In December 2005, Prosecutor Luis Moreno Ocampo reported to the Security Council that he had 'identified particularly grave events, involving, for example, high numbers of killings, mass rapes and other forms of extremely serious gender violence and other crimes within the jurisdiction of the Court'.[10]

The elaborate legal analysis in the Darfur Commission report constitutes an important contribution to the evolving law of genocide. Less than a year earlier, the Appeals Chamber of the International Criminal Tribunal for the Former Yugoslavia issued its first major ruling on genocide. The Tribunal confirmed that genocide had been committed in the final days of the war in Bosnia and Herzegovina, at Srebrenica. It said that General Radislav Krstić had not personally perpetrated the crime, but that he had aided and abetted in its commission, given that 'Krstic was aware of the intent to commit genocide on the part of some members of the VRS Main Staff, and with that knowledge, he did nothing to prevent the use of Drina Corps personnel and resources to facilitate those killings'.[11] The Darfur Commission was clearly influenced by the *Krstić Appeal Judgment*, and more specifically the Tribunal's refusal to convict in the absence of convincing evidence of genocidal intent.[12] Judge Shahabuddeen wrote a partially dissenting opinion in *Krstić* that considerably

---

6   'Report of the International Commission of Inquiry on violations of international humanitarian law and human rights law in Darfur', UN Doc. S/2005/60, para. 533 (emphasis in the original).

7   *Ibid.*, para. 569.

8   Rome Statute of the International Criminal Court, UN Doc. A/CONF.183/9.

9   UN Doc. S/RES/1593 (2005), para. 1. See: Luigi Condorelli and Annalisa Ciampi, 'Comments on the Security Council Referral of the Situation in Darfur to the ICC', 3 *Journal of International Criminal Justice*, p. 590.

10   'Second Report of the Prosecutor of the International Criminal Court, Mr. Luis Moreno Ocampo, to the Security Council Pursuant to UNSC 1593 (2005)', 13 December 2005. p. 2.

11   *Prosecutor v Krstić* (Case No. IT-98-33-A), Judgment, 19 April 2004, para. 134.

12   'Report of the International Commission of Inquiry on violations of international humanitarian law and human rights law in Darfur', UN Doc. S/2005/60, para. 503.

broadened the concept of genocide to include acts of forcible displacement, which would colloquially be called 'ethnic cleansing'.[13] The Darfur Commission did not cite the Shahabuddeen dissent.

Aside from the Darfur Commission, three Trial Chamber decisions are also part of the post-*Krstić* debates. One of them, *Brđanin*, issued on 1 September 2004, sticks to the relatively conservative approach of the Appeals Chamber, acquitting a Bosnian political leader with respect to a genocide count.[14] It is of interest that the Prosecutor has not appealed this aspect of the Trial Chamber decision. A second ruling, *Blagojević*, appeared a few days before the report of the Darfur Commission. It essentially followed the line taken by Judge Shahabuddeen in his dissent.[15] A third decision, issued in late-September 2006, dismissed charges of genocide against Bosnian Serb political leader Momčilo Krajišnik, who had been charged with participating 'in an enterprise to bring about the *partial* destruction of the Bosnian–Muslim and Bosnian–Croat groups in territories within Bosnia-Herzegovina'.[16] According to the Trial Chamber:

868 In the instances of extermination, the Chamber has considered whether a genocidal intent of the perpetrator could be inferred directly from the large number of killings. In this context, the Chamber has also considered the number of victims relative to the number of Muslims and Croats present in the village or detention centre where the killings took place, and the selection of the victims. *The Chamber* finds that in no instance are the killings themselves sufficient to make a conclusive finding on whether the perpetrator had a genocidal intent.

869 In addition to the acts themselves, the Chamber has considered the surrounding circumstances, including words uttered by the perpetrators and other persons at the scene of the crime and official reports on the crimes, in order to establish the *mens rea*. Considering the evidence as a whole, the Chamber can make no conclusive finding that any acts were committed with the intent to destroy, in part, the Bosnian–Muslim or Bosnian–Croat ethnic group, as such.[17]

If nothing else, these three decisions and the Darfur Commission report show how unsettled the law of genocide remains, despite what ought to have been an authoritative ruling of the Appeals Chamber.

One question that did not figure in these recent judgments, including the Appeals Chamber ruling in *Krstić*, is the role of a State plan or policy in the commission of genocide. At the International Criminal Tribunal for the Former Yugoslavia, the matter has been settled law since 2001, when the Appeals Chamber declared that 'the existence of a plan or policy is not a legal ingredient of the crime'.[18] Given the established case law of the *ad hoc* Tribunal holding that a State plan or policy

---

13 *Prosecutor v Krstić* (Case No. IT-98-33-A), Partial Dissenting Judgment of Judge Shahabuddeen, 19 April 2004, paras. 45–57.

14 *Prosecutor v Brđanin* (Case No. IT-99-36-T), Judgment, 1 September 2004.

15 *Prosecutor v Blagojević* (Case No. IT-02-60-T), Judgment, 17 January 2005.

16 *Prosecutor v Krajišnik* (Case No. IT-00-39-T), Judgment, 27 September 2006, para. 852.

17 *Ibid.* Also paras. 1089–1094.

18 *Prosecutor v Jelisić* (Case No. IT-95-10-A), Judgment, 5 July 2001, para. 48.

is not an element of genocide, it is intriguing to note that the Darfur Commission considered this issue in considerable detail. After all, one of its central conclusions was that 'the Government of Sudan has not pursued a *policy* of genocide'.[19]

The Commission said that there was evidence of two elements of the crime of genocide. The first was the presence of material acts corresponding to paragraphs in the definition of the crime set out in Article II of the 1948 *Convention for the Prevention and Punishment of the Crime of Genocide*. It observed that 'the gross violations of human rights perpetrated by Government forces and the militias under their control' included reports of killing, causing serious bodily or mental harm, and deliberate infliction of conditions of life likely to bring about physical destruction. The second was the subjective perception that the victims and perpetrators, African and Arab tribes respectively, made up two distinct ethnic groups. But, said the Commission:

> one central element appears to be missing, at least as far as the central Government authorities are concerned: genocidal intent. Generally speaking, the policy of attacking, killing and forcibly displacing members of some tribes does not evince a specific intent to annihilate, in whole or in part, a group distinguished on racial, ethnic, national or religious grounds. Rather, it would seem that those who planned and organized attacks on villages pursued the intent to drive the victims from their homes, primarily for purposes of counter-insurgency warfare.[20]

The Commission continued to consider whether crimes against humanity had been committed. Here too, it looked for the State plan or policy:

> However, as pointed out above, the Government also entertained the intent to drive a particular group out of an area on persecutory and discriminatory grounds for political reasons. In the case of Darfur this discriminatory and persecutory intent may be found on many occasions, in some Arab militias, as well as in the central Government: the systematic attacks on villages inhabited by civilians (or mostly by civilians) belonging to some 'African' tribes (Fur, Masaalit and Zaghawa), the systematic destruction and burning down of these villages, as well as the forced displacement of civilians from those villages attest to a manifestly persecutory intent. In this respect, in addition to *murder* as a crime against humanity, the Government may be held responsible for *persecution as a crime against humanity. This would not affect the conclusion of the Commission that the Government of Sudan has not pursued the policy of genocide in Darfur.*[21]

The Commission went on to acknowledge the theoretical policy that 'single individuals, including governmental officials',[22] or 'individual members of the militias supported by the Government, or even single Government officials',[23] pursued policies of genocide or crimes against humanity. But it proceeded no further

---

19 'Report of the International Commission of Inquiry on violations of international humanitarian law and human rights law in Darfur', UN Doc. S/2005/60, para. 518 (emphasis added).

20 *Ibid.*

21 *Ibid.*, para. 519 (emphasis in the original).

22 *Ibid.*, para. 520.

23 *Ibid.*, para. 521.

to speculate on this issue, and recapitulated its central conclusion 'that no genocidal policy has been pursued and implemented in Darfur by the Government authorities, directly or though the militias under their control'.[24]

Thus, while expressing fealty to the case law rejecting a State plan or policy as an element of genocide (or crimes against humanity), as a practical matter, the Darfur Commission situated the matter at the very centre of its analysis. This is all the more striking given that the Commission was not asked by the Security Council whether there was a State plan or policy of Sudan to commit genocide, but only whether 'acts of genocide have occurred'.[25]

It would be overstating the case to suggest that the Darfur Commission was arguing for a revision of the case law of the International Criminal Tribunal for the former Yugoslavia as to whether a State plan or policy is an element of the crime of genocide or, for that matter, of crimes against humanity. But even if the question was only raised indirectly and perhaps inadvertently, the Commission's discussion may help to prompt a reopening of the debate.

The discussion of the State plan or policy issue in the leading case on this matter, *Prosecutor v. Jelisić*, is thin and unsatisfactory. The Trial Chamber purported to base its analysis exclusively on a reading of the *travaux préparatoires*:

> In this respect, the preparatory work of the Convention of 1948 brings out that premeditation was not selected as a legal ingredient of the crime of genocide, after having been mentioned by the *ad hoc* committee at the draft stage, on the grounds that it seemed superfluous given the special intention already required by the text and that such precision would only make the burden of proof even greater. It ensues from this omission that the drafters of the Convention did not deem the existence of an organization or a system serving a genocidal objective as a legal ingredient of the crime. In so doing, they did not discount the possibility of a lone individual seeking to destroy a group as such.[26]

The *travaux préparatoires* are not nearly as conclusive as the Trial Chamber suggested. The debate it referred to did not contemplate the issue of a State plan or policy, but rather whether the reference to specific acts of genocide should include the adjective 'deliberate'. The Ad Hoc Drafting Committee, established in early 1948, had opted to use the word 'deliberate' rather than 'intent': 'In this convention genocide means any of the following deliberate acts directed against a national, racial, religious [or political] group, on grounds of national or racial origin or religious belief.'[27] On a proposal from the USA, the Committee later added the word 'intent': 'In this Convention genocide means any of the following deliberate acts committed with the intent to destroy a national, racial, religious or political group, on the grounds of the national or racial origin, religious belief, or political opinion of its members.'[28] The

---

24 *Ibid.*, para. 522.

25 UN Doc. S/RES/1564 (2004), para. 12.

26 *Prosecutor v Jelisić* (Case No. IT-95-10-T), Judgment, 14 December 1999, para. 100.

27 UN Doc. E/AC.25/SR.12, p. 12.

28 UN Doc. E/AC.25/SR.24, p. 3.

report of the Ad Hoc Committee stated that the proposed definition encompassed 'the notion of premeditation'.[29]

In the Sixth Committee of the General Assembly, the word 'deliberate' provoked a debate about whether genocide was a crime requiring premeditation. A range of opinions was expressed on the question of premeditation. At the close of the debate, the word 'deliberate' in the Ad Hoc Committee draft was deleted, but 'intent' retained.[30] These debates were confusing and sometimes contradictory and, as is often the case with the *travaux préparatoires*, it seems dangerous to rely on isolated remarks from certain delegations in attempting to establish the intent of the drafters. At no point was there a definitive and unambiguous decision by the Sixth Committee to exclude the concept of premeditation, which had been affirmed in the earlier report of the Ad Hoc Committee. The wording that resulted, in Article II of the *Convention*, represents a compromise aimed at generating consensus between States with somewhat different conceptions of the purposes of the instrument. Let us recall that in his partially dissenting opinion in *Krstić*, Judge Shahabuddeen warned of reliance on the *travaux* in applying the *Convention* to contemporary debates: 'On settled principles of construction, there is no need to consult this material, however interesting it may be.'[31]

But even assuming that the Trial Chamber in *Jelisić* was correct in deducing the absence of 'premeditation' from a definition requiring 'intent to destroy, in whole or in part, a national, ethnical, racial or religious group, as such', based on a scattered and inconclusive debate in the Sixth Committee, it seems far-fetched to extrapolate from the discussion a conclusion that there is no State plan or policy involved in the crime of genocide. Is it enough to conclude that this is not an element of the crime based upon the observation that the drafters 'did not discount the possibility of a lone individual seeking to destroy a group as such'? The Appeals Chamber ruling in the same case is hardly more edifying. It consists of a single sentence, without further discussion or authority: 'The Appeals Chamber is of the opinion that the existence of a plan or policy is not a legal ingredient of the crime.'[32]

From an inadequate discussion in a Trial Chamber decision, to an unsubstantiated confirmation by the Appeals Chamber, the International Criminal Tribunal for the former Yugoslavia then extended the same reasoning that it had applied with respect to genocide to crimes against humanity. After noting that '[t]here has been some debate in the jurisprudence of this Tribunal as to whether a policy or plan constitutes an element of the definition of crimes against humanity', the Appeals Chamber said that practice 'overwhelmingly supports the contention that no such requirement exists under customary international law'. Its discussion of this important matter lies buried in a footnote. The Appeals Chamber invoked a number of authorities in

29 UN Doc. E/794, p. 5.

30 UN Doc. A/C.6/SR.73 (twenty-seven in favour, ten against, with six abstentions).

31 *Prosecutor v Krstić* (Case No. IT-98-33-A), Partial Dissenting Judgment of Judge Shahabuddeen, 19 April 2004, para. 52.

32 *Prosecutor v Jelisić* (Case No. IT-95-10-A), Judgment, 5 July 2001, para. 48 (emphasis added). The Appeals Chamber's *obiter dictum* was followed in *Prosecutor v Sikirica* et al. (Case No. IT-95-8-T), Judgment on Defence Motions to Acquit, 3 September 2001, para. 62.

support, but without detailed explanation, and it is often not clear how and why such references buttress its position. And the Appeals Chamber cited itself: 'The Appeals Chamber reached the same conclusion in relation to the crime of genocide (*Jelisić Appeal Judgment*).'[33]

The absence of any reference to the *Rome Statute of the International Criminal Court* is telling here. When the *Rome Statute* appears to support arguments of the Appeals Chamber, it has had no compunction in relying upon its provisions.[34] On the State plan or policy issue, however, Article 7(2) of the *Rome Statute of the International Criminal Court* says that crimes against humanity must be committed 'pursuant to or in furtherance of a State or organizational policy'.[35] As for the crime of genocide, although the *Rome Statute* says nothing more specific than what appears in Article II of the 1948 *Convention*, it is surely significant that the Assembly of States Parties of the International Criminal Court insisted upon something resembling a plan or policy component in the Elements of Crimes, requiring that genocidal conduct take place 'in the context of a manifest pattern of similar conduct' directed against a protected group. [36] Indeed, these words in the Elements of Crimes were probably a reaction to the decisions of the International Criminal Tribunal for the former Yugoslavia in *Jelisić*. While perhaps not conclusive, these are relevant legal developments justifying some further attention to and reconsideration of the exclusion of the State plan or policy element from both genocide and crimes against humanity in the jurisprudence of the Appeals Chamber.

Serious questions have also been raised by leading academics. In his recent three-volume work, *The Legislative History of the International Criminal Court*, Cherif Bassiouni argues:

Contrary to what some advocates advance, Article 7 [of the *Rome Statute*] does not bring a new development to crimes against humanity, namely its applicability to non-state actors. If that were the case, the Mafia, for example, could be charged with such crimes before the ICC, and that is clearly neither the letter nor the spirit of Article 7. The question arose after 9/11 as to whether a group such as al-Qaeda, which operates on a worldwide basis and is capable of inflicting significant harm in more than one state, falls within this category. In this author's opinion, such a group does not qualify for inclusion within the meaning of crimes against humanity as defined in Article 7, and for that matter, under any definition of that crime up to Article 6(c) of the IMT, notwithstanding the international dangers that it poses ... The text [of Article 7(2)] clearly refers to state policy, and the words 'organisational policy' do not refer to the policy of an organization, but the policy of a state. It does not refer to non-state actors ....[37]

33 *Prosecutor v Kunarac* et al. (Case No. IT-96-23/1-A), Judgment, 12 June 2002, para. 98, fn. 114.

34 See *e.g.*, on the issue of 'joint criminal enterprise': *Prosecutor v Tadić* (Case No. IT-94-1-A), Judgment, 15 July 1999, paras. 222–223.

35 *Rome Statute of the International Criminal Court*, UN Doc. A/CONF.183/9, art. 7(2).

36 'Elements of Crimes, ICC-ASP/1/3, p. 113..

37 Cherif Bassiouni, M. Cherif (2005), *The Legislative History of the International Criminal Court: Introduction, Analysis and Integrated Text*, Vol. I, Ardsley: Transnational

In its landmark ruling on crimes against humanity, dated 28 June 2005, the Supreme Court of Canada considered the issue of whether there was a State plan or policy element with respect to crimes against humanity. It noted Professor Bassiouni's position with considerable deference,[38] but also acknowledged that the Appeals Chamber of the International Criminal Tribunal for the former Yugoslavia was taking the law in a different direction. 'It seems that there is currently no requirement in customary international law that a policy underlie the attack, though we do not discount the possibility that customary international law may evolve over time so as to incorporate a policy requirement,' said the Supreme Court of Canada.[39]

In his comment on the Darfur Commission report, Professor Claus Kress did not specifically consider the State plan or policy issue. But in stating his case for 'a fresh look on the meaning of genocidal intent', he explained that 'the way forward may lie in taking account of the fact that genocide, for all practical purposes, is a systemic crime. If a collective level of genocidal activity must normally be distinguished from the level of the individual genocidal conduct, it is worth asking whether the construction of the word "intent" should not be construed accordingly.' For Professor Kress, a workable interpretation of the mental element of the crime of genocide requires situating the acts of individual offenders within a collective enterprise. This is yet another argument for rejecting the *Jelisić* hypothesis of the lone perpetrator, an approach which lies at the origin of the rejection of the State plan or policy element.[40]

But reassessment of the jurisprudence on the State plan or policy element may prove inconvenient for the Office of the Prosecutor of the International Criminal Court that, for the first time in the history of international criminal justice, has focused the attention of an international tribunal on actors that are neither States nor even State-like entities. Rather, States have been encouraged by the Prosecutor to 'refer' cases against themselves or, rather, against rebel bands operating within their territory.[41] According to public sources, six arrest warrants have been issued by the International Criminal Court to date, all of them involving non-State war lords.[42] Thus, the substantive developments in the law of genocide and crimes against

---

Publishers, pp. 151–152. See also: M. Cherif Bassiouni (1999), *Crimes Against Humanity*, 2nd ed. (The Hague: Kluwer Academic Publishing), pp. 243–281.

38 *Mugesera v Canada (MCI)*, 2005 SCC 40, para. 157.

39 *Ibid.*, para. 158.

40 Kress, C. (2005), 'The Darfur Report and Genocidal Intent', 3 *Journal of the International Criminal Justice*, 562, at pp. 572–573.

41 Schabas, W.A. (2006), 'First Prosecutions at the International Criminal Court', 25 *Human Rights Law Journal*, p. 25.

42 *Situation in Uganda* (ICC-02/04-53), Warrant of Arrest for Joseph Kony Issued on 8 July 2005 as Amended on 27 September 2005; *Situation in Uganda (*ICC-02/04-54), Warrant of Arrest for Vincent Otti, 8 July 2005; *Situation in Uganda (*ICC-02/04-55), Warrant of Arrest for Raska Lukwaya, 8 July 2005; *Situation in Uganda* (ICC-02/04-56), Warrant of Arrest for Okot Odhiambo, 8 July 2005; *Situation in Uganda* (ICC-02/04-57), Warrant of Arrest for Dominic Ongwen, 8 July 2005; *Prosecutor v. Lubanga* (ICC-01/04-01/06-8), Decision on the Prosecutor's Application for a Warrant of Arrest, 10 February 2006.

humanity expressed in *Jelisić* and *Kunarac* have cleared the way for innovations in prosecutorial policy.

But perhaps this is not the direction that international criminal justice should be going. In other words, the arguments of Professor Bassiouni and others are not simply the pedantic declarations of scholars who are obsessed with the drafting history of archaic texts. They are also driven by compelling considerations of international criminal justice policy. At its origins, international criminal justice was developed to address 'crimes of state'. Indeed, that is precisely why criminal justice with respect to atrocities had to be internationalized. Such crimes went unpunished because the State where the crime took place was not only unwilling to prosecute, it was itself complicit in the offence. This is why the 'State plan or policy' element was always implied in the notion of genocide and crimes against humanity, even if the texts were silent on the point. Interpretations of the law that point us towards rebels, bandits, mafias and terrorists may be nothing more than a dangerous distraction. Of course, States themselves may find such legal developments to be rather comforting.

The Darfur Commission probably did not intend to ignite debate about all of this. Nevertheless, its approach to the State plan or policy element with respect to genocide makes the question unavoidable. It was not asked by the Security Council to determine whether there was a State plan or policy involved in the attacks on minorities in Darfur, but only whether 'acts of genocide' had occurred. By answering the question 'has genocide been committed' with the answer that 'the Government of Sudan has not pursued a policy of genocide,' it helped to confirm the existence of an implicit or unspoken element in the crime of genocide. At the very least, this should indicate that the debate on this matter did not end with the perfunctory pronouncements of the Appeals Chamber of the International Criminal Tribunal for the Former Yugoslavia.

Chapter 5

Sudan, the United States, and the International Criminal Court: A Tense Triumvirate in Transitional Justice for Darfur

Zachary D. Kaufman[1]

Introduction

More than two decades of civil war in Sudan have led to the death of over two million people. Since 2003 alone, when violence erupted in Sudan's western region of Darfur, hundreds of thousands of people have died and another two million individuals have been displaced. There is much debate on whether the mass atrocities in Darfur, which include widespread murder and rape, should be characterized – as the US Government (USG) has described them[2] – as 'genocide.'[3] Whatever the appropriate term, human rights organizations have been monitoring the ongoing

1   The author thanks the following individuals for comments on an earlier draft of this chapter: Ligia Abreu, Fahim Ahmed, Adrienne Bernhard, Samuel Charap, Phil Clark, Adam Cole, Mauro De Lorenzo, Cynthia DeGabrielle, Cassie Farrelly, David Fidler, Scott Grinsell, Benjamin Heineike, Howard Kaufman, Sarah Martin, Vipin Narang, Daniel Pastor, Katherine Southwick, Sharath Srinivasan, Pierre St. Hilaire, Yong Suh, Wilburn Williams, Lindsey Worth, and two anonymous reviewers. All statements and any errors are, of course, the responsibility of the author. This chapter is current as of 5 August 2005.
2   On 23 July 2004, the US Congress passed a joint US House of Representatives–US Senate resolution calling the atrocities in Darfur 'genocide.' In September 2004, both US President George W. Bush and former US Secretary of State Colin Powell characterized the Darfur atrocities as 'genocide.'
3   See: Schabas, W.A. (2005), 'Darfur and the "Odious Scourge": The Commission of Inquiry's Findings on Genocide?', 18:4 *Leiden Journal of International Law*, 871–85. See also, e.g.: International Commission of Inquiry on Darfur (25 January 2005), 'Report of the International Commission of Inquiry on Darfur to the United Nations Secretary-General,' http://www.ohchr.org/english/docs/darfurreport.doc; Prunier, Gérard (2005), *Darfur: The Ambiguous Genocide* (Ithaca, NY: Cornell University Press).

atrocities and lobbying the international community to take action, such as by bringing suspected perpetrators to justice.[4]

This chapter documents and assesses the controversy, compromise, and, ultimately, consensus within the United Nations Security Council (UNSC) that resulted in the UNSC's 31 March 2005 decision to adopt UNSC Resolution (UNSCR) 1593, through which the UNSC referred the situation in Darfur since 1 July 2002 to the Prosecutor of the International Criminal Court (ICC). This chapter considers the following: First, why did the USG initially propose the establishment of an alternative transitional justice option for addressing Darfur, in the form of an *ad hoc* hybrid tribunal to be established in Arusha, Tanzania, that would be jointly administered by the United Nations (UN) and the African Union and act as an extension of the UN International Criminal Tribunal for Rwanda (ICTR)? Second, given its opposition to the ICC, why did the USG ultimately abstain from voting on – rather than veto – UNSCR 1593, thus enabling the Darfur situation[5] to be referred by the UNSC to the ICC? Third, do the advent of the ICC and the UNSC's referral of the Darfur situation to it necessarily preclude the pursuit of other transitional justice options in this case? Finally, what is the significance of the UNSC referral of the Darfur situation to the ICC, and what political and legal precedents does it set?

In exploring these questions, this chapter focuses on the role of the USG because, for better or worse, its reaction to international crises often significantly shapes the global response due to the US's preponderance of resources in the post-Cold War era. This chapter will argue that the precedent-setting UNSCR 1593, on which the USG abstained for a combination of reasons, some self-interested, offers as much hope as doubt for the promotion of justice and accountability in Darfur.

UNSC Referral of the Darfur Situation to the ICC

On 31 March 2005, the UNSC, acting under Chapter VII of the UN Charter, adopted UNSCR 1593, which referred 'the situation in Darfur since 1 July 2002 to the Prosecutor of the International Criminal Court.'[6] Eleven states voted in favour of the resolution, none against, and four (Algeria, Brazil, China, and the US) abstained.

---

4   See, e.g.: Human Rights Watch (21 January 2005). 'Targeting the Fur: Mass Killings in Darfur', http://hrw.org/backgrounder/africa/darfur0105/; Human Rights Watch (November 2004), '"If We Return, We Will Be Killed": Consolidation of Ethnic Cleansing in Darfur, Sudan', http://hrw.org/backgrounder/africa/darfur1104/; Human Rights Watch (May 2004), 'Darfur Destroyed: Ethnic Cleansing by Government and Militia Forces in Western Sudan', Volume 16, Number 6(A), http://hrw.org/reports/2004/sudan0504/; International Crisis Group (8 March 2005), 'Darfur: The Failure to Protect', Africa Report Number 89, http://www.crisisgroup.org/home/index.cfm?id=3314&l=1; International Crisis Group (23 May 2004), 'Sudan: Now or Never in Darfur', Africa Report Number 80, http://www.crisisgroup.org/home/index.cfm?id=2765&l=1; International Crisis Group (25 March 2004), 'Darfur Rising: Sudan's New Crisis', Africa Report Number 76, http://www.crisisgroup.org/home/index.cfm?id=2550&l=1.

5   To be consistent with UNSCR 1593, this chapter refers to the conflict in Darfur as a 'situation.'

6   UN Security Council (31 March 2005). S/RES/1593 (2005).

After the vote, acting US Ambassador to the UN Anne Woods Patterson described the reasons for the USG's abstention. First, the USG believed that a superior transitional justice option would have been a hybrid tribunal located in Africa, which would incorporate local laws and procedures and employ staff from Africa and elsewhere. Second, the USG held the view that the ICC did not have jurisdiction over nationals of non-States Parties to the Rome Statute. Patterson also reiterated the USG's general objections to the ICC – for example, that this tribunal does not have sufficient safeguards to protect against politically-motivated prosecutions or frivolous cases. Despite these concerns, the USG did not vote against the resolution because, as Patterson explained, it recognized a need for the international community to cooperate in order to end impunity in Sudan and because it was confident that the wording of the resolution protected US nationals and members of the armed services of other non-States Parties to the Rome Statute (except Sudan) from the ICC's jurisdiction.[7]

The appearance of a near-consensus on the judicial response to the Darfur atrocities is only the latest chapter of the story. The UNSC decision to refer the case to the ICC was reached only after significant disagreement and consideration of alternative proposals. Because Sudan is not a State Party to the Rome Statute,[8] and the conflict is not of an international nature concerning a State Party, the ICC would only have jurisdiction over the Darfur situation if the UNSC, acting under Chapter VII of the UN Charter, referred the matter to the ICC.[9] In early 2005, the USG stated its opposition to such a referral. Instead, as early as 21 January 2005, the USG proposed that the international community establish an *ad hoc* tribunal in Arusha, Tanzania – the site of the ICTR – which would have jurisdiction over Darfur.[10] The USG proposed that the UN and the African Union jointly administer this new tribunal. Anticipating objections from UNSC members and others about the financial costs of establishing and operating such a tribunal, the USG offered to cover all such monetary expenses, estimated to range from US$40 to $150 million per year.[11] The USG claimed to be considering designing this *ad hoc* tribunal as an

---

7   United Nations (31 March 2005), Press Release SC/8351, 'Security Council Refers Situation in Darfur, Sudan, to Prosecutor of International Criminal Court', http://www.un.org/News/Press/docs/2005/sc8351.doc.htm.

8   Sudan signed the Rome Statute of the International Criminal Court on 8 September 2000, but has not ratified it. See: 'Rome Statute of the International Criminal Court: Participants', http://untreaty.un.org/ENGLISH/bible/englishinternetbible/partI/chapterXVIII/treaty10.asp.

9   See: Rome Statute of the International Criminal Court. Established 17 July 1998, entered into force 1 July 2002. UN Doc.A/CONF.183/9, http://www.un.org/law/icc/statute/romefra.htm. Part II (Jurisdiction, Admissibility and Applicable Law), Articles 12–15.

10   For more information on the USG proposal, see, e.g., Hoge, Warren (29 January 2005), 'US Lobbies U.N. on Darfur and International Court', *New York Times*, A8; Kralev, Nicholas (22 January 2005), 'US Balks at Global Court Use for Darfur', *Washington Times*, A1; US Department of State (21 January 2005), 'Daily Press Briefing, Richard Boucher, Spokesman, Washington, DC, January 21, 2005', http://www.state.gov/r/pa/prs/dpb/2005/41047.htm.

11   For estimates on the low side of this range, see, e.g., Punyasena, Wasana (Deputy Convenor, AMICC), and Jon Washburn (Convenor, AMICC) (3 February 2005), 'Message

expansion of or tied to the ICTR; the USG did not indicate that the tribunal should be completely separate.[12] Critics asserted that this alternative transitional justice institution would be slower, more expensive, less legitimate, and less effective than the already established ICC. Of course, these criticisms may be premature, as the ICC is not yet fully functional and has yet to try any cases. Nonetheless, in response to its proposal, some commentators accused the USG, which itself had characterized the crimes as 'genocide,' of promoting a purely self-interested position that neglected atrocities in Sudan and would delay justice in Darfur.[13] Consequently, instead of distributing the costs of pursuing transitional justice throughout the international system, the USG's optimal preference for the creation of a local, hybrid tribunal greatly drove up costs to itself − financially, politically, and logistically.

The direct monetary expense of permitting the UNSC to refer the case to the ICC would have literally been nothing for the USG. Because the US is not a State Party to the Rome Statute, the USG is not obligated to contribute funding to the ICC, a point reiterated in UNSCR 1593.[14] Yet the USG was prepared to spend US$40 to $150 million per year on an *ad hoc* tribunal in Arusha. The USG must therefore have initially calculated that indirect financial costs and other disadvantages of permitting the UNSC to refer the Darfur situation to the ICC would have been even greater. As calculated by the USG, those costs included 'legitimizing the ICC';[15] creating a precedent of pursuing transitional justice issues through the ICC instead of through, for example, the USG's preferred method of *ad hoc* tribunals established by the UNSC acting under Chapter VII of the UN Charter (as was done for the former Yugoslavia and Rwanda);[16] and creating a precedent of referring to the ICC cases concerning non-States Parties to the Rome Statute, which could include the US. Furthermore, if

on Darfur', Email to the Author. For estimates on the high side of this range, see, e.g., Power, Samantha (10 February 2005), 'Court of First Resort', Opinion Editorial, *New York Times*, A23.

12 For example, US Department of State spokesperson Richard Boucher stated on 21 January 2005 that the USG was considering expanding the ICTR to include jurisdiction over the atrocities in Darfur, as well as other options. See: United States Department of State (21 January 2005), 'Daily Press Briefing, Richard Boucher, Spokesman, Washington, DC, 21 January, 2005', http://www.state.gov/r/pa/prs/dpb/2005/41047.htm.

13 For criticisms of the USG proposal, see, e.g., Human Rights Watch (15 February 2005), 'US Proposal for a Darfur Tribunal: Not an Effective Option to Ensure Justice', http://hrw.org/english/docs/2005/02/15/sudan10179.htm; Kristof, Nicholas (2 February 2005), 'Why Should We Shield the Killers?,' Opinion Editorial, *New York Times*, A21; Power, Samantha (10 February 2005), 'Court of First Resort,' Opinion Editorial, *New York Times*, A23; *Washington Post* (29 January 2005), 'For the Triumph of Evil,' Editorial, *Washington Post*, A24.

14 UN Security Council (31 March 2005). S/RES/1593 (2005).

15 According to then US Ambassador for War Crimes Issues Pierre-Richard Prosper, as quoted in: Hoge, Warren (29 January 2005), 'US Lobbies U.N. on Darfur and International Court', *New York Times*, A8.

16 U.S. Department of State (2 August 2002), 'Fact Sheet, Bureau of Political-Military Affairs, Washington, DC, August 2, 2002, The International Criminal Court', http://www.state.gov/t/pm/rls/fs/2002/23426.htm; U.S. Department of State (30 July 2003), 'Fact Sheet, Bureau of Political-Military Affairs, Washington, DC, July 30, 2003, Frequently Asked

the USG had vetoed UNSCR 1593, international pressure on the USG to intervene – perhaps militarily – in Sudan might have increased. At least by abstaining during this vote, the USG could credibly deny that it was 'doing nothing' or obstructing action, even if the ICC referral was not the USG's optimal transitional justice option. Ultimately deciding to abstain, the USG apparently determined that the direct and indirect costs of cooperation did not exceed the costs of non-cooperation.

Alternative Transitional Justice Options for Darfur

On 1 June 2005, the first Prosecutor of the ICC, Luis Moreno Ocampo, officially opened the ICC's investigation into the situation in Darfur.[17] At the end of that month, Ocampo addressed the UNSC on his activities pursuant to UNSCR 1593. He stated that he had received 'a sealed envelope from the UN Secretary General containing the conclusions reached by the [International] Commission [of Inquiry on Darfur] as to persons potentially bearing criminal responsibility for crimes in Darfur' but added that he 'does not consider this list of names to be binding.'[18] The ICC is now considering which suspected atrocity perpetrators from Darfur to prosecute, and when and where to do so.

Contrary to popular belief, the advent of the ICC and referral of the Darfur situation to it do not preclude the pursuit of other transitional justice options with respect to Darfur. In fact, there are at least four reasons to believe that additional alternatives may be utilized.

First, the ICC's own jurisdiction limits the number of cases that the court can try concerning the Darfur situation. As they relate to Darfur, the ICC's subject-matter and temporal jurisdictions at the very least are restrictive factors. The jurisdiction *ratione materiae* of the ICC is limited to genocide, war crimes, crimes against humanity, and the still undefined crime of aggression.[19] The jurisdiction *ratione temporis* of the ICC, as reaffirmed in UNSCR 1593, is limited to crimes committed after the ICC came into force on 1 July 2002.[20] Crimes falling outside the ICC's subject-matter jurisdiction and/or committed before 1 July 2002 must therefore be addressed via alternative transitional justice options.

Second, the ICC will be limited by its own resources in the number of cases – and the number of defendants in those cases – that it can try within the Darfur

---

Questions About the U.S. Government's Policy Regarding the International Criminal Court (ICC)', http://www.state.gov/t/pm/rls/fs/23428.htm.

17 International Criminal Court (6 June 2005), Press Release OTP/LSU/066-05, 'The Prosecutor of the ICC Opens Investigation in Darfur', http://www.icc-cpi.int/press/pressreleases/107.html.

18 International Criminal Court (29 June 2005), 'Report of the Prosecutor of the International Criminal Court, Mr. Luis Moreno Ocampo, to the Security Council Pursuant to UNSCR 1593 (2005)', Section II (Preliminary Analysis and Initiation of the Investigation), Part 1 (Gathering of Information and Analysis), http://www.icc-cpi.int/library/cases/ICC_Darfur_UNSC_Report_29-06-05_EN.pdf.

19 Rome Statute, at Articles 5–8.

20 *Ibid.*, at Article 11.

situation. If more atrocities have been or are committed in Darfur than the ICC can investigate and prosecute, then either States Parties to the Rome Statute will have to increase the ICC's resources or those cases and suspected perpetrators will have to be addressed through alternative means.

Third, and related to the previous point, the total number of cases and suspected perpetrators that the ICC tries will be limited by the ICC Prosecutor's own discretion, not only because of the ICC's limited capabilities, but also due to political decisions that he may make not to try certain individuals. As Ocampo has stated, the ICC will try only a dozen or so 'big fish' of an atrocity, a policy consistent with that of other war crimes tribunals.[21] This guiding principle will leave all other suspected perpetrators of those atrocities to be addressed through alternative means, if at all. In Rwanda more than 120,000 suspects[22] were put in pre-trial detention after the 1994 genocide[23] and are being processed through either local (*gacaca*) or federal judicial systems. Similarly, for the vast majority of the perpetrators and victims of the Darfur atrocities, justice will have to be pursued outside the ICC. UNSCR 1593 seems to recognize this reality, as it emphasizes the 'need to promote healing and reconciliation and encourages in this respect the creation of institutions, involving all sectors of Sudanese society, such as truth and/or reconciliation commissions, in order to complement judicial processes and thereby reinforce the efforts to restore long-lasting peace, with African Union and international support as necessary.'[24]

Finally, some states may decide to pursue justice for crimes that fall within the ICC's jurisdiction. Furthermore, the Rome Statute's 'complementarity' principle, which provides that the ICC will have jurisdiction only if a state 'is unwilling or unable genuinely to carry out the investigation or prosecution,' may require the ICC to defer to these states because the ICC supplements, but does not claim primacy over, domestic proceedings.[25] These domestic proceedings could occur in several different ways. For example, as part of a compromise on the wording of what became UNSCR 1593, the USG obtained an exemption from the ICC's jurisdiction for any national, official, or personnel from a non-State Party to the Rome Statute (other than Sudan) suspected of committing atrocities in Sudan.[26] Some commentators have called this exemption, which was laid out in paragraph 6 of UNSCR 1593, a 'deferral within a referral.'[27] Patterson insisted that if any of its citizens violated international

21 Ocampo, Luis Moreno (27 June 2004), 'Remembering Rwanda: Justice for War Criminals and the Role of the International Criminal Court', Conference proceedings, Rhodes House, University of Oxford, Oxford, United Kingdom.

22 It is estimated by some Rwandan government officials that a total number of people several times that figure participated in the genocide. See: Gourevitch, Philip (1998), *We Wish to Inform You that Tomorrow We Will be Killed with our Families: Stories from Rwanda* (New York: Picador), 244–45.

23 'Rwandan Prisoners Endure Long, Cramped Wait in Jail for Trial', CNN.com, 15 September 1999, http://www.cnn.com/WORLD/africa/9909/15/rwanda.prison/.

24 UN Security Council (31 March 2005). S/RES/1593 (2005).

25 Rome Statute, at Article 17.

26 UN Security Council (31 March 2005). S/RES/1593 (2005).

27 See, e.g.: Gallavin, Chris (2 September 2005), 'The Stupefaction of the Law of Genocide through the Strangling of the International Criminal Court's Jurisdiction',

law, the USG would hold them accountable,[28] which it could do through domestic legislation designed specifically for this purpose.[29] However, if the US − or other non-States Parties to the Rome Statute besides Sudan − fails to bring to justice any of its citizens who might be involved in the Darfur atrocities, under this exemption the international community would have no recourse to do so through the ICC. In that case, these individuals may not be held responsible for their crimes.

Furthermore, Sudan itself is likely − and claims already to have begun − to investigate and prosecute some of its own citizens who are suspected of committing atrocities in Darfur. Sudan may do so through its domestic judiciary, a special court established for this singular purpose, or some combination thereof.[30] In stating his government's opposition to UNSCR 1593, the Sudanese representative to the UN, Ambassador Elfaith Mohamed Ahmed Erwa, claimed that his government was organizing trials and could ensure accountability.[31] Indeed, in mid-June 2005, Sudan established a special domestic tribunal, chaired by Judge Mahmoud Mohamed Saeed Abkam, to address claims against individuals suspected of perpetrating atrocities in Darfur.[32] The Sudanese Minister of Justice, Ali Mohamed Osman Yassin, announced shortly thereafter that this tribunal would try 160 suspects and that those trials had already begun.[33]

Some critics of this special court, such as Amnesty International, claim that the tribunal will not be fair, impartial, or independent. These critics also contend that the tribunal is 'doomed to failure' and is a deliberate attempt by the Sudanese Government to undermine the jurisdiction of the ICC.[34] If the ICC considers the Sudanese Government to be both willing and able genuinely to investigate and prosecute suspected atrocity perpetrators, however, it may defer to the Sudanese

---

Conference on 'The Criminal Law of Genocide—International, Comparative and Contextual Aspects', Nottingham Law School, Nottingham Trent University: Nottingham, UK.

28 United Nations (31 March 2005), Press Release SC/8351, 'Security Council Refers Situation in Darfur, Sudan, to Prosecutor of International Criminal Court', http://www.un.org/News/Press/docs/2005/sc8351.doc.htm.

29 See, e.g.: United States Code Title 18 (Crimes and Criminal Procedure), Part I (Crimes), Chapter 50A (Genocide), § 1091; Chapter 118 (War Crimes), § 2441; Chapter 113C (Torture), http://www.gpoaccess.gov/uscode/.

30 See, e.g.: Wax, Emily (2 April 2005), 'In Exploring a Solution for Darfur, Sudan Opts for Local Justice,' *Washington Post*, A16.

31 United Nations (31 March 2005). Press Release SC/8351.

32 See, e.g.: IRIN (15 June 2005), 'Sudan: National Court to Try Suspects of Darfur Crimes', http://www.alertnet.org/thenews/newsdesk/IRIN/ad0fcd5d9599a5d2e3400d7fea056351.htm; Saeed, Mohamed Ali (14 June 2005), 'Sudan's Own Darfur Crimes Court Starts Work, Rebels Cry Foul', *Agence France-Presse*, http://www.reliefweb.int/rw/RWB.NSF/db900SID/EVIU-6DCHDX?OpenDocument.

33 See, e.g.: Reuters (30 June 2005), 'Justice Minister Says Sudan to Try Darfur Suspects', http://www.alertnet.org/thenews/newsdesk/L30249394.htm; Oliver, Mark (30 June 2005), 'Sudan Rejects ICC Extradition Calls', *Guardian Unlimited*, http://www.guardian.co.uk/sudan/story/0,14658,1518327,00.html.

34 See, e.g.: Amnesty International (13 June 2005), 'Sudan: National Court for Crimes in Darfur Lacks Credibility', Press Release, http://t2news.amnesty.r3h.net/index/ENGAFR540592005.

domestic judiciary and/or Sudan's special court for Darfur to try these cases. If the ICC does not believe that to be the case (as suggested by the ICC Prosecutor's report of 29 June 2005[35]), tension will be likely to develop between the international community and Sudan, which the UNSC directed to 'fully cooperate' with the ICC. If Sudan is uncooperative, as Sudan's president, Omar al-Bashir, has pledged to be,[36] Sudan will be in breach of UNSCR 1593 and the ICC may therefore be limited in its ability to, *inter alia*, apprehend and transport suspects, acquire and preserve evidence, and recruit and protect witnesses. Since UNSCR 1593 was authorized under – and is therefore subject to enforcement through – Chapter VII of the UN Charter, the UNSC has the option, as a last resort, of threatening or using force to bring Sudan into compliance with the resolution.[37]

These and other attempts to promote justice for the Darfur atrocities outside the ICC need not be viewed as attempts to thwart the ICC, although, of course, they could be, especially given that some states, such as the US and Sudan, generally oppose the ICC. In fact, according to Ocampo, 'The number of cases that reach the Court should not be a measure of its efficiency. On the contrary, the absence of trials before this Court, as a consequence of the regular functioning of national institutions, would be a major success.'[38] Rather than simply trying as many cases as possible, then, a chief goal of the ICC appears to be encouraging and assisting states themselves to be willing and able to carry out genuine investigations and prosecutions of suspected atrocity perpetrators. The ICC would presumably also help prevent such heinous crimes by threatening to punish their perpetrators – a deterrent effect that is arguably stronger than that fostered by *ad hoc* tribunals established after the atrocities they adjudicate, such as the ICTR.

Precedents Established by UNSC Resolution 1593

The UNSC referral of the Darfur situation to the ICC and Sudan's declared initiative, whether genuine or not, to hold suspected Darfur atrocity perpetrators accountable are significant developments in international justice. The Darfur referral, the UNSC's

---

35 International Criminal Court (29 June 2005), 'Report of the Prosecutor of the International Criminal Court, Mr. Luis Moreno Ocampo, to the Security Council Pursuant to UNSCR 1593 (2005)', Section II (Preliminary Analysis and Initiation of the Investigation), Part 1 (Gathering of Information and Analysis), Paragraph 1.2 (Admissibility), http://www. icc-cpi.int/library/cases/ICC_Darfur_UNSC_Report_29-06-05_EN.pdf.

36 On 4 April 2005, Sudanese President Omar al-Bashir took a public oath, swearing, 'thrice in the name of Almighty God that I shall never hand any Sudanese national to a foreign court'. See: Hoge, Warren (6 April 2005), 'International War-Crimes Prosecutor Gets List of 51 Sudan Suspects', *New York Times*, A6.

37 Ocampo, Luis Moreno (16 June 2003), 'Statement by Mr. Luis Moreno-Ocampo, Ceremony for the Solemn Undertaking of the Chief Prosecutor', International Criminal Court, The Hague, The Netherlands.

38 Ocampo, Luis Moreno, 'Statement by Mr. Luis Moreno-Ocampo, Ceremony for the Solemn Undertaking of the Chief Prosecutor', International Criminal Court, The Hague, The Netherlands (16 June 2003).

first, affirmed the power and legitimacy of the UNSC to use its Chapter VII powers to refer cases to the ICC for prosecution of alleged offenders of atrocities.

That the first situation to be referred by the UNSC to the ICC did not concern a State Party to the Rome Statute and that the USG did not veto that initiative are particularly significant facts. Some commentators have suggested that the USG is hypocritical in insisting that Americans be shielded from the ICC (because the USG is not a State Party to the Rome Statute), while simultaneously allowing the ICC to try citizens of other non-States Parties to the Rome Statute (in this case, Sudan).[39] USG opposition to an international war crimes tribunal's having jurisdiction over Americans also provides ammunition to other states, including Sudan and Iraq, which oppose the involvement of the ICC or any other international court in crimes allegedly committed within their borders and/or by their citizens. Of course, this is not a new situation. The USG played a leading role in designing and establishing other international war crimes tribunals, including the International Military Tribunal for Germany at Nuremberg (the 'Nuremberg Tribunal'), the International Military Tribunal for the Far East at Tokyo (the 'Tokyo Tribunal'), the UN International Criminal Tribunal for the Former Yugoslavia (the ICTY), and the ICTR, each of which prevented American citizens and those of its allies from being tried for alleged atrocities, leading commentators to criticize these courts as 'victors' justice' or as otherwise being biased.[40]

Taken to its logical extreme, the possibility of bringing cases to the ICC through UNSC referrals means that the ICC could try individuals from any state that did not block such a referral – a capability that is limited to the five veto-wielding members of the UNSC (the US, the UK, France, China, and Russia) – and any other state that could successfully lobby against a referral. The USG's ultimate decision tacitly to agree to such referrals, combined with its unwillingness to let the ICC try its own or its allies' citizens, may in the future put it in a controversial and embarrassing position. If other UNSC members attempt to refer a case to the ICC concerning the USG or one of its allies, the USG may decide to use its veto power to obstruct the investigation and prosecution of particular suspected atrocity perpetrators. Nonetheless, as Patterson noted, UNSCR 1593 did include a 'precedent-setting' statement declaring that non-States Parties would not be subject to investigation or prosecution by the ICC without those states' consent or a referral by the UNSC,[41]

---

39 See, e.g.: Boucher, Richard (1 April 2005), 'Daily Press Briefing', U.S. Department of State, http://www.state.gov/r/pa/prs/dpb/2005/44132.htm. The relevant question posed to the U.S. Department of State spokesperson was, 'Can you explain why it is that the U.S. Government believes that citizens of Sudan, which signed the Rome Statute, but has not ratified it and therefore is not a state party to it, should be subject to its jurisdiction, when the crux of the American argument is that U.S. citizens should not be subject to its jurisdiction because the United States is not a state party to it… why should not Sudan continue to argue what is essentially your position, that because they're not a state party their citizens shouldn't be subject?'

40 See, e.g.: Minear, Richard H. (1971), *Victors' Justice: The Tokyo War Crimes Trial* (Princeton, New Jersey: Princeton University Press).

41 United Nations (31 March 2005), Press Release SC/8351.

a guarantee originally made in the Rome Statute itself.[42] Furthermore, as legal scholar Jack Goldsmith has observed, the USG may be able to use this resolution as a precedent to work through the UNSC to promote international justice without having to shoulder the burdens of doing so.[43] In asserting political control over the ICC by successfully lobbying for the inclusion of the aforementioned exemption in UNSCR 1593, the USG may thus have made the best out of a situation it did not desire. However, promoting the USG's interests in this way may also damage the ICC specifically and international justice generally. In the future, the other four veto-wielding members of the UNSC may mimic the USG in this respect. And, as has been proposed,[44] if the permanent membership of the UNSC expands to include, for example, Japan, Germany, Brazil, South Africa, and/or India, those additional states might also seize their prerogative within the UNSC to try to shield their own citizens from the ICC's jurisdiction while attempting to promote justice for certain atrocities in which they may have been involved.

The USG's policy shift from lobbying for an *ad hoc* hybrid tribunal for Darfur to abstaining during the vote on UNSCR 1593 also sets an important political precedent. The USG, especially under the current Bush administration, does not often publicly reverse itself on any issue. That the USG first resisted and then acquiesced to the international community's efforts to address the Darfur situation through the ICC may indicate that the Bush administration has become more supportive of international cooperation, at least on transitional justice issues.

The Darfur situation presents another important issue concerning US foreign policy: the USG's use of the word 'genocide' to describe certain atrocities. By referring to the Darfur situation as such, the USG raised domestic and international expectations that it would respond in some way, as it would be morally, politically, and – because the US is a party to the 1948 Convention on the Prevention and Punishment of the Crime of Genocide – legally compelled to act.[45] Consequently, by forcefully and repeatedly employing the term 'genocide,' regardless of whether the Darfur atrocities actually are, the USG created a situation in which the international community could pressure it to respond to the Darfur atrocities by supporting, *inter alia*, some sort of prompt and effective justice mechanism. As a result, the international community essentially forced the USG to accept the UNSC referral

---

42   Rome Statute of the International Criminal Court, Part II (Jurisdiction, Admissibility and Applicable Law).

43   Goldsmith, J. (24 January 2005), 'Support War Crimes Trials for Darfur', Opinion Editorial, *Washington Post*, A15.

44   See, e.g.: Annan, Kofi (21 March 2005), 'In Larger Freedom: Towards Development, Security and Human Rights for All', Report of the UN Secretary-General, A/59/2005, United Nations, http://daccessdds.un.org/doc/UNDOC/GEN/N05/270/78/PDF/N0527078. pdf?OpenElement, 42–3, Paragraphs 167–70.

45   See, e.g.: Cohen, Jared A., and Zachary D. Kaufman (15 July 2005), 'A Genocide by Any Other Name: Debating Genocide in Rwanda and Sudan', Opinion Editorial, *Broward Times*, 6; Cohen, Jared A., and Zachary D. Kaufman (3–4 April 2006), 'Of Rwanda and Sudan Genocide', Opinion Editorial, *New Times*, 8–9; Southwick, Katherine (Spring 2005), 'Srebrenica as Genocide? The Krstic Decision and the Language of the Unspeakable', 8 *Yale Human Rights & Development Law Journal*, 188–227, at 224.

of the Darfur situation to the ICC. If the USG is not satisfied with how this referral proceeds, or if it otherwise disapproves of future referrals, it may resist calling atrocities 'genocide' in order not to limit its options and not to allow other states to pressure it to support their preferred justice mechanisms. If such a situation occurs, the victims of genocide may continue to suffer from the neglect caused by power politics.

The UNSC referral of the Darfur situation to the ICC also presents one of the first test cases of the manner in which the ICC will interpret the Rome Statute's criteria for whether a state is genuinely willing and able to try suspected atrocity perpetrators who otherwise fall under the ICC's jurisdiction.[46] This case may present an ambiguous situation in which the UNSC and the ICC disagree over whether Sudan and other relevant states are fully cooperating with UNSCR 1593, and thus establish a precedent of what would occur in that case – specifically whether the evaluation of the ICC or the UNSC would take precedence, how, and why.

The Darfur referral will also be important in determining how the ICC would handle a potentially uncooperative state; what measures, if any, the UNSC would pursue to enforce its own resolution referring a case to the ICC; and how effective those measures would be. If the UNSC invokes its Chapter VII powers to coerce Sudan or another relevant state to cooperate with its first referral to the ICC, it would establish a significant political and legal precedent on the threat or use of force in international relations. Failure of the UNSC to enforce UNSCR 1593 could severely undermine its credibility in being an effective body, particularly in relation to transitional justice issues. Critics of the UNSC point out its many past failures to enforce its own resolutions.[47] UNSCR 1593 may therefore further undermine the strength and relevance of the UNSC and prompt additional calls for reforming or abandoning it as the central institution for maintaining international peace and security. All of this will depend on whether the UNSC is willing to back up its rhetoric with decisive action, which has not always been the case. If the ICC does not promote justice and accountability for the Darfur atrocities, alternative transitional justice mechanisms will provide the only hope for doing so. The international community therefore should be just as concerned about and supportive of these mechanisms as it is of the ICC.

If, as discussed above, the ICC tries some suspected Darfur atrocity perpetrators while other transitional justice institutions also address crimes committed in Sudan, then a precedent will be set for how the ICC functions alongside alternative transitional justice mechanisms. This situation would concern potential problems of, *inter alia*, double jeopardy, sharing evidence, and overlapping witnesses. These

---

46 For a list of the relevant criteria, see: Rome Statute, Part 2 (Jurisdiction, Admissibility and Applicable Law), Article 17 (Issues of Admissibility), Sections 2–3. For a consideration of another case, relating to Uganda, in which the ICC is currently interpreting these criteria, see, e.g.: Southwick, Katherine (Summer/Fall 2005), 'Investigating War in Northern Uganda: Dilemmas for the International Criminal Court', *Yale Journal of International Affairs*, Volume 1: 105–19; Southwick, Katherine (14 October 2005), 'When Peace and Justice Clash....' Opinion Editorial, *International Herald Tribune*, 6.

47 See, e.g.: Glennon, Michael J. (May/June 2003), 'Why the Security Council Failed', 82:3 *Foreign Affairs*, 16–35.

issues concern not only alternative prosecutorial transitional justice institutions, such as domestic courts within Sudan, but also non-prosecutorial transitional justice mechanisms. If, for example, as suggested in UNSCR 1593, Sudan establishes a truth and reconciliation commission to address the Darfur atrocities, then the ICC will need to institute precedent-setting policies on how to prosecute alongside amnesty provisions for individuals it may want to indict or have testify. In this respect, the ICC may look for guidance to the experience concerning atrocities in Sierra Leone, for which a hybrid war crimes tribunal has operated alongside a domestic truth and reconciliation commission, and to how several potential conflicts of interest or policy between these two institutions have been resolved.[48]

Finally, although the Darfur referral may represent an important precedent for the future of international justice, it comes after a long period of the world's indifference about and failure to address the Darfur atrocities. This episode, then, reinforces the precedent that the international community responds too late, if at all, to atrocities, including genocide.

Conclusion

The Darfur referral presents the opportunity to identify, try, and punish suspected atrocity perpetrators; to document the history of, and responsibility for, the Darfur atrocities; to deter future atrocities; and to promote reconciliation among the people of Sudan. On the other hand, this referral may lead to significant disagreements among Sudan, the ICC, and the UNSC about whether Sudan is cooperating and, if not, what can and should occur to remedy that problem. If the ICC and the UNSC are not successful in persuading Sudan to cooperate, the ICC and the UNSC will be discredited, the victims of the Darfur atrocities will continue to suffer, and future perpetrators of atrocities in other non-States Parties to the Rome Statute will be undeterred.

---

48   See e.g.: Schabas, W.A. (2004), 'A Synergistic Relationship: The Sierra Leone Truth and Reconciliation Commission and the Special Court for Sierra Leone', *Truth Commissions and Courts: The Tension Between Criminal Justice and the Search for Truth*, eds. W.A. Schabas and S. Darcy (Dordrecht, The Netherlands: Kluwer Academic Publishing), 3–54; Schabas, W.A. (December 2004), 'Conjoined Twins of Transitional Justice? The Sierra Leone Truth and Reconciliation Commission and the Special Court', 2:4 *Journal of International Criminal Justice*, 1082–99; Human Rights Watch (18 April 2002), 'Human Rights Watch Policy Paper on the Interrelationship between the Sierra Leone Special Court and Truth and Reconciliation Commission', http://www.hrw.org/press/2002/04/sierraleoneTRC0418.htm.

Chapter 6

The Major Powers and the Genocide in Rwanda

Roméo Dallaire and Kishan Manocha

The genocide in Rwanda, in which over 800,000 Rwandan men, women and children were brutally murdered in an orgy of violence almost beyond the capacity of the human heart to contemplate, was deliberately planned and ruthlessly executed by a powerful elite within a government that had gone out of control.

This contribution to the ongoing examination of the reasons for the Rwandan genocide will endeavour to explore why the major powers, when faced with incontrovertible evidence of the most clear-cut case of genocide possible, abjectly failed to denounce the evil and to take action to stop it. Among the major powers, this chapter only addresses the roles played by France, the US and the UK as it is the view of the authors that the level and type of involvement of these three Western countries in the genocide in Rwanda was unique and therefore worthy of special attention.

The Case against the Major Powers

The Rwandans who organized and carried out the genocide are ultimately responsible for the killing spree. However genocide, like any criminal act, is carried out within a context, whose creation and perpetuation is not simply or solely the work of the principal actors. In the case of Rwanda, the Hutu génocidaires were able to realize their murderous plans because three major powers helped create and sustain the necessary conditions – a context of impunity – that made it effortlessly easy.

Any 'indictment' of these powers is made more damning by the fact that none of them is in a position to plead ignorance as a defence. France, the US and the UK all knew about preparations for the slaughter,[1] and all three would have been

---

1   Des Forges, A. (1999) 'Human Rights,' *Leave None to Tell the Story: Genocide in Rwanda* (New York: Human Rights Watch, 1999) 18. France and the United States all had fully equipped and manned embassies in Kigali, Rwanda, with military and intelligence attachés; the United Kingdom had the same in Kampala, Uganda. Between human and signal intelligence on the ground and worldwide space- and air-based surveillance systems, it would be scarcely conceivable for these nations to claim that they did not have detailed knowledge as to what was going on, both before and throughout the genocide. See Lieutenant-General

aware of the reports of the International Commission of Investigation and the United Nations Special Rapporteur, released on 11 August 1993, which warned explicitly of a possible genocide.[2] But none of these powers chose to share what they knew more fully and openly with those Security Council members with no sources of information in Rwanda and with UNAMIR.

The Case Against France

How Much did France Know?

France certainly possessed the most detailed knowledge of what was going on in Rwanda both before and during the genocide.[3] Yet, despite this knowledge, France failed to heed and respond to early warnings of a systematic campaign of genocide against Tutsis and Hutu moderates. This suited French political interests, preferences and ambitions. For a government which enjoyed constant and cordial relations with the Hutu Power fanatics in Kigali throughout the genocide and which had armed and equipped the Rwandan Government and trained the military[4] and militia,[5] it was clearly in its best interests to play down the scale of the horror of the Rwandan killing fields. This was evidenced in President Francois Mitterrand's extraordinary remark that in countries such as Rwanda 'genocide is not too important,'[6] and in

R. Dallaire with Major B. Beardsley (2003), *Shake Hands with the Devil: The Failure of Humanity in Rwanda* (Toronto: Random House, Canada) 90.

2   Cited in Power, S. (2002) *A Problem from Hell: America and the Age of Genocide* (New York: Basic Books), 338. See report by Ndiaye W.B., Special Rapporteur, on his mission to Rwanda, 8–17 April 1993, *Extrajudicial, Summary or Arbitrary Executions*, UN doc. E/.4/1994/7/Add. 1, paras. 64, 78. See also Melvern, L. (2000), *A People Betrayed: The Role of the West in Rwanda's Genocide* (London: Zed Books) 56–57.

3   For examples, see Melvern, *ibid.*, pp. 43–44. It has been asserted that France had foreseen the risks of genocide from as early as 1990 and was aware of the implication of the most senior figures of the Rwandan regime in its preparation (Des Forges/Human Rights Watch, *ibid.*, pp. 175–176; McNulty, *ibid.*, p. 116.). Based on research done by Human Rights Watch, from the first hours after the killings began French policymakers knew that Tutsi were being slain because they were Tutsi (Des Forges/Human Rights Watch, *ibid.*, p. 19).

4   According to a Human Rights Watch report, in addition to combat troops, France sent military advisers to Rwanda to train Rwandan troops in combat techniques and commando operations. See (1994), Human Rights Watch, *Qui a armé la Rwanda? Chronique d'une tragédie annoncée* (Brussels: GRIP) 41.

5   See Melvern, *supra* note 2, 45. According to a witness in the trial of senior commanders of the Rwandan army at the International Criminal Tribunal for Rwanda, French military instructors trained Rwandan militia later to be blamed for the genocide. The tribunal was told that towards the end of 1992, in a forest near Camp Gabiro, Interhamwe militia received military training from French military instructors. The witness added that French instructors had also trained militia leaders at the base of the Presidential Guard at Kimihurura in Kigali ('France trained genocidal Rwandan militia, court told', *Agence France Presse Newswire Dispatch*, 13 January 2005).

6   Quoted in Gourevitch, P. (1998), *We Wish to Inform You that Tomorrow We Will Be Killed with Our Families: Stories From Rwanda* (New York: Farrar, Straus and Giroux) 325.

French military spokesmens' promotion of the idea of a 'two-way genocide'[7] – a tactic of misinformation that, through its influence of the media, non-governmental organizations and various political actors, who may otherwise have become involved at an earlier stage and with more weight, would further propel the killings and delay the response by the international community.

As the genocide raged, French diplomats and politicians, well aware of the magnitude of the bloodbath inside Rwanda, continued to actively shun the term in public fora or at least to ascribe it to the actions of the Hutu fanatics. Despite active pressure from within and without the Security Council to include the word 'genocide' in a presidential statement to be issued by that body in late April 1994, French resistance continued. The result was a watered-down, sanitized version of the truth. The Security Council could only bring itself to 'condemn' the killings, and while recognizing that the 'massacres' 'systematic' it failed to identify the perpetrators or the victims.

Aider and Abettor?

The full extent of the complicity of the French political and military establishment in the preparation and implementation of the butchery inside Rwanda may never been known, although documents have come to light confirming reports that a two hour high-level meeting took place on 9 May 1994 between Lieutenant-Colonel Ephrem Rwabalinda of the Rwandan Government Army and the head of the Military Mission of Cooperation in Paris even while the Rwandan armed forces were perpetrating genocide against their own people.[8]

The nature and magnitude of the French arm sales to Rwanda in the period immediately preceding the genocide and then subsequently as it unfolded speak volumes of France's role in that country's descent into hell and its responsibility for countless deaths.[9] Helicopters, mortars, armoured cars, light weapons and small arms of all sorts, anti-tank rocket launchers and ammunition were regularly dispatched, either directly from France or via willing third parties such as the former Zaire to the Rwandan armed forces between 1990 and 1994.[10]

---

7   Gourevitch, *ibid*, p. 156.

8   Details of this meeting can be found in de Saint-Exupéry, P. (1998), 'France-Rwanda: des silences d'Etat,' *Le Figaro* (14 January 1998) 4; Des Forges/Human Rights Watch, *supra*, note 1, 664; McNulty, M. (2000) 'French Arms, War and Genocide in Rwanda', 105 *Crime, Law & Social Change*, pp. 108–120.

9   Details of these arm sales, as well as the nature and scale of French military support and training to the Rwandan armed forces, are reviewed in de Saint-Exupéry, P. (2004) *L'inavouable: La France au Rwanda* (Paris: les arenas), pp. 201–203; McNulty, *ibid.*, p. 116.

10   According to de Saint-Exupéry, France delivered an equivalent of 14 million French Francs worth of military equipment to Rwanda in 1992 and a further 7 million French Francs worth of such equipment in 1993. In addition, during this period the French state-owned bank, Credit Lyonnais, financed arms transactions worth $6 million, and a French company, DYL-Invest, signed an arms contract for Rwanda worth $12.2 million in 1993 (de Saint-Exupéry, P. (1998) 'France-Rwanda: le syndrome de Fachoda', *Le Figaro* [13 January 1998], 4).

But the supply of arms to Rwanda did not just end with the onset of the genocide. Although strenuously denied by the French Government, a number of reliable sources attest to this fact. The leading French newspaper, *Le Figaro*, reported at least two instances in May 1994 of arms supplies to Rwanda involving French companies.[11] French arms traffic to Rwanda continued after 17 May 1994, in blatant violation of the arms embargo imposed by Security Council Resolution 918 to which, not surprisingly, France had initially been opposed.[12] According to Philip Gourevitch, on 16 and 18 June 1994, arms shipments for the Hutu Power regime were landed, with French connivance, in Goma, former Zaire, and quickly transported over the border to Rwanda.[13] Further, on 18 July 1994, at the height of *Opération Turquoise*, arms originating from France were delivered to the genocidal Hutu regime in exile.[14]

A French parliamentary commission set up to investigate France's military and political involvement before and during the genocide did conclude that certain 'errors of judgment' were indeed made by France in supporting the genocidal regime in Rwanda,[15] but the French Government was officially absolved of responsibility for the killings and the commission's report sadly shed little light on how decisions were made by political and military leaders in that country. Widely considered a whitewash,[16] the enquiry, in particular, failed to identify French arms supplies as instrumental in exacerbating the genocide.[17]

France was not a great fan of UNAMIR although it did initially express interest in the UN peacekeeping mission.[18] As the genocide reached its height, on 21 April 1994, France readily voted for Security Council resolution 912 which scaled down UNAMIR's troop strength by 90 per cent. The French Government then sat back and watched the US first block and later stall all efforts to get a reinforced UN presence (UNAMIR II) off the ground. However, France did eventually act by leading a

---

11 On 3 May 1994 an airplane landed in the former Zaire with $942,680 worth of arm supplies in its hold. The French firm DYL-Invest is alleged to have mediated this arms deal (de Saint-Exupéry, P. (1998) 'France-Rwanda: un genocide sans importance', *Le Figaro* [12 January 1998], 4).

12 Human Rights Watch (1995), *Rwanda/Zaire, Rearming with Impunity: International Support for the Perpetrators of the Rwandan Genocide* (New York: Human Rights Watch) pp. 6–7. Section B.13 of Security Council Resolution 918 stipulated that all States 'shall prevent the sale or supply to Rwanda by their nationals or from their territories or using their flag vessels or aircraft of arms and related *matériel* of all types, including weapons and ammunition, military vehicles and equipment, paramilitary police equipment and spare parts' (SC Res. 918, 17 May 1994).

13 Gourevitch, *supra* note 6, 155.

14 According to de Saint-Exupéry, on 18 July 1994 an aircraft landed in Goma, former Zaire, carrying arms from France and valued at $753,645. De Saint-Exupéry has evidence to show that this arms supply was funded by the Rwandan embassies in Paris and Cairo.

15 Assemblée nationale, *Rapport d'information déposé par la Mission d'information de la Commission de la défense nationale et des forces armées et de la Commission des affaires étrangères, sur les opérations militaires menées par la France, d'autres pays et l'ONU au Rwanda entre 1990 et 1994*, Paris, 15 December 1998.

16 Melvern, *supra*, note 2, p. 234.

17 McNulty, *supra*, note 8, pp. 105-106; Melvern, *ibid*, p. 234.

18 Dallaire, *supra*, note 1, p. 76.

coalition of French and African troops, with the blessing of the Security Council,[19] to conduct a humanitarian operation in Rwanda until UNAMIR II was brought up to strength.

Opération Turquoise did provide humanitarian assistance to a large number of internally displaced Rwandans.[20] However, it also acted as a screen behind which the génocidaires continued to pursue their deadly work, and to do so safe in the knowledge that their patrons in Paris would neither hand them over to the Tutsi government-in-waiting nor to the international community. Tutsis continued to be killed in the French-occupied zone in south-west Rwanda after the launch of *Opération Turquoise*.[21] The French forces were slow to prevent the massacres, apprehend the murderers, disarm the militia, and to stop the pro-genocide broadcasts of Radio Télévision Libre des Mille Collines (RTLM) from within the zone.

The Case Against the US

As the post-Cold War world's pre-eminent power, the US effectively dictated the international community's response at all stages of the Rwandan genocide, but particularly in its first weeks. Obsessively preoccupied by the loss of 18 American Rangers in Somalia in October 1993 and driven by an extraordinarily limited understanding of what constituted vital American interests, which in the area of multi-lateral peacekeeping initiatives had been formalized in the Presidential Decision Directive of 3 May 1994 (PDD-25), the US absolved itself of its moral responsibility to act for the sake of humanity and aggressively undermined any attempt by the United Nations to intervene in Rwanda.

In reviewing the full range of information and intelligence reports available to and relied upon by policymakers during the Rwanda crisis,[22] it is clear that the US was remarkably well-informed about the actual genocide.[23] US officials who followed Rwanda knew well that organized, systematic government-sponsored violence was under way and determined that the massacres constituted genocide within two weeks of the shooting down of the plane carrying the Presidents of Burundi and Rwanda.[24] This is confirmed by the view expressed by Joyce Leader on 7 April 1994, the then

---

19 United Nations Security Council Resolution, 929 (SC Res. 929, 22 June 1994).

20 Accounts vary as to the exact number of Tutsi saved by French soldiers. See Des Forges/Human Rights Watch, *supra*, note 1, 689; and Melvern, *supra*, note 2, 215.

21 Des Forges/Human Rights Watch, *ibid.*, pp. 679–681.

22 Ferroggiaro, W., 'The US and the Genocide in Rwanda 1994: The Assassination of the Presidents and the Beginning of the Apocalypse'. Available at: http://www.gwu.edu/nsarchiv/ NSA/EBB/NSAEBB119/index.htm (Accessed on 18 February 2005).

23 For a review of these sources, see Ferroggiaro, W. 'The US and the Genocide in Rwanda 1994: Information, Intelligence and the US Response', available online at http:// www.gwu.edu/nsarchiv/NSAEBB/NSAEBB117/index.htm (Accessed on 18 February 2005); Power, *supra*, note 1, pp. 354–355.

24 According to James Woods, deputy assistant secretary for African Affairs at the Department of Defense, the fact of the genocide was known as early as the second week (Melvern, *supra*, note 2, 230).

deputy to the US ambassador in Rwanda, that the killings involved not just political murders, but genocide.[25] Even the identity of those responsible for the high-profile political murders that laid the basis for the ensuing slaughter in Rwanda was known to the Clinton administration by the second day of the genocide.[26] The lack of an American response was even more scandalous in light of the fact that there had been information for a couple of years showing that the extremists had been planning and preparing the genocide for some time.[27] In one case a figure of 500,000 was predicted as the number of deaths in the case of a renewed conflict following the collapse of the Arusha Peace Agreement.[28]

As weeks went by, and despite a deluge of factual reports received by the US administration attesting to the nature and magnitude of the killings in Rwanda, State Department officials, rather than calling the evil by its real name, engaged in a farcical spectacle of word play after having been deliberately cautioned in writing by the government to avoid the word 'genocide' itself.[29] Genocide is not, and should never be allowed to become, a matter of semantics. The drawing of an artificial, meaningless distinction between 'acts of genocide' and 'genocide' may have started out as a convenient, self-serving means to escape the legal obligations to which the US had freely consented,[30] but its effect was to undermine the very moral foundation of the word itself.

Despite private admissions of the genocidal nature of the killings in Rwanda[31] and increasing calls for the denunciation of the slaughter in accurate terms by the highest international authority in the world, Madeline Albright, the US Ambassador

---

25 Power *supra*, note 1, 354.

26 A Central Intelligence Agency report of 8 April 1994 to top officials in the United States administration identified 'Hutu security elements from the Presidential Guard, gendarmerie and military' as killers of several government officials including the Prime Minister, cited in Ferroggiaro, *supra* note 44, Document 10 'Rwanda: Security Deteriorating', excerpt from Central Intelligence Agency, National Intelligence Daily (Freedom of Intelligence Act release).

27 According to James Woods, cited in Melvern, *supra*, note 2, p. 170.

28 Organisation of African Unity, *Rwanda: The Preventable Genocide*, OAU, Chapter 9, 5, quoted in Power, *supra*, note 1, p. 338.

29 The official formulation approved by the White House was: 'acts of genocide may have occurred' (cited in Gourevitch, *supra*, note 10, p. 152). For a review of the attitude of the American Government toward the use of the word 'genocide', see Power, *ibid.*, pp. 359–364. For illustrations of the attempts by the Clinton administration to avoid the use of the word 'genocide', see Transcript, State Department Press Briefing by Christine Shelley, Deputy Press Spokesperson, US Department of State, 29 April 1994, pp. 3–4, and State Department briefing, Federal News Service, 10 June 1994, pp. 1–4 (quoted in Power, *ibid.*, pp. 363–364).

30 A Defense Department discussion paper dated 1 May 1994 stated that the use of the word 'genocide' remained a concern and is full of cautions about the United States becoming committed to taking action: 'Be careful. Legal at State was worried about this yesterday – genocide finding could commit [the United States government] to actually "do something"' (quoted in Power, *ibid*, p. 359).

31 In a cable sent from the U.S.A mission at the United Nations to the State Department, a political adviser wrote: 'The events in Rwanda clearly seem to meet the definition of

at the United Nations, continued to resist using the word 'genocide' at meetings of the Security Council and led demands within the Council that the term be dropped from the presidential statement of 30 April 1994.[32] In failing to confront the reality head on, the US had showed the world that it was not prepared to take genocide seriously.

Having ensured that UNAMIR was never given the mandate or capacity to make any sort of meaningful contribution to the peace process in Rwanda,[33] the Americans then proceeded to promote full withdrawal of the United Nations presence very early on in the genocide and then subsequently to steadfastly oppose any plans for its reinforcement. In so doing, the US sought to avoid the two nightmare scenarios it feared the most. The one, the authorization of a new United Nations force replete with a fresh mandate but without the means to implement either. The other, the very real possibility of the US having to bail out a failed United Nations mission. Both outcomes would cost American money, and more importantly American lives, and the Clinton administration, already owing more than $800 million in dues to the United Nations[34] and having sustained 18 casualties in Somalia, was not going to contribute to another misguided 'invasion' of Africa.

Sensing a second Somalia in the making, the Clinton administration did not object to Belgian demands for the full withdrawal of UNAMIR troops following the murder of 10 Belgian peacekeepers by Hutu extremists. Tragically, on the very day the major powers effectively abandoned Rwandans to their fate as foreign nationals were safely escorted out of Kigali by approximately 1,000 French, Belgian and Italian soldiers, there were sufficient numbers of well-trained and well-equipped foreign troops, on or reasonably close to Rwandan soil, including at least 250 US Marines[35] in nearby Bujumbura, to bring an end to the killings.[36] US forces could have protected Rwandan civilians with very limited risk to themselves. There would have been no rerun of Somalia.

Satisfied that the unfolding apocalypse in Rwanda did not affect its interests enough to launch a unilateral intervention, the US then called for the full withdrawal of UNAMIR.[37] Issues of economics prevailed over issues of common humanity.

---

genocide in Article II of the 1948 Convention on the Prevention and Punishment of the Crime of Genocide' (quoted in Power, *ibid.*, p. 361).

32 Power, *ibid.*, p. 361.

33 The United States reluctantly voted for Security Council Resolution 872 on 5 October 1993 which authorized UNAMIR, but it failed to contribute either troops or money to this peacekeeping force. See Power, *ibid.*, 341.

34 UN Speech Monday will seek more caution in Peacekeeping, *Associated Press* (26 September 1993).

35 Power puts this number at 300, *supra*, note 1, 353.

36 In 1999, an international panel of senior military leaders in a report to the Carnegie Commission for Preventing Deadly Conflict concurred with the UNAMIR Force Commander's assessment that a joint force of 5000 experienced soldiers with air support, logistics and communications would have prevented the slaughter of 500,000 people (Carnegie Commission on Preventing Deadly Conflict, *Preventing Deadly Conflict: Final Report* [Washington DC: Carnegie Commission on Preventing Deadly Conflict, 1997] 6).

37 Power, *supra*, note 1, 366–368.

Short-sighted national interests prevailed over the defence and protection of universal human values. Domestic public opinion mattered more than the judges of history. The initial result was Security Council Resolution 912 which scaled down the peacekeeping presence in Rwanda by 90 per cent from 2,548 to a mere 270 troops. By adopting this breathtakingly senseless resolution the international community, at the insistence of the US, had declared to the génocidaires that it was now open season to kill Tutsis.[38]

The US remained under the naive impression that the solution to the Rwandan genocide was essentially a ceasefire between the warring factions.[39] Somehow, the fact of the genocide, as distinct from the civil war, had not penetrated the protective screens of the Clinton administration. Further, the US mistakenly believed that what worked for civil war also worked for genocide in the midst of a civil war. Only one official as can be determined among those in the United States Government whose eyes were supposedly fixed on Rwanda understood the reality of what was happening on the ground. Upon his return from a trip to Central and East Africa, John Shattuck wrote a memorandum on 9 May 1994 to the Acting Secretary of State in which he reported that 'Rwanda is a human rights catastrophe of the greatest magnitude', recommended an 'expansion and new mission for UNAMIR', and argued, contrary to the current policy, 'while a ceasefire … is of critical importance, it is still unlikely to end the killings'.[40]

But in rejecting any sort of intervention that could have cost American lives, the US also discounted action which should have incurred no American casualties yet would have saved thousands upon thousands of Rwandans.[41] On 5 May 1994, a Pentagon memorandum rejected proposals from the Force Commander of UNAMIR and Deputy Assistant Secretary of State Prudence Bushnell and her team to diminish the killings by using Pentagon technology to jam RTLM hate transmissions.[42] The neutralization of such a powerful instrument in the genocidal authorities' armoury would have significantly shattered their efforts to murder every last Tutsi in their midst. The terse Pentagon response was motivated by a desire to preserve and uphold the sovereignty of a regime that had long lost all claims to legitimacy because of the genocidal horror that it had so openly perpetrated upon its own citizens. The effect of the Pentagon decision was that the lives of an estimated 8,000–10,000 Rwandans being hacked to death each day were not worth the cost of the fuel or the violation of Rwandan airwaves.[43]

Unmoved by further appeals, particularly from a group of non-permanent members of the Security Council – Spain, New Zealand, Argentina, and the Czech Republic – and based on a plan recommended by the Force Commander of UNAMIR

---

38 Barnett, M. (2002), *Eyewitness to a Genocide: The United Nations and Rwanda*, Ithaca: Cornell University Press, p. 132; Power, *ibid.*, 369–370.

39 Power, *ibid.*, p. 347.

40 Ferrogiaro, *supra*, note 23, Document 19 'Shattuck Memo to Acting Secretary, 9 May 1994'.

41 Power, *supra*, note 1, pp. 370–371.

42 Memorandum of Frank Wisner, Undersecretary of policy at the US Defense Department, to Sandy Berger, 5 May 1994 (declassified), quoted in Power, *ibid.*, pp. 371–372.

43 Dallaires, *supra*, note 1, p. 375.

for a reinforced United Nations peacekeeping force in Rwanda to help rescue the thousands of helpless Rwandans facing imminent extinction,[44] the US responded to the ongoing slaughter by continuing to hold fast to an outmoded understanding of their traditional national interests.[45] This world view had been enshrined in PDD-25, which had the effect of restricting its support for other states that wished to conduct UN peacekeeping missions.[46] Rwanda had fast become the first casualty of this new doctrine.

As the genocidal authorities intensified their efforts to wipe out the last remaining Tutsis in Rwanda, all the US could do was to delay the Security Council vote by four days by seeking to impose a modified plan on the Council in the very final stages of the debate.[47] Unable to get its own way, the US then proceeded to undermine Security Council Resolution 918, adopted on 17 May 1994 and which created a new United Nations peacekeeping force (UNAMIR II) with 5,500 troops mainly drawn from Africa. By withholding any troops and strategic lift to the operation, the US succeeded in neutering the hard-won United Nations intervention. A matter as relatively straightforward as providing 50 Armoured Personnel Carriers (APCs) to the United Nations peacekeeping force proved to be an almost insurmountable challenge to the US. Unbelievably, it took a full month before the US was able to send the much-needed APCs to Africa and when they did arrive in July 1994, stripped of machine guns, radios, tools, and spare parts, the genocidal Government of Rwanda had ceased to exist.[48]

If the troops mandated in Resolution 918 had been speedily and effectively deployed, countless Rwandan lives could have been saved.[49] But the binding decision of the United Nations Security Council was conditional, on the insistence of the US, that 150 military observers be sent to Rwanda to oversee efforts towards a ceasefire.[50] Again, American fixation with traditional means to resolving civil wars cost the Rwandan people dearly.

The Clinton administration eventually did take action, of course, and when they did it was swift and impressive and in marked contrast with its failure to stir itself into action over the genocide. Keen to show the world that it could act decisively when the humanitarian stakes were high, the US began on 21 July 2004 a massive, magnificent and rapid airlift of humanitarian aid to the Rwandan refugees who had fled the country across the border to Goma, former Zaire,[51] regardless of the fact that among those displaced from their homeland were génocidaires, murderers, rapists and torturers and those who had trained, incited and directed them.

---

44 Dallaire, *ibid.*, pp. 354–359; Power *supra*, note 1, pp. 377–379.

45 Power, *ibid.*

46 Power, *ibid.*, p. 378.

47 Dallaire, *supra*, note 2, p. 372; Melvern *supra*, note 2, p. 195; Power, *ibid.*, p. 379.

48 Dallaire, *ibid.*, p. 376; Melvern, *ibid.*, pp. 195–196; Power, *ibid.*, p. 380.

49 This remains the firm conviction of the Force Commander of UNAMIR, see Dallaire, *ibid.*, p. 375, 514, and Melvern, *ibid.*, p. 198.

50 Melvern, *ibid.*

51 For accounts of the US response to the unfolding humanitarian disaster, see Power, *supra*, note 1, p. 381.

It is most regrettable that no serious efforts were ever made within the Clinton administration to examine why certain decisions were made (and not made for that matter) or what consequences they produced during the genocide.[52] The US has therefore never had to bring itself to an account over its failings in Rwanda.

The Case Against the UK

The role played by the UK in the Rwandan genocide remains ambiguous.[53] The British government's approach was characterized from the outset by a determination to play the matter down.[54] It maintained that it did not know what was going on in Rwanda: an astonishing response in light of the information and intelligence reports that would have clearly been available to it given its status as a major world power with a very well-equipped embassy in nearby Kampala, Uganda.

The UK allowed weapons to be supplied to the genocidal Rwandan government both before and during the 1994 genocide.[55] In November 1996 it emerged that a UK company, Mil-Tec, had brokered the sale of arms from Albania and Israel to the genocidal regime.[56] In January 1997, it was reported that the British government had 'failed to implement all the requirements of a United Nations arms embargo on Rwanda,[57] thus allowing Mil-Tec to supply weapons to extremist Hutu militia'.[58]

Like their American counterparts, UK representatives at the United Nations Security Council resisted the use of the word 'genocide' in debates on Rwanda. British diplomats and politicians also actively shunned the term. Knowing well the legal implications of a Security Council determination that genocide was under way in Rwanda, the UK objected to the inclusion of the term in the proposed statement by the president of the Council.[59] The UK argued that to use the word, but not to act on it, would be ridiculous.[60] What is particularly astonishing is that the British Foreign Office refused to label the events of 1994 as a 'genocide' a full year after the slaughter had ended.[61]

Rwanda was clearly not one of the UK's priorities. By his own admission, the UK representative at the United Nations at the time of the genocide, later admitted that

---

52 Power notes that although two officials in the Clinton administration did conduct internal studies on the administration's response to the Rwandan genocide, these were only paper exercises and their findings were never disclosed to the public (Power, *ibid.*, p. 510).

53 For a discussion of the British response to the Rwandan genocide, see Melvern, *supra*, note 2, 230–233.

54 Melvern, *ibid.*, p. 230.

55 McNulty, *supra*, note 8, 120.

56 McNulty, ibid.

57 Security Council Resolution, p. 918.

58 Evans, E., 'Whitehall Lapse Let UK Firm Sell Arms to Hutus', *The Times*, 22 January 1997, Approximately $5 million worth of arms and ammunition were supplied by Mil-Tec, a company with offices in London, to the interim government in Rwanda at various times during the genocide (Melvern, *supra*, note 2, 182).

59 Melvern, *ibid.*, p. 180; Power, *supra*, note 1, 361.

60 Melvern, *ibid.*

61 Melvern, *ibid.*, p. 230.

the British were 'extremely unsighted' over Rwanda.[62] The UK was reluctant about UNAMIR – it did not resource it and even opposed an increase in troop numbers as conditions in Rwanda deteriorated ahead of the genocide.[63] As the carnage spread through Rwanda, the British ambassador made known his preferred course of action, which was to withdraw most of the United Nations peacekeepers leaving behind 'some elements'.[64]

The UK then dragged its feet over UNAMIR II. It argued in the Security Council debates against the use of such terms as 'forceful action' and 'intervention', and supported American efforts to block and then stall the deployment of a reinforced United Nations presence in Rwanda.[65] In its view, any future action in Rwanda had to be taken primarily through the efforts of African countries.[66] It neither contributed troops nor strategic lift to UNAMIR II but it did offer some practical resources. However, the Bedford trucks it provided broke down one at a time until there were none left.[67]

A Sorry Tale Indeed

The failure of France, the US and the UK to apply the word and oppose the deed of genocide in the case of Rwanda is a sorry tale indeed. They tolerated the mass slaughter of the Tutsi people because it did not impinge on their narrowly defined national interests. Rwanda was clearly of no strategic value to these Western nations – not geographically, politically or economically. All that it had was a surplus of people and, in their view, this was clearly a most dispensable commodity.

By voting in favour of Security Council Resolution 912, these three major powers succeeded in emasculating the one means for preventing the bloodbath and then, when presented with two windows of opportunity to halt the ceaseless flow of Rwandan blood, they failed again. Hundreds of thousands of innocent men, women and children succumbed to unimaginable horror as the United Nations Security Council, under the influence of these powers, first authorized the dismantling of the United Nations presence in Rwanda. And then, to add insult to injury, when there was still time to save whatever remained of Tutsi life in Rwanda, the slowness and ineptness of the international community's response as manifested in the adoption of Security Council Resolution 918 on 17 May 1994 sealed their fate.

The sum total of the omissions and commissions of France, the US and the UK only served in the end to undermine the already weakened credibility of the United Nations as the custodian of the peace and well-being of mankind and the upholder and protector of human rights of every person on the planet.

---

62 Melvern, *ibid.*, p. 231.
63 Melvern, *ibid.*, p. 104.
64 Melvern, *ibid.*, pp. 153–154.
65 Dallaire, *supra*, note 1, p. 364.
66 Melvern, *supra*, note 2, p. 192.
67 Dallaire, *supra*, note 2, p. 376; Melvern, *ibid.*, p. 233.

Chapter 7

The Schism between the Legal and the Social Concept of Genocide in Light of the Responsibility to Protect

Larissa van den Herik

Introduction

During the Rwandan genocide, it took the international community several weeks to utter the 'G-word', afraid as it was that labelling the Rwandan massacres as genocide would entail an obligation to intervene. In a next situation of gross human rights violations in Africa, namely in the context of Darfur, the US did not want to be seen again as shying away from stating the obvious, and so on 22 July 2004, the US House of Representatives and the US Senate labelled the ongoing atrocities in Darfur a genocide. However, this was not followed by a US military intervention for humanitarian purposes. In contrast, some months later, the 'Cassese Commission', established by the UN Secretary-General to enquire whether genocide had taken place in Darfur, issued a report stating that no evidence of a genocidal policy had been found. This contradistinction is exemplary for the schism that exists between the broader concept of genocide as employed by social scientists (the 'social' concept) and the narrow concept of genocide as it emerges from the 1948 Genocide Convention (the 'legal' concept). In addition, the term 'genocide' bears a political connotation, as a result of the growing conviction that a determination that genocide is being committed places a special responsibility upon the shoulders of the international community and more specifically the UN Security Council to act and to protect. This chapter analyses and evaluates recent legal developments that appear to narrow the existing dichotomy between the legal and the social concept of genocide. It also investigates what the obligations are for the Security Council and the international community at large when certain atrocities are qualified as genocide either in legal, social or political terms.

The Schism

A discussion between lawyers and social scientists on genocide can have rather confusing results since each discipline employs its own definition. In other words: there is a schism between the legal and the social concept of genocide. Whereas the main characteristic of the legal concept of genocide is the specific intent to destroy a particular group in whole or in part, the social concept of genocide focuses more generally on the aspect of mass killing. Moreover, whereas the legal definition of genocide enumerates four specific groups that are protected by the prohibition of genocide, social scientists, such as Chalk and Jonassohn, include in the victim groups all human groups as targeted by the perpetrators.[1] Another social scientist, Charney, even departs entirely from the group element and refers to 'substantial numbers of human beings', taking the individual as the primary victim of genocide.[2] In contrast, the legal definition is wider than the social definition where it acknowledges that also an act other than killing, for instance rape, may constitute a genocidal act.

Recent developments that broaden the scope of the legal definition of genocide should be analysed in the light of the aforementioned schism. From the *Krstić* Appeal Judgement of 19 April 2004 and the *Blagojević* Judgement of 17 January 2005, it can be inferred that the International Criminal Tribunal for the Former Yugoslavia (the ICTY) is now inclined to interpret the genocide definition in a more lenient manner. Also the report of the Darfur Commission of Inquiry is a remarkable development, since it opened the door to identifying the victim group on the basis of a purely subjective approach. Below, these developments are studied more closely and put into their legal context.

The Legal Framework

The prohibition of genocide is laid down in the 1948 Genocide Convention. Article I of the Convention states:

> The Contracting Parties confirm that genocide, whether committed in time of peace or in time of war, is a crime under international law which they undertake to prevent and to punish.

Subsequently, Article II provides the legal definition of genocide, namely:

> ... genocide means any of the following acts committed with intent to destroy, in whole or in part, a national, ethnical, racial or religious group, as such:
>
> a) Killing members of the group;
>
> b) Causing serious bodily or mental harm to members of the group;
>
> c) Deliberately inflicting on the group conditions of life calculated to bring about its physical destruction in whole or in part;

---

1   Chalk, F. and Jonassohn, K. (1990), *The History and Sociology of Genocide: Analyses and Case Studies* (New Haven, CT: Yale University Press), pp. 23, 25, 26).

2   Charney, I.W. (1994), 'Toward a generic definition of genocide', in Andreopoulos, G.J. (ed.) *Genocide – Conceptual and Historical Dimensions*, (Philadelphia: University of Philadelphia Press), pp. 64–94, 75.

d)   Imposing measures intended to prevent births within the group;

e)   Forcibly transferring children of the group to another group.'

The prohibition of genocide did not exist as such in international law before the 1948 Genocide Convention came into force.[3] It has been argued though that over time the definition of genocide in customary international law became broader than the definition of the 1948 Genocide Convention in that it also included political groups as potential victim groups.[4] However, given that current international courts and tribunals all employ the definition of the 1948 Genocide Convention, this argument may have lost much of its merit. Still, as is illustrated below, recent developments are indirectly extending the prohibition of genocide to groups of victims that may not have been envisaged originally.

The definition of genocide as laid down in the 1948 Genocide Convention includes three main elements, namely: i) the intent to destroy in whole or in part; ii) a national, ethnic, racial or religious group, and iii) the genocidal acts enlisted in subs. (a) to (e). Below, case law of the International Criminal Tribunal for Rwanda (the ICTR), the ICTY and the report of the Darfur Commission of Inquiry are surveyed to determine how the first two of these elements have been interpreted and applied in practice.

ICTR Case Law

There is not much legal debate on whether the massacres in Rwanda in 1994 constituted genocide. Generally, one concurred in the opinion that genocide took place. Although this may have eased the legal task of the ICTR judges somewhat, these judges still faced some major juridical hurdles given that they were the first international judges to interpret and apply the legal definition of genocide in practice. Their pioneering work led to some remarkable results on the interpretation of the three elements. The ICTR's legal findings on the specific intent and on the protected groups are briefly set out in this sub-section with a view to providing a legal framework in which the more recent developments at the ICTY and the report of the Darfur Commission of Inquiry can be evaluated.[5]

The Specific Intent

The ICTR Trial Chambers have consistently held that the mental element of genocide is a special intent requirement and not a general intent requirement.[6] This means

---

3   As noted by the Commission of Experts for Rwanda in its final report, *UN Doc.* S/1994/1405 (9 December 1994), para. 150.

4   E.g., Van Schaak, B. (1997), 'The crime of political genocide: repairing the Genocide Convention's blind spot', 106 *Yale L J*, 2259–2291.

5   For a more elaborate analysis of the ICTR's case law on these and other elements, see van den Herik, L.J. (2005), *The Contribution of the Rwanda Tribunal to the Development of International Law* (Leiden: Martinus-Nijhoff Publishers).

6   E.g., *The Prosecutor v Akayesu*, Judgement (2 September 1998), para. 121; *The Prosecutor v Kambanda*, Judgement (4 September 1998), para. 16; *The Prosecutor v*

that a perpetrator must act with the individual desire to achieve the destruction of the group.[7] Having elucidated the standard to be applied, the question as to how it could be proved that a given perpetrator acted with the required intent was more problematic for the ICTR Trial Chambers.[8] In the *Akayesu* case, the Trial Chamber developed a method of inferring the specific intent from certain indicators. These indicators included:

- a general range of criminal acts systematically targeting the same group committed by the same perpetrator or others,
- the scale and nature of the acts committed,
- and the fact that victims were systematically and deliberately singled out because of their membership of a group, in contrast to non-group members.[9]

In the case of *Kayishema and Ruzindana*, the Trial Chamber referred to words and deeds of the accused and a 'pattern of purposeful action'.[10] It referred to the same sorts of indicators as the Trial Chamber in the *Akayesu* case, viz.:

- the physical targeting of the group or their property,
- the use of derogatory language toward members of the targeted group,
- the weapons employed and the extent of bodily injury,
- the methodical way of planning,
- the systematic way of killing,
- the number of victims from the group.[11]

Kayishema and Ruzindana, Judgement (21 May 1999), para. 91; *The Prosecutor v Rutaganda*, Judgement (6 December 1999), paras, 399–400; *The Prosecutor v Musema*, Judgement (27 January 2000), paras, 927–934.

7   *The Prosecutor v Rutaganda*, Judgement, para. 60.

8   *The Prosecutor v Akayesu*, Judgement (2 September 1998), para. 523, the Trial Chamber Stated 'intent is a mental factor which is difficult, even impossible, to determine'. In contrast, *The Prosecutor v Kajelijeli, Judgement* (1 December 2003), para. 805, and in *The Prosecutor v Kamuhanda*, Judgement (22 January 2004), para. 624, the Trial Chambers stated 'the intent to commit a crime, even genocide, may not always be difficult or impossible to discern from the circumstances of the case'.

9   *The Prosecutor v Akayesu*, Judgement (2 September 1998), para. 523. As approved in *The Prosecutor v Semanza*, Judgement (15 May 2003), para. 313, in *The Prosecutor v Kamuhanda Judgement* (22 January 2004), para. 623.

10   The Trial Chamber referred in this respect to Simon, T.W. (1996) 'Defining genocide', 15 *Wisconsin Int. L. J.*: 243–256, p. 247, who in his turn cited Fein, H. (1994), 'Genocide, terror, life integrity, and war crimes: the case for discrimination', in Andreopoulos, G.J. (ed.) *Genocide – Conceptual and Historical Dimensions* (Philadelphia: University of Philadelphia Press), pp. 95–107, 97.

11   *The Prosecutor v Kayishema and Ruzindana*, Judgement (21 May 1999), para. 93. This quotation was cited by the Trial Chambers in the *Kajelijeli* and *Kamuhanda* judgements. *The Prosecutor v Kajelijeli*, Judgement (1 December 2003), para. 806; *The Prosecutor v Kamuhanda*, Judgement (22 January 2004), para. 625.

Some of these indicators refer to contextual elements and not directly to the behaviour of an individual accused. Therefore, in the case of *Bagilishema*, the Trial Chamber cautioned, 'the use of context to determine the intent of an accused must be counterbalanced with the actual conduct of the accused'. The Trial Chamber held that intent had to be established above all by relying on the accused's own behaviour.[12] However valid this caution may be, it must also be noted that contextual elements do have relevance in proving a specific intent. An accused who acts with full knowledge of a genocidal context, contributes consciously and intentionally to that context, and so contextual elements may well serve to denote a genocidal intent.

In addition to the above-mentioned indicators, other indicators were also taken into account as evidence of a specific intent to destroy a group as such rather than a sum of individuals. The most important one was the sheer randomness of the killings, targeting not only men, but also pregnant women, elderly and children. In the *Kayishema and Ruzindana* case, the Trial Chamber observed:

> Not only were Tutsis killed in tremendous numbers, but they were also killed regardless of gender or age. Men and women, old and young, were killed without mercy. Children were massacred before their parents' eyes, women raped in front of their families. No Tutsi was spared, neither the weak nor the pregnant.[13]

In sum, to prove a specific intent, the Trial Chambers of the ICTR relied on specific statements of the accused in combination with their general pattern of conduct, their position in society and the general context of genocide in Rwanda.

The Protected Groups

The legal definition of genocide protects four specific groups, namely a national, ethnical, racial or religious group. It is this group-element of the legal definition of genocide that has always been subject to most criticism. Why is mass murder on these groups genocide and on other groups not?[14] When the ICTR judges applied the legal definition to the situation of Rwanda, they also encountered another problem, namely the problem of how to define which classes of groups could be qualified as protected groups. After an initial failed attempt to provide some sort of objective, static definition for each of the four classes of groups based on external factors,[15] the

---

12 *The Prosecutor v Bagilishema*, Judgement, para. 63.

13 *The Prosecutor v Kayishema and Ruzindana*, Judgement (21 May 1999), para. 532. Also see para. 542 ('Specifically, some testified about Ruzindana's statements about not sparing babies whose mothers had been killed because those attacking the country initially left as children').

14 This question is especially pertinent in light of the mass killings in Cambodia between 1975 and 1979, which according to the legal definition cannot be qualified as genocide, but which is a clear case of genocide for social scientists. See Schabas, W.A. (2001), 'Cambodia: was it really genocide?', in 23 *Human Rights Quarterly*, pp. 470–477, and Chalk, F. 'Redefining Genocide,' in Andreopoulos, G.J. (ed.) (1994), *Genocide – Conceptual and Historical Dimensions* (University of Philadelphia Press: Philadelphia), pp. 47–63.

15 *The Prosecutor v Akayesu*, Judgement, 2 September 1998, paras. 510–516. (A national group was defined as 'a collection of people who are perceived to share a legal bond based

ICTR Trial Chambers implicitly acknowledged that concepts such as ethnicity and race were mainly social artefacts. Consequently, the Trial Chambers took the victims' and the perpetrators' identification of the Tutsi as an ethnic group as a starting point.[16] Hence, these subjective factors started to play a preponderant role in the process of determining whether the Tutsi as a whole were a protected group. However, in the *Rutaganda* Judgement, the Trial Chamber indicated that a subjective definition alone was not sufficient, since the 1948 Genocide Convention was not intended to protect all groups, but only to protect the specific groups that were mentioned.[17] The subjective approach therefore had to be complemented and external (or 'objective') evidence relating to the political and cultural context was also taken into account in determining whether a certain group could be qualified as a protected group. In the words of the Trial Chamber in the *Semanza* Judgement:

> the determination of whether a group comes within the sphere of protection created by Article 2 of the Statute ought to be assessed on a case-by-case basis by reference to the *objective* particulars of a given social or historical context, and by the *subjective* perceptions of the perpetrators.[18]

Once it has been determined that a certain *group* can be qualified as one of the protected groups, a next question is how to determine in individual cases whether a specific *individual* is a victim of genocide or not. In the *Akayesu* case, the Trial Chamber held categorically that a Hutu could not be considered a victim of the 1994 genocide.[19] However, in later cases, Trial Chambers held that not only those individuals who actually belonged to the protected group could be considered as victims of genocide, but also those people who were perceived by the perpetrator as belonging to the protected group, even if this did not fully correspond to the perception of the group itself or of other elements of society.[20] Hence, the determination whether a specific

---

on common citizenship, coupled with reciprocity of rights and duties', an ethnic group was said to be 'a group whose members share a common language or culture', a racial group was based on 'hereditary physical traits often identified with a geographical region, irrespective of linguistic, cultural, national or religious factors', and members of a religious group 'share[d] the same religion, denomination or mode of worship').

16 *The Prosecutor v Kayishema and Ruzindana*, Judgement (21 May 1999), para. 98. ('An ethnic group is one whose members share a common language and culture; or, a group which distinguishes itself, as such (self identification); or, a group identified as such by others, including the perpetrators of the crimes (identification by others)'.) Also see *The Prosecutor v Akayesu,* Judgement (2 September 1998), para. 702 ('The Chamber further noted that all the Rwandan witnesses who appeared before it invariably answered spontaneously and without hesitation the questions of the Prosecutor regarding their ethnic identity.')

17 *The Prosecutor v Rutaganda*, Judgement (6 December 1999), para. 57.

18 *The Prosecutor v Semanza*, Judgement (15 May 2003), para. 317.

19 *The Prosecutor v Akayesu*, Judgement (2 September 1998) para. 712. ('... such acts as committed against victim V were perpetrated against a Hutu and cannot, therefore, constitute a crime of genocide against the Tutsi group.')

20 *The Prosecutor v Bagilishema*, Judgement (7 June 2001), paras. 61, 65; *The Prosecutor v Ndindabahizi*, Judgement (15 July 2004), paras. 466–469; *The Prosecutor v Kajelijeli*, Judgement (1 December 2003), para. 813.

individual can be considered as a victim is made solely on the basis of subjective factors, i.e., the perception of the perpetrator.

ICTY Case Law

In the ICTY Statute, the crime of genocide features in a less prominent place than in the ICTR Statute. This could reflect some hesitation about whether the events that took place in the former Yugoslavia can actually be qualified as genocide. The crimes in Yugoslavia were generally characterized as ethnic cleansing. Schabas maintained that ethnic cleansing as such does not constitute genocide, as the aim is not necessarily to exterminate a given group but rather to have this group leave a certain area.[21] So far, only two cases have resulted in a genocide conviction.[22] These are the *Krstić* case[23] and the *Blagojević and Jokić* case.[24]

The Specific Intent

The ICTY had more problems than the ICTR in construing the 'specific intent to destroy in whole or in part,' as the ICTY did not adjudicate crimes committed in a 'general context of genocide'. Therefore, three aspects of the mental element were broadly interpreted so as to come to the conclusion that genocide was committed.[25]

---

21 Schabas, W.A. (2001), *Genocide in international law: the crime of crimes* (Cambridge: Cambridge University Press), pp. 189–201. Also see Cassese, A. (2003), *International criminal law* (Oxford: Oxford University Press), pp. 98–100, who set out the different findings on this matter by various courts and tribunals, and adhered to the view that ethnic cleansing can be taken into account as indicating an intent to destroy.

22 For more information on the ICTY jurisprudence on genocide, see Schabas, W.A. (2001), 'The *Jelišić* case and the *mens rea* of the crime of genocide', 14 *Leiden Journal of International Law*, 125–139; Schabas, W.A. (2001), 'Was genocide committed in Bosnia and Herzegovina? First Judgements of the International Criminal Tribunal for the former Yugoslavia', in 25 *Fordham International Law Journal*, pp. 23–53; Jørgensen, N.H.B. (2002), 'Genocide acquittal in the Sikirica case', in 15 *Leiden Journal of International Law*, 289–408; Tournaye, C. (2003), 'Genocidal intent before the ICTY', 52 *International and Comparative Law Quarterly*, 447–462; and Sliedregt, E. van (2005), 'Commentary', in Klip, A. and Sluiter, G. (eds) *Annotated Leading Cases of International Criminal Tribunals, vol. VII*, (Antwerp: Intersentia), pp. 767–772).

23 *The Prosecutor v Krstić*, Judgement (2 August 2001). On appeal, Krstić was eventually convicted for aiding and abetting genocide, and the trial Judgement on this point was quashed, *The Prosecutor v Krstić*, Appeal Judgement (19 April 2004), para. 144.

24 *The Prosecutor v Blagojević and Jokić*, Judgement (17 January 2005).

25 Eventually, Krstić and Blagojević were convicted as accomplices having knowledge of the specific intent of the principal perpetrators, but without a specific intent themselves. The standard for aiding and abetting genocide was elucidated in *The Prosecutor v Krstić*, Appeal Judgement (19 April 2004), para. 140. It is noteworthy that a conviction on complicity can only be entered if it is proved that genocide has been committed. Another defendant before the ICTY, Stakić, was acquitted of complicity in genocide because it could not be proved that genocide had been committed, *The Prosecutor v Stakić*, Judgement (31 July 2003), para. 561.

These aspects concerned the factors from which the specific intent could be inferred, the interpretation of the word 'destroy,' and the application of the words 'in part'.

Evidence of the Specific Intent

Given the different context, the ICTY inferred the specific intent from different indicators. In the Krstić case, the ICTY Trial Chamber observed, 'where there is physical or biological destruction there are often simultaneous attacks on the cultural and religious property and symbols of the targeted group as well'.[26] Consequently, the Trial Chamber concluded that genocidal intent could also be inferred from such attacks on cultural and religious property and symbols. Thus, in addition to seeing the killing of all Bosnian Muslim men of Srebrenica as an indication of the genocidal intent, the Trial Chamber also took account of the destruction of the homes of Bosnian Muslims in Srebrenica and in Potočari and of the principal mosque in Srebrenica after the attack.[27] As indicated above, the ICTR also held that attacks on property can denote a specific intent. However, it did not need to rely to such a large extent on this indication, given that there was other, more convincing, evidence, such as specific statements of the accused. One should indeed be cautious to infer a specific intent to destroy a group from attacks on the property of that group. The fact that genocidal acts are often accompanied by other illegitimate acts, does not mean that these other illegitimate acts are always committed in the context of a genocide. Hence, property of a specific group may be attacked without a specific intent to physically destroy the group as such.

In the case of *Blagojević*, the Trial Chamber found 'that Colonel Blagojević knew of the principal perpetrators intent to destroy in whole or in part the Bosnian Muslim group as such.'[28] The Trial Chamber did not specify the factors from which it inferred the specific intent. In a footnote, it rather referred to some paragraphs mainly dealing with the physical act of genocide, causing serious bodily or mental harm.[29] Moreover, the Chamber held:

> the criminal acts committed by the Bosnian Serb forces were all parts of one single scheme to commit genocide of the Bosnian Muslims of Srebrenica, as reflected in the 'Krivaja 95' operation, the ultimate objective of which was to eliminate the enclave and, therefore, the Bosnian Muslim community living there.[30]

However, a plan to remove a group from a given area cannot serve to prove a specific intent to destroy this group physically. In fact, it might even be considered as counterevidence. The fact that Bosnian Muslims who were in the power of the Serbs were left alive can be held to demonstrate that the Serbs did not have the intention

---

26 *The Prosecutor v Krstić*, Judgement (2 August 2001), para. 580 (my emphasis).

27 *The Prosecutor v Krstić*, Judgement (2 August 2001), para. 595.

28 *The Prosecutor v Blagojević and Jokić*, Judgement (17 January 2005), para. 786.

29 *The Prosecutor v Blagojević and Jokić*, Judgement (17 January 2005), para. 78, especially fn. 2229.

30 *The Prosecutor v Blagojević and Jokić*, Judgement (17 January 2005), para. 674.

to destroy all Bosnian Muslims of Srebrenica. Hence, apart from the question which indicators can be used to denote a specific intent, another question is how the word 'destroy' must be interpreted.

The Interpretation of the Word 'Destroy'

In the *Kamuhanda* Judgement, an ICTR Trial Chamber emphasised that the word 'destroy' had to be understood as the 'material destruction of a group either by physical and biological means and not the destruction of the national, linguistic, religious, cultural or other identity of a particular group.'[31] Also the International Law Commission (ILC) in its 1996 report held:

> As clearly shown by the preparatory work for the Convention, the destruction in question is the material destruction of a group either by physical or by biological means, not the destruction of the national, linguistic, religious, cultural or other identity of a particular group. The national or religious element and the racial or ethnic element are not taken into consideration in the definition of the word "destruction", which must be taken only in its material sense, its physical or biological sense.[32]

While noting some developments that might point to an acceptance of cultural genocide, the Trial Chamber acknowledged:

> customary international law limits the definition of genocide to those acts seeking the physical or biological destruction of all or part of the group. Hence, an enterprise attacking only the cultural or sociological characteristics of a human group in order to annihilate these elements which give to that group its own identity distinct from the rest of the community would not fall under the definition of genocide.[33]

The Appeals Chamber confirmed this view stating:

> The Genocide Convention, and customary international law in general, prohibit only the physical or biological destruction of a human group.[34]

In sharp contrast, Judge Shahabuddeen stated in a Partial Dissenting Opinion that '[t]he intent certainly has to be to destroy, but, except for the listed act, there is no reason why the destruction must always be physical or biological.'[35] Disregarding the obligation to adhere to the Appeals Chamber's case law,[36] the Trial Chamber in the *Blagojević* case held:

---

31 *The Prosecutor v Kamuhanda*, Judgement (22 January 2004), para. 627. Also see *The Prosecutor v Semanza*, Judgement (15 May 2003), para. 315.

32 *UN Doc.* A/51/10 (6 May 1996–26 July 1996), pp. 90–91, as cited by the ICTY Trial Chamber in *The Prosecutor v Krstić*, Judgement (2 August 2001), para. 576.

33 *The Prosecutor v Krstić*, Judgement (2 August 2001), para. 580.

34 *The Prosecutor v Krstić*, Appeal Judgement (19 April 2004), para. 25.

35 *The Prosecutor v Krstić*, Appeal Judgement, Partial Dissenting Opinion of Judge Shahabuddeen (19 April 2004), para. 51.

36 *The Prosecutor v Aleksovski*, Appeal Judgement (24 March 2000), paras. 112–113. Also see Nollkaemper, A. and Zegveld, L. (2002), 'Commentary', in Klip, A. and Sluiter,

the physical or biological destruction of a group is not necessarily the death of the group members. While killing large numbers of a group may be the most direct means of destroying a group, other acts or series of acts, can also lead to the destruction of the group. A group is comprised of its individuals, but also of its history, traditions, the relationship between its members, the relationship with other groups, the relationship with the land. The Trial Chamber finds that the physical or biological destruction of the group is the likely outcome of a forcible transfer of the population when this transfer is conducted in such a way that the group can no longer reconstitute itself – particularly when it involves the separation of its members. In such cases the Trial Chamber finds that the forcible transfer of individuals could lead to the material destruction of the group, since the group ceases to exist as a group, or at least as the group it was.[37]

According to this view, genocide can also be committed without any killing, when members of a group are forcibly transferred and the group ceases to exist as a social unit. The Trial Chamber even held that this can be called physical or biological destruction of the group. However, since a group as such is not a tangible entity, the question is what exactly would be physically or biologically destroyed in such a case, if not the members of the group. True, the group as a social unit is destroyed, and so this would amount to the social destruction of the group. However, the adjectives 'physical' and 'biological' are intended to describe another form of destruction, namely the destruction of the group in which the group members are physically or biologically destroyed. There is a difference between destroying a group physically so that it ceases to exist in the world, and dispersing group members so the group ceases to exist in a specific place. It follows from the *travaux préparatoires*, the ICTR case law, the 1996 ILC report, and parts of the ICTY case law that the 1948 Genocide Convention only pertains to destroying a group by annihilating its members. Cultural genocide or social genocide for that matter are not prohibited under the 1948 Genocide Convention. Clearly, the Trial Chamber's interpretation in the Blagojević case exceeds the legal definition of genocide.

The Application of the Word 'In Part'

The application of the phrase 'in part' was challenged on appeal in the Krstić case. In the Judgement in first instance, the Trial Chamber had to determine whether the massacre of approximately 7,500 Bosnian Muslim men[38] in Srebrenica in July 1995 could be qualified as genocide. In so doing, the Trial Chamber decided that the group of men constituted a substantial part of the group of Bosnian Muslims in general, and that there was thus a specific intent to destroy the Bosnian Muslim group in part. As regards the fact that only the Muslim men of military age in Srebrenica were targeted, and not the women, children, and elderly people, the Chamber maintained:

G. (eds), *Annotated Leading Cases of International Criminal Tribunals, vol. IV* (Antwerp: Intersentia), pp. 411–418.

37 *The Prosecutor v Blagojević and Jokić*, Judgement (17 January 2005), para. 659.

38 This number is an estimate, see *The Prosecutor v Krstić*, Judgement (2 August 2001), paras. 80–84.

the combination of those killings with the forced transfer of the women, children and elderly would inevitably result in the physical disappearance of the Bosnian Muslim population in Srebrenica.[39]

Various scholars have criticized the Trial Chamber's approach.[40] They pointed out that the disappearance of a group from a certain place does not necessarily constitute genocide, but is actually an indication of ethnic cleansing. Genocide is the annihilation of a group, not the removal of a group.[41]

On appeal, the defence argued that the 7,500 men did not constitute a substantial part of the Bosnian Muslims in general. However, the Appeals Chamber held that there had been an intent to destroy all the Bosnian Muslims of Srebrenica. It stated:

> the Trial Chamber treated the killing of the men of military age as evidence from which to infer that Krstić and some members of the VRS Main Staff had the requisite intent to destroy all the Bosnian Muslims of Srebrenica, the only part of the protected group relevant ...[42]

As set out above, the word 'destroy' must be interpreted as referring to the physical or biological destruction of the group, that is of the members of the group. The key question is the following. How could the Appeals Chamber find that there was convincing evidence of a specific intent to physically eliminate the women, children and elderly Muslims and some wounded Muslim men of Srebrenica, if all of these people had been authorized to leave? In comparison, one of the indicators from which the ICTR deduced the genocidal intent was that even newborn babies and pregnant women had not been spared.[43] Both the ICTY Trial Chamber and the Appeals Chamber explained the decision not to kill the women, children and elderly on the ground of 'the Bosnian Serbs' sensitivity to public opinion',[44] and a lack of manpower on the side of the Bosnian Serbs.[45] But the conclusion could also have been that there was just not a specific intent.

In the *Krstić* case, the Appeals Chamber acknowledged:

---

39 *The Prosecutor v Krstić*, Judgement (2 August 2001), para. 595.

40 Schabas, W.A. (2001), 'Was genocide committed in Bosnia and Herzegovina? First Judgements of the International Criminal Tribunal for the former Yugoslavia', 25 *Fordham International Law Journal*, 23–53; Tournaye, C. (2003), 'Genocidal intent before the ICTY', 52 *International and Comparative Law Quarterly*, 447–462; and Sliedregt, E. van (2005), 'Commentary', in Klip, A. and Sluiter, G. (eds) *Annotated Leading Cases of International Criminal Tribunals, vol. VII* (Antwerp: Intersentia), pp. 767–772.

41 In the *Stakić* case, the Trial Chamber also observed that the expulsion or dissolution of a group does not constitute genocide, *The Prosecutor v Stakić*, Judgement (31 July 2003), para. 519.

42 *The Prosecutor v Krstić*, Appeal Judgement (19 April 2004), para. 19.

43 *The Prosecutor v Akayesu*, Judgement (2 September 1998), para. 121.

44 *The Prosecutor v Krstić*, Appeal Judgement (19 April 2004), para. 31. *The Prosecutor v Krstić*, Judgement (2 August 2001), para. 547.

45 *The Prosecutor v Krstić*, Judgement (2 August 2001), para. 546.

The decision by Bosnian Serb forces to transfer the women, children and elderly within their control to other areas of Muslim-controlled Bosnia could be consistent with the Defence argument[46] [namely that there was no genocidal intent].

The Appeals Chamber continued:

> This evidence, however, is also susceptible of an alternative interpretation. As the Trial Chamber explained, forcible transfer could be an additional means by which to ensure the physical destruction of the Bosnian Muslim community in Srebrenica. The transfer completed the removal of all Bosnian Muslims from Srebrenica, thereby eliminating even the residual possibility that the Muslim community in the area could reconstitute itself.[47]

Yet, as demonstrated above and as acknowledged by the Appeals Chamber itself, genocide is not about the physical removal of a group from a specific place, but about the physical disappearance of the group from the earth. This aim does not have to be achieved, but it must be the aim, or in legal terms, the specific intent.

Ultimately, the question of whether the ICTY came to the correct conclusion in the *Krstić* case that genocide had been committed is a question of how to evaluate the evidence that was presented. Basic principles of criminal law require that a conviction is only entered if guilt has been proved beyond reasonable doubt.[48] Since the Appeals Chamber acknowledged that the defence argument that there was no genocidal intent could also be plausible, it should not have entered a conviction on genocide.[49]

The Protected Groups

With regard to another element of the crime of genocide, the ICTY also displayed a willingness to interpret broadly. Like the ICTR, the ICTY generally used the subjective approach complemented by the objective approach to determine whether the victim group was a group protected by the 1948 Genocide Convention.

In the *Jelišić* case, an ICTY Trial Chamber demonstrated that the groups mentioned in the Convention were originally supposed to be objectively defined. However, the Trial Chamber held that such an objective classification might not correspond to the perceived reality for the persons concerned. For that reason, the Trial Chamber opted for the subjective approach.[50] In the case of *Krstić*, the Trial Chamber held that the relevant group could be identified 'by using as a criterion the stigmatisation of the

---

46 *The Prosecutor v Krstić*, Appeal Judgement (19 April 2004), para. 31.

47 *The Prosecutor v Krstić*, Appeal Judgement (19 April 2004), para. 31.

48 Or in the words of the Appeals Chamber itself, 'Genocide is one of the worst crimes known to humankind, and its gravity is reflected in the stringent requirement of specific intent. Convictions for genocide can be entered only where that intent has been unequivocally established'. *The Prosecutor v Krstić*, Appeal Judgement (19 April 2004), para. 134.

49 This conclusion does not mean, of course, that what happened in Srebrenica in July 1995 was not atrocious or impermissible. Undoubtedly, it was. As expressed by Special Rapporteur Whitaker: '[o]ther attacks and killings do, of course, remain heinous crimes, even if they fall outside the definition of genocide.' *UN Doc.* E/CN.4/Subs.2/1985/6 (2 July 1985), para. 29.

50 *The Prosecutor v Jelišić*, Judgement (14 December 1999), paras. 69–70.

group, notably by the perpetrators of the crime, on the basis of its perceived national, ethnical, racial or religious characteristics.'[51] It thus emphasized that the subjective approach should prevail in identifying a group. However, the Trial Chamber also noted that 'a group's cultural, religious, ethnical or national characteristics must be identified within the socio-historic context which it inhabits.'[52] This statement might reveal that objective criteria, i.e., criteria that are not directly related to the perpetrator or the victim's perception, should still play a complementary role. The Trial Chamber in the *Blagojević* case also held:

> The Trial Chamber finds that the correct determination of the relevant protected group has to be made on a case-by-case basis, consulting both objective and subjective criteria.[53]

The Trial Chamber in the *Krstić* case further maintained that the list of the four groups in the 1948 Genocide Convention 'was designed more to describe a single phenomenon, roughly corresponding to what was recognised, before the Second Word War, as "national minorities", rather than to refer to several distinct prototypes of human groups'.[54] Even though the four adjectives were considered to describe the same phenomenon, it was still specified that the Bosnian Muslims constituted a *national* group.[55]

A whole list of legal sources were named as a basis for the conclusion that in fact national minorities were protected in the 1948 Genocide Convention, and not four distinct groups. However, the question is, if the drafters of the Convention meant to say national minorities, why did they not just say so?

The Darfur Report

Upon the request of the UN Security Council,[56] the Secretary-General established an International Commission of Inquiry. This Commission, whose president was the former ICTY President Antonio Cassese, was given the specific task to investigate whether genocide had been committed in Darfur. The recent practice of establishing commissions of enquiry in cases of gross human rights violations that report to the Security Council has been welcomed as bridging the gap between the Security Council and the former Human Rights Commission, now replaced by the Human Rights Council.[57] In the face of a detailed report on the facts and applicable legal principles in a given humanitarian crisis, it will not be so easy for the permanent

---

51 *The Prosecutor v Krstić*, Judgement (2 August 2001), para. 557.

52 *Ibid.*

53 *The Prosecutor v Blagojević and Jokić*, Judgement (17 January 2005), para. 667.

54 *The Prosecutor v Krstić*, Judgement (2 August 2001), paras. 554–560.

55 *The Prosecutor v Krstić*, Judgement (2 August 2001), para. 559. *The Prosecutor v Krstić*, Appeal Judgement (19 April 2004), para. 15. The Trial Chamber in the *Blagojević* case concluded that the Bosnian Muslim were a protected group without specifying what kind of group, *The Prosecutor v Blagojević and Jokić*, Judgement (17 January 2005), para. 667.

56 *UN Doc*. S/RES/1564 (18 September 2004), para. 12.

57 Alston, P. (2005), The Darfur Commission as a Model for Future Responses to Crises Situations', 3 *Journal of International Criminal Justice*, 600–607.

members of the Security Council to obstruct appropriate action. In fact, the Darfur report led to the first ICC referral, something that was considered hypothetical until almost the very moment it happened. The Darfur Commission of Inquiry presented its report in January 2005. In this report, it cautiously came to the conclusion that the Government of Sudan had not pursued a genocidal policy in Darfur.[58] The Commission explicitly stated that:

> The conclusion that no genocidal policy has been pursued and implemented in Darfur by the Government authorities, directly or through the militias under their control, should not be taken as in any way detracting from or belittling the gravity of the crimes perpetrated in that region.[59]

Despite this statement, the report has been heavily criticized for its conclusion that no genocide was committed on a State level and even misunderstood. The following quote of Prunier in his book on Darfur may serve to illustrate this:

> ... a UN Commission of Inquiry gave its answer as to whether the Darfur horror deserved to be called a genocide and the answer was negative; it was merely a routine matter of some war crimes and assorted violations of human rights.[60]

The Commission's conclusion on genocide is analysed in this section. In the subsequent section the question is answered how this conclusion affects the new doctrine on 'the responsibility to protect'.

The Specific Intent

The Commission's conclusion that no there was no governmental genocidal policy resulted mainly from lack of a finding of a genocidal intent. The Commission acknowledged that:

> the scale of atrocities and the systematic nature of the attacks, killing, displacement and rape, as well as racially motivated statement by perpetrators that have targeted members of the African tribes only, could be indicative of the *genocidal intent*.[61]

However, the Commission also observed that there were some counterindications. It noted:

> in a number of villages attacked and burned by both militias and Government forces the attackers refrained from exterminating the whole population that had not fled, but instead selectively killed groups of young men ...[62]

---

58 *Report of the International Commission of Inquiry on Darfur to the United Nations Secretary-General*, Geneva, 25 January 2005 (hereinafter *Darfur Report*), *UN Doc.* S/2005/60, (1 February 2005), para. 519.

59 *Darfur Report*, para. 522.

60 Prunier, G. (2005), *Darfur: The Ambiguous Genocide* (London: Hurst).

61 *Darfur Report*, para. 513 (emphasis added).

62 *Darfur Report*, para. 513.

And it added:

> Another element that tends to show the Sudanese Government's lack of a genocidal intent
> can be seen in the fact that persons forcibly dislodged from their villages are collected
> in IDP camps. In other words, the population surviving attacks on villages are not killed
> outright, so as to eradicate the group; they are rather forced to abandon their homes and
> live together in areas selected by the Government.[63]

The Commission concluded:

> generally speaking the policy of attacking, killing and forcibly displacing members of
> some tribes does not evince a specific intent to annihilate.[64]

In addition to this finding, the Commission also stated that single individuals could
have acted with genocidal intent.[65] The scholar Kress criticized this statement in the
Darfur Report that followed the purpose-based approach of the ICTR and ICTY as
the standard for the specific intent. He advocated that the proper standard for the
specific intent to commit genocide should be knowledge-based, namely knowledge
of a genocidal campaign in combination with at least the awareness that his act
could contribute to the destruction of the group.[66]

Next to determining the correct standard, the question whether there is a
genocidal intent is also to a very large extent an evidentiary question and it may be
that the judges of the ICC, to which the Darfur issue has now been referred,[67] reach
a different conclusion. Nevertheless, at first sight the way the Darfur Commission
of Inquiry evaluated the evidence at hand appears to be different from the ICTY's
appreciation of similar evidence.[68]

The Protected Groups

In its report, the Commission recalled the case law of the *ad hoc* Tribunals that the
protected groups were 'no longer identified only by their objective connotations but
also on the basis of the subjective perceptions of members of the group.'[69] It thus
appeared to confirm the case law that a group could be identified by the subjective
approach complemented with the objective approach.

However when investigating whether the victim tribes could be considered a
protected group, the Commission enquired:

---

63 *Darfur Report*, para. 514.

64 *Darfur Report*, para. 518.

65 *Darfur Report*, para. 520.

66 Kress, C. (2005), 'The Darfur Report and Genocidal Intent', 3 *Journal of International Criminal Justice*, 562–578.

67 *UN Doc.* S/RES/1593 (31 March 2005).

68 Also see Schabas, W.A. (2005) 'Darfur and the "Odious Scourge": The Commission of Inquiry's Findings on Genocide', in 18 *Leiden Journal of the International Law*, 871–885.

69 *Darfur Report*, para. 501.

if objectively the two sets of persons at issue do not make up two distinct groups, the question arises as to whether they may nevertheless be regarded as such subjectively, in that they perceive each other and themselves as constituting distinct groups.[70]

This enquiry marks a shift to a purely subjective approach. This choice might be justified with the argument that concepts such as race and ethnicity are viewed as social constructs rather than as scientific phenomena that can be defined purely objectively. However, to regard race and ethnicity as social constructs does not mean that they are not scientifically identifiable, but rather that they cannot be retraced to biological or natural particulars. Even if the latter is considered true, it is still not correct to identify a racial or an ethnic group solely on the basis of a subjective approach, i.e., solely on the basis of the perception of the victim and the perpetrator. Such identification should to a certain extent also be embedded in a socio-historical discourse.

Therefore, the *ad hoc* Tribunals also had regard to circumstances outside the perpetrator and/or the victim, the so-called 'objective factors'. Taking these objective factors, such as socio-historical context, into account does serve a certain goal. Besides the fact that the purely subjective approach risks going beyond the legal definition of genocide, a more serious disadvantage is that identification of a group solely on the basis of the perception of the victim and the perpetrator risks loosing touch with reality. If the government of a certain State propagates that all lawyers constitute a religious group and that this group should be physically destroyed, and if consequently this policy is implemented, this does not constitute genocide, even if the perpetrators and the lawyers themselves have started to believe that they form a religious group. If in this hypothetical case, an international tribunal has to qualify the massacres afterwards, it would not be beneficial to the society concerned, if this tribunal took the propaganda of the government as a basis for its findings, and in so doing reinforced it. Therefore, objective factors, such as socio-historical facts, should also be taken into account, albeit in a complementary fashion.

Another observation is that, on the basis of the purely subjective approach, the Commission determined that 'the tribes who were victims of attacks and killings subjectively make up a protected group.'[71] The Commission did not specify which of the four classes of groups were concerned, thereby adhering to the ICTY's view that in fact the 1948 Genocide Convention aims to protect one group, namely national minorities. In practice, this novel interpretation leads to a reconceptualization of genocide as a crime that protects much more groups than originally envisaged, if not all human groups. As indicated with regard to the ICTY case law on this point, even if welcome, it is questionable whether this wide interpretation is completely at ease with the text of the Convention.

---

70 *Darfur Report*, para. 509.
71 *Darfur Report*, para. 512.

Genocide and the Responsibility to Protect

As is apparent from the foregoing, the notion of genocide bears special social significance in two respects. First of all, it denotes extreme gravity. Secondly, with the Rwandan cries for help still echoing, the qualification of genocide has been understood to imply a duty to act for the international community. These social connotations of genocide are, however, not reflected in legal duties or qualifications.

As regards the first connotation of the notion of genocide, namely that it is the worst crime, both *ad hoc* Tribunals have maintained that there is no abstract hierarchy between genocide and crimes against humanity. As the ICTR Appeals Chamber stated, 'there is no hierarchy of crimes under the Statute, and that all of the crimes specified therein are serious violations of international humanitarian law, capable of attracting the same sentence.'[72] Hence, from a legal perspective, genocide is not a graver crime than crimes against humanity. However, even the Tribunal judges cannot do away with the feeling that there is something special about genocide that makes it more serious than other crimes, as illustrated by the following excerpt from the *Krstić* Trial Judgement:

> The [Genocide] Convention thus seeks to protect the right to life of human groups, as such. This characteristic makes genocide an exceptionally grave crime and distinguishes it from other serious crimes, in particular persecution, where the perpetrator selects his victims because of their membership in a specific community but does not necessarily seek to destroy the community as such.[73]

As regards the second connotation of the notion of genocide, a wide perception exists that qualifying massacres as genocide means that there is a duty to act. There is of course no doubt that such a duty exists on a moral level. However, the question is whether that moral duty has been translated into a legal obligation.

The argument that there is a unilateral legal obligation to intervene in cases of genocide could be based on Article I of the 1948 Genocide Convention which includes the duty to prevent genocide. However, Article I is phrased in rather general terms, and it might be argued that the duty to prevent genocide is addressed first of all to the territorial State. This would be in line with the enforcement system of Article VI of the Convention which principally grants jurisdiction over genocide to territorial States.[74] Moreover, to understand Article I as granting individual States

---

72 *The Prosecutor v Kayishema and Ruzindana*, Appeal Judgement (1 June 2001), para. 367. Also see Van den Herik, L.J. (2005), *The Contribution of the Rwanda Tribunal to the Development of International Law* (Leiden: Martinus Nijhoff Publishers), pp. 245–249.

73 *The Prosecutor v Krstić*, Judgement (2 August 2001), para. 553.

74 In the case of *Bosnia-Herzegovina v Yugoslavia*, the International Court of Justice held that the obligation to prevent was not territorially limited. ICJ, *Case Concerning Application of the Convention on the Prevention and Punishment of the Crime of Genocide (Bosnia-Herzegovina v Yugoslavia)*, Judgement on Preliminary Objections (11 July 1996), 1996 ICJ Reports 595, para. 31. However, this statement should be read in the context of the case, since Bosnia-Herzegovina alleged that Yugoslavia committed genocide in Bosnia, which renders this case a so-called case of inter-State genocide as opposed to Darfur which is a case of intra-State genocide.

the right or even the duty to intervene would conflict with the system of collective security of the UN Charter, and more directly with the prohibition of the use of force as laid down in Article 2(4) of the UN Charter. Given that this latter provision is generally accorded a *jus cogens* status, another rule that is intended to derogate from this provision should at the very least do so explicitly and it should also have a *jus cogens* status. Of course, the prohibition of genocide can be said to constitute *jus cogens*.[75] However, it would be harder to maintain that the right or duty of third States to intervene in case of genocide is *jus cogens*. In fact, this right or duty may not even exist under customary international law, given the lack of State practice in this regard.

The argument that there is a collective legal obligation to intervene in case of genocide can first of all be based on Article VIII of the 1948 Genocide Convention in relation with Chapter VII of the UN Charter and the new doctrine on the responsibility to protect. Article VIII of the 1948 Genocide Convention reads:

> Any Contracting Party may call upon the competent organs of the United Nations to take such action under the Charter of the United Nations as they consider appropriate for the prevention and suppression of acts of genocide or any of the other acts enumerated in Article III.

The competent UN organ to authorize the use of force is the Security Council.[76] It may do so under Chapter VII of the UN Charter after it has determined that a threat to peace exists under Article 39. On occasion, the Council has already qualified genocide as a threat to peace.[77] However, its power to authorize the use of force under Article 42 is a discretionary one and the text of the UN Charter does not oblige the Security Council to act. Yet, the International Commission on Intervention and State Sovereignty (ICISS) discerned an emerging norm of a collective international responsibility to protect.[78] This new doctrine was endorsed by the High Level Panel on Threats, Challenges and Change in its report of December 2004,[79] by the Secretary-General in his follow-up report of March (2005),[80] and most importantly,

---

75 See *Armed Activities on the Territory of the Congo (New Application: 2002)*, (*Democratic Republic of the Congo v Rwanda*), Judgement on Jurisdiction of the Court and Admissibility of the application (3 February 2006), para. 64. See more specifically on the issue of *jus cogens* the Separate Opinion of Judge *ad hoc* Dugard.

76 The UN General Assembly (UNGA) has a secondary responsibility for the maintenance of international peace and security. In case of paralysis of the Security Council, the UNGA may take matters in its own hands under the *Uniting for Peace Resolution, UN Doc.* 377(A) (3 November 1950). However, this is a highly controversial procedure.

77 See, e.g., *UN Doc.* S/RES/955 (8 November 1994).

78 ICISS (2001), *The Responsibility to Protect: report of the International Commission on Intervention and State Sovereignty* (hereinafter *ICISS Report*), *UN Doc.* A/59/565 (2 December 2004), para. 135.

79 *A more secure world: our shared responsibility* (hereinafter *High Level Panel Report*), *UN Doc.* A/59/565 (2 December 2004), para. 203.

80 *In larger freedom: towards development, security and freedom for all*, (hereinafter *Secretary-General's Report, UN Doc.* A/59/2005) (31 March 2005), para. 135.

by the General Assembly in the 2005 World Summit Outcome.[81] In all reports though, it was underlined that when the responsibility to protect requires enforcement action, the Security Council is the appropriate body to authorize such action. All reports emphasized the Council's special responsibility and the serious consequences that might ensue if the Council did not properly take up this responsibility.[82] In this vein, proposals were issued, such as a code of conduct for the five permanent members that they should not use their veto in cases of genocide or other forms of gross human rights violations.[83] Unsurprisingly, these proposals have not been translated into a legal obligation.

In sum, there is no clear legal right for third States to intervene in case of genocide, nor is there a clear legal obligation for the Security Council to act. Propagating that there is might not only be wishful thinking, but may also raise expectations that will not be fulfilled. This can turn out to be even more harmful to those expecting to be saved than being honest about the disappointing current state of the law.

Conclusion

Currently, there is a gap between the legal and the social concept of genocide, as well as between the moral duty to act in case of genocide and the legal framework in this regard. The recent legal developments analysed in this chapter are welcome from a social perspective given that they narrow the dichotomy between the legal and the social concept of genocide. However, from a legal perspective, it must be acknowledged that the developments were not always the result of sound legal reasoning. Should these recent developments nevertheless be sustained to unite the legal and the social concept, or does the current dichotomy serve a function? The answer to this question varies depending on the purposes of the prohibition of genocide.

The purposes of the 1948 Genocide Convention are twofold, namely to prevent and to punish genocide. Initiatives to fulfil the first purpose, namely to prevent genocide, fall within the ambit of human rights law and the law on peace and security. Projects to implement the second purpose, namely to punish genocide, come within the realm of international criminal law. Of course, the legal definition of genocide is the one given in the 1948 Genocide Convention, and is the same for all fields of international law. Nevertheless, strict adherence to the definition may be more important with regard to punishing genocide, and less important when prevention is at stake.

In addresses to the General Assembly on 21 and 22 September 2004, the UN Secretary-General and the Representative of Canada, respectively, addressed the situation in Darfur. Both emphasized that real action to prevent human catastrophes is far more important than any legal debate on whether certain mass killings do or do not constitute genocide. Moreover, in all legal discourses on whether States have

---

81 *World Summit Outcome, UN Doc.* A/60/1 (20 September 2005), paras. 138–139.

82 *ICISS Report*, para. 6.13–6.40; *High Level Panel Report*, paras. 199–203 and 256; *Secretary-General's Report*, paras. 126, 135. *World Summit Outcome*, para. 139.

83 *High Level Panel Report*, para. 256.

a right or a duty to intervene in case of gross human rights violations, such right or duty is assumed for both genocide and crimes against humanity.[84] Finally with regard to prevention, it may be noted that the mandate of the recently appointed Special Advisor on Genocide, Juan Mendez, is to develop an early-warning mechanism for potential genocide situations and to make recommendations on how to prevent genocide in these cases. The Special Advisor must thus especially act in situations where no genocide has been committed yet, and therefore the precise legal definition of what constitutes genocide is less relevant to the adequate fulfilment of his mandate. Hence, where prevention of genocide is concerned, the social concept of genocide, i.e., understanding genocide as being the mass killing of a group of people, can prevail and the legal concept need not be emphasized.

In contrast, it remains important to adhere strictly to the legal concept of genocide in the context of international criminal law, because of the special character of criminal law as a separate field of law. Criminal law aims to qualify a prohibited act in legal terms, while taking account of any relevant circumstances in which the act was committed. A sophisticated national system penalizes a whole number of prohibited acts. Different circumstances may lead to a different qualification. For instance, if a man is murdered this may be qualified as a different crime depending on the circumstances. It may be simple murder, or patricide, or even terrorism. In a similar vein, at the international level a distinction should be maintained between the different crimes of genocide and crimes against humanity. Not because genocide is necessarily a more serious crime than crimes against humanity, but because it is a different crime pertaining to different circumstances.

One of the basic principles of criminal law is that there can only be a conviction if guilt has been proven beyond reasonable doubt. This principle calls for a strict construction of the specific intent. There can only be a conviction for genocide, if all the evidence that is taken into account leads almost automatically to the conclusion that there was a specific intent to destroy a certain group. In the ICTY judgements, this was not the case. As illustrated above, the evidence available in the relevant cases could also have led to other plausible conclusions.

From a broader, sociological perspective, it is also important that the definition of genocide in international criminal law is clear-cut. Criminal tribunals, be they international or national, play an important educative role. They can only fulfil this role properly if their case law is not controversial. Yet, for the ICTY, eminent scholars as well as ICTY staff displayed their disagreement on the genocide judgements. In addition, it may be noted that a clear and strict definition can help preventing that the term genocide is popularly used to denote the gravity of a certain event that has nothing to do with genocide as a legal concept, such as the AIDS crisis in Africa. Finally, adhering consistently to a strict definition may eventually bring the

---

84 *ICISS Report*, paras. 4.10–4.43, and in particular paras. 4.19–4.20. Also see *High-level Panel Report*, para. 203; *Secretary-General's Report*, paras. 122, 125, 134–135. In this respect Article 4(h) of the Charter of the African Union is also illustrative. This provision stipulates: 'the right of the Union to intervene in a Member State pursuant to a decision of the General Assembly in respect of grave circumstances, namely: war crimes, genocide and crimes against humanity.'

message across to society that not all forms of mass murder constitute genocide. It may temper expectations and thus avoid disappointment on the part of survivors and relatives when a certain crime is not qualified as genocide.

In sum, this author pleads for a strict legal definition of the crime of genocide. It must be noted though, that the distinction between crimes against humanity and genocide is only relevant in the domain of international criminal law. In the field of peace and security, both crimes against humanity as well as genocide can constitute a threat to peace and the commission of both crimes trigger the UN Security Council's responsibility to protect.

PART III

ASPECTS OF THE CRIME

Chapter 8

Is the Emerging Jurisprudence on Complicity in Genocide before the International *Ad Hoc* Tribunals a Moving Target in Conflict with the Principle of Legality?

Michael G. Karnavas

Introduction

The international community codified the crime of genocide under international law through the Convention on the Prevention and Punishment of the Crime of Genocide.[1] The crime of genocide is unique from other crimes because it requires a distinctive mental element commonly referred to as the *dolus specialis* or special genocidal intent. Both the International Criminal Tribunal for the Former Yugoslavia ('ICTY') and the International Criminal Tribunal for Rwanda ('ICTR'), referred to herein as '*ad hoc* Tribunals', incorporated, *verbatim*, Articles II and III of the Genocide Convention into their Statutes,[2] essentially being the first legal institutions (national or international) to apply the Genocide Convention to individuals.

Any application of the crime of genocide, as with any crime set out by the Statutes of the *ad hoc* Tribunals, must comport with the principal of legality, forbidding the judging or punishing of a person unless an extant law: i) preceded the act in question; ii) defined the crime at the time of its commission by setting out the objective elements (*actus reus*) and the subjective mental element (*mens*

---

1   Convention on the Prevention and the Punishment of the Crime of Genocide of 9 December 1948, 78 UNTS 277 (hereinafter: 'the Genocide Convention').

2   Both the ICTY and the ICTR draw their provisions on genocide *verbatim* from the Genocide Convention, stating, in Article 4 of the ICTY Statute, and Article 2 of the ICTR Statute: 'The International Tribunal shall have the power to prosecute genocide as defined in paragraph 2 of this article or of committing any of the other acts enumerated in paragraph 3 of this article.' Sub-paragraphs 2 and 3 correspond to Articles II and III of the Genocide Convention respectively.

rea); and iii) specifically expressed the nature and scope of the punishment.[3] This chapter examines the confusion resulting from the application of two apparently overlapping provisions in the Statutes of the *ad hoc* Tribunals: Article 4(3)(e)/2(3) (e), which lists 'complicity in genocide' as an act that shall be punishable under the heading of genocide, and ICTY Article 7(1)/6(1) which provide for individual criminal responsibility, including the application of 'aiding and abetting' to all of the crimes listed in the Statute.[4]

It is submitted that the Chambers of the *ad hoc* Tribunals are interpreting the Genocide Convention in a broad and contradictory fashion and are diluting the essence of the crime when they apply the statutory modes of liability to the crime of genocide.

Key Concepts

Genocide and the Special Genocidal Intent

The Genocide Convention specifically states in Article I that genocide is a crime under international law, reflecting customary international law and *jus cogens*.[5] The Genocide Convention requires that three elements be proven: i) the perpetrator must commit one of the underlying offences enumerated in Article II against a member of a protected group (*actus reus*); ii) the perpetrator must possess the requisite intent to commit the underlying offence (*mens rea*); and iii) during the commission of the underlying offence, the perpetrator must possess the 'special genocidal intent,' that is, *the intent to destroy, in whole or in part, a national, ethnical, racial or religious group, as such*. The special genocidal intent, which is part of the *chapeau*, distinguishes genocide as a specific crime under international law. Incorporating Article III of the Genocide Convention, the Statutes of the *ad hoc* Tribunals designate five punishable acts: genocide, conspiracy to commit genocide, direct and public incitement to commit genocide, attempt to commit genocide and complicity in genocide. Similar to the Genocide Convention, the Statutes do not provide definitions distinguishing the *mens rea* requirements for any of the enumerated acts other than the special genocidal intent found in the *chapeau*.[6]

---

3   *See Prosecutor v Vasiljević*, Case No. IT-98-32-T, Trial Judgement, 29 November 2002, at para. 193.

4   For the sake of brevity, unless noted otherwise, this paper will refer to the ICTY Statute.

5   *Reservations to the Convention on the Prevention and Punishment of the Crime of Genocide* (Advisory Opinion) [1951] ICJ Reports 16, at p. 23.

6   Article III of the Genocide Convention states:
The following acts shall be punishable:

(a) Genocide;
(b) Conspiracy to commit genocide;
(c) Direct and public incitement to commit genocide;
(d) Attempt to commit genocide;
(e) Complicity in genocide.

Forms of Participation in Genocide/Punishable Other Acts

As a general principle, irrespective of the crime charged, it is well known that participants other than the direct perpetrator of the criminal act may also incur liability for a crime, and in some cases different *mens rea* standards may apply to direct perpetrators and to other persons.[7] In parallel, the ICTY and ICTR Statutes provide modes of liability for crimes referred to in each Statute. Article 7(1) for the ICTY and Article 6(1) for the ICTR assign individual criminal responsibility as follows:

> A person who planned, instigated, ordered, committed or otherwise aided and abetted in the planning, preparation or execution of a crime referred to in Article 2 to [5/4] of the present Statute, shall be individually responsible for the crime.[8]

The modes of liability contained in Articles 7(1) and 6(1) are not defined in either Statute. Consequently, judges at the *ad hoc* Tribunals are entrusted with determining the *actus reus* and *mens rea* for each mode of liability. For the crime of genocide, the ICTY and ICTR Statutes spell out the various modes of participation or punishable acts, which, from the ordinary meaning of the adopted text in Articles 4 and 2 for the ICTY and ICTR, respectively, share the same *mens rea* without qualification.

Thus, with regard to the crime of genocide and the modes of liability, the ICTY and ICTR Statutes create a problem: while the genocide provisions – being adopted wholesale from the Genocide Convention – are self-contained with their own forms of participation sharing the same *mens rea*, Articles 7(1) and 6(1) provide modes of liability for a 'crime referred to' in the other articles of the Statute, which, unconditionally, includes the crime of genocide. Consequently, unlike other crimes listed in the ICTY and ICTR Statutes, there seems to be an overlap (or collision, as it were) between the forms of participation contained in the provisions of genocide and levels/modes of liability contained in the provisions for individual liability. This overlap leaves it up to the Chambers to determine when and how each applies and begs the question of whether aiding and abetting in Article 7(1)/6(1) is applicable to the crime of genocide or whether it is encompassed by the provision for complicity in genocide under Article 4(3)(e)/2(3)(e). The interpretive task is further complicated by the requirement of the special genocidal *mens rea* that, according to the language of the Statute, applies to all of the modes of liability contained in the genocide provisions.

---

7   *Prosecutor v Brdjanin*, Case No. IT-99-36-A, Decision on Interlocutory Appeal, 19 March 2004, at para. 5.

8   ICTY Statute Article 7(1), ICTR Statute Article 6(1). The 'crimes referred to in articles 2 to [5/4]' are: ICTY – Article 2 'Grave Breaches of the Geneva Conventions of 1949', Article 3 'Violations of the Laws or Customs of War', Article 4 'Genocide', Article 5 'Crimes Against Humanity'; ICTR – Article 2 'Genocide', Article 3 'Crimes Against Humanity', Article 4, 'Violations of Article 3 Common to the Geneva Conventions and of the Additional Protocol II'.

The Principle of Legality in International Criminal Law

The principle of legality is an established principle recognized in the common law and civil law systems as well as in international law. It encompasses, *inter alia*, the maxim *nullum crimen sine lege*, requiring criminal rules to unambiguously indicate the prohibited conduct. This principle forms the basis of the general interpretive rule that criminal law must not be construed expansively to the detriment of the accused.[9]

When faced specifically with an interpretation of the genocide provisions, the *ad hoc* Tribunals should interpret according to the principles enumerated in Article 31 of the Vienna Convention.[10] Since the ICTY and ICTR Statutes adopted the Genocide Convention *verbatim* and the Genocide Convention is an international treaty, it stands to reason that the Vienna Convention on Treaties applies.[11] The Vienna Convention provides (1) that treaty interpretation should follow good faith adherence to the ordinary meaning of the terms in their context and in light of the treaty's object and purpose;[12] and, 2) to confirm or determine meaning not resulting from application of the ordinary meaning, interpreters may refer to the preparatory work of the treaty or the circumstances of its conclusions.[13]

It is accepted that the principle of legality does not prevent a court (national or international) from clarifying the elements of a particular crime, so long as it is a measured clarification or interpretation and the result is consistent with the essence of the offence and could be reasonably foreseeable.[14] Under certain circumstances, this may be an acceptable approach to determine whether certain conduct falls within the elements of a crime, but it should not permit judges the freedom to create law aimed at correcting *lacunae* of international criminal law.[15]

---

9 *See Prosecutor v Kayishema*, Case No. ICTR-95-1-T, Decision on the Motion of the Prosecutor to Sever, to Join in a Superseding Indictment and to Amend the Superseding Indictment, 27 March 1997, at para. 3.

10 Vienna Convention on the Law of Treaties, May 23, 1969, Arts 3, 1155 UNTS 331 (hereinafter 'Vienna Convention'). The Vienna Convention provisions dealing with interpretation are generally considered to codify principles of customary international law.

11 For a counter-argument *see* Charles Lister (2005), 'What's in a Name? Labels and the Statute of the International Criminal Tribunal for the Former Yugoslavia', 18 *Leiden Journal Int'l Law*, 77.

12 Vienna Convention Article 31(1).

13 Vienna Convention Article 32.

14 *See* Mohamed Shahabuddeen (2004), 'Does the Principle of Legality Stand in the Way of Progressive Development of Law?' 2 *J. Int'l .Crim. Just.*, 1007, 1012–13; *see also Prosecutor v Hadžihasanović*, Case No. IT-01-47AR72, Decision on Interlocutory Appeal Challenging Jurisdiction in Relation to Command Responsibility, 16 July 2003, at para. 34; *Prosecutor v. Vasiljević*, Case No. IT-98-32-T, Trial Judgement, 29 November 2002, at paras. 193 and 294; *Prosecutor v Aleksovski*, Case No. IT-95-14/1-A, Appeal Judgement, 24 March 2000, at para. 127.

15 Audaciously, Judge Mohamed Shahabuddeen advocates what he self-classifies as a non-majority view, arguing that when the authorized sources of law are wanting, the policy-oriented approach provides an independent basis of decision-making. Judge Shahabuddeen postulates that a policy approach cannot violate the principle of *nulla crimen sine lege* because

In establishing the first *ad hoc* Tribunal, the ICTY, the United Nations Secretary-General indicated that 'the principle *nullum crimen sine lege* requires that the international tribunal should apply the rules of international humanitarian law.'[16] In determining what constitutes a customary international law norm, it is generally accepted that two requirements must be met: 1) the prohibition of the conduct must be well established in state practice, and 2) the state practice must be recognized as based on *opinio juris*. If the principle of legality applies to the *ad hoc* Tribunals, then only those criminal elements recognized as *opinio juris* and practiced as customary international law at the time of the alleged offence,[17] should be applied.[18] Thus, assuming that a particular rule of customary international law exists, a Trial Chamber should only enter a conviction if the law meets the requirements of the principle of legality, that is, the prohibited act is defined with sufficient precision to put the accused on notice. A Trial Chamber is expected to examine the jurisprudence of numerous jurisdictions before articulating an accurate definition of a crime based on the principle of specificity.[19] Further, when determining the nature of customary international law at a relevant time, a Trial Chamber should only rely on state practice that was in existence when the acts at issue occurred.[20] Thus, the imperative question is whether the *ad hoc* Tribunals' jurisprudence on complicity in genocide and aiding and abetting genocide comport with the principle of legality.

Complicity, Aiding and Abetting and the Special Genocidal Intent

The following analysis will focus on illustrating the confusion and contradiction in the jurisprudence of the *ad hoc* Tribunals created through attempts to justify their holdings (or *dicta*) on the *mens rea* requirements for complicity in genocide and aiding and abetting genocide. The enquiry will begin with a cursory look at the

---

he sees the law as a complex process of decision making rather than as an established body of rules. Mohamed Shahabuddeen (2003), 'Policy Oriented Law in the Tribunal for the Former Yugoslavia', in *Man's Inhumanity to Man: Essays on International Law in Honour of Antonio Cassese*, Lal Chand Volrah et al. (eds) 893–898, (Kluwer Law International).

16 *See* The Secretary-General, *Report of the Secretary-General of the United Nations on the ICTY Statute* (S/25704), at para. 34 (emphasis added). He confirms his view of the implications of the principle, though the justification he offers in terms of non-adherence to specific conventions is not an integral element of the principle.

17 *Prosecutor v Vasiljević*, Case No. IT-98-32-T, Trial Judgement, 29 November 2002, at para. 199.

18 *See Prosecutor v Delalić et al.*, Case No. IT-96-21-A, Appeal Judgement, 20 February 2001, at para. 170.

19 *Prosecutor v Furundžija*, Case No. IT-95-17/1, Trial Judgement, 10 December 1998, at para. 177.

20 *Prosecutor v Kordić and Čerkez*, Case No. IT-95-14/2-PT, Decision on the Joint Defence Motion to Dismiss the Amended Indictment for Lack of Jurisdiction Based on the Limited Jurisdictional Reach of Articles 2 and 3, 2 March 1999, paras. 20 and 22. *See also* The Secretary-General, *Report of the Secretary-General Pursuant to Paragraph 2 of Security Council Resolution* 808 (1993), at para. 29; *see also Prosecutor v Delalić et al.*, Case No. IT-96-21-A, Appeal Judgement, at para. 170.

relevant ICTR and ICTY cases, followed by a more critical examination of two recent Judgements on genocide from the ICTY: the *Krstić* Appeal Judgement[21] and the *Blagojević* Trial Judgement.[22] It is suggested that a genocide jurisprudence is emerging that is precariously clashing with the principle of legality: an accused charged with genocide can be convicted without the special genocidal intent based on aiding and abetting genocide, complicity in genocide, command responsibility, and joint criminal enterprise (category III) ('JCE III').[23]

Relevant Decisions on Complicity and Aiding and Abetting from the ICTR/ ICTY

Even a cursory review of the genocide jurisprudence at the *ad hoc* Tribunals reveals a fluctuating appreciation for and application of what constitutes the appropriate *mens rea*. For example, in *Akayesu*,[24] the first ever genocide conviction before an international tribunal, the Trial Chamber, in *dicta*, stated that an accomplice need not possess the special genocidal intent to be convicted of complicity in genocide, so long as the accomplice knew or had reason to know that the principal offender was acting with the special genocidal intent.[25] The Trial Chamber distinguished between aiding and abetting under Article 6(1) and complicity in genocide under Article 2(3)(e). For complicity, it found that the perpetrator need only possess knowledge, or presumed knowledge, that the principal perpetrator was acting with genocidal intent; while for aiding and abetting, it found that a perpetrator must share the genocidal intent of the principal perpetrator.[26]

Similarly, in *Musema*,[27] the Trial Chamber found that an accused is liable for genocide if he voluntarily aided and abetted a person to commit genocide while knowing that the person was committing genocide even if he did not have the special genocidal intent himself.[28] The Trial Chamber further found that knowledge was sufficient for a conviction for genocide of a superior under Article 6(3), if the superior 'knew or had reason to know' that his subordinates were going to or had in fact

---

21 *Prosecutor v Krstić*, Case No. IT-98-33-A, Appeal Judgement, 19 April 2004.

22 *Prosecutor v Blagojević*, Case No. IT-02-60-T, Trial Judgement, 17 January 2005.

23 JCE III extends the liability of a perpetrator involved in a common plan to all the crimes that are a 'natural and foreseeable consequence' of the criminal enterprise, irrespective of the perpetrator's participation in the crime itself. The *mens rea* is more than 'negligence' but far from the special genocidal intent. While the perpetrator did not intend to bring about a certain result, he was (or would have been) 'aware that the action of the group were likely to lead to the result but nevertheless willingly took the risk'. *See Prosecutor v Tadić*, Case No. IT-94-1-A, Appeal Judgement, 15 July 1999, at para. 11.

24 *Prosecutor v Akayesu*, Case No. ICTR-96-4-T, Trial Judgement, 2 September 1998, at paras. 530–532.

25 *Id.*, at paras. 539–541.

26 *Id.*, at paras. 541–547.

27 *Prosecutor v Musema*, Case No. ICTR-96-13-T, Trial Judgement, 27 January 2000, at paras. 168–183.

28 *Id.*, at para. 887.

committed acts of genocide.[29] Command responsibility under Article 6(3) requires only that the commander knows, or has reason to know, that the subordinate was about to commit an act or had done so and the commander failed to take measures to prevent such acts or to punish the perpetrators.[30]

In other genocide cases, courts have held that the special genocidal intent is required for all forms of committing genocide but not for the alternate modes of liability. For instance, in *Kayishema and Ruzindana*,[31] the Trial Chamber took the opposite position from *Akayesu*, noting that the specific genocidal intent is required for all forms of committing genocide under Article 2(3), including complicity in genocide; while for aiding and abetting under Article 6(1), mere 'knowledge' of the principal's genocidal intent is sufficient.

Still other chambers have found that knowledge of the principal perpetrator's intent is a sufficient *mens rea* for an accomplice or an aider and abettor. For example, in *Bagilishema*,[32] as in *Akayesu*, the Trial Chamber held that complicity requires that the accused act with knowledge and not with special genocidal intent.[33] It also found that knowledge of the principal's intent is sufficient for aiding and abetting genocide under ICTR Article 6(1). In other words, under *Bagilishema*, the *mens rea* for all forms of accomplice liability to the crime of genocide simply requires 'knowledge'. Similarly, in *Semanza*,[34] the Trial Chamber held that there is 'no material distinction' between aiding and abetting genocide and complicity in genocide.[35] The Trial Chamber then took issue with *Akayesu* and *Ntakirutimana*, noting that there was no legal basis for distinguishing aiding and abetting from complicity by elevating the *mens rea* requirement for aiding and abetting.[36] On the other hand, in *Sikirica*, the Trial Chamber acquitted the accused of genocide and complicity in genocide pursuant to a defence motion for a judgement of acquittal.[37] The Trial Chamber, proclaiming 'what is a relatively simple issue of interpretation of the *chapeau*'[38] found that the text of Article 4(2) requires that an accomplice must also have the special genocidal intent.[39] Giving the words of the Statute their ordinary meaning, the

---

29 *Id.*, at paras. 894–895.

30 *See ICTR* Article 6(3).

31 *Prosecutor v Kayishema and Ruzindana*, Case No. ICTR-95-1-T, Trial Judgement, 21 May 1999, at paras. 91, pp.205–207.

32 *Prosecutor v Bagilishema*, Case No. ICTR-96-13-T, Trial Judgement, 7 June 2001, at paras. 36 and 71.

33 *Id.*

34 *Prosecutor v Semanza*, Case No. ICTR-97-20-T, Trial Judgement, 15 May 2003.

35 *Id.*, at paras. 388 and 394.

36 *Id.*, at n. 648. Notably, Semanza was not convicted as a principal perpetrator though the factual findings certainly warranted such a conviction. The Trial Chamber reasoned that Semanza supposedly lacked the *actus reus*: he did not personally kill.

37 *See Prosecutor v Sikirica et al.,* Case No. IT-95-8-T, Judgement on Defense Motions to Acquit, 3 September 2001.

38 *Id.*, at para. 58.

39 *Id.*, at para. 60.

Trial Chamber stated that very specific intent is required for complicity in genocide, in part to distinguish it from persecution.[40]

The dilution of the special genocidal intent before the *ad hoc* Tribunals also seems evident in the ease with which guilty pleas are accepted where the factual basis may not necessary support the *mens rea* requirements, or where the guilty plea is used as a vehicle of lowering the *mens rea* threshold. In *Serushago*, the Trial Chamber accepted a guilty plea to genocide under both ICTR Articles 6(1) and 6(3) from the accused who was a *de facto* leader of the Interahamwe. However the facts supported a conviction only under Article 6(1).[41] Additionally, in *Kambanda*,[42] the Trial Chamber accepted a guilty plea to genocide and complicity in genocide, though the facts supported a conviction for genocide under Article 6(1) as a principal offender and not for superior responsibility under Article 6(3). By accepting the plea for both 6(1) and 6(3) the Trial Chamber inadvertently suggests that the special genocidal intent need not apply to one in command over a principal perpetrator of genocide.

In *Jelisić*,[43] the Trial Chamber found that there was insufficient evidence to find that the accused was motivated by the special genocidal intent.[44] The Appeals Chamber disagreed with the Trial Chamber's assessment of the evidence,[45] but avoided the opportunity to consider whether 'commission of genocide' means genocide under Article 4 or committing under Article 7(1) of the ICTY Statute.[46]

In *Ntakirutimana*, the Trial Chamber held that aiding and abetting requires the special genocidal intent.[47] However, the Appeals Chamber following its own reasoning from *Krstić*, as discussed below, reversed the Trial Chamber. The Appeals Chamber in *Ntakirutimana* held that modes of participation in Article 6(1) should be read into Article 2(3), that the text of Article 6(1) includes the liability of aiding and abetting, and that Article 6(1) expressly applies the mode of aiding and abetting liability to any crime referred to in the Statute.[48]

Application of JCE III to genocide is a further example of the dilution of genocidal intent in the *ad hoc* Tribunals' jurisprudence. An instructive interpretation of this can be found in *Stakić*.[49] In that case, the Trial Chamber acquitted the accused

---

40 *Id.*

41 *Prosecutor v Serushago*, Case No. ICTR-98-39-S, Sentence, 5 February 1999, at paras. 28–29.

42 *Prosecutor v Kambanda*, Case No. ICTR-9-23-S, Trial Judgement, 4 September 1998, at para. 40.

43 *Prosecutor v Jelisić*, Case No. IT-95-10, Trial Judgement, 14 December 1999.

44 *Id.*, para. 108.

45 *Prosecutor v Jelisić*, Case No. IT-95-10, Appeal Judgement, 5 July 2001, at para. 72.

46 *Id.*, at n.82, stating that its opinion only applied to the 'commission of genocide as reflected in Article 4 of the Statute'.

47 *Prosecutor v Ntakirutimana*, Case No. ICTR-96-10-T & ICTR-96-17-T, Trial Judgement, 21 February 2003, at paras. 788–789.

48 *Prosecutor v Ntakirutimana*, Case No. ICTR-96-10-A & ICTR-96-17-A, Appeal Judgement, 21 March 2003, at paras. 500–501.

49 *Prosecutor v Stakić*, Case No. IT-97-2-T, Trial Judgement, 22 March 2006, at para. 561.

of genocide and complicity in genocide having found that genocide as set forth in the Indictment did not occur.[50] The Trial Chamber's *dictum is* nevertheless instructive because it gives a well-reasoned approach to interpret the crime of genocide. After noting that Article 4 of the ICTY Statute was taken *verbatim* from the Genocide Convention,[51] the Trial Chamber listed four sources to rely on when interpreting genocide because of the 'non-retroactivity principle of substantive criminal law': i) the Genocide Convention according to the rules of interpretation set out in the Vienna Convention; ii) the purpose of the Genocide Convention as evidenced by the *travaux préparatoires*; iii) subsequent jurisprudence of the *ad hoc* Tribunals and national courts; and iv) the publications of international authorities.[52] Importantly, the Trial Chamber found that Article 4 of the ICTY Statute must be interpreted within the context of the unique nature of the crime of genocide.[53] Discussing criminal liability under JCE III as it relates to the crime of genocide, the Trial Chamber commented on the interplay between Articles 4(3)(e) and 7(1). It noted that when considering the relationship between Articles 4(3) and 7(1) of the ICTY Statute, Article 4(3) can be regarded as '*lex specialis*' in relation to Article 7(1) as '*lex generalis*', and accordingly, 'reading the modes of participation under Article 7(1) into Article 4(3), whilst maintaining the *dolus specialis* prerequisite, would lead to the same result.'[54] Thus, correctly in the view of the author, the Trial Chamber proclaimed that modes of participation cannot replace core elements of a crime, and importing JCE III into genocide would result in diluting the special genocidal intent.[55]

In *Brdjanin*, the Appeals Chamber, disagreeing with the logic expressed by the *Stakić* Trial Chamber, extended liability for genocide without the special genocidal intent to joint criminal enterprise. The *mens rea* for JCE III is based on *dolus eventualis*; it confers liability on an accused who did not intend to commit the crime or even knew with certainty that the crime was to be committed, but who only entered into a joint criminal enterprise to commit a different crime with the awareness that the commission of that agreed upon crime made it reasonably foreseeable to him that the crime would be committed by other members of the joint criminal enterprise, and that it was in fact committed.[56] In an interlocutory appeal in *Brdjanin*, the Appeals Chamber found that JCE III could be imported into genocide without a finding of the special genocidal intent.[57] Judge Shahabuddeen dissented stating that 'genocide

---

50 *Id.*

51 *Id.*, at para. 500.

52 *Id.*, at para. 501. This outline of how genocide should be interpreted is not found in most ICTY and ICTR jurisprudence, specifically the *Krstić* Appeal Judgement and the *Blagojević* Trial Judgement.

53 *Id.*, at para. 502.

54 *Prosecutor v Stakić*, Case No. IT-97-24-T, Decision on Rule 98 *bis* Motion for Judgement of Acquittal, 31 October 2002, at para. 49.

55 *Prosecutor v Stakić*, Case No. IT-97-24-T, Trial Judgement, 22 March 2006, at para. 530.

56 *Prosecutor v Brdjanin*, Case No. IT-99-36-A, Decision on Interlocutory Appeal, 19 March 2004, at para. 5.

57 *Prosecutor v Brdjanin*, Case No. IT-99-36-A, Decision on Interlocutory Appeal, 19 March 2004, at paras. 7–10. *See also Prosecutor v Stakić*, Case No. IT-97-24-A, Appeal

is a crime of specific intent, a conviction for it is therefore not possible under the third category of joint criminal enterprise.'[58] Months after the Interlocutory Appeal Decision in *Brdjanin*, the Trial Chamber acquitted the accused of genocide and complicity in genocide.[59] However, irrespective of the acquittal in this case, the Trial Chamber felt compelled to declare, in *dicta*, that a person can be convicted of genocide without genocidal intent under command responsibility and complicity in genocide based on aiding and abetting.[60] The Trial Chamber noted that the absence of command responsibility from the Genocide Convention was due to a 'play of factors'; conspicuously, the Trial Chamber failed to reveal these 'factors'.[61]

The *Krstić* and *Blagojević* Judgements

On 17 January 2005, the ICTY handed down the *Blagojević* Trial Judgement, convicting Vidoje Blagojević, the Commander of the Bratunac Brigade of the Bosnian-Serb Army (VRS) of 'complicity in genocide by aiding and abetting' under Article 4(3)(e) of the Statute.[62] This judgement relied heavily on the ICTY's first genocide conviction of General Krstić who was Blagojević's superior officer during the events at Srebrenica. Krstić, who was tried for genocide and in the alternative complicity in genocide, was initially convicted by the Trial Chamber for genocide. The Appeals Chamber overturned Krstić's conviction for genocide and found instead that Krstić had aided and abetted genocide, applying 'knowledge' as the *mens rea*.[63]

Arriving at a conviction for aiding and abetting genocide, the *Krstić* Appeals Chamber found an overlap between Article 4(3) and Article 7(1). The Appeals Chamber rejected the possibility that the discrepancy between Articles 4(3)(e) and 7(1) could be the product of poor draftsmanship, resulting in an unintentional

---

Judgement, 22 March 2006, at para. 38.

58 *Id.*, at paras. 2–4. Judge Shahabuddeen reasoned:

The third category of Tadić does not, because it cannot, vary the elements of the crime; it is not directed to the elements of the crime; it leaves them untouched. The requirement that the accused be shown to have possessed a specific intent to commit genocide is an element of that crime. The result is that the specific intent always has to be shown; if it is not shown, the case has to be dismissed.

59 *Prosecutor v Brdjanin*, Case No. I-99-36-T, Trial Judgement, 1 September 2004, at para. 989.

60 *Id.*, at paras. 721 and 730.

61 *Id.*, at para. 712.

62 *Prosecutor v Blagojević*, Case No. IT-02-60-T, Trial Judgement, 17 January 2005, at para. 140, where for aiding and abetting under Article 7(1) the Appeal Chamber held that for accessorial liability, the requirements are met when:

• The accused carried out an act which consisted of practical assistance, encouragement or moral support to the principal that had a 'substantial effect' on the commission of the crime;

• The accused had knowledge that his or her own acts assisted in the commission of the specific crime by the principal offender;

• The accused knew that the crime was committed with specific intent.

63 *Prosecutor v Krstić*, Case No. IT-98-33-A, Appeal Judgement, 19 April 2004, at para. 138.

inconsistency.[64] Rather, without authority, it reasoned that while there may be an overlap, any discrepancies could be reconciled because complicity under Article 4(3)(e) encompasses the narrow concept of aiding and abetting under Article 7(1).[65] The Appeals Chamber further held that liability for aiding and abetting under Article 7(1) applied to the criminal offences of genocide in Article 4, and that mere 'knowledge' was the appropriate *mens rea* for aiding and abetting genocide.[66]

Relying on the *Krstić* Appeal Judgement, the Trial Chamber imported the lower standard of accessorial liability and applied it in *Blagojević*. Blagojević was found guilty of complicity in genocide by aiding and abetting, where, consequently, only knowledge of the principal perpetrator's specific intent was required.[67] Concluding that 'some heads of responsibility listed under Article 7(1) are necessarily included in those forms of liability listed in Article 4(3), or vice versa,'[68] the Trial Chamber then held that '[t]he conviction for aiding and abetting genocide upon proof that the defendant knew about the principal perpetrator's specific intent is permitted by the Statute and case-law of the Tribunal.'[69] It continued, '[a]ccordingly, the count of complicity in genocide is limited to an allegation of Blagojević's guilt as an aider and abettor'.[70] Interestingly, the Trial Chamber adopted identical *actus reus* elements for complicity in genocide as those required for aiding and abetting by the *Krstić* Appeals Chamber.[71]

---

64 *Id.*, at para. 139.

65 *Id.*

66 In *Krstić*, the Appeals Chamber concluded that the *mens rea* required for an aider and abettor, as set out in other (non-genocide) Judgements, i.e., that 'an individual who aids and abets a specific intent offence may be held responsible if he assists the commission of the crime knowing the intent behind the crime', applies to the Statute's prohibition of genocide. *Id.*, at para. 140, citing *Prosecutor v Krnojelac*, Case No. IT-97-25-A, Appeal Judgement, 17 September 2003, at para. 52, *Prosecutor v Vasiljević*, Case No. IT-98-32-A, Appeal Judgement, 25 February 2004, at para. 142. The Appeals Chamber in *Ntakirutimana*, without any independent statutory interpretation, simply relied on the *Krstić* Appeal Judgement in finding that the genocidal intent is not required for aiding and abetting genocide. *See Prosecutor v Ntakirutimana*, Case No. ICTR-96-10-A & ICTR-96-17-A, Appeal Judgement, at para. 501.

67 *Prosecutor v Blagojević*, Case No. IT-02-60-T, Trial Judgement, 17 January 2005, at para. 780.

68 *Id.*, at para. 679. In discussing complicity in the context of genocide, the *Blagojević* Trial Chamber noted that while the principal perpetrator has been defined as one who fulfils a key coordinating role and whose participation is of an extremely significant nature and at the leadership level, the accomplice has been defined as someone who associates him or herself in the crime of genocide committed by another. *Id.*, at para. 776 (citations omitted).

69 *Id.*, at para. 779, citing *Prosecutor v Krstić*, Case No. IT-98-33-A, Appeal Judgement, at para. 140 and *Prosecutor v Ntakirutimana*, Case No. ICTR-96-10-T & ICTR-96-17-T, Trial Judgement, 21 February 2003, at paras. 500–501.

70 *Supra* note 75, at para. 679.

71 *Prosecutor v Brdjanin*, Case No. IT-99-36-A, Decision on Interlocutory Appeal, 19 March 2004, at n. 21. It is noteworthy that the ICTY treats 'aiding and abetting' collectively (*see Prosecutor v Tadić*, Case No. IT-94-I-T, Opinion and Judgement, 7 May 1997, at para. 689) while the ICTR treats them in the disjunctive: 'aiding' involving the giving of assistance to someone, and 'abetting' facilitating the commission of an act or omitting to act

The authority relied by the *Krstić* Appeal Judgement is dubious, and does not rise to the level of *opinio juris*: 'to hold that principle was part of customary international law, it has to be satisfied that State practice recognized the principle on the basis of *opinion juris*.'[72] The *Krstić* Appeals Chamber only produced two state practices, those of France and Germany, which were directly relevant to the issue, before citing other authority that provided no support for the proposition that 'knowledge' was the appropriate *mens rea* for aiding and abetting genocide or complicity in genocide.[73] Furthermore, no authority was cited by the Appeals Chamber in support of its pronouncement that:

> The texts of the Tribunal's Statute and of the Genocide Convention, combined with evidence in the Convention's travaux préparatoires, provide additional support to the conclusion that the drafters of the Statute opted for applying the notion of aiding and abetting to the prohibition of genocide under Article 4.[74]

In his dissent, Judge Shahabuddeen went even further. Reasoning that complicity in genocide includes aiding and abetting and does not require genocidal intent,[75] he noted that under customary international law there is a crime called aiding and abetting in complicity in genocide, yet provided no reference or authority for the claim.[76]

The *Krstić* and *Blagojević* Judgements appear to also violate the principle of legality because they suggest that there are two possible levels of *mens rea* for complicity in genocide – *special intent* and *knowledge* – which does not comport with the plain language of the Genocide Convention.[77] While acknowledging that

---

(*see Prosecutor v Akayesu*, Case No. ICTR-96-4-T, Trial Judgement, 2 September 1998, at para. 484; *Prosecutor v Kayishema and Ruzindana*, Case No. ICTR-95-1-T, Trial Judgement, 21 May 1999, at para. 197).

72 *Prosecutor v Hadžihasanović*, Case No. IT-01-47AR72, Decision on Interlocutory Appeal Challenging Jurisdiction in Relation to Command Responsibility, 16 July 2003, at para. 12.

73 *Prosecutor v Krstić*, Case No. IT-98-33-A, Appeal Judgement, 19 April 2004, at para. 141.

74 *Id.*, at para. 142. Oddly enough, the Appeals Chamber noted that the *travaux préparatoires* indicated that the drafters intended the charge of complicity in genocide to require proof of genocidal intent.

75 *Id.*, at para. 65.

76 *Id.*, In ten paragraphs of discussion, Judge Shahabuddeen used four footnotes evincing more of a personal opinion than an authoritative judgement. *Id.*, at paras. 59–68.

77 In *Milošević*, for example, the Trial Chamber entertained in its Rule 98*bis* Decision on Motion for Judgement of Acquittal, the issue whether the Accused aided and abetted in the commission of the crime of genocide or was complicit in its commission. The Trial Chamber in *Milošević* noted that though the Appeals Chamber convicted *Krstić* as an aider and abettor in the crime of genocide, the Appeals Chamber's finding was '*obiter dicta*' as it was 'confined to the facts of that case.' Commenting on the Appeals Chamber's finding that complicity in genocide can encompass broader conduct than the offence of aiding and abetting, the Trial Chamber noted that the Appeals Chamber took no position as to the *mens rea* of complicity, and found 'no authoritative decision within the Tribunal as to whether there is a difference in the *mens rea* for aiding and abetting genocide and complicity in genocide, either when the latter is broader than aiding and abetting, or indeed, when it is of the same scope as aiding

there is authority to suggest that complicity in genocide requires proof that the accomplice possessed the special genocidal intent ('where it prohibits conduct broader than aiding and abetting'), the *Krstić* Appeals Chamber held that such intent was not a prerequisite if the accomplice was charged with aiding and abetting.[78]

Holding that the special genocidal intent is 'not a prerequisite' for a conviction of genocide does not appear to be the natural and ordinary meaning of the language in the genocide provisions, which state: 'genocide means any of the following *acts committed with intent* to [...]".[79] Accepting that the special genocidal intent forms an element of the *chapeau* of the offence of genocide which characterizes it as an international crime, it *must* apply to all five forms of criminal participation in committing genocide. Such an interpretation is true to the intentions of the drafters of the Genocide Convention and respects the plain language of the Statutes.

Additionally, *Krstić* and *Blagojević* may overstep the bounds of legal interpretation and tread the path of legislating from the bench by not recognizing the significance of the *dolus specialis* enumerated in Article II of the Genocide Convention. Requiring special genocidal intent does not obviate accomplice liability for genocide. An accomplice may aid or abet a principal with only knowledge of their intention to commit the *underlying offence*, such as murder. To be an accomplice to genocide, however, it is submitted that the accomplice must possess the special genocidal intent.[80] There is no explicit statutory language providing for a lowered *mens rea* requirement for accomplice liability, rather, it is a development that has resulted from judicial decisions of the *ad hoc* Tribunals that *read in* principles of accomplice liability distilled from general principles of criminal law and national jurisdictions.[81] Notably, such an application of accomplice liability draws a false

---

and abetting'. The Trial Chamber went on to find that '[i]n the absence of anything to indicate that complicity in genocide is broader than aiding and abetting in the circumstances of this case [...] there is merit in the Prosecution's submission that the two are essentially the same'. Interestingly, the *Milošević* Trial Chamber accepted the *Stakić* Trial Judgement, in which the Trial Chamber held that complicity in genocide under Article 4(3)(e) is the *lex specialis* in relation to liability under Article 7(1), and accordingly did not confine itself to a determination of the Accused's responsibility as an aider or abetter. *See Prosecutor v Milošević*, Case No. IT-02-54-T, Decision on Motion for Judgement of Acquittal, 16 June 2004, paras. 295–297 (citations omitted).

78 *Prosecutor v Krstić*, Case No. IT-98-33-A, Appeal Judgement, 19 April 2004, at paras. 139, 142 and 143. The Appeals Chamber in *Krstić*, departed from *Stakić*, where the Trial Chamber rejected the Prosecution's argument that under JCE III, proof of genocidal intent is not required because the accused is not the principal perpetrator. It further stated that in order to commit genocide, proof of genocidal intent is required and that modes of participation cannot replace core elements of a crime. *See Prosecutor v Stakić*, Case No. IT-97-24-T, Trial Judgement, at paras. 529–530.

79 ICTY Statute Article 4(2); ICTR Statute Article 2(2) (emphasis added).

80 For further support for this viewpoint, *see also*, Schabas, W.A. (2000), *Genocide in International Law*, (Cambridge University Press) 300.

81 See *Prosecutor v Blagojević*, Case No. IT-02-I60-T, Trial Judgement, 17 January 2005, at para. 776, citing *Prosecutor v Brdjanin*, Case No. IT-99-36-A, Decision on Interlocutory Appeal, 19 March 2004, at para. 724.

and impermissible equivalence between the *mens rea* for specific intent offences in domestic jurisdictions, and the *dolus specialis* for genocide.

The reasoning in the *Krstić* Appeal demonstrates the lengths to which the Appeals Chamber was willing to go to frame the legal analysis to fit a desired result, rather than allow the result to be a pure product of the law. While having no choice but to follow the holding in *Krstić*, the Trial Chamber in *Blagojević* went even further in re-defining the law. Commenting on both holdings, one eminent scholar notes, more generously, that they are based on less than convincing legal reasoning and seem to hint of compromises among a divided bench.[82] These holdings underscore an observation made by one author, which, exquitivally, encapsulates the general sentiments held by the defence bar at the *ad hoc* Tribunals: 'the judgements of the ad hoc Tribunals frequently appear […] to be largely declaratory of nascent and previously unexpressed customary principles.'[83]

Conclusion

Under the guise and protection of international criminal prosecution, the *ad hoc* Tribunals seem to be stretching the crime of genocide beyond its intended limit. This cursory look at the incongruent genocide decisions and the tortuous reasoning of the various Chambers suggests that application of the Genocide Convention is in both a state of flux and a state of confusion, leading to unforeseeable and inconsistent results.

Whether an accused is convicted or not on a charge of genocide before the *ad hoc* Tribunals (or the ICC) is not necessarily a zero sum game, where a not guilty verdict results in the non-accountability for proved criminal acts. There are many other equally reprehensible crimes encompassed under the umbrella of crimes against humanity which carry a stigma that is just as repugnant as genocide and where a sentence may be as severe as for genocide.[84] However, it seems that a genocide conviction has a certain *cache* value,[85] which may give rise to a false notion that

---

82 *See* Schabas, W.A. (2006), 'The "Odious Scourge": Evolving Interpretations of the Crime of Genocide', paper presented to the Fourth Law Congress of the Ankara Bar Association Conference, Ankara, 4–6 January 2006, available at http://www.nuigalway.ie/human_rights/Docs/genocide.ankara.1.06.doc, last visited April 28, 2006.

83 Lamb, S. (2002), 'Nullum Crimen, Nulla Poena Sine Lege', in *International Criminal Law*, in *ICC Commentary*, I, (Cassese et al., eds, Oxford University Press), p.745. Interestingly, citing W.J. Bosch, *Judgement on Nuremburg* 49 (1970) at p. 49, Lamb points out: 'This recalls, in the ICTY context also, the truism applied to the IMT that "[t]he diplomat's past reluctance to codify international law resulted in Nuremburg's applying retroactive law"'. *Id.*, at n. 47.

84 Perhaps the delegate from Brazil to the Genocide Convention said it best when he noted that genocide is 'characterized by the factor of particular intent to destroy a group. In the absence of that factor, whatever the degree of atrocity of an act and however similar it might be to the acts described in the convention, that act could still not be called genocide.' *See* Summary Records of the meetings of the Sixth committee of the General Assembly, 21 September–10 December 1948, at p.109 (*travaux préparatoires* of the Genocide Convention).

85 *See* e.g. comments of Secretary-General Kofi Annan posted on the home page of the ICTR website: 'The ICTR delivered the first ever judgement on the crime of genocide. This

without genocide convictions the *raison d'être* of the *ad hoc* Tribunals may be called into question.[86] Thus, it may be that a genocide conviction is a desired result and that it will be sought even when the law and facts do not support it without contorting the law and facts in a procrustean bed.

---

judgement is a testament to our collective determination to confront the heinous crime of genocide in a way we never have before', available at http://69.94.11.53/default.htm, last visited 28 April 2006.

86 *See generally*, Schabas, W.A. (2001), 'Was Genocide Committed in Bosnia and Herzegovina? First Judgements of the International Criminal Tribunal for the Former Yugoslavia', 25 *Fordham Int'l L.J.*, 23, commenting that initial indictments were parsimonious in making accusations of genocide, *Id.* at 25, and that in at least one case, the youthful ICTY which was hungry for work, invited the prosecutor to consider broadening the scope of the characterization of genocide to include more of the alleged criminal acts, *Id.*, at p.28.

Chapter 9

Telling Stories and Hearing Truths: Providing an Effective Remedy to Genocidal Sexual Violence against Women

Fiona de Londras

Genocide characterized the 1990s. In Rwanda and the Former Yugoslavia genocide and ethnic cleansing forced the international community to think in more depth about the appropriate way in which to enforce the United Nations Convention on the Prevention and Punishment of Genocide. To this end two *ad hoc* tribunals were established – the International Criminal Tribunal for the Former Yugoslavia (ICTY) in The Hague and the International Criminal Tribunal for Rwanda in Arusha. Both of these tribunals faced immense challenges – how would the crime of genocide be interpreted to adhere to the spirit and objects of the Convention in light of these atrocities? How could people be adequately represented in these tribunals? How would indicted individuals be apprehended? How would the challenge of sexual violence, so prevalent in both of these circumstances, be met by the tribunals?

This chapter addresses only one of those challenges – that of sexual violence. In both Rwanda and the Former Yugoslavia gender and genocide proved a potent mixture; sexual violence was used not only as an ancillary weapon in these conflicts but as a fundamental one – a means of committing genocide. How would the tribunals deal with the challenges of recognizing and punishing this use of sexual violence, gender and sex within its legal and (at least *quasi-*) adversarial structure? I contend that while the Tribunals have attempted to deal with sexual violence several challenges have stood in the way of success – prosecutorial unwillingness to prioritize sexual violence being primary among them. In addition I suggest that a commitment to an intersectional understanding and analysis of this use of sexual violence is fundamental to changing this mindset, particularly in light of the future potential for genocide-related proceedings before the International Criminal Court.

The Nature of Genocidal Sexual Violence

At first glance there appears to be a tendency to conflate wartime sexual violence, sexual violence *simpliciter* (if this nomenclature can be excused) and genocidal sexual violence. While international tribunals have often recognized that sexual violence can constitute torture, a crime against humanity and a war crime it is rarely recognized as genocide. The nature of what I term genocidal sexual violence must, therefore, be grappled with in the first instance.

It is important to note that all of these three forms of sexual violence are *similar* but not *the same*. All three emanate from an underlying assumption that women and girl children are rapeable, abuseable and possessable[1] and, in this way, reflect peacetime sexual violence in an exacerbated violent context.[2] Genocidal sexual violence is different, however, because it carries with it the unique *mens rea* of the crime of genocide. This *mens rea* (or *dolus specialis*) is provided for in Article 2 of the Genocide Convention, which defines the crime (emphasis added):

> Any of the following acts committed *with intent to destroy in whole or in part a national, ethnical, racial or religious group*, as such
>
> a) Killing members of the group;
> b) Causing serious bodily or mental harm to members of the group;
> c) Deliberately inflicting on the group conditions of life calculated to bring about its physical destruction in whole or in part;
> d) Imposing measures intended to prevent births within the group;
> e) Forcibly transferring children of the group to another group.

In other words, acts will only carry the legal colour of genocide if they are carried out with the intention of destroying a particular group of people with a shared character identity. As a result sexual violence will only qualify as *genocidal* sexual violence if it is done with this intent.

Women who suffer genocidal sexual violence therefore suffer not only as women, but also as agents for the destruction of their community group. This experience is

---

1 The targeting of women in conflict, and especially the predominance of the use of sexual violence against women does not come from nowhere, it does not spontaneously arise. In fact, this method of treating women could not come to light were there not already a practise or perception of women as being subordinate, sexualized, weak and possessed. Writing in the midst of the Balkan conflict, Catherine MacKinnon expressed this hypothesis thus: '[T]he rapes in this war are not grasped as either a strategy in genocide or a practice of misogyny, far less both at once. They are not understood as continuous both with this particular ethnic war of aggression and with the gendered war of aggression of everyday life. Genocide does not come from nowhere, nor does rape as a ready and convenient tool of it. Nor is a continuity an equation. These rapes are to everyday rape what the Holocaust was to everyday anti-Semitism. Without everyday anti-Semitism a Holocaust is impossible, but anyone who has lived through a pogrom knows the difference.' MacKinnon, K. (1994), 'Rape, Genocide and Human Rights', 17 *Harvard Women's Law Journal*, 5, p.8.

2 *C.f.* Holter, G. (2002), 'A Theory of Gendercide', 4:1 *Journal of Genocide Research*, 11. Holter claims that as war or persecution turns into a situation of gendercide, 'sex stratification, the race-gender link and the victimization aspect all become manifest. In this perspective, 'gendercide' is interpreted as an outcome of civil-life processes as well as conflict and war events. Gendercide is an extreme that also says something about normal conditions' (p.13). While this argument is being made in the context of the targeting of men in genocide, it applies equally the targeting of women in genocide.

distinct. It is the use of the womb and the vagina as grenades. It is the objectification of the woman not only as an object of sexual plunder, but also as border and honour and blood and kin and race and ethnicity and religious icon. This is the truth of the experience of a woman victim of genocidal sexual violence.

This truth was (at least implicitly) recognized by the Office of the Prosecutor at a relatively early stage in the history of the Yugoslav tribunal. In *Prosecutor v Tadic*[3] the indictment originally charged the defendant with crimes against humanity for a 'campaign of terror which included killings, torture, sexual assaults, and other physical and psychological abuse' and for his part in the 'torture of more than 12 female detainees including several gang rapes'.[4] Although acts of sexual violence were explicitly prohibited in the Statute as crimes against humanity, the Office of the Prosecutor determined that these acts could be prosecuted implicitly as, *inter alia*, genocide. This broad interpretation expanded the ICTY's ability to prosecute sexual assaults despite the fact that rape was only enumerated as a crime in Article 5(G) of the Statute. Leaving aside for the moment the fact that the independent rape charges were later withdrawn because the witness was allegedly too afraid to testify, this early acknowledgement of the occurrence of sexual violence and its physical and psychological effects can be seen as having paved the way for the successful prosecution of gender-based crimes in both of the *ad hoc* tribunals.

What Survivors Want

In any situation where procedures are being put in place to re-establish the Rule of Law in light of atrocity some competing interests co-exist. These are seen in both the decision-making process as to what kind of institution should be established *and* the priorities and aims of that institution. The former question tends to concentrate on the relative merits of national trials, international trials, truth and reconciliation commissions with or without amnesties and doing nothing at all. The relative merits of each of these have long been debated and need little consideration here,[5] but the latter issue – institutional priorities – is at the core of the notion of effective remedy.

All transitional justice mechanisms have responsibility to law, the peopled state and the individual rights and needs of survivors, with the needs and desires of these constituents regularly being incompatible within traditional judicial mechanisms.[6] Julie Mertus claims that survivors look to post-atrocity mechanisms, and particularly

---

3   *Prosecutor v Tadic*, IT-94-1-T, December 14 1995.

4   Second Amended Indictment, PP4, 4.3.

5   *C.f.* for example Cherif Bassiouni, M. (1996), 'Searching for Peace and Achieving Justice: The Need for Accountability' 59 *Law and Contemporary Problems* 4; Kirsch, S. (2001), 'The International Criminal Court – Central Issues and Perspectives' 64 *Law and Contemporary Problems* 1; Landsmann S. (1996), 'Alternative Responses to Serious Human Rights Abuses; of Prosecution and Truth Commissions', 59 *Law and Contemporary Problems* 81.

6   See generally Humphrey, M. (2002), *The Politics of Atrocity and Reconciliation: From Terror to Trauma* (London: Routledge).

judicial mechanisms, to receive public acknowledgement of their experiences, achieve revenge and retribution, receive a remedy for their suffering, (re)establish the principle that law exists over force and power, and record their truths and the collective truth. In contrast, she claims, the international community and local power-brokers tend to be more concerned with the reassertion of the position of international and domestic law.[7] It is my contention that, through the integration of more imaginative and victim orientated methodologies, these desires can be better reconciled.

Remedy as a Function of Law

The expectations of survivors are, to some extent, based on the premise that law has a function in providing a remedy. This might be said to be a basic corollary of the statement that law has a function of settling disputes, whether one sees that as the main function of law (like Jerome Frank[8]) or one of many functions of law (like R. S. Summers): once the law has decided on the outcome of a dispute it settles it in some way by making good whatever harm/detriment has accrued. That is the notion of remedying a situation. Generally speaking, that remedy will take a financial or material form: compensation, return of stolen property, enforced compliance with a contractual obligation, *etc.* ....

The law has predominantly tended to see the notion of remedy in a rather restrictive manner, fixated to some extent with notions emerging from *restitutio in integrum*, or returning someone to how they were before the wrong was done onto them. This type of restitution or remedy attempts to put someone in the position in which they would have been had the contract never been entered into. But an act of genocidal sexual violence is not a contract, and notions of remedy predicated on ideas of freedom of choice and autonomous involvement are unsuitable in this context. In domestic legal systems the remedy for sexual violence tends to be imprisonment (in criminal law) and monetary compensation (in civil law) – again reflecting the *restitution* notion and a narrow legal interpretation of remedy. These are reflected in the Statutes of the Tribunals, both of which include details of the punishment to be handed down to those found guilty by the Tribunal, but do not expressly mention the notion of providing a remedy to victims of such crimes. It is, of course, possible that punishing the perpetrator can be conceived of as a remedy, but if we revert to the notion of remedy as healing it has only a small part to play in the process. The main virtue of punishment as remedy is that it can re-empower the victim: the perpetrator is being punished on the basis of the narrative that is revealed to the court/tribunal.

However the notion of remedy is not merely one of financial or material compensation; rather it has a much broader remit: the remit of healing. I contend

---

7   See generally Mertus, J. (2000), 'Truth in A Box: The Limits of Justice through Judicial Mechanisms', in Amadiume, I. and An-Na'im, A. (eds), *The Politics of Memory: Truth, Healing and Social Justice* (New York and London: Zed Books), pp.142–161.

8   See generally Frank, J. (1949), *Courts on Trial: Myth and Reality in American Justice* (Princeton: Princeton University Press); Frank, J. (1930), *Law and the Modern Mind* (New York: Coward-McCann Inc.).

that the real role of the law in situations of genocide or other atrocities is to act, in conjunction with other legal and social innovations, as an agent for collective and individual healing, and that it is in this healing that the remedy is evident and provided by the Law. The use of the tribunals to hear and appreciate the holistic truth of one's experiences is what I term the 'effective remedy'.

The Notion of Truth

Survivors have noted their desire for the truth to out in the tribunals.[9] What is vital, therefore, is that the institutions hear the victim's narrative and, in doing so, hear the entire truth thereof. It is not enough to simply deal with genocidal sexual violence in a vacuum – to see it as an incident. Such an approach does not acknowledge or appreciate the real truth of that experience. It does not understand or try to understand the reasons for that violence. It does not understand or try to understand the ramifications of that violence – for there is a potential to destroy a group in the ramifications of sexual violence against women as much as there is in the actual act.

An act of sexual violence does not become freeze framed in someone's consciousness: rather it becomes a canvas upon which much of the remainder of one's life experiences and narrative is painted. Equally the collective, or the community, does not forget. Where sexual violence becomes systemic, as was the case in both Rwanda and the Former Yugoslavia, it becomes a permanent marker on the collective consciousness: the permanent canvas upon which all-subsequent gender relations are performed and an ink by which they are coloured.

To carry out the act of healing that constitutes the effective remedy in such cases the tribunals must be prepared to acknowledge where that violence comes from and where it leads. This is the significance of using the theory of intersectionality in this context: appreciating that a woman suffers genocidal sexual violence not only because of her sex (i.e., her biological make up and capacity to reproduce) and her gender (i.e., her position within a particular society, or at least her constructed position within that society),[10] but also because of her position within one of the protected groups. It is the intersection of all of those characteristics that make women and girl children perfect targets in genocides that occur within 'traditional' societies, i.e., within societies such as those targeted in Yugoslavia and Rwanda.

The inherent political characteristics of the tribunals have necessary implications for the capacity of the tribunal to find, hear and appreciate the truth of what victims have experienced. In the words of Mahmood Mamdani this politicization can result

---

9   *C.f.* Mertus (*op. cit.*), See also Lusby, K. (1995) 'Hearing the Invisible Women of Political Rape: Using Oppositional Narrative to Tell a New War Story', 25:4 *University of Toledo Law Review*, 911 and Osiel, M. (1997), *Mass Atrocity, Collective Memory and the Law* (New York: Transaction Publishers).

10 On the conflation between gender and sex in international legal scholarship generally see Askin, K. and Koenig, D. (1999), 'International Criminal Law and The International Criminal Court Statute: Crimes Against Women' in Askin, K and Koenig, D (eds), *Women and International Human Rights Law: Volume 1* (New York: Transnational Publishers Inc.).

in the construction of compromised truth. Reflecting on the South African Truth and Reconciliation Commission, Mamdani notes that by virtue of being a political exercise and seeking political compromise the Truth and Reconciliation Commission has created a compromised truth, which obscures the larger truth.[11] When this political aspect is combined with the necessary geographical and temporal limitations of the tribunals' jurisdictions the capacity for the truth to be obscured is further increased. While jurisdictional limitations are unavoidable in any situation of legal arbitration, it is important that decisions as to indictments, the content of indictments and the operation of the tribunals (down even to how much funding they receive to operate on a daily basis) are not taken in a manner that reduces the capacity for the lived experiences of women to be told, heard and appreciated. Prosecutorial decisions, described by Andrew Ashworth as 'gatekeeping decisions',[12] have an important role to play in the provision of effective remedy as they dictate, to some extent, what stories are chosen for investigation and how they are told.

The Importance of Facilitating the Narrative

The first step in the provision of this remedy is the provision of a supportive theatre in which the narrative or the 'violence story'[13] can be told. It is not enough to simply provide a legal atmosphere in which the normal process of translation can be undertaken. Rather the performative nature of telling the violence story must be appreciated and taken into account. Equally the re-constitution of the self as victim by virtue of telling the story must be acknowledged, particularly since the process of transition and re-establishment of law is contingent upon the willingness of survivors/ victims to share that story, reveal the truth and have the law applied thereto.

In recognizing the performative nature of telling the violence story the theory is quite simple: by exposing her experiences the victim allows those scars to once more be placed on her body. It is not simply an experience of retelling a story, but reliving an experience through one's words. Genocides and other atrocities depend to a large extent on traumatizing and terrorizing groups of people, therefore acts of genocide are generally carried out in a manner that would maximize humiliation, degradation and trauma. This is bound to have an effect on the victim who reveals her truth to the tribunal, or any other kind of transitional justice body for that matter. The revelation of one's violence story can also be performative after the fact of the exposition: the abuse can be repeated either literally (through the targeting of

---

11 Mamdani, M. (2000), 'The Truth According to the TRC' in Amadiume, I and An-Na'im, A (Ed.s), *The Politics of Memory* (London: Zed Books) p.178.

12 Ashworth, A. (1998), *The Criminal Process: An Evaluative Study*, 2nd edn, Oxford: Oxford University Press) Chapter 5.

13 Cobb uses the term 'violence story' to describe a victim's retold experience of violence and notes that, through this retelling, victims 'must mark themselves as victims, which in turn excludes them from the very communities that are brought forth through their own sacrifice'. Cobb, S. (1997), 'The Domestication of Violence in Mediation', 31:3 *Law and Society Review* 397, p.406.

now 'sullied' women by other men in their community) or figuratively (through the ostracization of women from their communities).

To facilitate truth telling leading to healing, tribunals must ensure that women are protected after giving evidence and that they are prepared for the traumatic nature of the experience of testifying to their experiences.

This is very much also the case in relation to the recognition of the fundamentality of the violence story in the process of reconstitution of the state based on the Rule of Law. Generally speaking, trials emphasize the weapon rather than the wound: the act rather than the repercussions. In this way the trials can establish responsibility for the acts performed and assign, or recognize, legal guilt. We therefore rely on the testimony of the victims to use the law in reconstituting legal and political authority by showing that nobody is above the law, in other words, by re-establishing the Rule of Law. It is all too easy to see the role of the victim as merely this; merely an agent for the reconstruction of the state; and to ignore the needs of the victim herself. It is vital, however, to ensure that we appreciate the experience of the victim both during the trial and during the atrocity to ensure that we facilitate the telling of the narrative and that victims can carry out this function resulting in the healing of the collective consciousness.

Intersectionality, Adjudication and the Facilitation of Truth

The theory of intersectionality can be effectively invoked in order to provide the effective remedy sought by victims. Kimberle Crenshaw championed intersectional theory in legal discourse in her writings on critical race theory. This theory essentially states that the lives of women of colour are shaped by their identity-based characteristics (such as gender and race), and that as such many (if not all) of their experiences occur on the intersection between these identities. The central point to her analysis, however, is that these experiences are not simply incidental to gender and race, but resultant from the distinct vulnerabilities created by the overlapping of these identities.[14]

In her analysis Crenshaw discusses three elements of the subordination of women: 'the structural dimensions of domination (structural intersectionality), the politics engendered by a particular system of domination (political intersectionality), and the representations of the dominated (representational intersectionality)'[15] and highlights the importance of an intersectional analysis of women's experiences, stressing that the traditional analysis of these experiences in the context of gender *or* race marginalizes women of colour within both categories. It is her contention that an analysis that neglects one of a woman victim's identity-based characteristics or fails to adequately consider the effect of the intersection between these characteristics does

---

14 Crenshaw, K. (1993), 'Beyond Racism and Misogyny: Black Feminism and 2 Live Crew' in Matsuda, M., Lawrence, C., Delgado, R. and Crenshaw, K. (eds) *Words That Wound: Critical Race Theory, Assaultive Speech, and the First Amendment* (Boulder: Westview Press), p.111.

15 Crenshaw, K., (1991), 'Mapping the Margins: Intersectionality, Identity Politics, and Violence against Women of Color', 43 *Stanford Law Review*, p.1241.

not fully appreciate women's experiences. To provide an effective remedy to women victims of genocidal sexual violence international criminal law must acknowledge that women experience genocide in a very particular way *because of* the intersection between their gender and their identity within one of the protected groups, and tailor its response to sexual violence as genocide in order to fully appreciate and respond to these experiences. As Chandra Mohanty has stated '[w]omen are constituted as women through the complex interaction between class, culture, religion and other ideological institutions and frameworks.'[16]

Intersectional theory has been particularly popular in the context of racial discrimination. Gay McDougall has advocated the use of this methodology by the Race Convention Committee, claiming that such an analysis would allow the Committee to properly understand the 'compound effects of gender and race factors combined'.[17] According to McDougall, such a methodology would focus the attention of the Committee on '1) the form a violation takes, 2) the circumstances in which a violation occurs, 3) the consequences of a violation, and 4) the availability and accessibility of remedies and complaint mechanisms'.[18]

The theory of intersectionality is now beginning to gain currency in the context of genocide law as well. Writing about the use of gender hate propaganda in Rwanda, Green recommends the use of the theory of intersectionality to accurately appreciate the impact of this propaganda on the events that transpired in the Rwandan genocide.[19] According to Green, the advantage of employing this methodology is that it contributes to judicial decision-making bodies' ability to accurately assess the impact of this propaganda by highlighting its effect on women because of *both* their gender and their race. In other words, such a methodology would enhance the tribunals' understanding of the reality of women's experiences and ability to accurately assess the damage caused by this propaganda.

This theory also has the potential to enhance the effectiveness of the Genocide Convention to appreciate, understand and punish genocidal sexual violence. By employing a method of thinking and interpreting law that considers the effect of sexual violence on all of a victim's identity characteristics, the international criminal justice system will be empowered to understand the full ambit of the reasons for targeting women in this way, and properly comprehend the injuries caused.

Intersectionality and the Office of the Prosecutor

If such thinking were employed by the Office of the Prosecutor it is sensible to presume that there would be less apprehension about charging defendants with

16 Mohanty, C. (1988), 'Under Western Eyes: Feminist Scholarship and Colonial Discourses', 30 *Feminist Review*, pp. 61, 74.

17 McDougall, G. (1999), 'Commentary to the CERD General Recommendation on Gender Related Dimensions of Racial Discrimination, Comm. on the Elimination of Racial Discrimination', 7, U.N. Doc. CERD/C/54/Misc, 31.

18 *Ibid.*

19 Green, L. (2002), 'Gender Hate Propaganda and Sexual Violence in the Rwandan Genocide: An Argument for Intersectionality in International Law', 33 *Columbia Human Rights Law Review*, 733.

sex crimes and that the Prosecutor would begin to formulate a managed, strategic prosecutorial policy that aims to recognize women's experience and thereby accurately allocate responsibility for the crimes committed during the genocide. A brief consideration of the history of a number of indictments before the Rwandan tribunal reveals a relative failure on the part of the Prosecutor to aid the provision of effective remedy to women victims of genocidal sexual violence.

While the ICTR is hailed as being the theatre in which rape was first defined as genocide in the *Akayesu* case,[20] there had been an earlier opportunity to do this in the ICTY case of *Kunarac*.[21] While the Tribunal held, for the first time, that rape could be a crime against humanity, the evidence showed that individual incidents of rape in Foca formed part of a larger policy to terrorize Muslims, evict them from the area and convert the region into a Serb stronghold – after raping one Muslim woman Kunarac 'told her she should enjoy being "fucked by a Serb" ... [adding] that she would carry a Serb baby and would not know who the father would be'.[22] All the evidence available in the case pointed towards the use of this sexual violence as part of the genocidal campaign and the failure on the part of the Prosecutor not to include genocide on the indictment is telling.

The history of the *Akayesu* indictment also reveals prosecutorial failure in this regard. The original indictment included no charges relating to sexual violence. This led to the submission of an *Amicus Curae* brief requesting that the Rwandan Tribunal exercise its supervisory authority under its Statute and Rules to request that the Office of the Prosecutor amend the indictment to include charges of 'rape and other serious acts of sexual violence as crimes within the competence of the Tribunal'.[23] According to the brief the failure to indict Akayesu in relation to sexual violence would produce unfairness and constitute a miscarriage of justice.[24]

In light of this brief and evidence elicited in judicial questioning the Indictment was amended during the trial to include three extra charges and three additional paragraphs. The fact that it took a substantial amount of political pressure for these charges to be added to the Indictment led to Defence arguments that '[t]he charges of offences of sexual violence ... were added under the pressure of public opinion and were not credibly supported by the evidence' (para. 42). This submission was understandable inasmuch as it would seem logical that where there was sufficient evidence of sexual violence, the Office of the Prosecutor would have included sexual violence in the original indictment and not have been forced to amend the indictment as happened in this case. Therefore, the failure of the Office of the

---

20 *Prosecutor v Akayesu* (Case No. ICTR-96-4-T), Judgment, 2 September 1998.

21 *Prosecutor v Kunarac, Kovac and Vukovic* (IT-96-23-T & IT-96-23/1-T), Judgment, 22 February 2001.

22 *Ibid.*, para 583.

23 *Amicus* Brief Respecting Amendment of the Indictment and Supplementation of the Evidence to Ensure the Prosecution of Rape and Other Sexual Violence Within the Competence of the Tribunal. This brief was prepared by Joanna Birenbaum and Lisa Wyndel of the Working Group on Engendering the Rwanda Tribunal, (Toronto); Rhonda Copelon of the International Women's Human Rights Law Clinic, City University of New York, and Jennifer Green of the Centre for Constitutional Rights (New York).

24 *Ibid.*, para. 5

Prosecutor to include charges of sexual violence in the original indictment cast doubt on the credibility of the testimony of women who suffered sexual violence in the Taba commune and thereby failed to appreciate both the reality of these women's experiences *and* the importance of recognizing these experiences through prosecution to begin the healing process and to end the circle of impunity for genocidal sexual violence against women.

In the aftermath of *Akayesu* very few Indictments have been amended to include charges of genocide for sexual violence. In a number of high-profile cases however the Indictments have been amended to include charges of rape and sexual violence as crimes against humanity and violations of the Geneva Conventions.[25] There have been a number of exceptionally high-profile cases where there were no charges relating to sexual violence despite the solid evidence that the accused in these cases were responsible for genocidal sexual violence.[26]

The Tribunals and Intersectional Theory

It would be unfair to say that the tribunals have not attempted to engage with intersectional theory in their work. To concentrate solely on the ICTY, it has clearly incorporated intersectional analysis into its decision making processes – but has it done so successfully?

The case of *Kunarac, Kovac and Vukovic*[27] dealt with acts commissioned at the Foca rape camp to the south-east of Sarajevo. The defendants were charged with torture, as a crime against humanity, under Article 5(f) of the Statute of the Tribunal, and as a violation of the laws or customs of war, under Article 3 of the Statute and recognized by Common Article 3 (1) (a) of the 1949 Geneva Conventions. They were also charged with rape, as a crime against humanity, under Article 5(g) of the Statute and as a violation of the laws or customs of war, under Article 3 of the Statute. Finally, two of the defendants (Kunarac and Kovac) were charged with enslavement as a crime against humanity, under Article 5(c) of the Statute.

Having overrun the town of Foca in April 1992, Serb forces transferred women and girls to a number of locations around Foca, including the local high school and private residences. While in detention these women were repeatedly raped and threatened with knives and guns, indeed Judge Florence Mumba, in her statement at the end of the case, said that '[w]hat the evidence shows, are Muslim women and girls, mothers and daughters together, robbed of their last vestiges of human dignity. Women and girls,

---

25 For example the indictment of Pauline Nyiramasuhoko, former Minister for Women's Development and Family Welfare was amended to include two charges of rape – one as a crime against humanity and one as a violation of the Geneva Conventions. *Prosecutor v Nyiramasuhoko* (ICTR-97-21-I), Indictment.

26 *Prosecutor v Kanyabashi*; *Prosecutor v Ndayambaje*; *Prosecutor v Ntezirayayo*; *Prosecutor v Nsabima*; *Prosecutor v Renzaho*. *Prosecutor v Kanyabashi* Case No. ICTR-96-15-T; *Prosecutor v Ndayambaje* Case No. ICTR-96-8-T; *Prosecutor v Nteziryayo* Case No. ICTR-97-29-T; *Prosecutor v Renzaho* Case No. ICTR-97-31-I.

27 *Prosecutor v Kunarac, Kovac and Vukovic* (IT-96-23-T & IT-96-23/1-T), Judgment, 22 February 2001.

treated like chattels, pieces of property at the arbitrary disposal of the Serb occupation forces, and more specifically at the beck and call of the three accused.'

In its Judgment the Tribunal noted that the repeated rape of women and girls 'were one of the many ways in which the Serbs could assert their superiority and victory over the Muslims' (para. 579), thereby acknowledging to some extent the potency of sexual violence within conflict and genocide. This decision reflects an awareness on the part of the Tribunal of how gender and ethnicity might coincide, and could therefore be said to be an intersectional analysis. As is so often the case, however, this intersectional analytic framework fell into the essentialist trap in the later decision in *Krstic*.[28]

The potential for intersectional theory to result in essentialism should not be overlooked, despite its capacity to constitute the theoretical framework in which an effective remedy to genocidal sexual violence can be provided. Indeed, essentialism might be said to be one of the limitations of intersectional theory, particularly as it is anathema to the nature of intersectional analysis to view categories of people as having essential characteristics as opposed to viewing the personal experience upon the intersection of personal characteristics. Davina Cooper[29] has recently stated that intersectionality has three basic weaknesses:

1. An understanding of inequality or experience as structured by different axes of oppression 'produces only two, bipolar positions: powerful and powerless',[30] but many people occupy contradictory positions. For example, would a wealthy, independent, respected Muslim woman in Srebrenica have experienced the patriarchal community identified by the Tribunal in its envisaged manner given the contradictions between powerful and powerless on her intersection?

2. Intersectional analysis sees only the intersections of axes and not the axes themselves, which are also formed by entanglements of various natures as a result of their existence within society itself. So if, for example, one of the axes of oppression is gender how can we begin to understand an experience formed on the intersection of gender with another characteristic unless we understand and appreciate the nature of gender itself as informed by and related to society itself?[31]

3. Cross-intersectional comparison is impossible: an understanding of the relative positioning of people with vastly different intersectional experiences cannot be engaged in as a result of their differences. This difficulty or limitation is inherently related to the concentration on the intersection of axes and lack of concentration on the formation of the axes themselves.[32]

---

28 *Prosecutor v Radislav Krstic* (Case No. IT-98-33-A.) Judgment, 19 April 2004, Appeals Chamber.

29 Cooper, D. (2004), *Challenging Diversity: Rethinking Equality and the Value of Difference* (Cambridge: Cambridge University Press).

30 *Ibid.*, p.47.

31 *Ibid.*, pp.48–49.

32 *Ibid.*, p.49.

Each of these weaknesses presents a distinct challenge for intersectional theorists and should neither be ignored nor cited as reasons why intersectional methodology should not be used by judicial institutions. Rather they should be considered as warning signs of essentialist and reductionist thinking in the application of intersectional theory: the points at which one's reasoning requires refreshing and rethinking.

Conclusion

It is apparent then that, in order to be complete, intersectional analysis must be personal, in-depth, expansive and non-reductionist: a heavy task for already over-burdened judicial institutions. I contend, however, that the weight of this task is matched by its benefits in terms of the provision of an effective remedy to women victims of genocidal violence: the chance to tell their story and have that story heard in its complete, personal, intersectional and societal truth.

Genocides are made up of many stories and many truths. Judicial institutions can hear only some of them. But in hearing these stories they can contribute to the act of collective and personal healing by selecting them well, protecting their tellers, recognizing their truths, and convicting their protagonists.

Chapter 10

A Moment of Kindness?
Consistency and Genocidal Intent

Paul Behrens

Introduction

Soon after the *ad hoc* Tribunals had taken up their work, the question of genocidal intent claimed its place as one of the most significant and complicated aspects of a crime which, in the eyes of some Trial Chambers, was at the very apex of the hierarchy of international crimes.[1] There are reasons for that. Specific genocidal intent – the 'intent to destroy, in whole or in part, a national, ethnical, racial or religious group, as such'[2] is seen by the international tribunals as the element which

---

1 ICTR (Trial Chamber), Case No. ICTR-98-39-S, *The Prosecutor v Omar Serushago*, Judgment 5 February 1999 [*Serushago* (Trial Chamber)], para. 15. For a discussion of a possible hierarchical relationship between war crimes on the one hand and crimes against humanity and genocide on the other, see Matthew Lippman (2000–2001), 'Genocide: The Crime of the Century. The Jurisprudence of Death at the Dawn of the New Millenium', 23 *Houston Journal of International Law*, p. 508. But *cf.* ICTR (Appeals Chamber), *The Prosecutor v Clément Kayishema* and *Obed Ruzindana*, Case No. ICTR-95-1-A, Judgment 1 June 2001, para. 367 ['[...] there is no hierarchy of crimes under the Statute [...]']. See also Adil Ahmad Haque, 'Group Violence and Group Vengeance: Towards a Retributivist Theory of International Criminal Law', 9 *Buffalo Criminal Law Review* (2005–2006), p. 309.

2 Article 4(2) of the Statute of the ICTY, Article 2(2) of the Statute of the ICTR. On the differentiation between 'specific intent' as understood in common law systems and the *dolus specialis* of genocide, see William Schabas (2001–2002), 'Was Genocide Committed in Bosnia and Herzegovina? First Judgments of the International Criminal Tribunal for the Former Yugoslavia', 25 *Fordham International Law Journal* [Schabas (2001/2002)], p. 48. On the use of 'special intent' in civil law systems, see Nina H.B. Jørgensen (2001), 'The definition of genocide: Joining the dots in the light of recent practice', 1 *International Criminal Law Review*, p. 292. In line with common usage of the terms by the international criminal tribunals, the terms 'specific intent', 'special intent' and 'dolus specialis' of genocide are used interchangeably in this chapter. On the necessity of 'clear intent' to destroy a protected group in whole or in part, see David L. Nersessian (2002), 'The Contours of Genocidal Intent: Troubling Jurisprudence from the International Criminal Tribunals', 37 *Texas International Law Journal* [Nersessian (2002)], p. 264

gives genocide its speciality and distinguishes it from an ordinary crime and other crimes against international humanitarian law.[3]

And this speciality lies in the particularly high threshold which the *dolus specialis* requires. Attempts by the Prosecution to widen the concept of genocidal intent to include the mere awareness of a genocidal result or a form of recklessness have met with no acceptance by the Tribunals;[4] specific intent means, as the Trial Chamber found in *Akayesu*, that 'the perpetrator clearly seeks to produce the act charged'.[5]

The significance of intent is also apparent in the deliberation of the question whether genocide can be committed through the acts of a single perpetrator. The respective instruments of the International Criminal Tribunal for the Former Yugoslavia (ICTY), the International Criminal Tribunal for Rwanda (ICTR) and of the International Criminal Court (ICC)[6] do not exclude this possibility and may therefore put the legal definition of genocide at odds with its historical and social understanding. The ICTY in *Jelisic* expressly referred to this situation as a 'theoretical' possibility[7] and relied in this context on the *Genocide Convention* itself,

---

3   ICTY (Trial Chamber), Case No. IT-95-10-T, *The Prosecutor v Goran Jelisic*, Judgment 14 December 1999 [*Jelisic* (Trial Chamber)], para. 66. See also Margaret A. Lyons (2001), 'Hearing the Cry Without Answering the Call: Rape, Genocide and the Rwandan Tribunal', 28 *Syracuse Journal of International Law*, at p. 119; Mark A. Drumbl / Kenneth S. Gallant (2001), 'Appeals in the *Ad Hoc* International Criminal Tribunals: Structure, Procedure and Recent Cases', 3:2 *The Journal of Appellate Practice and Process*, p. 596; Lippman, p. 506 and Lucy Martinez (2002–2003), 'Prosecuting Terrorists at the International Criminal Court: Possibilities and Problems', 34 *Rutgers Law Journal*, p. 23. On the meaning of specific intent, see Alexander K. A. Greenawalt (1999), 'Rethinking Genocidal Intent: The Case for a Knowledge-Based Interpretation', 99 *Columbia Law Journal*, p. 2266; Caroline Fournet (2006), *International Crimes*, (London: Cameron May) p. 86 (with references to the drafting history).

4   In *Krstic*, the Prosecution maintained that it sufficed that the perpetrator 'knew his acts were destroying, in whole or in part, the group, as such; or he knew that the likely consequence of his acts would be to destroy, in whole or in part, the group, as such', ICTY (Trial Chamber), Case No. IT-98-33-T, *The Prosecutor v Radoslav Krstic*, Judgment, 2 August 2001 [*Krstic* (Trial Chamber)], para. 569. The Trial Chamber rejected this view. 'For the purpose of this case, the Chamber will therefore adhere to the characterisation of genocide which encompass [sic] only acts committed with the *goal* of destroying all or part of a group' [emphasis by the Trial Chamber], *Krstic*, para. 571.

5   ICTR (Trial Chamber), Case No. ICTR-96-4-T, *The Prosecutor v Jean-Paul Akayesu*, Judgment, 2 September 1998 [*Akayesu* (Trial Chamber)], para. 498.

6   Article 6 of the Rome Statute of the International Criminal Court. It is apparent from the *Elements of Crime* that the concept of genocide as codified in the Statutes of ICTY and ICTR has not changed in this regard: the final sentences in Articles 6(a) to 6(e) of the *Elements of Crime* have the following identical version: '5. The conduct took place in the context of a manifest pattern of similar conduct directed against that group *or was conduct that could itself effect such destruction.*' (Emphasis added.)

7   *Cf.* ICTY (Appeals Chamber), Case No. IT-95-10-A, *The Prosecutor v Goran Jelisic*, Judgment, 5 July 2001 [*Jelisic* (Appeals Chamber)], para. 61. See also Kriangsak Kittichaisaree (2000), 'The NATO Military Action and the Potential Impact of the International Criminal Court', 4 *Singapore Journal of International & Comparative Law*, p. 513.

which 'did not discount the possibility of a lone individual seeking to destroy a group as such'.[8] The meaning of genocidal intent in cases of this kind is evident: the very question whether genocide may have been committed in a particular location may turn on the specific intent of the one lone perpetrator.

Intent however – and indeed, *mens rea* in general – encompasses a certain difficulty. Ascertaining what a particular defendant may have intended at a particular point in time is a problematic task; some debate therefore exists on the question whether it can be achieved at all. The ICTR Trial Chamber in *Kamuhanda* showed great confidence in this regard.[9] The better (and more modest) view is perhaps expressed by the Canadian Judge Advocate in the case of *Johann Neitz*:

> Intention is not capable of positive proof, and, accordingly, it is inferred from the overt acts. Evidence of concrete acts is frequently much better evidence than the evidence of an individual for, after all, an individual alone honestly knows what he is thinking. The Court cannot look into the mind to see what is going on there.[10]

The question of suitable elements of evidence has therefore become of crucial importance to the adjudication of genocide;[11] and even the existence of evidence can only ever lead to an approximation of the true intent at the time of the commission

---

8   *Jelisic* (Trial Chamber), para. 99. Askin however points out that a hesitation 'to find a low level actor guilty of genocide, particularly when it was not firmly established that genocide had been committed in the region', might have impacted on the Trial Chamber's decision to acquit Jelisic of genocide Kelly D. Askin (1999–2000), 'Judgments Rendered in 1999 by the International Criminal Tribunals for the Former Yugoslavia and for Rwanda', 6 *ILSA Journal of International and Comparative Law*, p. 499. The possibility of the lone génocidaire has met with criticism in the literature; it has been called 'an extremely unlikely scenario' (Guglielmo Verdirame (2000), 'The Genocide Definition in the Jurisprudence of the *Ad Hoc* Tribunals', 49 *International and Comparative Law Quarterly*, p. 587); and in Schabas' view, it 'might be called the "Lee Harvey Oswald theory of genocide"', Schabas (2001/2002), p. 31.

9   'The Chamber generally approves of this statement [by Trial Chamber I in the *Akayesu* case] adding only that intent to commit a crime, even genocide, may not always be difficult or impossible to discern from the circumstances of the case', ICTR, Case No. ICTR-95-54A-T, *The Prosecutor v Jean de Dieu Kamuhanda*, Judgment 22 January 2004 [*Kamuhanda* (Trial Chamber)], para. 624.

10 *Record of Proceedings of the Trial by Canadian Military Court of Johann Neitz* held at Aurich, Germany, 15–20 March 1946. See Cassese (2003), *International Criminal Law*, p. 177. For an earlier version of the beginning of this quote, see *Blake v Albion Life Assurance Society*, 27 W.R. 321, L.R. 4, C.P. D. 94 (quoted in 9 *Central Law Journal*, p. 420 [1879]) and *In Re Debaun* (1888), 11 *Crim. L. Mag. and Rep* [1889], p. 62 (referring to *Archbold's Criminal Evidence*). See also *The Journal of Criminal Law*, 'Courts of Summary Jurisdiction', vol. XII, no. 4 (October–December 1948), p. 341 and Nersessian (2002), p. 265. See also David L. Nersessian (2003), 'The Razor's Edge: Defining and Protecting Human Groups Under the Genocide Convention', 36 *Cornell International Law Journal*, p. 314.

11 See Lippman, p. 506. The *ad hoc* tribunals have looked to a variety of strands of evidence to establish genocidal intent. The main categories will be discussed later. For a summary, see Nersessian (2003), p. 314 and Martinez, p. 24 as well as the extensive discussion in David Alonzo-Maizlish (2002), 'In Whole or in Part: Group Rights, the Intent Element of

of the crime. Cases certainly exist in which the evidence seems to be overwhelming. In the 2003 ICTR Judgment of the *Ntakirutimanas*, reference is made to armed attackers who chased Tutsi refugees while singing: 'Exterminate them; look for them everywhere; kill them; and get it over with, in all the forests'.[12] In the 1999 ICTY Judgment of *Goran Jelisic* reference was made to his statement that he hated Muslims and wanted to kill them all.[13]

And yet, cases have come into existence where the apparent alignment between evidence and true intent has proven to be more complicated. This happens in particular when other, possibly contradictory, factors coincide with evidence for genocidal intent. Human behaviour is not always consistent, and the behaviour of génocidaires is no exception in this regard.

1. The Problem of Consistency

The case of *Jelisic* is in fact the most prominent example in this field. Jelisic, a former farm mechanic, had become a guard at the Luka prison camp in Northern Bosnia.[14] Before the ICTY, he stood accused of genocide. The evidence against him seemed overwhelming. Jelisic, a man who called himself the 'Serbian Adolf' (and presented himself as 'Adolf' at his initial hearing), had made in his time at the camp statements which appeared to leave little doubt about his intentions: he 'hated Muslim women [...] wanted to sterilise them all in order to prevent an increase in the number of Muslims but [...] before exterminating them he would begin with the men in order prevent any proliferation'.[15] He kept a tally of the Muslims he had killed.[16] He claimed he had to execute 'twenty to thirty persons before being able to drink his coffee each morning'[17].

But Jelisic also gave – 'against all logic', as the Tribunal observed – *laissez-passers* to some detainees, including one Muslim who was first forced to play Russian roulette with him, and another detainee who had first been beaten by Jelisic.[18]

It is this form of inconsistency that causes difficulties if, on the basis of the available evidence, the specific intent of genocide is to be established.

Genocide, and the "quantiative criterion"', 77 *New York University Law Review*, pp. 1386–1390; and *cf.* Fournet, p. 90.

12 ICTR (Trial Chamber), *The Prosecutor v Elizaphan and Gérard Ntakirutimana*, Cases No. ICTR-96-10 and ICTR-96-17-T, Judgment 21 February 2003 [*Ntakirutimana* (Trial Chamber)], para. 828. Elizaphan Ntakirutimana's involvement in this situation consisted in the transporting of the attackers and the pointing out of the refugees.

13 *Jelisic* (Trial Chamber), para. 102.

14 *The Seattle Times*, 14 December 1999, 'Bosnian Serb gets 40 years for war crimes', and *Jelisic* (Trial Chamber), para. 123. On the background of Jelisic, *cf.* Drumbl/Gallant, p. 638 and Askin, p. 499.

15 *loc. cit.*, para. 102.

16 *loc. cit.*, para. 103.

17 *loc. cit.*, para. 103.

18 *loc. cit.*, para. 106.

In the case of *Kayishema and Ruzindana*, one of the accused, Clément Kayishema, had been governor (*prefet*) of the Kibuye Province at the time of the atrocities in Rwanda.[19] The evidence against Kayishema was again partly formed by incriminating utterances. The defendant had referred to Tutsis as 'Tutsi dogs' and 'Tutsi sons of bitches' and had exhorted attackers to 'get down to work' – which in this particular context was understood to mean to begin to kill Tutsis.[20]

However, his behaviour too seems to have been subject to certain inconsistencies. At the Appeals stage, the Defence maintained that the Trial Chamber had not properly taken into account that Kayishema had also rescued '72 Tutsi children, who had survived the massacre at Home St Jean Complex',[21] as evidenced by the statement of a witness.

A third case may be of interest in this context. Georges Ruggiu, a Belgian journalist (the only European to be tried by the ICTR) stood accused of incitement to genocide in connection with his broadcasts for the *Radio Television Libre des Milles Collines* (RTLM).[22] On 15 May 2000, Ruggiu pleaded guilty to the counts of the indictment, having signed a plea agreement with the Prosecution.[23] Ruggiu admitted that there was a link between his broadcasts and the deaths of victims in Rwanda.[24] The phrase 'go to work' makes its appearance in his case, as it had been used by him in public broadcasts. The Trial Chamber found that with 'the passage of time, the expression came to mean "go kill the Tutsis and Hutu political opponents of the interim government."'[25]

Ruggiu had however, also 'personally assumed responsibility' for the hiding and transport of Tutsi children in his jeep to a mission, to keep them protected. The feeding of some farmers and refugees in Kigali, including Tutsis, was also carried out under his responsibility.[26]

It is perhaps not surprising that the inconsistencies at the level of the available evidence were mirrored at the level of its treatment by the international tribunals. The Trial Chamber in *Jelisic* was the one who accorded the greatest weight to the existence of negative evidence. Having referred to the fact that Jelisic had let some detainees go free, it stated that Jelisic had killed arbitrarily rather 'than with the clear intention to destroy a group'; and in view of this uncertainty, the Chamber found that

---

19 *Africa News/Inter News* (Tanzania), 'Rwanda; Profile of a Genocide Convict', 21 May 1999.

20 ICTR (Trial Chamber), *The Prosecutor v Clément Kayishema and Obed Ruzindana*, Case No. ICTR-95-1-T, Judgment 21 May 1999 [*Kayishema* (Trial Chamber)], para. 539.

21 *Kayishema* (Appeals Chamber), para. 147.

22 ICTR (Trial Chamber), *The Prosecutor v Georges Ruggiu*, Judgment 1 June 2000, Case No. ICTR-97-32-I, [*Ruggiu* (Trial Chamber)], para. 44.

23 *loc. cit.*, para. 10.

24 *loc. cit.*, para. 45.

25 *loc. cit.*, para. 44.

26 *loc. cit.*, paras. 73 and 74.

The benefit of the doubt must always go to the accused and, consequently, Goran Jelisic must be found not guilty on this count.[27]

Very different the Appeals Chamber in *Kayishema*:

> The Appeals Chamber observes that in light of the overall evidence, the fact that the 72 children *may* have been taken to the hospital pursuant to Kayishema's instructions has little direct bearing on the question whether he possessed the requisite *mens rea*.[28]

Finally, in *Ruggiu*, the 'Accused's assistance to Victims' was of relevance as part of 'mitigating circumstances' only.

It would therefore appear that the *ad hoc* tribunals have adopted widely differing approaches when they were faced with the task of evaluating contradictory evidence in the context of genocidal intent. The result is a situation which allows for little legal certainty and which provides inadequate guidance for future cases of this kind.

2. Towards an Understanding of Contradictory Evidence

2.1 Does Contradictory Evidence Exist?

Not every situation in which *prima facie* evidence of genocidal intent is joined by other pieces of evidence, leads by necessity to a contradictory outcome. There are cases where an *actus reus* of genocide was based on a variety of reasons without eliminating the determinative specific intent to destroy a group in whole or in part.

The very consideration of motives behind the *actus reus* has met with criticism in the jurisprudence of the tribunals. The *Kayishema* Appeals Chamber for instance noted that criminal intent 'must not be confused with motive' – without, however, examining where, in the case of genocide, the dividing line is to be drawn.[29] The problem with this view lies in the fact that by accepting a *dolus specialis* the

---

27 *Jelisic* (Trial Chamber), para. 108. See also Kittichaisaree, p. 513.

28 *Kayishema* (Appeals Chamber), para. 149. Emphasis by the Appeals Chamber.

29 *loc. cit.*, para. 161. See also *Jelisic* (Appeals Chamber), para. 49. Similarly Beth van Schaack, 'Darfur and the Rhetoric of Genocide', 26 *Whittier Law Review* (2004–2005), p. 1128. In fact, the question whether 'motive' forms part of the elements of the crime of genocide, has caused one of the 'major controversies' in the debate of this crime; George E. Bisharat, 'Sanctions as Genocide', 11 *Transnational Law and Contemporary Problems*, pp. 379, at p. 416. *Alonzo-Maizilish* states that there was 'great debate' during the drafting of the *Genocide Convention* on the question whether a 'motive element' should be included; Alonzo-Maizlish, p. 1382, fn. 58. *Greenawalt* points out that the record of the Ad Hoc Committee of ECOSOC which considered the draft of the *Genocide Convention*, does not reveal any discussions on the meaning of 'intent' or 'motive', Greenawalt, p. 2275. See also Nersessian (2002), p. 267. Some authors refer to genocidal intent as a 'purpose' (Haque, p. 310), which adds to the approximation of 'intent' and 'motive'. For a detailed discussion of the reasons in favour and against an inclusion of motives in the consideration of elements of a crime (with reference to English criminal law), see Jonathan Herring (2006), *Criminal Law*, (Oxford: Oxford University Press) pp. 213–216 and (with reference to American law), Wayne R. LaFave (2003), *Criminal Law*, (St Paul, Minnesota: West Group), pp. 256–257.

drafters of the Genocide Convention do call for the exploration of reasons behind the objective genocidal acts, which go well beyond the simple voluntative element pertaining to the *actus reus*. It is not enough that the perpetrator (for example) killed members of the group and wanted to do that; he must have possessed the intent to destroy the protected group, in whole or in part, as such. But if this is the case, then motives do carry significance. The existence of certain motives may demonstrate that the reason behind the *actus reus* was not the destruction of the group and that therefore the *dolus specialis* is negated; while the existence of other motives may not be harmful to a finding of specific genocidal intent.[30]

With regard to the latter alternative, the Appeals Chamber had occasion to note that the existence of personal motives,[31] economic benefits or political advantages[32] does not necessarily exclude the presence of genocidal intent.[33] The co-existence of these reasons is certainly in principle possible. The defence in the case of *Ruzindana* for instance, who stood accused of genocide before the ICTR, had claimed that it was the 'elimination of business competitors' that had influenced his actions. It is however difficult to see why it should not be possible for a perpetrator to appoint the destruction of a protected group as his goal and, at the same time, to intend to gain economic benefits from this action.

However, there is reason to believe that every case will need to be examined on its individual merits. In the case of *Ruggiu* for instance, the Belgian journalist had at some stage drawn the attention of the Gikondo population to the fact that RPF members were in the area; a statement which resulted in the killing of many people, women and children among them. It seems however that Ruggiu had acted to warn one person in particular – the editor-in-chief of RTLM, who lived in this area. In a case like this it is at least conceivable that personal concerns rather than the desire to destroy a protected group had formed the intent of the perpetrator; additional evidence would be required to reach an appropriate assessment of this instance.

---

30 See also Schaack on the obscuring of 'evidence for genocidal intent,' if alternative explanations for the behaviour in question can be identified; Schaack (2004–2005), 26 *Whittier Law Review*, p. 1128. See also Greenawalt, p. 2285 and Nersessian (2003), p. 315 (on motives which can indeed be considered as evidence for genocidal intent). It is interesting to note that the international criminal tribunals were able to accept the significance of motives in the context of the subjective element of the perpetrator relating to the policy element of crimes against humanity. There, it was found that the perpetrator must not have acted 'for purely personal motives completely unrelated to the attack on the civilian population'. ICTY (Trial Chamber), *The Prosecutor v Duko Tadic*, Case No. IT-94-1-T, Judgment, 4 May 1997 [*Tadic* (Trial Chamber)], paras. 658, 659.

31 *Kayishema* (Appeals Chamber), para. 161.

32 ICTY (Appeals Chamber), *The Prosecutor v Goran Jelisic*, Case No. IT-95-10-A, Judgment 5 July 2001, [*Jelisic* (Appeals Chamber)], para. 49. See also Nersessian (2002), p. 268 (on acts motivated by 'financial gain' and ideological motives) and Nersessian (2003), p. 315.

33 See also Gunael Mettraux (2001), 'Current Developments', 1 *International Criminal Law Review*, p. 279 and Greenawalt, p. 2288 (on 'ideological or political motives').

Two situations in particular, in which assumed genocidal intent may have been joined by another consideration, have proven to be cumbersome for the international tribunals.

The first concerns the potential co-existence of considerations of military or security concerns and genocidal intent. The case of *Ruggiu* may again serve as an illustration of the complexities of this situation. The language used in Ruggiu's broadcasts was frequently of a military nature: there was a move to encourage 'civil defence',[34] there were references to the 'enemy', the RPF and their allies.[35] It is significant that the Trial Chamber states that, as time went past, the exhortations to fight the RPF and their allies assumed the meaning of exhortations to kill Tutsis and oppositional Hutus.[36] The relationship between the perception of military advantages and the intent to destroy a protected group may therefore be very close. The situation is in so far similar to the assessment of a co-existence of economic or political benefits: it is not inconceivable that a perpetrator might desire the destruction of a group and see in this at the same time a military advantage.

It should, however also be noted that there were cases in which the international tribunals were content to accord greater weight to the military intention and to even allow it to exclude genocidal intent. Thus, the Trial Chamber in *Brdjanin* agreed that the fact that the greater part of the detainees in camps had been of military age

> could militate further against the conclusion that the existence of genocidal intent is the only reasonable inference that may be drawn from the evidence. There is an alternative explanation for the infliction of these acts on military-aged men, and that is that the goal was rather to eliminate any perceived threat to the implementation of the Strategic Plan in the ARK and beyond.[37]

Whereas the Appeals Chamber in *Krstic* pointed out that the male Muslim prisoners who had been killed, had been killed on the basis of their identity only; the victims had included civilians, old and young men.[38] The evaluation of the co-existence of military and genocidal intent therefore becomes a question of a case-by-case analysis. If it can be proven that the perpetrator directed his acts solely against those members of the protected group who posed a military threat, and left other parts of the group unharmed, the finding for a specific genocidal intent will be much more difficult to support.[39]

---

34 *Ruggiu* (Trial Chamber), para. 44 (iv).

35 *loc. cit.*, para. 44 (i).

36 *loc. cit.*, para. 44 (iv).

37 ICTY (Trial Chamber), *The Prosecutor v Radoslav Brdjanin*, Case No. IT-99-36-T, Judgment 1 September 2004, [*Brdjanin* (Trial Chamber)], para. 979.

38 ICTY (Appeals Chamber), *The Prosecutor v Radislav Krstic*, Case No. IT-98-33-A, Judgment 19 April 2004 [*Krstic* (Appeals Chamber)], para. 37.

39 It should be noted that the assertion that the perpetrator acted to avert a military threat, causes further complications. One may ask if child soldiers and human shields may be embraced by the definition of a 'military threat'. If that were the case, then the difference between 'military considerations' and the intention to destroy a protected group may be considerably diminished.

Perhaps the most complicated case of a co-existence of intentions is that of the ethnic cleanser. The international tribunals – in particular the ICTY – have struggled long to evaluate the phenomenon of ethnic cleansing in the context of genocide. The Appeals Chamber in *Krstic* adopted the view that the forcible transfer of Bosnian Muslims from Srebrenica eliminated 'even the residual possibility that the Muslim community in the area could reconstitute itself'.[40] The Trial Chamber in *Brdjanin* spelled it out: 'forcible displacement', in its view, 'could be an additional means to ensure the physical destruction'.[41] In the case of *Blagojevic*, Trial Chamber I of the ICTY accepted that 'intent to destroy' means the physical or biological destruction of the group, but it also found that physical or biological destruction was the likely outcome of a forcible transfer if the group could no longer reconstitute itself.[42]

Not everybody agrees with this assessment. The Trial Chamber in *Stakic* saw a clear difference between the 'mere dissolution' of a group and physical destruction.[43] In this context, it went back to the *travaux préparatoires* and pointed out that a proposal to include 'measures intended to oblige members of a group to abandon their homes […]' had been rejected by the drafters of the *Genocide Convention*.[44] Nor could it be said that academic opinion unequivocally supports such an extensive view of genocidal intent. *Schabas* indeed went so far as to say that '[Ethnic cleansing] is intended to displace a population, [genocide] to destroy it. The issue is one of intent and it is logically inconceivable that the two agendas co-exist'.[45]

A co-existence of motives in this regard is perhaps not entirely 'inconceivable'. If the perpetrator expels a protected group into a territory were certain death awaits its members – one may think of a desert[46] – then it would appear entirely possible that genocidal intent and the intent of 'ethnic cleansing' share a place in the mind of the author of the act. In the vast majority of cases however, the assessment of the Trial Chamber in *Stakic* appears more convincing. Including ethnic cleansing in the definition of 'physical or biological destruction' puts a considerable linguistic strain on the phrase in question. 'Destruction' carries a distinct notion of permanence which does not inhabit the concept of 'expulsion': the group still exists, and it cannot even be said with certainty that it will never again re-form on its accustomed territory.

2.2 Does Contradictory Evidence Exist at the Same Time?

If the apparent conflict between evidence in support of genocidal intent and evidence to the contrary cannot be resolved by the assumption of co-existence of the two

---

40 *Krstic* (Appeals Chamber), para. 31.

41 *Brdjanin* (Trial Chamber), para. 976.

42 ICTY (Trial Chamber), *The Prosecutor v Vidoje Blagojevic* and *Dragan Jokic*, Case No. IT-02-60-T, Judgment 17 January 2005 [*Blagojevic* (Trial Chamber)], para. 666.

43 ICTY (Trial Chamber), *The Prosecutor v Milomir Stakic*, Case No. IT-97-24-T, Judgment 31 July 2003 [*Stakic* (Trial Chamber)], para. 519.

44 *Stakic* (Trial Chamber), para. 519.

45 Schabas (2000), *Genocide in International Law: The Crime of Crimes*, Cambridge, p. 200.

46 Instances of this kind reportedly occurred featured during the Herero massacres between 1904 and 1907.

strands of evidence, then a real situation of contradictory evidence may exist. This is however only the case if the two strands of evidence refer to the same moment in time.

The principle of simultaneity (or contemporaneity), which is well known to major legal systems in the world[47] must claim its validity in the realm of international criminal law as well. It is mandatory that the *mens rea* extends to the period in which the *actus reus* is performed. In other words, if a perpetrator kills a victim because he bore a personal grudge against him, and later develops a general desire to destroy the entire group to which the victim belongs, it would be inapposite to apply this desire to the act in question; it comes too late. If, on the contrary, a racist whose intention it was to destroy a protected group in whole or in part, repents his views, but then kills a member of the group in order to gain an economic advantage, his views before the performance of the *actus reus* will not matter; they no longer existed at the crucial time.

It is suggested that a strict application of the principle of simultaneity can resolve a number of cases of apparently contradictory evidence. If Goran Jelisic declares that he 'must have been mad to dirty his hands with a "balija" [a Turk, as a term for Muslims, used in a derogatory way]' before then executing his victim,[48] he leaves little doubt that his act followed the singling out of the victim because of his membership in the group. The giving of *laissez-passers* to other detainees is a different act at a different stage[49] and is therefore irrelevant for the evaluation of genocidal intent with regard to the Muslim victim whom Jelisic called *balija*.

Similarly, the alleged saving of 72 Tutsi children by Kayishema after the massacre at the St Jean complex[50] is quite different from an act which occurred at the Stadium in Kibuye, when the prefect ordered gendarmes to 'fire on these Tutsi dogs'[51]. If genocidal intent is inferred in the latter case, the former case will be unable to exert any influence on the finding.

Nor could it be different in the case of *Ruggiu*. His intent at the time of his broadcasts can be inferred from the nature of his utterances. His invitations to the population to 'go to work' – with the destructive connotations which this phrase carried[52] – are an act quite different from his protection of Tutsi children and his

---

47 For a discussion of the principle of contemporaneity in various domestic jurisdictions see Alan R. White (1977), 'The Identity and Time of the Actus Reus', 148 *Criminal Law Review*; Geoffrey Marston (1970), 'Note, Contemporaneity of Act and Intention in Crimes,' 86 *Law Quarterly Review*, 208; G.R. Sullivan (1993), 'Cause and Contemporaneity of *Actus Reus* and *Mens Rea*', 52:3 *Cambridge Law Journal*, pp. 487–500; Claus Roxin, (2006), *Strafrecht Allgemeiner Teil. Band 1, Grundlagen. Der Aufbau der Verbrechenslehre*, München, pp. 478–479; Adolf Schönke/Horst Schröder/Peter Cramer (2006), *Strafgesetzbuch. Kommentar*, München, p. 269, paras. 48–49; Hans-Heinrich Jescheck/Thomas Weigend (1996), *Lehrbuch des Strafrechts. Allgemeiner Teil*, Berlin, p. 294.

48 *Jelisic* (Trial Chamber), para. 75.

49 *loc. cit.*, para. 106.

50 *Kayishema* (Appeals Chamber), para. 147.

51 *Kayishema* (Trial Chamber), paras. 364, 538.

52 *Ruggiu* (Trial Chamber), para. 44 (iv).

assistance to Tutsi farmers,[53] and as such, the intent in the latter case cannot detract from his intent during the broadcasts for RTLM.

A clear division of this kind does however necessitate sufficiently precise evidence for the existing intent of the perpetrator at the time of the *actus reus*. This appears easy enough when the author of the act accompanied the material part of the crime with utterances which revealed his intention – the example of the singing attackers in the case of the *Ntakirutimanas* has been mentioned above. But it is a fair assumption that in the majority of cases the best evidence that is available leads only to an approximation of the intent as it existed at the time of the act.

In the case of *Jelisic* for instance, it would be reasonable to see his boasts on the number of Muslim victims he had killed in the context of his most recent victims, even though the utterances were apparently made after the act.[54] But there are cases in which no such statements existed – nor a confession by the perpetrator before the tribunal, nor any other piece of evidence that could be convincingly linked to a particular act at a particular time. Instead, a number of evidential strains may exist, referring to roughly the same, more general, timeframe. In situations of this kind, the phenomenon of contradictory evidence may indeed emerge; and it is then of importance to accord a value to the various forms of evidence that an international criminal tribunal may accept.

3. Towards an Assessment of Contradictory Evidence

The jurisdiction of the international criminal tribunals provides a certain guidance as to the elements of human behaviour which can be appropriately considered in the determination of incriminating evidence.[55] The tribunals are less clear about the evaluation of negative evidence; evidence that seems to negate the existence of genocidal intent. However, the principles of international criminal law are quite clear on situations which, after all due care has been taken to assess the significance of different strands of evidence, still present an insoluble evidentiary conflict pertaining to the *mens rea* of the perpetrator: if reasonable doubt attaches to the existence of his intent, it must be resolved in favour of the defendant.[56]

Among the pieces of evidence accepted by the international tribunals, two seem to merit particular attention in this respect: the existence or otherwise of an action and the existence or otherwise of a statement by the alleged genocidal perpetrator.

---

53 *Ruggiu* (Trial Chamber), para. 73.

54 *Jelisic* (Trial Chamber), para. 103.

55 For an overview of evidence accepted by the *ad hoc* tribunals in the case of genocide, see Bisharat, p. 414. See also Jørgensen, p. 297 (with references to the *Report of the Commission of Experts on the Former Yugoslavia* and the 1985 *Whitaker Report*).

56 *Cf. Jelisic* (Trial Chamber) para. 108. See also *Kayishema* (Appeals Chamber), para. 148, 'On the basis of such evidence, it found that it had been established beyond reasonable doubt that the requisite *mens rea* was present.'

The *ad hoc* tribunals have for a long time accepted that the acts of the defendant themselves allow an inference of his intent at the time of commission.[57] This position however, may require qualification. In view of the opinion expressed above – that it is the specific intent which 'gives genocide its speciality'[58] and that distinguishes it from certain crimes against humanity (extermination, persecution), it would appear strange and contradictory to assume genocidal intent exclusively from the existence of, e.g., killings. The view expressed by some Trial Chambers, that the 'scale of the atrocities'[59] and the 'manner of killing'[60] can allow an inference of genocidal intent is particularly unsatisfactory. Crimes against humanity can be committed in an equally cruel fashion, and are indeed, because of the requirement of a 'widespread and systematic attack',[61] likely to result in large scale atrocities.

That does not mean that the facts of a case are without any value at all for the determination of the specific intent; but an assessment of intent which relies on only one of the above mentioned elements is capable of yielding misleading results. The opinion of the *Akayesu* Trial Chamber, which favoured a more contextual view, is more convincing in this regard.[62]

There is however one element on the material side of the crime which may carry greater weight in the assessment of genocidal intent than the others. On some occasions, the defendant had adopted a process of selection before proceeding with the genocidal act. Thus, Semanza at one stage 'instructed soldiers to separate Hutu from Tutsi, who were then killed by gunfire and grenades'.[63] In the *Bagambiki* case the Trial Chamber made reference to massacres committed on a football field; on the eve of the atrocities, soldiers had come to the field and had 'asked the refugees whether they were all Tutsis'.

If a perpetrator separates members of a protected group from other persons, he certainly does engage in an act of discrimination. If he then proceeds to kill the members he had thus selected, he will, by this act, have created a strong assumption

---

57 ICTR (Trial Chamber), *The Prosecutor v Laurent Semanza*, Case No. ICTR-97-20-T, Judgment 15 May 2003 [*Semanza* (Trial Chamber)], para. 313; earlier *Akayesu* (Trial Chamber), para. 523.

58 *Jelisic* (Trial Chamber), para. 66, see *supra*, p. 126.

59 'large number of victims,' ICTR (Trial Chamber), *The Prosecutor v André Ntagerura, Emmanuel Bagambiki, Samuel Imanishimwe*, Case No. ICTR-99-46-T [*Ntagerura* (Trial Chamber)], Judgment 25 February 2004, para. 689. See also Lawrence J. LeBlanc (1984), 'The Intent to Destroy Groups in the Genocide Convention: The Proposed U.S. Understanding', 78 *American Journal of International Law*, p. 382; Nersessian (2002), p. 266; Nersessian (2003), p. 314 and Verdirame, p. 586. The 'scale of the atrocities' was mentioned in *Jelisic* (Appeals Chamber), para. 47. For a critical assessment of these strands of evidence see Jørgensen, p. 298.

60 The 'manner in which the soldiers killed the refugees', *Ntagerura* (Trial Chamber), para. 689.

61 *Cf.* Article 7 of the Rome Statute.

62 'The Chamber considers that it is possible to deduce the genocidal intent inherent in a particular act charged from the general context of the perpetration of other culpable acts systematically directed against that same group', *Akayesu* (Trial Chamber), para. 523.

63 *Semanza* (Trial Chamber), para. 429.

that his action had indeed been based on an intent to destroy, in whole or in part, a protected group as such.

It may be more difficult to decide whether the lack of a particular action – in those cases where the perpetrator had the opportunity to act – can be taken as evidence for a lack of genocidal intent.

This situation has not received uniform treatment by the Trial Chambers. In the *Krstic* case for instance, the Appeals Chamber did not accept the possibility that the perpetrator could have done more to effect genocide, as an argument against the assumption of genocidal intent. 'Ineffectiveness' did not militate against the existence of specific intent.[64] In the case of *Stakic* on the other hand, the Trial Chamber appeared more welcoming towards the acceptance of negative evidence. With regards to killings in the Prijedor area, the Chamber found:

> Had the aim been to kill *all* Muslims, the structures were in place for this to be accomplished.[65]

and it pointed out that, while 23,000 people had passed through the Trnopolje Camp, the killings in Prijedor were limited to about 3,000 persons.[66]

In a similar vein, the Trial Chamber in *Brdjanin* pointed to the fact that the Bosnian Serbs in the ARK (Autonomous Region of Krajina) had the logistical resources to displace 'tens of thousands of Bosnian Muslims and Bosnian Croats, [...] resources which, had such been the intent, could have been employed in the destruction of all Bosnian Muslims and Bosnian Croats of the ARK'.[67]

Context is again of great importance if the accurate value of the omission of a fact is to be ascertained. The omission of the destruction of a group when the perpetrator had the means at his proposal to proceed, may serve as a *prima facie* negation of genocidal intent. However, the consideration of contextual factors may change the picture. Thus, the Appeals Chamber in *Krstic* pointed out that the international attention which the situation in Srebrenica had attracted, may well have prevented the perpetrators from adopting a more 'efficient way' of implementing a genocidal plan.

Of more importance for the determination of genocidal intent may in fact be the second piece of evidence which is frequently invoked by the international tribunals – the existence of utterances at the commission of an *actus reus* of genocide. The various statements by Jelisic, Kayishema and Ruggiu have been mentioned above.[68] In the case of *Jelisic* in particular, it is difficult to dismiss – as the Trial Chamber did – the value of his utterances for the assessment of genocidal intent; one may assume

---

64 *Krstic* (Appeals Chamber), para. 32.
65 Emphasis added by the Trial Chamber. *Stakic* (Trial Chamber), para. 553.
66 *loc. cit.*, para. 553.
67 *Brdjanin* (Trial Chamber), para. 978.
68 See *supra*, p. 128, 129; Lyons, p. 119.

that there could hardly be clearer evidence of such an intent than the phrase that the perpetrator hated all members of the group and wanted to kill them all.[69]

The lack of utterances on the other hand, appears not to have been seen as greatly significant in the determination of genocidal intent.[70] A contextual view may again yield different results – in situations, in which a statement had been expected of, but was denied by, the defendant (such as the refusal to take an oath on a genocidal leader), the omission of utterances might allow an insight into the mind of the perpetrator and may cast doubt on the existence of genocidal intent.

Apart from these two elements of evidence, the international tribunals have in the past considered the existence of a genocidal plan,[71] the existence of a pattern (a systematic targeting of members of a group),[72] and the repetition of particular acts[73] as relevant for the assessment of the defendant's intent. These factors should perhaps be considered together with the degree of independence of the perpetrator's decision. It is one of those areas where, again, sentencing considerations meet elements of evidence. A certain lack of independent thinking – in cases of indoctrination[74] or of perpetrators who 'allowed themselves to be drawn into a maelstrom of violence'[75] – has been accepted as a relevant reason for the mitigation of a sentence. This will certainly account for the majority of cases in which a lack of independence could be invoked by the Defence. However, it is at least conceivable that a perpetrator, without profound indoctrination, commits murders on a victim group because his peers (his corps, his clique) do – but would refrain from so doing if he were on his own. He would thus certainly have awareness of the fact that he contributed to the destruction of the group, but his specific intent – and only this counts in a consideration of the *mens rea* of genocide – would attract much greater doubt.

Finally, there are strands of evidence which have been dismissed by the international tribunals in the past. The Trial Chamber in *Jelisic* had, among other considerations, relied on the 'disturbed personality', the 'anti-social' and 'narcissistic' elements of his character, which had led him to commit the crime.[76] The Appeals Chamber rejected this line of reasoning and referred to the fact that no defence of insanity had been used by Counsel for *Jelisic*.[77]

---

69 'Goran Jelisic remarked to one witness that he hated the Muslims and wanted to kill them all', *Jelisic* (Trial Chamber), para. 102.

70 'The Defence also argues that the record contains no statements by members of the VRS Main Staff indicating that the killing of the Bosnian Muslim men was motivated by genocidal intent to destroy the Bosnian Muslims of Srebrenica. The absence of such statements is not determinative'. *Krstic* (Appeals Chamber), para. 34.

71 *Jelisic* (Appeals Chamber), para. 48.

72 *loc. cit.*, para. 47, 'a pattern of purposeful action', *Kayishema* (Trial Chamber), para. 93.

73 *Jelisic* (Appeals Chamber), para. 47.

74 *Ruggiu* (Trial Chamber), para. 63.

75 *Krstic* (Trial Chamber), para. 711.

76 *Jelisic* (Trial Chamber), para. 106.

77 *Jelisic* (Appeals Chamber), para. 70.

It seems a preferable view. What must count in the assessment of criminal responsibility is whether the perpetrator is capable of forming intent. A disturbed personality may allow a finding that this ability did not exist and that therefore criminal responsibility cannot be assumed. But once the Trial Chamber is convinced that the perpetrator is capable of forming intent, the remaining disorders in his personality cannot serve to negate the finding of the requisite *mens rea*.

The Appeals Chamber also rejected the argument that Jelisic had killed his victims at random.[78] This seems to be in line with its general position on the evidentiary value of the *omission* of genocidal acts (*supra*, p. 137). The Chamber concluded that a

> reasonable trier of fact could have discounted the few incidents where he showed mercy as aberrations in an otherwise relentless campaign against the protected group. [79]

This, however, requires further qualification. In the light of the great significance that the absence of genocidal acts can carry,[80] it seems particularly unsatisfactory that the Appeals Chamber would permit a 'discounting' of such an important element of evidence.[81] The preferable question would be one about the underlying motive to which the 'aberrations' seem to point.

The motive, it will be found, was, in the case of *Jelisic*, far from altruistic. Giving *laissez-passers* to a victim whom Jelisic had at first beaten and to another, who had been forced to engage in a game of Russian roulette, is hardly the ephemeral moment of kindness that seems to be suggested in the Judgment of the Appeals Chamber. The likely motive is caused by the fact that Jelisic, in these few cases, had become master over life and death. The likely motive was Jelisic's enjoyment of this exercise of power, which was made possible only by the dehumanization of his victims. The likely motive was racism, and is as such entirely compatible with the specific intent required for the crime of genocide.

Conclusion

From the above examination it appears that the problem of specific intent and the impact of inconsistencies in the behaviour of the perpetrator is a problem of evidence as much as of material law. Its particular difficulty lies in the proper evaluation of evidentiary elements which may point to other, possibly contradictory motives behind the *actus reus*. To simply disregard this evidence or to state that motives are 'irrelevant'[82] is an unsatisfactory approach; more so, as (as the case of *Stakic* has

---

78 *loc. cit.*, para. 71. See, on a discussion of the Appeals Chamber's Judgment in the *Jelisic* case, Fournet, p. 87. *Cf.* also Kittichaisaree, p. 513.

79 *loc. cit.*, para. 71.

80 See *supra*, p. 137.

81 See however the interpretation of the Appeals Chamber's Judgment in Mettraux, p. 282.

82 *Kayishema* (Appeals Chamber), para. 161, *Jelisic* (Appeals Chamber), para. 49. But see for a different approach (regarding crimes against humanity), *Tadic* (Trial Chamber), paras 658, 659.

shown) a particular motive (ethnic cleansing) may be held to deny the existence of genocidal intent.

The preferable view is an approach which would allow a detailed examination of evidence both in support of and against the assumption of genocidal intent. In some cases, it will be found that evidence for a different reason behind the acts of the perpetrator (*e.g.*, economic, political or military advantages) may in fact co-exist with the specific intent required for genocide. In other cases (as in the majority of cases of ethnic cleansing), the motive thus established militates against a finding of specific genocidal intent.

Even if contradictory evidence has been found to exist, a strict application of the principle of simultaneity may help to resolve the difficulty. A motive which would deny genocidal intent, but which arose at a point in time different from that of the genocidal act, is irrelevant and cannot enter into the consideration of the *dolus specialis*. It is suggested that a scrupulous application of this principle would, at least in the case of *Jelisic*, have led to a different judgment by the Trial Chamber.

There are finally factors which may aid in the determination of genocidal intent or of the existence of a different motive. The existence and omission of facts, the existence and omission of statements, a plan or a pattern, repetitive acts and the independence of the perpetrator's decision, have been mentioned above. The value of other factors however – the 'disturbed personality' of a perpetrator or the 'randomness' of his actions, has been disputed by the international tribunals.

The *dolus specialis* of genocide retains its position as one of the most complex phenomena with which the international criminal tribunals have been confronted. The inconsistent judicial treatment which contradictory evidence and the apparent co-existence of several motives have received gives little room for confidence in the future of its adjudication. There is little doubt that, based on the judgments up to this date and the different strands of opinion they represent, it will continue to haunt the evaluation of the crime and will constitute the cause of major difficulties in genocide cases before the Permanent International Criminal Court.

Chapter 11

Freedom of Speech v Hate Speech: The Jurisdiction of 'Direct and Public Incitement to Commit Genocide'

Tonja Salomon

In January 1994 General Dallaire who was leading the UNAMIR, the UN mission for Rwanda, sent a fax to New York in which he informed the UN Headquarters that a massive killing was being prepared in the tiny country in East Africa. The department of peacekeeping operations ignored the information. The UN's refusal to interfere allowed the perpetrators to establish huge weapon stores which subsequently enabled the realization of the genocide. Rwandan party, media and military people meanwhile created a dense and deadly atmosphere that provided the perfect background for their plan to kill the Tutsi.

All perpetrators of genocide know that what is necessary is to prepare people by means of propaganda to kill their neighbours, to torture and rape. That task is not easy to accomplish. It requires the creation of a certain state of mind that enables the killers to dehumanize their victims. The Rwandan genocidaires started their psychological and physical preparation months, if not years, before the actual massacres began, enabled, and no doubt encouraged, by the silence of – among others – the UN, the USA and France.

The Rwandan genocide began on 6 April 1994 after president Juvénal Habyarimana's plane was shot down in Kigali, by actors unknown until today. What followed was the murder of at least 800,000 human beings. The first stage of genocide has always been the preparation and mobilization of the masses by means of propaganda. In Germany, the Nazis had started a long propaganda campaign against Jews long before they were deported and murdered. They created a 'Feindbild' of Jews by using established anti-Semitic stereotypes. The Germans ultimately pictured Jews as 'Ungeziefer' (vermin). The Rwandan perpetrators used similar methods. They asserted that the Tutsi dominated Rwandan business, that they had a plan to regain political power in Rwanda and to push the Hutu out of their well-deserved place in society; besides, Tutsi women were accused of being seducers.

The six men sentenced by the International Criminal Tribunal for Rwanda (ICTR) for the crime of direct and public incitement to commit genocide knew these ingredients well. They dehumanized Tutsis and labelled them as 'bloodthirsty', 'evil', 'arrogant' and 'lusting for power'. They created fear of the Tutsi as an ethnic group. They argued that what was necessary was 'self defence' of the Hutu. Ultimately 'self defence' came to mean to kill Tutsi, whether they were members of the Tutsi rebel army or not. Akayesu, Kambanda, Ruggiu, Kajelijeli, Barayagwiza, Nahimana and Ngeze, urged people one way or another 'to lose their pity' for the 'milk drinking small nose' Tutsi.[1]

Speeches and writings by influential members of society such as government officials, party members, intellectuals and journalists are powerful instruments for spreading racism and hate. Genocidaires publish infamous newspapers and give horrifying speeches, especially on radio. In Rwanda, where at least one-third of the population is illiterate, radio has a very prominent function in this respect.

What is freedom of speech worth if a genocide is prepared and committed in its name? The subject of this chapter is the fine line between freedom of speech and protection against atrocities. It deals with crimes against humanity induced in part by words. If words have the potential to enable and indeed to induce mass murder then at what point do words start to be murder instruments?

The answers to this question differ in the various legal cultures, reflecting the individual histories of states. In Germany, for example, denial of the Holocaust is with good reason liable to prosecution, while it is – comprehensibly as well – not in most other countries. As regards incitement to genocide in international criminal law, the judgments of the ICTR answer that question by taking into account the standard of incitement jurisprudence developed worldwide. In this text, I will address the legal findings of the Arusha based tribunal, focusing on the criteria used by the judges to define the elements of the crime.

Direct and public incitement to commit genocide is expressly defined as a specific crime, punishable as such, pursuant to Article 2(3)(c) of the Statute of the International Criminal Tribunal for Rwanda.

The first definition of the elements of this crime was established by Trial Chamber I in the judgment against Jean Paul Akayesu. This judgment was historic the day it was delivered, on 2 September 1998. It was the first judgment in international criminal law that convicted a defendant with the crime of genocide and direct and public incitement to commit genocide. Among its most important legal findings is the decision that the crime of direct and public incitement to commit genocide is punishable even if the genocide in question is never actually committed or even attempted.[2] By doing so, the judges acknowledged that words alone can have the effect of bullets. The inciters of Rwanda's genocide were found guilty for their words *and* deeds as well as for their words *as* deeds.[3]

---

1   One of the most disturbing propaganda publications was seen by President Habyarimana as proof of Rwanda's 'freedom of the press' and therefore he championed their publication: 'The Hutu Ten Commandments'. It reads like an instruction for the state of mind mentioned above. The most often quoted commandment said: 'Hutus must stop having mercy on the Tutsis.' Gourevitch, P (1998), *We wish to inform you that tomorrow we will be killed with our families* (New York: Farrar, Straus and Giroux).

2   *Prosecutor v Akayesu* (Case No. ICTR-96-4-T) 2 September 1998, paras. 561–562.

3   MacKinnon, C.A. (2004), 'International Decisions: *Prosecutor v Nahimana, Barayagwiza & Ngeze (American Journal of International Law)*'; Butler, J. (1997), *Excitable*

The Trial Chamber found that Akayesu incited genocide by leading and addressing a public gathering in Taba on 19 April 1994, during which he urged the population to unite to eliminate what he referred to as the 'sole enemy': the accomplices of the 'Inkotanyi' – a derogatory reference to Tutsis. That was understood to be a call to kill the Tutsis in general.[4]

The judges started their legal finding recalling 'the most famous conviction for incitement to commit crimes of international dimension'. The International Military Tribunal in Nuremberg sentenced Julius Streicher for the virulently anti-Semitic articles that he had published in his weekly newspaper *Der Stürmer*. The Nuremberg Tribunal found that: 'Streicher's incitement to murder and extermination, at the time when Jews in the East were being killed under the most horrible conditions, clearly constitutes persecution on political and racial grounds in connection with War Crimes, as defined by the Charter, and constitutes a Crime against Humanity'.[5] The ICTR Chamber examined the Genocide Convention and stated that the delegates 'agreed to expressly spell out direct and public incitement to commit genocide as a specific crime, in particular, because of its critical role in the planning of a genocide, with the delegate from the USSR stating in this regard that 'it was impossible that hundreds of thousands of people should commit so many crimes unless they had been incited to do so and unless the crimes had been premeditated and carefully organized'.[6] However, it is useful to call attention to the fact that the drafters of the Genocide Convention could not agree to criminalize hate speech. A Russian proposal intending to include all forms of propaganda as punishable hate speech was dismissed.[7] With regard to the 'direct' element of the crime the rejection of including hate speech still causes legal problems, as perpetrators may use this argument.

To define the elements of the crime of direct and public incitement, the judges focused on specific incitement definitions both under Common and Civil law. While under Common law systems incitement tends to be viewed as a particular form of punishable criminal participation, in Civil law systems it is most often treated as a form of complicity. In some Civil law countries, provocation, which is similar to incitement, is a specific form of participation in an offence.[8] The Chamber recalled that incitement is defined in Common law systems as encouraging or persuading another to commit an offence. One line of authority in Common law would also view threats or other forms of pressure as a form of incitement. Civil law systems punish direct and public incitement assuming the form of provocation, which is defined as an act intended to directly provoke another to commit a crime or a misdemeanour through speeches, shouting or threats, or any other means of audiovisual communication. Such a provocation, as defined under Civil law, is made up of the same elements as

<hr>

Speech – a politics of the perfomative (New York: Routledge).

4   *Prosecutor v Akayesu, supra*, note 2, para. 673.

5   *Prosecutor v Akayesu, supra*, note 2, para. 550.

6   Ad Hoc Committee on Genocide, 6th Meeting, UN ESCOR, UN Doc. E/AC.25/SR. 15 (1948).

7   See for the Genocide Convention's drafting history: Schabas, W.A. (2000), 'Hate speech in Rwanda – The road to Genocide', *MacGill Law Journal*.

8   *Prosecutor v Akayesu, supra*, note 2, para. 552.

direct and public incitement to commit genocide as those covered by Article 2 of the Statute, that is to say it is both direct and public.

The Chamber stated that the public element of incitement to commit genocide 'may be better appreciated in light of two factors: the place where the incitement occurred and whether or not assistance was selective or limited'.[9] A line of authority commonly followed in Civil law systems regards words as being public when they are spoken aloud in a place that is public by definition. According to the International Law Commission, public incitement is characterized by a call for criminal action to a number of individuals in a public place or to members of the general public at large by such means as the mass media, for example, radio or television.

The crucial element of the crime is the 'direct' element of incitement. It was and still is the main point of discussion, as mentioned above. 'Direct' literally means 'explicit'. Ambiguous phrases and expressions that are open to various interpretations are rarely direct in the above sense, as they tend to merely imply their meaning. Under a strictly dogmatic approach, it is difficult to subsume such phrases under direct incitement.[10] The Chamber's approach took into account that the law has to deal with a wide variety of issues, many of them of great complexity. It is inevitable that this results in a development of a vocabulary of technical terms, what many would call legal jargon. In other words: Judges must give effect to the grammatical and ordinary or, where appropriate, the technical meaning of words in the general context of a statute. That is exactly what Trial Chamber I did. It established a workable definition of direct incitement.

The Chamber stated that incitement is direct where it assumes a direct form and specifically provokes another to engage in a criminal act. More than mere vague or indirect suggestion is necessary to constitute direct incitement. The judges argued 'However, the Chamber is of the opinion that the direct element of incitement should be viewed in the light of its cultural and linguistic content. Indeed, a particular speech may be perceived as "direct" in one country, and not so in another, depending on the audience.' The Chamber further recalled that incitement might be direct, and nonetheless implicit.[11]

The Chamber came to the conclusion that in order to be able to come to an exact evaluation of a speech it is necessary to 'consider on a case-by-case basis whether, in light of the culture of Rwanda and the specific circumstances of the instant case, acts of incitement can be viewed as direct or not, by focusing mainly on the issue of whether the persons for whom the message was intended immediately grasped the implication thereof.'[12]

Applying the standards and definitions it developed, the Chamber found that 'it has been established that Akayesu clearly urged the population to unite in order to eliminate what he termed the sole enemy: the accomplices of the Inkotanyi, that the population understood Akayesu's call as one to kill the Tutsi'. The judges were

---

9   *Ibid.*, para. 556.

10   The statutory interpretation in civil law does not allow an interpretation of criminal law that goes beyond the plain or literal meaning of the legal text.

11   *Ibid.*

12   *Ibid.*

satisfied beyond a reasonable doubt that, by his speeches, Akayesu had the intent to directly create a particular state of mind in his audience necessary to lead to the destruction of the Tutsi group.[13]

The next person who was convicted for the crime of incitement was Jean Kambanda. Kambanda is the first head of government to be convicted and punished for genocide and direct and public incitement to commit genocide. In his guilty plea, Jean Kambanda acknowledged that as Prime Minister of the Interim Government of Rwanda from 8 April 1994–17 July 1994, he was head of the 20 member Council of Ministers and exercised *de jure* authority and control over the members of his government. The Chamber stated that Jean Kambanda acknowledged that in his capacity as Prime Minister, he gave clear support to Radio Television Libre des Mille Collines (RTLM), with the knowledge that it was a radio station whose broadcasts incited killing, the commission of serious bodily or mental harm to, and persecution of Tutsi and moderate Hutu. On this occasion, speaking on this radio station, Jean Kambanda, as Prime Minister, encouraged the RTLM to continue to incite the massacres of the Tutsi civilian population, specifically stating that this radio station was 'an indispensable weapon in the fight against the enemy'.[14]

Kambanda further admitted that in his particular role of making public engagements in the name of the government, he addressed public meetings, and the media, at various places in Rwanda directly and publicly inciting the population to commit acts of violence against Tutsi and moderate Hutu. He acknowledged uttering the incendiary phrase, which was subsequently repeatedly broadcast: 'You refuse to give your blood to your country and the dogs drink it for nothing.' Again, this phrase shows the problem raised by the inevitable ambiguity of human language. Kambanda acknowledged that the content of the phrase was meant to incite. Thus, the Trial Chamber simply stated that Kambanda's speech satisfied the Akayesu standard.

The third person to be convicted was George Ruggiu, a Belgian. He was a social worker who worked for the Belgian Social Security Administration. While in Rwanda, the accused worked as a journalist and broadcaster for RTLM radio from 6 January 1994–14 July 1994. In his guilty plea he assumed full responsibility for all the relevant acts alleged in the indictment. He admitted 'that all broadcasts were directed towards rallying the population against the "enemy", the RPF and those who were considered to be allies of the RPF, regardless of their ethnic background'.[15] He admitted that RTLM broadcasts generally referred to those considered being RPF allies as *RPF 'accomplices'*. The Trial Chamber found that the meaning of this term gradually expanded to include the civilian Tutsi population and Hutu politicians opposed to the Interim Government. Ruggiu stated that in the months following his arrival in Rwanda, he noticed changes in the Rwandan political scene. The country was slipping senselessly into further violence against a background of increasing ethnic problems and rifts. The trial Chamber argued that the widespread use of the term 'Inyenzi' conferred the *de facto* meaning of 'persons to be killed'. Within the context of the civil war in 1994, the term 'Inyenzi' became synonymous with the

13 *Prosecutor v Akayesu, supra*, note 2, para. 559.
14 *Prosecutor v Kambanda* (ICTR 97-23-S), para. 39(vii).
15 *Prosecutor v Ruggiu* (ICTR-97-32-I), para. 44.

term 'Tutsi'. Ruggiu confirmed this interpretation. He acknowledges that the word 'Inyenzi' as used in a certain socio-political context, came to designate the Tutsis as 'persons to be killed'. Ruggiu admitted that as part of the move to encourage 'civil defence', he made a public appeal to the population on several occasions to 'go to work'. The phrase 'go to work' is a literal translation of the Rwandan expression that Phocas Habimana, Manager of the RTLM, expressly instructed the accused to use during his broadcasts. With time, this expression came to clearly signify 'go fight against members of the RPF and their accomplices'. With the passage of time, the expression came to mean 'go kill the Tutsis and Hutu political opponents of the interim government'.

Again, the speeches and broadcasts given by Ruggiu did not require an intense analysis by the Trial Chamber. However, the Trial Chamber stated that the legal questions concerning an incitement conviction were 'extensively discussed in *Prosecutor v Akayesu*'.[16] Further, the Chamber noted that 'in the instant case, the accused's acts constitute public incitement. His messages were broadcast in a media forum and to members of the general public'.[17]

The fourth incitement judgment was delivered on 1 December 2003 convicting Juvénal Kajelijeli. *The Accused* was a founder and leader of Interahamwe in the Mukingo commune from 1991 to July 1994. During meetings Kajelijeli made speeches inciting his audience who were predominantly members of MRND and Hutus, to assault, rape and exterminate the Tutsi who were excluded from such meetings on account of their ethnicity.[18] He instructed a crowd during a meeting to 'kill and exterminate all those people in Rwankeri' and 'to start to work'. As Kajelijeli used clear and non-ambiguous phrases there was no need to exhaustively analyse his speeches. There simply is no clearer phrase to constitute direct incitement than to ask people to go and exterminate people. A phrase like this can without doubt be subsumed under the legal definition developed by the Tribunal in the Akayesu decision.

One of the most complex trials of the ICTR was the Media trial that opened in October 2000 and ended on 22 August 2003 after 230 trial days. Trial Chamber I found Jean-Bosco Barayagwiza, Ferdinand Nahimana and Hassan Ngeze guilty of genocide, direct and public incitement to commit genocide, conspiracy to commit genocide, persecution and extermination as crimes against humanity. The judgment is more than 350 pages long of which 300 are dedicated to a detailed description of how the three Rwandan media leaders acted and how they used their positions to help to kill the Tutsi. Appeals are pending and the Appeals judgment is not expected before next year.

In 1992, Nahimana and others founded a comité d'initiative to set up the company known as Radio Télévision Libre des Mille Collines. Jean-Bosco Barayagwiza was a member of the committee which organized the founding of RTLM. During this time, he also held the post of Director of Political Affairs in the Ministry of Foreign Affairs,

---

16 *Prosecutor v Ruggiu* (ICTR-97-32-I), para. 13.

17 *Ibid.*, para. 17.

18 *Prosecutor v Kajelijeli* (ICTR-98-44 A-T), para. 856.

while Hassan Ngeze worked as a journalist, and in 1990, founded the newspaper Kangura and held the post of Editor-in-Chief.

The media, particularly RTLM radio, were a key tool used by extremists within the political parties to mobilize and incite the population to commit the massacres. 'Radio hate' or 'Radio Machete', as the radio was called, had a large audience in Rwanda and became an effective propaganda instrument. RTLM vigorously pursued ethnic hatred and violence. In its broadcasts journalists encouraged setting up roadblocks and congratulated perpetrators of massacres of the Tutsis at these roadblocks. They continued to call upon the population, particularly the military and the *Interahamwe* militia, to finish off the 1959 revolution.

Kangura means 'to wake others up'. It was a widely circulated newspaper. The most impressive description of the editor's state of mind and intention gives a cartoon that was first published in another newspaper but picked up by Kangura's editor Hassan Ngeze and republished in Kangura. It shows the editor himself with a psychotherapist who is asking him what he is sick of. And Ngeze answers: 'Tutsi, Tutsi, Tutsi'. Ngeze described Tutsi people as 'hypocrites, thieves and killers'. The Trial Chamber found – amongst other things – that Kangura suggested that 'Tutsi women intentionally use their sexuality to lure Hutu men into liaisons in order to promote the ethnic dominance of the Tutsi over the Hutu'.[19]

The Media judgment is the first to consider the role of mass media in the preparation and execution of a genocide since the Streicher conviction by the Nuremberg International Military Tribunal in 1946. The ICTR Trial Chamber developed important principles with respect to the conflict between hate speech and freedom of speech in the context of mass media. Taking the Akayesu standard as a base, and applying specific elements, it finally established a way of defining at what point the fine line between incitement and freedom of speech is crossed. It also made clear that there is no easy recipe and that there are many factors that need to be considered. The Chamber recalled the important protections of international law of the right of freedom of expression and noted that some of the communications cited by the Prosecution were protected, for example an interview of Barayagwiza's broadcast on RTLM, which is described as 'a moving personal account of his experience of discrimination as a Hutu'. The judgment held that it was 'critical to distinguish between the discussion of ethnic consciousness and the promotion of ethnic hatred' and that some broadcasts fell squarely within the scope of protected speech.

The Chamber stressed the crucial point it was dealing with: 'Unlike Akayesu and others found by the Tribunal to have engaged in incitement through their own speech, the accused in this case used the print and radio media systematically, not only for their own words but for the words of many others, for the collective communication of ideas and for the mobilization of the population on a grand scale'. It pointed out, and I believe this to be important, that it needs to consider the contents of broadcasts and articles as well as the responsibilities inherent in ownership and institutional control over media.

---

19 *Prosecutor v Barayagwiza, Nahimana and Ngeze* (ICTR-99-52-T), para. 211.

The Trial Chamber not only cited the Streicher case but also referred to the judgment of Hans Fritsche, a broadcaster during the Third Reich, who had a weekly radio programme. Unlike Streicher he was acquitted. The reason given for his acquittal was basically that he did not know about the extermination of the Jews, that he tried to avoid anti-Semitism in his programme and that he had actually refused requests from Goebbels to incite antagonism and arouse hatred. The main argument remained that he had no control over the formulation of propaganda policies. Thus, he was merely a conduit to the press of directives passed down to him.[20]

The Trial Chamber also recalled the UN Conventions such as the Universal Declaration of Human Rights and the International Covenant on Civil and Political Rights (ICCPR) and the International Convention of the Elimination of all Forms of Racial Discrimination (CERD).[21] It could be said that those international treaties complemented the Genocide Convention.[22] The essence of these conventions could be described as the frame for balancing freedom of speech and protection against racist discrimination. The Chamber noted that freedom of expression and freedom from discrimination are not incompatible principles of law. Hate speech is not protected speech under international law. In fact, governments have an obligation under the International Covenant on Civil and Political Rights to prohibit any advocacy of national, racial or religious hatred that constitutes incitement to discrimination, hostility or violence. Similarly, the Convention on the Elimination of all Forms of Racial Discrimination requires the prohibition of propaganda activities that promote and incite racial discrimination.[23] The Chamber gave an almost worldwide overview over domestic law on freedom of expression and protection against discrimination. A great number of countries around the world, including Rwanda, have domestic laws that ban advocacy of discriminatory hate, in recognition of the danger it represents and the harm it causes.

The Trial Chamber cited a decision of the Human Rights Committee. In the case of *Robert Faurisson v France*, the Human Right Committee considered the meaning of the term incitement in Article 20(2) of the ICCPR. Faurisson argued that his right of freedom of expression was violated because he was convicted in France for publishing articles in which he doubted the existence of gas chambers.[24] The Human Right Committee came to the conclusion that the restriction on publication of these views did not violate right to freedom of expression in Article 19. In addition, it stated that it was indeed necessary to restrict this kind of speech under Article 19(3).[25]

The Chamber further examined six decisions of the European Court for Human Rights. Under the European Convention on Human Rights restricting speech is justified 'for the protection of the reputation or rights of others'. In *Jersild v Denmark*[26] the

---

20 *Ibid.*, para. 980.

21 *Ibid.*, para. 984.

22 Schabas *supra*, note 7.

23 *Prosecutor v Barayagwiza, Nahimana and Ngeze, supra*, note 19, para. 1074.

24 *Ibid.*, para. 988.

25 *Ibid.*, *Robert Faurisson v France*, CCPR/C/58/D/550/1993 (1996).

26 *Ibid.*; *Jersild v Denmark*, European Court of Human Rights (EHCR), Judgment of 22 August 1994.

Court overturned the conviction of a journalist who had interviewed members of a racist youth group. The main argument for the ruling was that the introduction of the programme 'clearly disassociated' the journalist from the persons he interviewed. But there were two dissenting votes stating that the conviction should be upheld as 'not enough was said in the program to condemn the racist views'. Thus, the background of a speech is a factor that helps to define the directness of an ambiguous speech. Another potential justification for speech restriction is national security concerns. Article 10 of the European Convention protects the right to express support for, and to disseminate expression of support for, political goals that are identified with violent means used in an effort to attain them. In *Zana v Turkey*, the Court considered that the defendant not only made contradictory and ambiguous comments but had a certain standing in society as he was a former mayor. In the context of ongoing attacks his statements 'had to be regarded as likely to exacerbate an already explosive situation in that region'.[27] The other Turkish cases cited by the Trial Chamber all allow us to conclude that a decision about speech restriction requires us to consider the 'need for the closest scrutiny' in cases involving opposition parties. The Court stressed that criticism of the government should be given additional latitude. Furthermore, the Court argued that where statements incite to violence, there is a 'wider margin of appreciation' for interference with freedom of expression.

The Trial Chamber also focused on the impact as a defining factor: A book, for example, is a literary work rather than mass media, a factor limiting the potential impact on national security and public order.[28] In *Sürek and Özdemir v Turkey* where journalists made statements supporting the PKK the Court expressed that 'particular caution is called for when consideration is being given to the publication of the views of representatives of organisations which resort to violence against the State lest the media become a vehicle for the dissemination of hate speech and the promotion of violence. At the same time, where such views cannot be categorised as such, contracting States cannot with reference to the protection of territorial integrity or national security or the prevention of crime or disorder restrict the right of the public to be informed of them by bringing the weight of the criminal law to bear on the media.'[29] Nevertheless, five judges concurred stating that 'less attention should be given to the form of the words used and more attention to the general context in which the words were used and their likely impact'. The key questions, as the Trial Chamber cited, are: 'Was the language intended to inflame or incite to violence?' and 'Was there a real and genuine risk that it might actually do so?'

In *Sürek v Turkey* the Court addressed the question of shareholder responsibility. While the defendant argued that he should be exonerated from any criminal liability for the content of statements made by others and published by him, the Court found 'he was the owner and as such had the power to shape the editorial direction of the review. For that reason, he was vicariously subject to the duties and responsibilities which the review's editorial and journalistic staff undertake in the collection and dissemination of information to the public and which assume an even greater

---

27 *Ibid.*, para. 994, *Zana v Turkey*, EHCR, Judgment of 25 November 1997.

28 *Ibid.*, para. 996, *Arslan v Turkey*, ECHR, Judgment of 8 July 1999.

29 *Ibid.*, para. 997, *Sürek and Özdemir v Turkey*, ECHR, Judgment of 8 July 1999.

importance in situations of conflict and tension'.[30] The Chamber used the rulings of these cases as a basis and concluded: Hate speech expressing ethnic and other forms of discrimination violates the norm of customary international law prohibiting discrimination. Within this norm of customary law, the prohibition of advocacy of discrimination and incitement to violence is increasingly important as the power of the media increases and is increasingly acknowledged.

To recapitulate: to decide whether a pronouncement constitutes the crime of direct and public incitement to commit genocide it is necessary to define the term 'direct'. The Trial Chamber I presented in detail the factors that need to be considered to assess ambiguous Media statement as direct incitement.

These factors help to refine the sensitive criteria of crime 'directness'. An ambiguous pronouncement may only be evaluated as direct incitement when all of these factors have been considered cumulatively. The application of these criteria allows an exact evaluation of statements which are ambiguous, to find out if a statement is protected speech or discrimination. To legally define 'direct', a court has to take into account the background of the pronouncement, the tone used by the speaker, his or her standing in society. Another important legal finding of the Trial Chamber is that the speaker's intent allows to evaluate the pronouncement in question. If the speaker has a genocidal intent, this intent indicates that his statement is more likely to be incitement to commit genocide. On the other hand, when the pronouncement was made to inform, it does not constitute incitement. In the context 'incitement to commit genocide', therefore, the judges focus on intent, content and consequence. In addition to what was ruled in the Akayesu case the Trial chamber developed these additional criteria to deal with the complexity of media pronouncements. The Chamber for example stated that the power of the human voice adds a quality and dimension beyond words to the message conveyed. It found that 'the radio heightened the sense of fear, the sense of danger and the sense of urgency giving rise to the need for action by listeners. The denigration of Tutsi ethnicity was augmented by the visceral scorn coming out of the airwaves – the ridiculing laugh and the nasty sneer. These elements greatly amplified the impact of RTLM broadcasts'.[31]

The assessment of evidence followed those principles and was done in a scrupulous manner, thus, in some cases, coming to the finding that some broadcasts were actually intended to inform. When analysing articles and editorials of Kangura, the Chamber differentiated between 'information about Tutsi privilege and Hutu disadvantage (that) was conveyed in a manner that appears as though intended to raise consciousness regarding ethnic discrimination against the Hutu' and other articles which incorporated messages of ethnic hatred.

The UN inactivity in 1994 was the organization's most painful failure since its founding. The International Criminal Tribunal for Rwanda was established – amongst other reasons – to restore the tarnished reputation of the UN. The judgments presented in this text are part of that task. It is also helpful to bear in mind that the principles and standards developed by the ICTR have the potential to impact

---

30 *Ibid.*, para. 999, *Sürek v Turkey (No. 1)*, ECHR, Judgment of 8 July 1999.
31 *Ibid.*, para. 1032.

and influence both international and domestic law. The ruling that hate speech can constitute the crime of genocide as well as the crime of direct and public incitement to commit genocide is critical.

The media judgment has been praised as well as criticized. The critics claim that the established definition of incitement is too broad and endangers freedom of speech but it does in fact comply with the strictest standard of protection by the First Amendment of the United States Constitution. Therefore, most legal scholars agree that it will serve as a workable guideline. Though some points of the judgment, which were not address in this text – such as causation or the discussion about incitement being an inchoate offence – seem rather unclear, it does not constitute a serious risk of doctrinal abuse in the future. I agree with those who point out that the judgment's reasoning allows for broad conviction in circumstances as extreme as Rwanda's while simultaneously establishing limits for less atrocious situations. It presents an example for how courts and tribunals should undertake inquiries concerning questions of intent, as well as circumstances, content, potential impact and tone.

The conflict incitement jurisdiction involves questions that cannot be answered by logic alone. The clash of freedom of speech and protection against atrocities is fundamentally about a collision of responsibility and freedom. How we respond to this clash is of existential significance to humanity on both global and local scales. One needs to keep in mind that although it is a legal discourse it is in fact everything but abstract or merely symbolic. The conflict between freedom of speech and protection against atrocities is not a paradox but a dilemma. It cannot be solved easily. One may think, with Ingeborg Bachmann 'history teaches but it does not have pupils'. The judgments can be seen not only as a result of hard work but also of the legal community's learning process. They have a clear message: that scrupulous legal argumentation and meticulous examination of law and facts have the power to protect not only freedom of speech but freedom from atrocities. Ideally, the judgments will also have an effect on the collective conscience in terms of moral and social values and help to prevent genocide in the future.

Chapter 12

The Prohibition of Genocide under the Legal Instruments of the International Criminal Court[1]

Tuiloma Neroni Slade

... at all periods of history genocide has inflicted great losses on humanity ...[2]

This is a personal contribution setting out my own views and in no way suggesting what the Court, or the other Judges, may consider or do.

Introduction

Article VI of the 1948 Convention on the Prevention and Punishment of Genocide (the Genocide Convention) provides that persons charged with genocide shall be tried 'by a competent tribunal of the State in the territory of which the act was committed, or by such international penal tribunal as may have jurisdiction'. Now, more than 50 years after the Genocide Convention came into force, a permanent International Criminal Court (ICC) with the ability to try an *individual*[3] for the crime of genocide has been created. The ICC carries with it great promise for international justice and has the potential to play a pivotal role in the strengthening, refining and developing of international criminal law and the law of genocide in particular. But it also faces enormous challenges, including how to exercise its jurisdiction over the most serious crimes of concern to the international community.

This chapter proposes to examine how the crime of genocide has been incorporated into the jurisdiction of the ICC through the Court's primary legal instruments, the Rome Statute and the Elements of Crimes; and to highlight some of the issues that this incorporation may raise and the possible impact on the future development of the crime of genocide at a national and international level.

---

1 I am deeply indebted to Ms Leanne McKay, former intern in the Pre-Trial Division of the ICC, for the assistance she gave me in the preparation of this chapter.

2 Preamble, *Convention on the Prevention and Punishment of Genocide*, adopted by Resolution 260 (III) A of the United Nations General Assembly on 9 December 1948.

3 The Court shall have jurisdiction over natural persons: article 25.1, Rome Statute.

The Rome Statute and the Convention

The inclusion of the crime of genocide in the jurisdiction of the ICC, and the adoption of the Convention definition, was probably a foregone conclusion given the fact that for many delegations at the Rome conference in 1998 there was much more to commend acceptance of what had been recognised by the International Law Commission, the International Court of Justice (ICJ) and the statutes of the *ad hoc* International Criminal Tribunal for the former Yugoslavia (ICTY) and the International Criminal Tribunal for Rwanda (ICTR), as part of customary international law.

But it would be clear that there could be issues of contention that may arise from the manner of incorporation. Unlike the statutes of the *ad hoc* Tribunals, for instance, the Rome Statute does not reproduce article III of the Genocide Convention, which lists the various forms of punishable criminal participation. Instead, the forms of criminal participation which entail individual criminal liability are provided for separately in the Rome Statute under article 25, and in a way intended to reflect article III of the Convention. The genocide-specific article 25.3 (e), for example, allows for a person to be responsible and liable for punishment for 'directly and publicly' inciting others to commit genocide, in the way as is found in article III (c) of the Genocide Convention.

However, it has been suggested that article III has not been entirely incorporated, there being a material difference in the 'conspiracy' provision in article III (b) of the Convention (which uses the term 'conspiracy') compared to the provision under article 25.3 (d) of the Rome Statute. Under article III (b), the Convention seems to have adopted the common law approach, by which the offence is completed when there is conspiracy, whether or not that offence is actually committed.[4] In contrast, article 25.3 (d) of the Rome Statute provides for criminal responsibility if the person 'contributes' to the 'commission or attempted commission of such a crime by a group of persons acting with a common purpose', adopting more of the civil law standard that requires the offence to be completed only when the underlying crime is also committed or attempted. Whether 'contributes' bears the same meaning as 'conspiracy' would be another issue. But, at any rate, commentators have noted that the matter was not fully debated in Rome, and perhaps the inconsistency is inadvertent.[5] The outcome, it would seem, is that a different and stricter approach may have been set under the Rome Statute.

Is Genocide of 'Special Status'?

The debate whether genocide is the 'crime of crimes' seems to have been settled by the Appeal Chamber of the ICTY (in the case of *Kayishema* and *Ruzindana*), with the clarification that 'there is no hierarchy of crimes under the Statute, and that all

4   See Schabas W.A. (1999), 'Article 6: Genocide' in O. Triffterer (ed.), *Commentary on the Rome Statute of the International Criminal Court*, (Baden-Baden, Nomos Verlagsgesellschaft), 115–116.
5   Triffterer, *supra*, note 3, 116.

of the crimes specified therein are 'serious violations of international humanitarian law'.[6]

The ICC system does not confer any obvious 'special status' to the crime of genocide. Under the Rome Statute, genocide is *one* of the listed most serious crimes of concern to the international community as a whole, and is equalised in the Statute under article 5, although it does come first in the definitions of each crime within the Court's jurisdiction, and thus arguably retaining some primacy. Further, by virtue of article 77 of the Rome Statute, the same penalties are applicable for persons convicted of any of the crimes under the Court's jurisdiction, including genocide. Article 25 also, which deals with individual criminal responsibility, has general application to all ICC crimes, although there is the special inclusion of the incitement clause under paragraph 3 (e) in respect of genocide.

Elements of Crimes

The Elements of Crimes are a special feature of the ICC system. They were adopted for the purpose of assisting the Court in the interpretation and application of the definition of genocide and of the other core crimes under the Rome Statute. There was widespread agreement that the Genocide Convention provided strong guidance, and that this be reflected in the Elements.

Some general observations may be made of some of the elements, as follows.

Genocide by Killing

The Elements is an innovation in international practice; and it has introduced innovations to the constituent features of the crime of genocide.

The act of 'killing members of the group' referred to in article 6 (a) of the Statute has been expanded upon in the Elements to explicitly cover the killing of one or more persons. In addition, a footnote to this Element states that the term 'killing' is interchangeable with the term 'caused death'. Both of these notions reflect developments in the case law of the *ad hoc* Tribunals,[7] *Akayesu* in particular.

Some commentators[8] have disputed that article II of the Genocide Convention permits such an expansion, noting the reference to 'killing of members (plural) of the group' and have noted that this broadening of the scope of genocide could be seen to be inconsistent with the definition enshrined in customary international law and the Genocide Convention.

---

6 *Prosecutor v Kayishema and Ruzindana* (Case No. ICTR-95-1-A), Appeals Chamber, 1 June 2001, p. 367.

7 *Akayesu*: that the act of killing must be committed against one or several individuals ...'; and *Semanza*: that 'the prosecutor must show the following elements: (1) the perpetrator intentionally killed one or more members of the group ...'.

8 Schabas W.A. (2000), *Genocide in International Law*, (Cambridge: Cambridge University Press), 158.

Genocide by Causing Serious Bodily or Mental Harm to Members of the Group

The element relating to the causing of 'serious bodily or mental harm' to members of the group (article 6 (b)) includes footnote 3, which states that the conduct may include, but is not necessarily restricted to, 'acts of torture, rape, sexual violence or inhuman and degrading treatment'. This footnote is also based on the case law of the *ad hoc* Tribunals.[9] The extension of the notion of bodily and mental harm to cover especially rape and other acts of sexual violence would be in line with the emphasis given to these matters in the provisions and scheme of the Rome Statute.

As the decisions of the Tribunals have explained, the harm need not necessarily be permanent and/or irremediable, although this point might need to be confirmed or otherwise pronounced upon by the ICC Judges in view of the fact that both the Elements and Rome Statute are silent on the matter.

It is important also to note that this particular element demonstrates the affirmation in paragraph 9 of the general introduction to the Elements that a particular conduct may constitute one or more crimes under the Court's jurisdiction, i.e., torture can be a crime against humanity, a war crime and, in the appropriate context and with the necessary intent, could also amount to genocide.

Genocide by Deliberately Inflicting Conditions of Life Calculated to Bring about Physical Destruction

Footnote 4 to this element states that 'conditions of life' may include, but is not necessarily restricted to 'deliberate deprivation of resources indispensable for survival, such as food or medical services, or systematic expulsion from homes'. This footnote expands upon the meaning of the phrase found in the *Akayesu* decision (where the Chamber stated that 'deliberately inflicting on the group conditions of life calculated to bring about its physical destruction in whole or in part' should be construed as 'methods of destruction by which the perpetrator does not necessarily intend to immediately kill the members of the group' but which are ultimately aimed at their physical destruction, such methods including, for instance, subsistence diet, systematic expulsion from their homes and deprivation of essential medical supplies below a minimum vital standard).[10]

It is not obvious whether the use in this element of the term 'calculated' creates a mental element, or whether the use of the term relates not so much to the mind or calculations of the perpetrator but more to the character of the measures or conditions of life imposed. It would seem that the matter has been left to the Judges to decide upon the character of the element and its interpretation and implications.

---

    9   *Akayesu*: that the crime of genocide includes 'acts of torture, be they bodily or mental, inhumane or degrading treatment, persecution', that when rape and other acts of sexual violence are used as methods to destroy a protected group by causing serious bodily or mental harm to the members of the group, it may constitute genocide; and followed in the *Krstic* case.

    10 *Akayesu*, pp. 505–506.

The Common Elements

The three common elements for each of the five forms of genocide covered by the Rome Statute are:

1. Such person or persons (who suffered from the listed acts of genocide) belonged to a particular national, ethnical, racial or religious group;
2. The perpetrator intended to destroy, in whole or in part, that national, ethnical, racial or religious group, as such;
3. The conduct took place in the context of a manifest pattern of similar conduct directed against the group or was conduct that could itself effect such destruction.

As to the first common element, it should be noted that political groups remain unprotected. In the Rome negotiations, some States had suggested enlarging the list of groups protected to include social and political groups but this was opposed by other States. Part of the fear was that expansion of the list of groups would go beyond customary international law and that this might open the possibility, for instance, of the ICC and the ICJ rendering conflicting decisions on the same set of facts. It was noted that crimes committed against these additional groups could be considered crimes against humanity and thus the seriousness of such crimes would still be recognised.

The second common element requiring the intent to 'destroy, in whole or part' merely repeats the requirement stated in article 6 of the Statute with no expansion or additional interpretation provided. The way in which the second common element will be interpreted however, is likely to be affected by the inclusion of the third common element, next to be discussed.

Contextual Element

The third common element introduces a contextual setting, i.e., the requirement that 'the conduct took place in the context of a manifest pattern of similar conduct directed against that group or was conduct that could itself effect such destruction'.

Article 9.3 of the Rome Statute states that the Elements shall be consistent with the Statute, but it would appear that by virtue of the third common element, the drafters of the Elements of Crimes have introduced a requirement not stated, perhaps not envisaged, in the Statute, or for that matter in the Genocide Convention.

Neither article 6 of the Rome Statute nor the Genocide Convention expressly requires the existence of a plan or policy to destroy a group. The *ad hoc* Tribunals have ruled that proof of a plan or policy is not a legal ingredient of the crime although admitting that, in fact genocidal acts are seldom isolated or sporadic events and are normally part of a widespread policy, often approved of or condoned by governmental authorities.[11]

---

11 See *Kayishema and Ruzindana*, 94 and 276. 'Although a specific plan to destroy does not constitute an element of genocide, it would appear that it is not easy to carry out a

Theoretically then, according to the case law of the *ad hoc* Tribunals, and also from a reading of the Genocide Convention, an individual acting alone may still perpetrate the crime of genocide, provided he or she intends to destroy a protected group in whole or in part. On the other hand, the inclusion of this common element would seem to limit the risk that an individual might ever be charged before the ICC with genocide in relation to isolated acts or events of limited criminal magnitude.

The Introduction to the Elements for article 6 includes three additional notes to the contextual element requirement.

Firstly, the term 'in the context of' is defined as including the 'initial acts in an emerging pattern', thus ensuring that the initial perpetrators of genocide may still be covered by the crime of genocide. This provision would have practical importance in catching the initiators of evil deeds, for they are as culpable as the later perpetrators of genocidal acts when the 'pattern' has been established. Secondly, the term 'manifest' is specified as being an objective qualification, which was introduced to avoid the potential situation of a 'pattern' referring to a few isolated crimes occurring over, say, a period of years. And finally there is reference to the general mental element required under article 30, stating that knowledge of the circumstances will usually be addressed in proving specific genocidal intent, however 'the appropriate requirement, if any, for a mental element regarding this circumstance will need to be determined by the Court on a case-by-case basis'. We know from the record that there was disagreement among the States participating in the Preparatory Commission on how to deal with the mental element requirement; and the matter was left to the Court to decide. Whether 'case-by-case' is to be taken literally or might mean that the Court could decide to settle a general principle and apply the same in subsequent decisions on the authority of article 21.2, by which the Court may apply principles and rules of law as interpreted in its previous decisions is a matter that remains for determination.[12]

There might also be a problem in defining 'similar conduct'. Must the pattern be of the same form of acts, or can it consist of different acts though no less genocidal? Whilst States apparently agreed that 'similar' clearly referred to all five acts listed in article 6 and that no explanation or repetition of these acts was deemed necessary, it would seem to be an issue that remains open to interpretation.

---

genocide without such a plan, or organization ... the existence of such a plan would be strong evidence of the specific intent requirement for the crime of genocide'; *Prosecutor v. Goran Jelisic* (Case No.: IT-95-10-A) Appeals Chamber, 5 July 2001, 48: 'the existence of a plan or policy is not a legal requirement of the crime. However, in the context of proving specific intent, the existence of a plan or policy may become an important factor in most cases. The evidence may be consistent with the existence of a plan or policy, or may even show such existence, and the existence of a plan or policy may facilitate proof of the crime'; *Prosecutor v Blagojevic* (Case No.: IT-02-60-T), Trial Chamber, 17 January 2005, 656 reaffirmed the finding of the appeals chamber in *Jelisic* that the existence of a plan or policy is not a legal requirement of the crime.

12 See generally Clark R.S. (2002), 'The Mental Element in International Criminal Law: The Rome Statute of the International Criminal Court and the Elements of Offences', 12 *Criminal Law Forum*, p. 291.

In reality, it seems difficult to imagine genocide that is not planned or organised, and therefore the practical effect of this third common element might turn out to be generally limited.

However, its existence does raise some interesting questions with regards to the role of the Elements, and the issues that the Judges will need to consider when faced with conflicts between the Rome Statute, the Elements and developing customary international law.

Article 9 of the Rome Statute

Article 9 of the Statute was proposed, in part because of the concern to ensure the definitions of crimes within the subject-matter jurisdiction of the ICC conformed with the *nullum crimen sine lege* principle. To this end it was felt that the definitions and elements of crimes should be stated with clarity, precision and the specificity required by criminal law. However, while many delegations agreed that the crimes should be defined with clarity and precision not all agreed that there should be further elaboration of their constituent elements. There were also issues relating to the legal force of the Elements, and their placement, whether in the Statute, in an annex or elsewhere. It would seem that at the time of its proposal not many delegations had a completely clear idea of what 'elements' were.

According to article 9.1, the Elements is to be adopted by a two-thirds majority of the members of the Assembly of States Parties. In fact, the Elements were adopted on 9 September 2002 by consensus of the States participating in the Preparatory Commission, and to that extent it could be taken as reflecting the consensus view of the international community. It is required under article 9.3, that the Elements and amendments thereto 'shall be consistent' with the Statute. If there is inconsistency, which the Judges will need to determine, the Statute will prevail.

The wording of article 9 reflects the compromise of political negotiations. Initially, it had been proposed that the Elements 'shall be applied by the Court in reaching determinations of guilt', thus granting them the same binding force as the provisions of the Statute. But this was challenged on the grounds that it would deprive the Judges of the necessary flexibility in applying the Elements and will increase in substance the chances of unsolvable contrasts with the Statute.

Article 9.1 now states that the 'Elements of Crimes *shall assist* the Court in the interpretation and application of articles 6, 7 and 8'. This wording suggests that it is the definitions of crimes, first of all, that are to be applied, that the Court has discretion in their interpretation, and that the Elements are of the nature of guidelines intended to 'assist' the Judges and therefore not having binding force. The overall impression gathered is that the drafters of the Elements may not have been entirely faithful to their responsibility to 'assist' the Court.

Elements of Crimes and the Applicable Law (Article 21)

The relationship between article 9 and article 21 of the Statute, which deals with the applicable law of the ICC, is unclear and seems to raise further questions concerning the relationship between the Elements, the Statute and other sources of law.

Article 21 details the sources of law that the Court may rely upon in the interpretation and application of the Statute. It holds that, in the first place, the Court *shall apply*, the Statute, Elements of Crimes and its Rules of Procedure and Evidence. There is no apparent hierarchy of application of these three sources, although it is clear that ultimately the Statute takes precedence. Article 51.5, states that where there is a conflict between the Statute and the ICC Rules, the Statute prevails; and, as noted before, article 9.3, requires the Elements to be consistent with Statute. It will be for the Judges to determine whether or not there is consistency in any given situation.

The language of articles 9 and 21 import different connotations in describing the weight that must be give to the Elements. Article 9 provides that the Elements 'shall assist' the Court; and article 21 requires that the Court 'shall apply' the Elements along with the Statute and the Rules, thus adopting terminology that arguably is of a more binding nature than that used in article 9. In the context of the discussions in Rome on these provisions, article 21 can probably be read as laying down what the applicable law is and merely enumerating the various sources which the Court shall apply without defining the status of such sources. It means that it will be up to the Judges to find a reading that determines a coherent relationship between the two provisions.

With respect to the crime of genocide and its contextual element, there would also be the need to understand the relationship in light of the case law of the *ad hoc* Tribunals. In the absence of explicit reference in article 21, the case law of the *ad hoc* Tribunals could be interpreted as falling within the 'principles and rules of international law' found under article 21.1 (b), where such principles and rules are 'appropriate'. In practice it would be unlikely that the ICC Judges would fail to give the closest and the most serious consideration to the jurisprudence of the *ad hoc* Tribunals, which has had such a critical role in the development of the law and principles relating to genocide, crimes against humanity and war crimes.

At the same time, it can be expected that the experience of the *ad hoc* Tribunals will not always be beneficial, or necessarily determinative, where there is silence in the provisions or discrepancy between the Statute and the Elements. For example, does the Court have discretion in developing the original Elements of Crimes, and if so, to what extent? Article 9.2 sets out what seems to be a strict rule regarding amendments, requiring proposed amendments to be made by any State Party, the Judges acting by an absolute majority or the Prosecutor, and ultimately requiring a two thirds majority of the members of the Assembly of States Parties. This provision would seem to treat any amendments to the Elements as a matter of subsequent legislation. Arguably, such a strict rule is needed to ensure consistency with the principle of *nullum crimen sin lege* and to reflect the consent of sovereign States, which may then imply that the Court is to *apply* the law, not develop the law, nor create it.

Still, the Elements are only a guide to assist the Judges. As a product of State consensus, the Judges will undoubtedly show deference to the Elements. However, where the Judges are convinced that a particular provision of the Elements is clearly not consistent with the Statute, or not required by the Statute, I should think they must apply the Statute as they interpret it.

This possibility also raises the issue of the role of the ICC in the development of international law and norms.

Articles 10 and 22.3 of the Rome Statute are relevant here. Although distinct in terms of their scope and effect, these provisions act together, in the words of one commentator, to 'prevent the perception that the Statute would rob general international law of its power to criminalise behaviour, or would narrow the scope of any such criminalisation outside the ICC regime...'.[13] It means that the Statute does not exclusively codify or exhaust international criminal prohibitions.

Of course, this does not mean that international law outside of the Statute is irrelevant to the functioning of the ICC. On the contrary, article 21.1 (b) requires the Court to apply the rules and principles of international law; and under paragraph 3 to apply and interpret the law consistent with internationally recognised human rights standards.

Further, it seems clear that the jurisprudence of the ICC will inevitably impact on developing international law and customary international law, especially bearing in mind the fact that the *ad hoc* Tribunals will cease to exist, seemingly in the near future, leaving the ICC as the sole international Court with jurisdiction over individuals who commit genocide or other serious crimes. As such the question is raised as to what extent and how the Court should attempt to align itself with customary international law and State practice and to what extent the Court's role is one of harmonising international rules and norms.

It is clear that the Rome Statute reflects an attempt at harmonising universal principles and standards derived from the world's major legal systems and heritage in order to establish an international criminal justice system. At the same time there is also the acknowledged duty of every State to exercise its own criminal jurisdiction over those responsible for international crimes. The state of domestic law and, for instance, the incorporation of genocide definitions from the Convention and from the Rome Statute will no doubt have significance in the exercise of that jurisdiction. The authorities in my own country, Samoa, have begun work on proposed domestic legislation to implement the Rome Statute, drawn mainly from existing models and the experience of countries in my part of the world like Australia and New Zealand, but also from other Commonwealth countries.

Conclusion

From these observations, one has to acknowledge that it is too soon to tell how the Judges of the International Criminal Court might approach any of these issues, or, indeed, other issues; in particular whether, and to what extent there might be a continuation of the type of what has been seen as an 'expansive' trend observable with the jurisprudence of the *ad hoc* Tribunals.[14]

---

13 Triffterer, *supra*, note 3, p. 460.

14 See, e.g., Schabas W.A. (2005), 'The "Odious Scourge": Evolving Interpretations of the Crime of Genocide'. Paper delivered at the International Conference, Yerevan, Armenia, 20–21 April 2005.

The warning against broad reading and over-application of norms likely to risk dilution of the original prohibition of crimes has been sounded for the Tribunals.[15] Yet, there will be others who point to history and the undeniable fact of a particularly odious crime; and the need to liberate humankind from the scourge of genocide,[16] and to put an end to impunity for the sake of present and future generations.[17]

It is clearly not possible to say in advance when and how the ICC and the Judges will respond to any of the issues touched on. However, there cannot be any question of the priority and importance that must be given to the case law and jurisprudence of the ICTY and the ICTR. What can be said with certainty is that the first charge of genocide that comes before the Court will be given the closest and most serious attention by the Judges.

It is necessary also to add that in other respects the success of the Court rests, to a large extent on the willingness of States Parties, and other States, to assist and not to undermine the Court, to participate in ICC enforcement, to ensure domestic implementation, and to support the Court with its requests for co-operation.

---

15 Schabas, *ibid.*
16 Preamble, Genocide Convention.
17 Preamble, Rome Statute.

PART IV

INTERNATIONAL AND DOMESTIC PROSECUTION OF GENOCIDE

Chapter 13

ICC Investigations and a Hierarchy of Referrals: Has Genocide in Darfur been Predetermined?

Chris Gallavin

In light of the Security Council's (SC) shock referral of the Darfur situation to the International Criminal Court (ICC), and the Court's manifest preference for state self referrals I argue here that a hierarchy between the 'trigger' mechanisms of the Rome Statute of the International Criminal Court (Rome Statute) will inevitably develop. In dealing with such referrals the ICC prosecutor, and consequently the judicial arm of the Court, must be on guard against pressure to conform with the wishes of the referring body.

With a court whose credibility is so intrinsically related to its ability to secure state cooperation, the risk of political manipulation is great. As a consequence it is in the interests of the Court to secure a strong mandate before commencing an investigation and/or prosecution. Under such circumstances I contend that SC referrals will provide the Court with significant surety. Self referrals by States will likewise provide the Court with a powerful and co-operative partner. I suggest that third party referrals will, in all likelihood, be either avoided by the Prosecutor, or used in a similar way to his *proprio motu* authority, to obtain a more secure mandate by way of a self-referral or SC referral. However, if such a hierarchy of referrals were to develop, the practical opportunity for the Prosecutor to act truly independently of referring parties may be limited.

Security Council Referrals

The issue of the relationship between the SC and the Court resulted in significant controversy. In the 1994 draft statute, the SC had a controlling interest in the operation of the Office of the Prosecutor (OTP).[1] Draft Article 23 established that

---

1   1994 Draft Statute. Part 3 Jurisdiction of the Court, *Report of the International Law Commission on the work of its forty-sixth Session*, 2, May–22 July 1994, General Assembly Official Records, Forty-ninth Session, Supplement No.10 (A/49/10).

the SC, acting under Chapter VII, was able to trigger the investigatory mechanisms of the Court.[2] Paragraph (2) of the draft article provided for jurisdiction over the crime of aggression, however, the Court could only exercise jurisdiction over the crime subsequent to the SC determining that an act of aggression had taken place. Additionally, paragraph (3) stated that the ICC was prohibited from commencing a prosecution when the particular situation was, at that time, before the SC as a matter involving a threat or breach of the peace, or an act of aggression, under Chapter VII of the Charter. When commenting on the inclusion of paragraph (3) the International Law Commission stated that it was 'an acknowledgement of the priority given by Article 12 of the Charter, as well as for the need for co-ordination between the Court and the Council in such cases'.[3]

The finally agreed system of SC referral is manifest in the ability of the Council to refer situations to the Court under Article 13(b) of the Statute. The Court and SC relationship potentially widens the scope of the Court's jurisdiction as SC referrals are not limited by the provisions of Article 12. This article provides that for a State Party referral or *proprio motu* investigation to be valid the crime must have been committed by a State Party national or within the territory of a State Party. While not expressly limited to such a restriction, SC referrals are nonetheless similarly limited to a 'situation' and not an individual.

Article 16 of the Rome Statute details the final element of the Court and Council relationship. The article vests the SC with the ability to defer the Court's jurisdiction for a renewable period of 12 months. Pursuant to Article 16 such a request must be made by the SC when acting under Chapter VII of the United Nations Charter.

State Referrals

State referrals are provided for under Article 13 of the Statute and are elaborated upon in Articles 12 and 14. Article 13(a) provides for a State Party referral in accordance with Article 14. While not expressly provided for self-referrals by State Parties were, at the very least, unexpected.

The Prosecutor's Proprio Motu Authority

At the Rome Conference the question of the prosecutor's *proprio motu* authority arose as an issue closely related to the doctrines of complementarity and state

---

2   Daniel Derby has said of this provision that '… when the theoretical clutter is stripped away and realistic probability is considered, the court may never have occasion to deal with any cases except upon affirmative action by the Security Council', Derby, D. (1995), 'An International Criminal Court for the Future', 5 *Transnat'l L & Con. Probs* 307, 311.

3   Watts, A. (1999), *The International Law Commission 1949–1998, Vol. II; The Treaties*, (Oxford: Oxford University Press), 1491. Article 12 (1) of the United Nations Charter provides that '[w]hile the Security Council is exercising in respect of any dispute or situation the functions assigned to it in the present Charter, the General Assembly shall not make any recommendations with regard to that dispute or situation unless the Security Council so requests.'

sovereignty.[4] If acting under his *proprio motu* powers, and if satisfied that there are sufficient grounds to mount an investigation, the prosecutor is to seek authorization for the commencement of an investigation from the Pre-Trial Chamber.[5]

Within this request for authorization the Pre-Trial Chamber will review the evidential before the prosecutor and will also consider matters of jurisdiction and admissibility along with evidential material presented by the prosecutor in reaching a decision on whether to authorize an investigation.[6] If authorization is granted the prosecutor must first notify those States to which the information reveals a primary responsibility to investigate. Such States have one month to notify the prosecutor of an investigation, past or present, of the alleged offenders and/or situation referred. If such notification is forthcoming then the prosecutor is prohibited from instigating an investigation pursuant to the doctrine of complementarity.[7]

Securing Co-operation

The Court's success will depend upon the prosecutor's ability to build strong relationships with states. Effective Court and State cooperation is therefore vital.[8] Unfortunately, the political will to assist the Court will not always be present, particularly where State authorities represent the main suspects in an investigation. The Court is therefore presented with an almost impossible situation. With little resources and a highly critical opposition the OTP must ensure successful prosecutions (convictions) within an environment where State cooperation may be, at best, problematic. In such an environment the prosecutor will, in all likelihood, seek to instigate investigations only in those situations that present him with the most favourable conditions.

As the primary responsibility for the maintenance of international peace and security rests with the SC any referral by the Council will present the ICC with the strongest mandate upon which to base an investigation. This will be so for either of two reasons. First, for a situation to involve the SC it must be of significant international significance. Therefore, any SC referral is likely to be symbolic of a wider call for action. Second, irrespective of whether support for juridical action is

---

4   The 'trigger' mechanisms of the Rome Statute of the International Criminal Court can be found in Article 13.

5   Articles 15(2) and (3) and Rule 50 of the ICC Rules of Procedure and Evidence.

6   Article 15(4). This system would be referred to by Davis as 'the principle of check'. See Davis, K.C. (1980), *Discretionary Justice: A Preliminary Inquiry* (Westport, CT: Greenwood) p. 142.

7   Article 18(2).

8   *Statement of the Prosecutor of the International Criminal Court Mr Luis Moreno Ocampo to the Security Council on 29 June 2005 Pursuant to UNSCR 1593 (2005)*. Available at http://www.icc-cpi.int. See also, *Report of the Prosecutor of the International Criminal Court Mr Luis Moreno Ocampo to the Security Council on 29 June 2005 Pursuant to UNSCR 1593 (2005)*. Available at http://www.icc-cpi.int and Brubacher, M. (2004), 'Prosecutorial Discretion within the International Criminal Court' 2(1) *JICJ*, 7; Danner, A. (2003), 'Enhancing the Legitimacy and Accountability of Prosecutorial Discretion at the International Criminal Court', 97 *AJIL*, 510.

present within the wider international community, a SC referral represents a promise of cooperation. A SC referral will therefore give a prosecutor access to a level of political will that may be absent from a State Party referral or where the prosecutor exercises their *proprio motu* authority.

The unusual phenomenon of self-referrals will provide the ICC prosecutor with the next level of surety. While broad State cooperation is important, it is the cooperation of the state within which the alleged atrocity occurred that is vital. Of the three situations currently the subject of the ICC's investigative interest two are a result of self-referrals.[9] Self-referrals present states with a unique opportunity. First, it sends a strong signal to the global community that the self-referring state is open and willing to co-operate with an institution representing the rule of law. Second it represents a willingness to be investigated themselves.[10] This second point may, however, be a little optimistic. States who recognize the inevitability of an ICC investigation may opt for a self-referral in the hope that they may, more easily, control the Court and its conduct within their territory. Irrespective of the motivation of such States it is contended that self-referrals present the OTP with a strong and reassuring mandate.

State referrals of situations that perhaps fall within the interest but not the territory of the referring State are likely to provide the Court with a less secure basis of legitimacy. Co-operation from the territorial State under investigation cannot be assured with any confidence when the basis of such an investigation is, for example, a referral of an unfriendly neighbour.

While the prosecutor's *proprio motu* authority may, for some states, represent the opportunity for tyranny and arbitrary decision making through a lack of accountability the weak mandate it provides means that it is unlikely to be relied upon by the OTP. Where a lack of political will within the international community means that no SC referral is forthcoming, the state in question is unwilling to refer itself, and any neighbouring State Parties fail to make a referral to the prosecutor, the application of the prosecutor's inherent jurisdiction is hardly likely to engender the significant state cooperation required. The thought of exposing the Court to the realities of conducting a largely unsupported investigation will act as a strong deterrent to 'going it alone'. As the challenge for the Prosecutor will be to ensure the success of the Court by, for example, ensuring convictions while maintaining the integrity of prosecutorial independence, such a lack of mandate and state cooperation will inevitably place the Prosecutor's *proprio motu* authority in a very unattractive light.

Referrals and Predeterminations

By recognizing the Court's need to secure state cooperation and the fact that SC referrals are likely to provide the Court with the strongest mandate, a number of unfortunate implications become apparent. Security Council referrals potentially

---

9   Darfur region of Sudan (SC referral), the Republic of Uganda (self-referral), Democratic Republic of the Congo (self-referral).

10 The compatibility of self-referrals and the requirement of 'unwilling and unable' pursuant to Article 17 of the Rome Statute are beyond the scope of this article.

place a significant burden upon the OTP. While providing a strong, enforceable mandate for the Court SC referrals also act to potentially limit the ambit of prosecutorial discretion.

Here I will first examine the difficulty in dealing with an investigation when a prior determination of law appears to have been made. Second, I will attempt to delineate the scope of the Prosecutor's authority when faced with a manipulating SC referral.

Security Council Resolution (1593)

The horrific atrocities that have occurred within the Darfur region of Sudan have been the subject of significant international attention. As a result of these atrocities and the alleged culpability of the Sudanese Government a commission of enquiry on Darfur was established at the request of the SC.[11] Subsequent to the submission of the Commission's report the SC referred the Darfur situation to the ICC.[12] Although the referral resolution presents the Court with a number of potential difficulties I will only focus on one issue here.[13]

Article 6 of Resolution 1593 states that:

> ... nationals, current or former officials or personnel from a contributing State outside Sudan which is not a party to the Rome Statute of the International Criminal Court shall be subject to the exclusive jurisdiction of that contributing State for all alleged acts or omissions arising out of or related to operations in Sudan established or authorized by the Council or The African Union, unless such exclusive jurisdiction has been expressly waived by that contributing State.

Two things may be initially said about this provision. First, it appears to conform with the current limits of the ICC's jurisdiction.[14] Therefore, the practical implications of

---

11 See the Report of the International Commission of Inquiry on Darfur to the United Nations Secretary-General Pursuant to Security Council Resolution (1564) of 18 September 2004, 25 January 2005. See also the Report of the United Nations High Commissioner for Human Rights and Follow-up to the World Conference on Human Rights: Situation of Human Rights in the Darfur Region of the Sudan 7 May 2004, UN Doc. E/CN.4/2005/3, and the Report of the Secretary-General completed pursuant to UNSC resolution 1556 (2004), S/2004/703. The mandate of the International Commission of Inquiry was established pursuant to paragraph 12 of UNSC resolution 1564. The paragraph requested the Secretary-General to '... rapidly establish an international commission of inquiry in order immediately to investigate reports of violations of international humanitarian law and human rights law in Darfur by all parties, to determine also whether or not acts of genocide have occurred, and to identify the perpetrators of such violations with a view to ensuring that those responsible are held accountable', S/Res/1564 (2004).

12 Pursuant to Res (1593) on 31 March 2005.

13 For further discussion of the remaining issues see Gallavin, C. (2006), 'Prosecutorial Discretion within the ICC: Under the Pressure of Justice', 17:1 *Crim LF* 43, and Gallavin, C. (2005), 'The Security Council and the ICC: Delineating the Scope of Security Council Referrals and Deferrals', 5 *NZAFLR*, 19.

14 Refer to the jurisdictional requirements under Article 12 of the Rome Statute.

the provision are potentially inconsequential. However, the provision may also be interpreted as signalling an intention of the SC to authoritatively confine the ambit of the Court's jurisdiction. This is problematic. In answer to this second interpretation I submit that the ICC Prosecutor is bound by the provisions of the Rome Statute only. Apparent limitations contained in a SC or State referral that go beyond the jurisdiction of the Court as provided for by the Rome Statute ought to be treated, at the very most, as merely recommendatory.[15]

The paragraph ought not to be interpreted as authority for the principle that the SC may legitimately limit the jurisdiction of the Court beyond that which is provided for by the Rome Statute. The ICC is not a tool of the SC. Neither is the Court an organ of the UN. Given these facts I submit that no contravention of Article 103 of the UN Charter would arise if the ICC were to fail to adhere to a provision of a SC referral that attempted to extend or limit the jurisdiction of the Court beyond that which the Rome Statute provides.

Article 103 of the Charter provides:

> In the event of a conflict between the obligations of the Members of the United Nations under the present Charter and their obligations under any other international agreement, their obligations under the present Charter shall prevail.

Not only does this provision apply to 'Members' of the UN, of which the ICC is not, but I suggest that Article 103 does not empower the SC with an unlimited authority to use any organization as a tool in any way it sees fit. The first element of this contention is, I suggest, the most persuasive. The ICC is not a state and is therefore not a member of the UN. Undoubtedly, decisions of the SC will affect the work of the ICC but only to the extent provided for by the provisions of the Rome Statute, or the extent to which SC resolutions may pragmatically bare upon the work of the ICC.

As an international organization it could be argued that the ICC is inferior to the international personality enjoyed by States. This, it may be said, means that the ICC ought not to avoid obligations imposed by the SC that would be undoubtedly binding upon Member States particularly in the area of maintaining international peace and security. I believe that this argument can be discounted. The SC retains the ability to establish *ad hoc* tribunals such as the International Criminal Tribunals for the former Yugoslavia and Rwanda (ICTY and ICTR). To allow the SC to ostensibly use the ICC as an *ad hoc* facility would leave the jurisdiction of the Court unworkable. If the SC had such an authority there could be no limits placed upon the SC's ability to amend the Rome Statute. Two objections to this proposition are immediately apparent. First, the complexity of the Rome Statute and the accompanying Rules of Procedure and Evidence and Elements of Crimes means that substantial reworking of the Court's jurisdiction may be required in the case of each SC referral. This could give rise to an impossible situation in which the ICC becomes a substantively and administratively different beast from one investigation to the next. Second, such a controlling interest by the SC was specifically proposed and rejected by the

---

15 I have argued elsewhere that a limitation within a SC referral may also be treated as a deferral pursuant to Article 16. See Gallavin, C. (2006), 17:1 *Crim LF*, 43.

negotiating states at the Rome Conference of 1998. Additionally, consideration was also given to the possibility of the ICC being an organ of the UN. This was likewise rejected in favour of an independent treaty basis for the Court.

By way of observation it may also be noted that there was discussion within the SC of establishing a separate, *ad hoc*, tribunal to investigate Darfur.[16] Although ultimately rejected due to cost and delay it does indicate that there was concern that the jurisdiction of the ICC was not fit for the purpose. Despite the objections of the USA which represented the principal motivating state behind such a suggestion, if there had been universal recognition that the SC could manipulate the jurisdiction of the Court as it saw fit, then the suggestion of an *ad hoc* tribunal may not have been forthcoming. Additionally, although paragraph 6 of resolution 1593 may be interpreted as an attempt to control the jurisdiction of the Court, it may still be interpreted as an attempt by the SC to work within the boundaries of the SC and ICC relationship as delineated by the Rome Statute. The resolution does not reveal any express acknowledgment that the ICC is subject to the unilateral will of the SC pursuant to Article 103 of the Charter.

Whether the Court has the ability to disregard any resolution of the SC that may purport to extend the jurisdiction of the Court beyond that provided for by the Rome Statute is likely to be a moot point. As I have argued elsewhere, the traditionally loose nature of SC resolutions combined with the referral and deferral provisions of the Rome Statute, provide the ICC with a liberal margin of interpretative flexibility.[17] Only in the event of a SC resolution so pointed that the Court was unable to use the deferral provision of Article 16 or the limiting affect of Articles 12, 17 and 19 would the issue of the ICC's incompatibility with Article 103 of the Charter arise. I suggest that this would be an extremely rare event indeed. Under most circumstances, if the Court were to adopt a policy not to publicly classify elements of a resolution, then the inherent flexibility within the Statute would act to avoid a SC/ICC crisis. Even if the ICC Prosecutor were to accept the limiting elements of a SC referral then he could invoke the pragmatic constraints associated with the very limited resources available to the OTP to constrict the application of the offending provision.

The Report of the Commission of Inquiry on Darfur

A further difficulty surrounds SC resolution 1593, not in the words used in the resolution, but in the possible effect of the Report of the Commission of Inquiry which gave rise to its passing. I have previously discussed much of the substantive detail of the Report and do not propose to provide such an overview again here.[18] Suffice to say, the Commission concluded that, '[b]ased on a thorough analysis of the information gathered in the course of its investigations, the Commission established that the Government of the Sudan and the Janjaweed are responsible for serious violations of international human rights and humanitarian law amounting to crimes

---

16 See Cryer, R. (2006), 'Sudan, Resolution 1593 and International Criminal Justice', 19 *Leiden Journal of International Law*, 195, see also Gallavin (2005), 5 *NZAFLR*, 19.

17 Gallavin (2005), 5 *NZAFLR*, 19.

18 *Ibid.*

under international law'.[19] The Commission further noted that, '[t]he measures taken so far by the Government to address the crisis have been both grossly inadequate and ineffective, which has contributed to the climate of almost total impunity for human rights violations in Darfur'.[20]

In recognition of the difficulty in establishing the necessary elements of the crime of genocide, the Commission went so far as to say that genocide could not be established.[21] The difficulty such a conclusion presents relates to the influence it may have upon the ICC investigation. Having received a strong and influential mandate from the SC the OTP may be inclined to confirm those findings upon which a SC referral may be based. Considering that the Court will be under significant pressure to ensure successful convictions and the fact that the US, Russia and China have failed to ratify the Rome Statute the future existence of the Court may be in the balance. From this perspective prosecutorial discretion in the ICC is potentially limited.

While under pressure to produce tangible results the ICC prosecutor has stood firm in his Darfur investigation. He has ensured transparent decision making through regularly reporting to the SC and clearly indicating that he sees himself bound by the provisions of the Rome Statute.[22] Such resistance to the implicit pressure associated with the referral by the SC will perhaps be difficult to maintain.

Conclusion

Proprio motu authority vesting with the ICC Prosecutor caused considerable controversy at the Rome Conference of 1998. One could go so far as to say that this authority is ultimately responsible for the failure of the US and China to ratify the Rome Statute. However, far from being the Court's Achilles Heel, I suggest that this prosecutorial authority will inevitably be sidelined as it provides the OTP with a weak mandate upon which to instigate an investigation and consequent prosecution. Third party State referrals will likewise fail to fulfil the pragmatic requirements of the Prosecutor who must conduct investigations with minimal resources. Only in the case of State self-referrals or SC referrals will the Prosecutor be assured of the necessary state cooperation required.

However SC referrals represent a double edged sword. While providing significant surety as to the successful instigation and completion of an investigation the pressure to conform with the political will of the SC will be great. Such political will, is likely to be manifest expressly by the SC through any referring resolution, or implicitly

---

19 *Report of the International Commission of Inquiry on Darfur*, p. 3. See also generally, Kaufman, Z. (2005), 'Justice in Jeopardy: Accountability for the Darfur Atrocities', 16 *Crim LF.* p. 343.

20 *Ibid.*, p. 6.

21 *Report of the International Commission of Inquiry on Darfur*, paras. 489–522. See also Schabas, W. (2005), 'Darfur and the "Odious Scourge": The Commission of Inquiry's Findings on Genocide', 18 *LJIL*, p. 871.

22 *Statement of the Prosecutor of the International Criminal Court Mr Luis Moreno Ocampo to the Security Council on 29 June 2005 Pursuant to UNSCR 1593 (2005).*

through the determinations of SC investigatory bodies or political statements of member states. While the ICC Prosecutor has, so far, taken a clear and transparent stance on how the OTP will deal with SC referrals this will be difficult to maintain.

The pragmatic complexities associated with a poorly resourced prosecutions office may be exacerbated by claims that the SC can dictate, at will, the ambit of the ICC's jurisdiction. I believe that such a conclusion is unfounded. The Prosecutor is bound by the provisions of the Rome Statute. Additionally, a failure to implement an aspect of an overly restricting or liberalizing SC resolution would not place the Court in breach of Article 103 of the Charter. The ambit of SC referrals, the deferral mechanism under Article 16 of the Rome Statute and the significant flexibility that comes with the prioritization of limited resources should combine with the fact that the ICC is not an organ of the UN and is not a state actor to see it avoid any accusation of inconsistency with the UN Charter.

Chapter 14

Specificity of Indictments in ICTR Genocide Trials

Paul Ng'arua[1]

In the period between 1 April and 31 July 1994, and particularly following the death of President Habyarimana in a plane crash on 6 April 1994, widespread and systematic killings targeting ethnic Tutsis occurred throughout Rwanda. In addition to the rampant killings, many Tutsis in different parts of Rwanda were raped and subjected to other acts of sexual violence during wholesale attacks against their ethnic group. As a result of this, the United Nations Security Council established the International Criminal Tribunal for Rwanda ('the Tribunal') on 8 November 1994.[2]

The Tribunal is governed by its Statute, annexed to the Security Council Resolution 955 and by its Rules of Procedure and Evidence ('the Rules'), adopted by the judges on 5 July 1995 and subsequently variously amended.

Legal Challenges Brought by the ICTR Completion Strategy

The focus of this chapter is the significant challenges the ICTR Prosecutor faces in respect of the specificity of indictment and amendment thereof in the face of a completion strategy imposed by the Security Council, and the resulting inevitable exclusion of evidence. I have particular interest in the Casmir Bizimungu, Justin Mugenzi, Jerome Bicamumpaka and Prosper Mugiraneza trial (Government II),

---

1 The views expressed are those of the author and not those of the ICTR

2 In this respect, the Prosecution submitted that the *Krstić* Trial chamber was correct in stating that 'by incorporating Article 4 (3) in the Statute, the drafters of the Statute ensured that the Tribunal has jurisdiction over all forms of participation in genocide prohibited under customary international law'. The consequence of this approach, however, is that certain heads of individual criminal responsibility in Article 4 (3) overlap with those in Article 7 (1). *Krstić Trial Judgement*, para. 640. *see* also *Bagilishema Trial Judgement*, paras. 67–70. Cite also to *Stakić* Rule 98bis decision (the distinction [between Article 7(1) aiding and abetting and Article 4(3)(e) complicity in genocide] is not sustainable, but unfortunately for us he turned the analysis on its head: despite the jurisprudence of *Akayesu* and *Musema*, Schomburg strongly suggested that he believes that special intent is required for all forms of genocide including complicity (paras. 47–48, 60, 63–67).

all former cabinet ministers of the 1994 Rwanda interim government. In effect I will deal primarily with the challenges of specificity of indictments in the Rwandan Genocide trials at the ICTR. To better manage this very wide subject, I have elected to use my experience in the Government II Trial that I lead as a point of reference.

ICTR Indictments

The Government II indictment is a lengthy 70 page document divided into the following themes:

a) The four accused are charged with 'conspiracy to commit genocide; Genocide or alternatively complicity in genocide; direct and public incitement to commit genocide; crimes against humanity and violations of Article three common to the Geneva conventions and additional protocol II offences stipulated in Articles 2, 3, and four of the Statute of the Tribunal'.

b) Historical context, 'the revolution of 1959 marked the beginning of a period of ethnic clashes between the Hutu and the Tutsis in Rwanda causing hundreds of Tutsi to die and thousands to flee the country in the years immediately following. the revolution resulted in the abolition of the Tutsi monarchy and the proclamation of the first republic in 1961 …'.

c) Territorial, Temporal and material jurisdiction 'that the crimes referred to in this indictment took place in Rwanda between 1 January and 31 December 1994'.
    'During the events referred to in this indictment Rwanda was divided into 11 prefectures: Butare, Byumba, Cyangugu, Gikongoro, Gisenyi, Gitarama, Kibungo, Kibuye, Kigali-Ville, Kigali rural and Ruhengeri. Each prefecture was subdivided into communes and secteurs.'

d) The power structure, here the constitution of 10 June 1991 and Its definition of executive power and devolution of power is addressed; it states in part that:
    '3.1 according to the Constitution of June 1991, the executive power is exercised by the President of the Republic, assisted by the Government, composed of the Prime Minister and the ministers. the Government determines and applies national policy. To that effect it controls the civil service and the armed forces …'
    '3.2 the ministers implement the Government policy as defined by the Prime Minister. They are answerable to the Head of the government for doing so. In the discharge of their duties, the ministers stand by the President of the Republic. Before taking up their posts, they take an oath promising to uphold the interest of the Rwandan people and to respect the constitution and the law …'

The term 'global' indictment is indeed metaphorical rather than specific in that it is a working term describing the drafting style of some of ICTR indictments instead of the substance in those indictments. It could be more specifically defined as the style of drafting before 'Kupresic'. The style of the global indictments took root to accommodate the ambitious project of trying in one fell swoop, Bagosora and 28 others. The Government II accused formed part of the 29 persons in that ambitious global indictment. Subsequently, Bagosora and 28 others became Bagasora and three others and styled military I trial. Four other military Officers were charged under the military II indictment, whilst other persons charged were re-grouped into thematic titles characterized by certain aspects such as either their prefecture of origin like *Kibuye, Butare, Cyangugu*, or by their positions and roles, such that senior politicians are in government I and II, military I and II, media, Akazu, etc.

The *Theoneste* Bagosora and 29 others indictment submitted on 6 March 1998, fitted the 'global' indictment label, in that firstly, it attempted to encompass 29 accused persons and secondly, defined the historical back ground to the commission of the offences and thirdly, it generally described the modes of participation and the concept of joint criminal responsibility, of the 'superior responsibilities' of those most responsible for the genocide. As such, the indictment tended to include sweeping statements as to the mode of participation of the accused, and the circumstances surrounding the commission of the crimes. This is understandable in a setting designed to embrace a multitude of persons engaged in various aspects of the genocide in Rwanda.

The Completion Strategy

The statute of the International Criminal Tribunal for Rwanda (Security Council resolution 955 of 08 November 1994) established the ICTR for '… the sole purpose of prosecuting persons responsible for genocide and other serious violations of international humanitarian law committed in the territory of Rwanda and Rwandan citizens responsible for genocide and other such violations committed in the territory of neighboring states between 1 January and 31 December 1994.' Resolution 1,503 (2003) adopted by the Security Council at its 4,817 meeting on 28 August 2003, was 'urging the ICTR to formalize a detailed strategy, modeled on the ICTY completion strategy, to transfer cases involving intermediate and low rank accused to competent national jurisdictions as appropriate, including Rwanda, in order to allow the ICTR to achieve its objective of completing investigations by the end of 2004, all trial activities at first instance by the end of 2008, and all of its work in 2010 – ICTR Completion Strategy.'

Government II trial started on 6 November 2003. Prior on 26 August 2003, the Prosecutor filed a request for leave to file an amended indictment pursuant to Rules 50 and 73 of the Rules. On 6 October 2003, Trial chamber II ('the chamber') delivered its decision dismissing the Prosecutor's request for leave to file an amended Indictment.[3] On 29 October 2003, the chamber granted certification to the Prosecutor to appeal against its decision of 6 October 2003 denying the Prosecutor

---

3   *See* Decision on the Prosecutor's Request for Leave to File an Amended Indictment, 6 October 2003 [hereinafter 'Impugned Decision').

to file an amended Indictment. In dismissing the Prosecutor's motion for leave to file an amended Indictment, Trial chamber II held that:

(a) noting that the trial date has been set for 3 November 2003, the Trial chamber held that to permit the Prosecutor to amend the Indictment would result in *undue delay* for the commencement of the trial and thus prejudice the accused.
(b) The expansions, clarifications and specificity made in support of the remaining counts amounted to *substantial changes* which would cause prejudice to the accused persons. The Trial chamber noted that the substantial changes would necessitate that the accused persons be given adequate time to prepare their defence.

Amended Indictment would Cause Undue Delay to the Prejudice of the Accused

In rejecting the Prosecutor's leave to file an amended Indictment, the Trial chamber held that as the trial date had been set for 3 November, allowing the Prosecutor's application would cause undue delay for the commencement of the trial, occasioning prejudice the accused persons.[4] The Prosecutor did not challenge the existence of discretion on the part of the Trial chamber to determine whether to grant leave to amend an Indictment after the initial appearance of the accused pursuant to Rule 50 (a) of the Rules of the ICTR.

In paragraph 27 of the impugned Decision, after highlighting the rights of the accused under Articles 19 and 20 of the Statute, the chamber concluded that '*these rights are balanced with the complexity of the case*'.[5] The Prosecutor submitted that the chamber's approach was erroneous in that it failed to take into account a multiplicity of other material considerations or values against which the rights of the accused must be balanced to reach a correct decision. The rights of the accused to a trial without undue delay must be balanced not only with the complexity of the case, but others important/material values or rights, including, *the gravity or seriousness of the crimes with which the accused is/are indicted; the mandate or fundamental purpose of the Tribunal to bring to justice all those responsible for the heinous crimes in Rwanda in 1994; the rights of victims; the obligation of the Prosecutor to prosecute the accused to the full extent of the law and to present before the Tribunal all relevant evidence reflecting the totality of the accused's participation in the crimes; and establishing the totality of truth of what happened in Rwanda and those who are responsible in order to promote justice and reconciliation.*

In its decision delivered about four days before its delivery of the impugned Decision, Trial Chamber II Decision on Prosper Mugiraneza's *motion to Dismiss the Indictment for Violation of* Article 20(4)(c) of the *Statute, Demand for Speedy Trial and for Appropriate Relief*[6] pursued a correct approach to the balancing test, contrary

---

4 *See* Impugned Decision, para. 35.
5 Italicization added.
6 Decision of 2 October 2003.

to its approach in the impugned Decision. In finding that there was no undue delay in trying the accused, the chamber held that any enquiry into the alleged breach of the right:

> [...] will necessarily involve a consideration of a number of factors, including *the fundamental purpose of the Tribunal, which is* 'prosecuting persons responsible for genocide and other serious violations of international humanitarian law committed in the territory Rwanda and Rwandan citizens responsible for genocide and other such violations committed in neighbouring States, between 1 January 1994 and 31 December 1994.' *This entails balancing the rights of the accused with other important considerations of interest all of which serve the ends of justice.*[7]

Allowing the Prosecutor to amend his Indictment and add 11 counts two and half year after the confirmation thereof in *Kajelijeli*, a differently impanelled Trial chamber II held thus:

> As to the propriety of the timing of the Prosecutor's motion, the chamber concurs with the jurisprudence of the *tribunal in prosecutor v Musema*, ICTR – 96–13-T (6 May 1999) (Decision on the Prosecutor's Request for leave to amend the Indictment), which held at para. 17 that, '[...] Rule 50 of the Rules did not explicitly prescribe a time limit within which the Prosecutor may file to amend the Indictment, leaving it open to the Trial chamber to consider the motion in light of the circumstances of each individual case. *A key consideration would be whether or not, and to what extent, the dilatory filing of the motion impacts on the rights of the accused to a fair trial. In order that justice may take its proper course, due consideration must also be given to the Prosecutor's unfettered responsibility to prosecute the accused to the full extent of the law and present all relevant evidence before the Trial chamber.*'[8]

Error in failing to deliberate and to determine whether allowing the Amendment would occasion impermissible delay and the Trial chamber's overemphasis on the start of trial failed to balance the rights of the accused with other vital and material considerations discussed above, including the overall interest of justice, the gravity of the crimes with which the accused are indicted, the mandate and overall purpose of the Tribunal, the need to determine the truth of what happened in Rwanda and all four accused person's participation therein and the need to give due consideration to the Prosecutor's unfettered responsibility to prosecute the accused to the full extent of the law and present all relevant evidence before the Trial chamber.

The Prosecutor submitted that the Appeal chamber's approach in *prosecutor v Milan Kovacevi*[9] is instructive and persuasive. In that case, one aspect of its *ratio decidendi* is that the fact that a trial date has been fixed alone is insufficient in the determination of the issue whether the Prosecutor can amend an Indictment and

---

7 At paragraph 11 of the Decision.

8 *Prosecutor v Kajelijeli*, Case No. ICTR-98–44 A-T, *Decision on Prosecutor's motion to Correct the Indictment Dated 22 december 2000 and motion for leave to file an amended Indictment*, Decision of 25 January 2001, para. 35. Italicization added.

9 *The Prosecutor v Milan Kovacevic, Decision Stating Reasons for Appeal Chamber's Order of 29 May 1998*, Decision of 2 July 1998.

whether the amendment will result in undue delay. The Appeal chamber emphasized that the delay to the trial of the accused resulting from the amendment was not unreasonable in light, *inter alia* of the complexity of the case. In his separate concurring opinion, Judge Shahabuddeen emphasized that in light of the complexities inherent in unearthing and assembling materials for war crimes prosecutions, a flexible approach to the question of amending indictments is particularly important.[10]

While there are differences between the above case and Government II with regard to the number of years the accused had spent in pre-trial detention, the principles of the decision are relevant and applicable. In any event, as submitted and discussed above, the reasonableness of the delay to try an accused cannot be translated into a fixed number of days, months or years. The Prosecution therefore requested that the Appeals chamber reverse the impugned Decision and allow the proposed amendments, or in the alternative, rule that the evidence of the material allegations is admissible provided it relates to allegations previously communicated to the accused in a timely, clear and consistent manner.[11] The following instances are instructive:

i)   The proposed paragraph 15 alleges that the attacks on wounded Tutsi refugees in the vicinity of University Hospital in Butare occurred between April and May 2004. Previously, the Prosecutor alleged that these attacks occurred on or about 15 April 1994.[12]

ii) The proposed Paragraph 16 alleges that the accused mandated hospital staff to halt treatment of Tutsi refugee patients and later ordered their evacuation with no provision for their care. While the current indictment mentions an attack on wounded Tutsi at the hospital, it says nothing about orders or instructions that the accused might have given to hospital staff.[13]

iii) The proposed paragraph 18 alleges that the establishment of roadblocks was ordered by the Interim Government on or about 7 April 1994. The current indictment categorically states that the Interim Government ordered roadblocks to be created on 27 April 1994.[14]

(v) The proposed Paragraph 25 alleges the accused's involvement in the abduction of Tutsi civilians from various communes and their torture at the brigade cell or ESO Camp. The proposed Paragraph 26 alleges the accused's involvement in the abduction of family members of Tutsi soldiers from ESO camp who were later on killed at an unknown location. The current indictment only indicates one abduction at the Beneberkia Convent.

(vi) The proposed Paragraph 27 alleges that Jean Baptiste Habyalimana was detained at the brigade cell which was under the control of the accused. It further alleges that Habyalimana was taken away from the cell and never

---

10 *Prosecutor v Kovacevic* (supra), *Separate Opinion of Judge Mohamed Shahabuddeen, 2 July 1998.*

11 *Ibid.*, para. 5.

12 Impugned Decision, para, 41.

13 Impugned Decision, para, 41.

14 Impugned Decision, para, 41.

seen again. The current indictment refers to Habyalimana's dismissal from his position as prefect of Butare, yet no mention is made of the accused's involvement is his detention or disappearance.

vii)   The proposed Paragraph 41 alleges that the accused himself 'provided weapons for local militiamen' at the Nyakizu meeting in April 1994, and that these weapons were later used 'to kill Tutsi civilians'. Conversely, Paragraph 3.26 of the existing indictment alleges that 'during the events referred to in this indictment' the accused participated directly in the provision of weapons.[15]

As the Appeals chamber held in the *Karemera* case, 'although Rule 50 did not require the Prosecution to amend the indictment as soon as it discovers evidence supporting the amendment, neither may it delay giving notice of the changes to the Defence without any reason'.[16] Under some circumstances, the Prosecution might justifiably wait to file an amendment while it continues its investigation so as to determine whether further evidence either strengthens its case or weakens it. But here the Prosecution has not demonstrated that such delay was justified by the circumstances; it has not provided any evidence that it acted with due diligence.

The Impact of the Bizimungu Decision on the Genocide Cases

The first most fundamental challenge in the case came by way of Casimir Bizimungu's 2 motions to exclude certain witnesses who would testify to Casimir Bizimungu's criminal conduct in Ruhengeri Prefecture:
The Testimonies of witnesses GKB, GAP, GKC, GKD and GFA and a second subsequent motion excluding the testimonies of witnesses AEI, GKE, GKF and GKI all implicating Casimr Bizimungu in crimes in the Ruhenger Prefecture on the ground that Casimir Bizimungu had no notice of any charges against him emanating from the prefecture of Ruhengeri because in the indictment, Ruhengeri prefecture had not been specifically pleaded in the indictment. The trial chamber on 26 January 2004 delivered a decision in favour of Casimir Bizimungu. Following the decision of these two motions in favour of the defence, the Prosecutor was subsequently inundated by a flood of other similar motions filed by Bizimungu's co-accused Mugiranez to exclude a total of 17 Kibungo prefecture witnesses on similar grounds. These matters went on cross appeals to the Appeals chamber.
The Prosecutor challenged the findings of the chamber excluding evidence as falling outside the Indictment, and thus inadmissible. We submitted that the Indictment contains several paragraphs, which clearly plead allegations of criminal conduct on the part of the accused Casimir Bizimungu throughout Rwanda for which the expunged evidence is material and relevant. Furthermore, bearing in mind the nature of the Prosecutor's case, supported by well established jurisprudence (including by

---

15 Ibid.

16 *Prosecutor v Karemera*, No ICTR-98–44-AR73, *Decision on Prosecutor's Interlocutory Appeal Against Trial Chamber III Decision of 8 December 2003 Denying Leave to File An Amended Indictment*, 19 December 2003, para. 20.

the Appeals chamber), the facts contained in the expunged witness statements and their testimonies in court have been sufficiently pleaded in those paragraphs of the Indictment. It is thus an error on the part of the Trial chamber to exclude any relevant and material evidence that falls within the ambit of the Indictment.

In the *Prosecutor v Kupreskic*, the Appeals chamber has explained that whether evidence is relevant to an Indictment and the degree of specificity required of an Indictment:

> [...] is dependent on the nature of the Prosecution case. A decisive factor in determining the degree of specificity with which the Prosecution is required to particularize the facts of its case in the indictment is the nature of the alleged criminal conduct charged to the accused. For example, in a case where the Prosecution alleges that the accused personally committed the criminal acts, the material facts, such as the identity of the victim, the time and place of the events and the means by which the acts were committed, have to be pleaded in detail. *Obviously, there may be instances where the sheer scale of the alleged crimes makes it impracticable to require a high degree of specificity in such matters as the identity of the victims and the dates for the commission of the crimes.*[17]

Indeed, in dealing with a similar motion brought by another accused person, prosper Mugiraneza, the chamber found that a number of paragraphs cited in the table above, namely: 6.14, 6.23, 6.25, 6.31 and 6.68, adequately set out the material facts in relation to the commission of the offences of complicity in genocide and conspiracy to commit genocide.[18] The very same paragraphs, among others, form the basis of the charges of complicity in genocide and conspiracy to commit genocide brought against Casmir Bizimungu. Although the Prosecutor in both his written and oral submissions cited virtually all the said paragraphs as containing allegations of criminal conduct of Casimir Bizimungu for which the expunged evidence would go to prove, it was erroneous that the same Trial chamber rejected the Prosecutor's case and expunged in entirety all the witnesses regarding criminal liability of Bizimungu emanating from his activities in Ruhengeri.

Conclusion

The writing is on the wall now, that the Tribunal has been pushed to a corner and will be reluctant to allow the Prosecutor to invoke the provisions of Rule 50 of the Rules to amend the indictment before the close of the prosecution's case. The implementation of the limitations set by the exit strategy may have been interpreted by the Tribunal as 'judicial economy'. There may be several and diverse points of view to explain this. This is unsettling, as there is now no certainty that Rules have their ordinary and direct meaning. The timing of this strategy on the Tribunal will reflect on Security Council resolution to close down the ICTR trials by 2008. This

---

17 *The Prosecutor v. Kupreskic* et al, Appeal Chamber Judgement, para. 89.

18 *The Prosecutor v Casimir Bizimungu* et al., *Decision on Prosper Mugiraneza's Motion to Exclude Testimony of Witnesses Whose Testimony is Inadmissible in view of the Trial Chamber's Decision of 23 January 2004 and for other Appropriate Relief*, Decision of 5 February 2004.

is a very drastic measure in dealing with such an indelible tragedy as the Rwandan genocide. This will affect the jurisprudence in pending cases. The Rwamakuba trial immediately comes to mind. The question that begs an answer is why has the Security Council called for a sacrifice of this enormity twice on the same genocide. is there wisdom in the sacrifice of due process and justice on the altar of appearances and expediency?

The ruling in Bizimungu points at the drastic impact of the Security Council's pressure on due process. This echoes on the part of the Security Council the same elevation of financial considerations that were made in 1994 that resulted in insufficient action to stop genocide, as the world watched in the comfort of their homes the gory dispatch of over a million souls in the unfolding Rwanda genocide. To repeat this mistake in the judicial arena is a fundamental issue upon which the Security Council's performance and influence over international criminal law will be assessed by posterity.

From another perspective, if indeed this is a wake up call for all organs and parties in the Tribunal to get on with the expeditious delivery of 'favorable trial statistics', it misses the mark for failing to take into account the inertia and difficulties experienced by the *ad hoc* Tribunal to set up in 1995, and the logistical nightmare involved in setting up an institution of this magnitude. These difficulties should be adequately considered before any drastic formulation of a completion strategy is adopted. If the Security Council took into account the enormity of the indelible mark the Rwandan genocide will leave on the face of Humanity, no steps of this nature should have been taken or construed in isolation of due process. What will appear, after all this, is a hurried and compromised justice. This decision reinforces the view that the Security Council is now satisfied that their gesture of the atonement for a guilty conscience in failing to stop genocide is now satisfied by the salutary gesture and that a drastic exit strategy will now do.

In Response to these drastic and frightful developments, the Prosecutor reinforced steps to be taken before any indictment is presented for confirmation. These steps include the following:

- peer review of pending indictments at an open forum where all Senior Trial Attorneys will lead their teams to critically review all the aspects of their case before their peers.
- Scrutiny at a second level of all witness statements and documentary evidence available.
- A comprehensive Review of case theory and pre-trial briefs.
- Clarification and expansion of indictments should be done before confirmation.
- Attention to be given to quality of investigations of crimes and special measures to be taken in dealing with counts pleading sexual violence.
- Use of modern technology tools such as text map and case map to assist in mapping or matching evidence to specific paragraphs of the indictment.

These steps will buttress the Prosecutor's commitments to efficiency and will have a positive impact on the remaining trials at the ICTR.

Chapter 15

Cambodia's Extraordinary Chamber: Is it the Most Effective and Appropriate Means of Addressing the Crimes of the Khmer Rouge?

Alex Bates[1]

Introduction

Between 1975 and 1979, during what is colloquially known as the Cambodian genocide,[2] 1.7 million people perished. Yet more than 27 years after the downfall of Pol Pot's Khmer Rouge no one has been brought to justice in a credible criminal trial.

Over three years have passed since the signing of the agreement between the Royal Government of Cambodia and the United Nations ('RGC-UN Agreement') concerning the prosecution of crimes committed during the period of Democratic Kampuchea.[3] Accountability will be sought through the newly-created, but controversial, Extraordinary chamber ('EC'). At time of writing – early July 2006 – the remaining financial and personnel issues have recently been resolved, and prosecutions before the EC appear months rather than years away.

Many compromises were made in the negotiations leading up to the RGC-UN Agreement. The operation of the EC is faced with numerous challenges which will undoubtedly have a bearing on the effectiveness of the prosecutions. I aim to examine some of these compromises and challenges and to discuss what the trials may achieve. I shall argue that it is important to be realistic about the potential achievements of the prosecutions, and that an appropriate response to the atrocities of the Pol Pot era must include a wider process of national reconciliation and education.

---

1   The views expressed in this chapter are entirely the author's own.

2   Colloquially rather than legally – problems still exist as to the legal classification of the crimes committed in Cambodia, but it is beyond the scope of this essay to discuss: see Schabas, W. (2001), 'Problems of International Codicfication – Were the atrocities in Cambodia and Kosovo genocide?', 35 *New England Law Review*, p.286.

3   Full text http://daccessdds.un.org/doc/UNDOC/GEN/N03/358/90/PDF/N0335890. pdf?OpenElement.

Why Prosecute 30 Years On?

The particular matrix of factors in Cambodia – the length of time since the atrocities were committed, the integration of many tens of thousands of former Khmer Rouge cadre into the population, the perceived weaknesses and distrust of the criminal justice system, the particular political power wielded by the government – combine to make any contemporary response to the crimes of the Pol Pot era less than straightforward. Any examination of accountability for massive human rights violations in the region must confront these realities in the face of the obvious moral imperative for punishment.[4]

The now well-recognized duty to prosecute human rights violations is no less imperative even when some 30 years have elapsed since the commission of the offences, especially where the effects are still being felt throughout all sections of Cambodian society. Obvious difficulties created by the delays in accountability should not stand in the way of bringing perpetrators to justice. Regardless of compromises in the format, jurisdiction and scope of the EC, and in spite of the considerable evidential, legal and political challenges facing prosecutors, the contemporary response to the atrocities of the Khmer Rouge era is long overdue, necessary and important. For the Cambodian people who desire 'justice and memory,' to quote the twin aims of the Documentation Centre of Cambodia, the forthcoming trials will provide a focus for these goals. For the wider international community, and for the development of international criminal law, the trials will hopefully reflect an establishing tendency to ensure that the language of human rights is not reduced to empty rhetoric.

Although there have been many academic and historical studies of the crimes committed during Democratic Kampuchea,[5] to date there has been no official, authoritative assessment which stands as Cambodia's own domestic account. Criminal trials within Cambodia may therefore provide the impetus for Cambodians to create such an authoritative domestic history. However, although the history of the Khmer Rouge has not been taught in Cambodian schools since 1991,[6] the notoriety of Pol Pot and the other senior leaders in Democratic Kampuchea is proclaimed so frequently that the impression can be given that only a handful of individuals were responsible for the deaths of the millions of victims. The wisdom of limiting the jurisdiction of the forthcoming trials to the prosecution of senior leaders of the Khmer Rouge, together with 'those most responsible', is a matter of considerable debate, as I shall discuss.

---

4   Ratner, S. and Adams, J. (2001), *Accountability for Human Rights Atrocities in International Law: Beyond the Nuremberg Legacy*, 2nd edn, (Oxford: Oxford University Press) at p.xliv.

5   Kiernan (1999), *The Pol Pot Regime: Race, Power and Genocide in Cambodia under the Khmer Rouge, 1975–79* (New Haven: Yale University Press); Marks, S., 'Elusive Justice for the Victims of the Khmer Rouge', 52 *Journal of International Affairs*, 691; Ratner, S. and Adams, J. (2001), *ibid.*

6   Fawthrop and Jarvis (2004), *Getting Away With Genocide? Elusive Justice and the Khmer Rouge Tribunal*, (London: Pluto Press, Ann Arbor) at p. 146.

The Compromises of the Extraordinary Chamber

The theoretical side of the duty to prosecute massive human rights violations will always encounter the hard realities of geo-politics, logistics and legal and procedural complexities, not to mention particular cultural factors which may have an influence upon how prosecutions are received within the society in which the atrocities occurred. Additionally, pursuing justice through criminal trials of alleged perpetrators is seldom sufficient for wronged communities affected by the initial violence itself, particularly where crimes have been compounded by decades of subsequent inaction. For Cambodia, the question is whether the many anticipated compromises in the nature and scope of the prosecutions before the EC will significantly devalue the principle of accountability.

The EC has no exact parallel amongst any of the world's other criminal tribunals specifically established to address accountability for genocide. The EC will be situated within the existing Cambodian justice system; the majority of the EC's judicial and administrative personnel will be Cambodian; and the total number of suspects for which trials will be held will be small. These features are the result of significant compromises between the negotiating parties, and will have an important bearing on how the trials will unfold.

Notwithstanding the recommendations of the United Nations' Group of Experts,[7] the EC is a domestic court, established pursuant to Cambodian law and operating within the pre-existing Cambodian judicial framework, but internationalized in composition. It has been argued that the United Nations, many international NGOs and most international experts and commentators would rather have seen a model based on the Yugoslav or Rwandan Tribunals, insulated as it would have been from any perceived undue influence from the Cambodian Government, albeit distant from and inaccessible to the Cambodian people. The opposing, and ultimately successful, position was that it was necessary to site the trial process within the Cambodian judicial system, albeit with international assistance, to allow Cambodia to feel a sense of ownership of the process. Although the UN-RGC Agreement could not have taken place without compromise on both sides, it is likely that there would have been no tribunal at all had it not been recognized that this sense of ownership was a source of intense national pride and principle. Additionally, there exists in Cambodia a functioning state and judicial system (despite the problems well-documented by Amnesty International and the UN's Group of Experts), which there was not after the break-up of the former Yugoslavia. The passage of three decades since the atrocities will also hopefully enable Cambodia's EC to achieve a sense of perspective that, for example, the domestic courts in Rwanda immediately after the genocide may not have been able to achieve.

Cambodian criminal procedure is modelled on the civil law system, with prosecutions initiated by prosecutors but transferred to investigating judges who follow the inquisitive legal tradition. Prosecutions before the EC will consist of one

---

7   Ratner, S.R. (1999), 'The United Nations Group of Experts for Cambodia', *American Journal of International Law*, 93, p. 948.

Cambodian and one foreign co-prosecutor,[8] each of equal standing. There will also be co-investigating judges, one Cambodian and one foreign.[9] At the pre-trial stage, official prosecutorial or judicial investigation decisions must be taken by agreement of both co-prosecutors or co-investigating judges, respectively. In the event of any disagreement, the matter will be resolved by a Pre-Trial chamber consisting of three Cambodian and two foreign judges.[10] The EC will consist of the Trial chamber, comprised of three Cambodian and two foreign judges, and the Supreme Court Chamber, comprised of four Cambodian and three foreign judges.[11] Decisions can only be passed though a 'super-majority'[12] of four judges in the Trial chamber, or five in the Supreme Court Chamber, to ensure that at least one international judge will be in agreement.[13]

The Pre-Trial chamber regulation of disputes between co-prosecutors or co-investigating judges and the super-majority rule in decision-making have no precedent in international criminal law. Their operation is bound to be fraught with difficulty and disagreement, potentially impeding the smooth-running of the judicial process. Furthermore, the EC does not yet have a uniform procedural code by which it will operate.

Finally, and most significantly in terms of who will actually be prosecuted, there are jurisdictional compromises. The two qualifying categories for personal jurisdiction – that suspects should be either 'senior leaders of Democratic Kampuchea' or 'those most responsible [for serious crimes]' – will also mean that the thousands, possibly tens of thousands, of lower-ranking Khmer Rouge cadre will not face any form of criminal justice for crimes they may have committed. Additionally, temporal jurisdiction is strictly limited to crimes committed between 17 April 1975 and 6 January 1979, which will in effect preclude any possible prosecution of non-Cambodian suspects.[14]

The suspects alleged to be the most responsible, most of whom did indeed hold senior positions in the Khmer Rouge, have long been identified[15] and are now all in their 70s and 80s. Obvious questions may be asked about the benefits of prosecuting

---

8   Articles 16–22 of the Law on the Establishment of the Extraordinary Chambers in the Courts of Cambodia for the Prosecution of Crimes Committed during the Period of Democratic Kampuchea, Adopted by the Cambodian National Assembly on 2 January 2001 (as amended) (hereafter 'ECDK Law').

9   Articles 23–28 ECDK Law.

10   Articles 20 and 23 ECDK Law respectively.

11   Article 9 ECDK Law.

12   Article 14 ECDK Law.

13   See also Scott Worden (2005), *An Anatomy of the Extraordinary Chambers* in Ramji and van Schaak (eds), *Bringing the Khmer Rouge to Justice: Prosecuting Mass Violence before the Cambodian Courts*, (Lewiston: Criminological Studies Volume 27, the Edwin Mellen Press).

14   This will therefore limit the scope of any examination of the actions of the USA, China or Thailand (see Kiernan, 1996 *ibid.*, at p. 25 and Kiernan 'Conflict in Cambodia, 1945–2003', 34 *Critical Asian Studies*, pp. 483–4; Fawthrop and Jarvis, 2004 *ibid.*, pp. 5–6).

15   See Heder and Tittemore (2004), *Seven Candidates for Prosecution*, 2nd edn (Phnom Penh: Documentation Centre of Cambodia).

such elderly defendants when any punishment could never hope to be commensurate with the crimes they may have committed. Clearly, however, the age of any individual suspect is but one factor when considering the obligation to prosecute. Where grave crimes have been committed, the symbolic effect of prosecution is far more important than the practical effect on the individual accused or their ability to repay their debt to society, despite the inevitably selective nature of all prosecutions for mass atrocity.

Additionally, given the all-pervasive nature of the Khmer Rouge regime, it would not be practicable, productive nor in the best interests of Cambodia to prosecute every Khmer Rouge cadre member for each act of barbarity perpetrated. All justice is necessarily selective, and each situation calls for an individual examination of the circumstances leading to the atrocities. For Cambodia, the passage of such a lengthy period of time since the crimes, together with the resultant re-integration into society of the vast majority of low-ranking Khmer Rouge, calls for a form of accountability limited to those bearing the greatest responsibility.

Principles of natural justice demand that egregious criminality is addressed rather than ignored, minimized or forgotten. If we accept that there is a duty to prosecute massive human rights violations, such as undoubtedly occurred in Democratic Kampuchea, even the considerable practical compromises of the EC must in principle be better than silence and impunity. The practical application of this duty, however, faces many challenges, and it is to these I now turn.

The Challenges Faced by the Extraordinary Chamber

The Challenges for Cambodian Society

There has been no systematic review conducted of the Cambodian population to gauge their support for prosecutions of the Khmer Rouge *per se* or for the EC in its current form. However, numerous relatively small-scale and largely unscientific surveys[16] have concluded that ordinary Cambodians are broadly in favour of prosecutions, provided the trials are fair. A common theme to emerge from these surveys was an insistence that the trials be conducted according to international standards, or with some form of international participation.[17] It is unclear whether this indicates simply a distrust of domestic governmental interference or an understanding that this will result in the respect for the rights of the suspects as well as fair trials. Historically, the Cambodian criminal justice system has been governed by political rather than judicial power, and the concepts of the presumption of innocence and other defendant rights have been neither well-known, nor it would seem, well-practised.[18] It may be difficult for many of the victims and their families, particularly those outside

---

16 For example: Linton (2004), 'Reconciliation in Cambodia' (Phnom Penh: Documentation Centre of Cambodia); the Khmer Institute of Democracy (http://www.bigpond.com.kh/users/kid/KRG-Tribunal.htm).

17 Question 13 of the DC-Cam Survey in Linton (2004), *ibid.* At p.10.

18 Marks, S.P. (1994), 'Forgetting "The Policies and Practices of the Past": Impunity in Cambodia', 18 *Fletcher Forum for World Affairs*, p.17.

educated communities and local NGOs, to comprehend how it is that former Khmer Rouge leaders are allowed to defend themselves in fair trials when the regime itself failed to deliver fair justice – particularly if evidential or legal challenges may result in some of the suspects being acquitted of the most serious charge of genocide.

As far as the prosecution of the main suspects is concerned, expectations are high that they will be convicted of genocide and sentenced to imprisonment for the rest of their natural lives. The prevailing theory of responsibility for the atrocities preached by successive post-Khmer Rouge governments is that the summary execution, forced labour and deliberate starvation was ordered and directed from the highest-ranking members of the Khmer Rouge, and that the responsibility for the genocide starts and ends with this select group of suspects. In many ways, this is a more palatable hypothesis: for the current political leaders of Cambodia, many of whom were lower-ranking members of the Khmer Rouge, their own actions or inactions are not subjected to examination. For the wider population, whatever criminal acts those amongst them may have performed as Khmer Rouge cadre are excused as having been committed under pain of death from their superiors.

However, it must be expected that during any trial before the EC defence lawyers will seek to argue that their clients were not aware of the individual acts of slaughter in the fields, however numerous, and that the chain of command responsibility was therefore broken. Should a more nuanced picture emerge during the trials, pointing to what has been suggested[19] may be a 'bottom-up' rather than 'top-down' model of responsibility for the crimes, whereby lower-ranking cadre do indeed bear significant responsibility, potentially an extremely challenging version of history may face the Cambodian nation. This in itself may have a severe impact on any process of reconciliation. A comprehensive programme of education is therefore needed to disseminate the aims, principles and methods of the EC in advance of the forthcoming trials so that awareness, and not simply expectation, is raised.

Cultural and Religious Challenges

Cambodia is still today almost exclusively a Buddhist country. To understand Cambodian attitudes towards justice, accountability and reconciliation, the historical and religious context must therefore be appreciated.[20] Customarily, monks have been the most well-regarded and least corruptible sector of society. Notwithstanding the fact that their order was almost entirely wiped out by the Khmer Rouge, monks retain a prominent place in Cambodia's daily life, and their views carry significant weight. Scepticism of the international dimension to the trials, a desire to ground accountability in Buddhist principles, and an urge to seek reconciliation rather than

---

19 Steve Heder, *Reassessing the Role of Senior Leaders And Local Officials in Democratic Kampchea Crimes: Cambodian Accountability in Comparative Perspective*, in Ramji van and Schaak (*ibid.*)

20 I am very grateful to Ian Harris, Reader in Buddhist Studies, University of St Martin, Lancaster, for his insights shared in discussions in Phnom Penh, 9–14 July 2005.

retribution provide an alternative perspective on the EC.[21] Other commentators have picked up on this theme, urging a re-focusing away from the ideas of victimhood and vengeance towards a culture of peace, justice and truthfulness through an anticipation of a shared future community.[22] Such concepts of reconciliation can seem challenging to the tradition of prosecuting crimes of mass atrocity, but where such prosecutions are to be as limited as they are in Cambodia, this vast wealth of indigenous cultural and religious practice may be an extremely useful means of achieving society-wide understanding.

Political Challenges

Leading NGOs have long argued that the prosecution of the Khmer Rouge in the present form threatens not only the requirements of fair trials for the specific accused, but also the credibility of the system of international criminal law. Amnesty International's report of 23 April 2003 in particular highlighted continuing concerns over the abilities of Cambodian judges and their susceptibility to political influence.[23] These political challenges have not disappeared. The Cambodian Government may wield significant control over the EC: in the selection of judges (both Cambodian and foreign), in the office of the prosecutor (the limited independence of which may have a bearing on the course of the investigations, identification of evidence and selection of suspects), and in the appointment of local investigators who will work for the investigating judges and prosecutors. The numbers of international personnel are strictly limited, no doubt much to the dismay of those who criticized the compromises of the RGC-UN Agreement.

Furthermore, views have been expressed that there has to date only been a limited concept of accountability of public officials in Cambodia. It has been argued that law was seen as 'an instrument to affirm the rightfulness of the power-holders'[24] rather than as the means of regulating relations between the individual and the state. Although there are offences of coercion of witnesses (Article 55 of 1992's UNTAC Law), perjury (Article 56) and bribery (Article 58),[25] no specific criminal offence of interfering with the course of justice exists.

The impunity for crimes committed by the Khmer Rouge can therefore be seen in the context of a long history of Cambodia's rulers being above the law: those with the power and influence to intervene have always been able to do so. Relatively recently, a withering attack on the independence of the judiciary was launched by the

---

21 Harris, I. (2005), '"Onslaught on Beings": A Theraveda Buddhist Perspective on Accountability for Crimes Committed in the Democratic Kampuchea Period', in Ramji and van Schaak (*ibid.*).

22 Rigby (2002), '"Forgiving the past"? Pathways Towards a Culture of Reconciliation', *The Stockholm International Forum for Truth*.

23 See http://web.amnesty.org/library/index/ENGASA2300 52003.

24 Rajagopal (1998), 'The Pragmatics of Prosecuting the Khmer Rouge', *The International Humanitarian Law Yearbook*, (The Hague: Asser Institute).

25 Provisions Relating to the Judiciary and Criminal Law and Procedure Applicable in Cambodia During the Transitional Period, 10 September 1992, passed during the United Nations Transitional Authority in Cambodia (UNTAC).

Cambodian Bar Association in 1999 after the UN's Group of Experts had submitted their report, demanding certain minimum standards of independence and fairness for any prospective trials.[26]

How such criticisms will impact upon the course of the proceedings is uncertain. Whether the investigations and trials are allowed to run their course, with both exculpatory and inculpatory evidence permitted and alternative theories of responsibility considered equally, is a matter of speculation. It is clear that the whole process will be under close scrutiny from both domestic and international observers, and such trial monitoring and training initiatives there exist are to be applauded and encouraged as concrete examples of a developing and more independent civil society.

Legal and Procedural Challenges

The 2001 ECDK Law lists the crimes that are to be prosecuted in the EC.[27] The domestic crimes from the Cambodian Criminal Code of 1956 to be prosecuted include homicide, torture and religious persecution. Additionally, from international law, the crimes of genocide, crimes against humanity, war crimes, destruction of cultural property in armed conflict and crimes against internationally protected persons will be the subject of the eventual indictments.

Judicial unfamiliarity with the applicable law may be a major problem. The 1956 Code has not been applied since before the days of the Khmer Rouge, and it is feared that few Cambodian judges will be conversant with the principles of international criminal law. Additional legal challenges for all judges will include determining the state of customary international law in 1975; examining how command responsibility applied to senior leaders of the Khmer Rouge; and, in respect of the crime of genocide, analysing the issue of whether a specific genocidal intent was made out or whether the victims belonged to one of the four protected groups specified under Article 4 of the ECDK law.

Furthermore, the status of the defence is uncertain. Cambodia has still not yet recovered from the decimation of the legal profession during the days of the Khmer Rouge. Very few domestic practitioners will have any experience in international criminal law. There may also be a considerable stigma attached to Cambodian lawyers who seek to defend any of the high-profile suspects. Only recently, with the proposals for the eventual trial of the Khmer Rouge taking shape, have training programmes for the Cambodian legal community commenced. It is likely that there will still be a considerable shortage of appropriately experienced defence counsel. Clearly, if there is to be any equality of arms, it would appear that non-Cambodian lawyers will be needed to make up the shortfall but, according to current domestic legislation, foreign attorneys are restricted to an advisory role and have no rights of

---

26 The Cambodian Bar Association Statement, Published in the *Phnom Penh Post*, Issue 8/20 of October 1–14 1999, requested that all judges would be appointed by the United Nations, that there would be an international chief prosecutor and the investigations would be conducted by non-Cambodians.

27 Articles 3–8 inclusive, ECDK Law.

advocacy in court.[28] This law may have to be changed to allow greater participation and representation by specialist international criminal lawyers from overseas if the principle of equality of arms is to have any effect. Justice for international as well as domestic crimes is best served by the presence of a strong and independent Defence Bar as well as rigorous and even-handed prosecution.

Evidential Challenges

Trials of crimes that were committed decades earlier are not uncommon in either domestic or international tribunals. Trials of crimes attributed to the leaders of an entire regime, whilst more complex, have also taken place in recent times.[29] But the combined factors of antiquity and complexity will provide a serious challenge for even the most experienced and diligent tribunals. The EC will face considerable challenges: poor memories, lost documents, uncertain identification, and reluctant, frightened and confused witnesses. Enormous efforts have been made by the Documentation Centre of Cambodia ('DC-Cam')[30] to preserve hundreds of thousands of pages of documents and to identify and to take histories from victims and their families. It is anticipated that such information will play a significant part at the forthcoming EC trials. But the legal status of the 'histories' taken by DC-Cam's staff may be uncertain. The weight of any such evidence presented before the EC will very much depend upon the manner in which it was taken. DC-Cam staff are not full-time police officers and although many have attended courses on the collection of evidence,[31] it is unrealistic to expect the same degree of rigour in questioning where there were no formal rules of procedure applied. The evidence collected by DC-Cam, and the means by which it was collected, can therefore be expected to be the subject of considerable legal argument before the EC.

What Will the Extraordinary Chamber Achieve?

With so many challenges facing the new tribunal, which is itself a product of so many compromises, it is tempting to agree that the EC will be 'just another political sideshow'.[32] But the appalling nature of the crimes committed demand some form of official response, particularly where a culture of impunity has blighted Cambodian society for so many years in respect of one of the worst atrocities in modern times.

Nevertheless, it is important to be realistic. The compromises made will not in themselves result in punishment for the crimes of many thousands of former Khmer Rouge cadre. Nor will any complete historical perspective emerge from the

---

28 Article 6, Cambodian Law on the Bar, adopted by the National Assembly of Cambodia on 15 June 1995.

29 Most notably of Jean Kambanda in the ICTR and Slobodan Milosevic in the ICTY.

30 Initially a field office of Yale University's Cambodian Genocide Programme, DC-Cam became an independent research institute in 1997. See http://welcome.to/dccam.

31 From the author's conversations with DC-Cam staff, 11–22 July 2005.

32 Short (2000), 'Devil's Advocate: there should be no Khmer Rouge Trial', *Phnom Penh Post*, November, 10–23.

prosecutions alone: trials will seek to ascribe responsibility to individuals for distinct criminal acts, rather than providing an exhaustive chronology. Although it has been remarked that reconciliation begins with the rule of law,[33] given that it has already been decided that there will be no wholesale prosecutions, additional means must be sought to promote wider reconciliation.

The formation of an official truth commission initially appears an attractive option as a more flexible means to gather evidence attuned to the particular cultural, social and historical environment. But whilst there has been much academic debate concerning such a commission for Cambodia, there has been no actual progress.[34] Undeniably, the extreme delay in addressing the wrongs of the Khmer Rouge era has had profound effects upon Cambodian society. An attempt to examine the wider truth would undoubtedly provide both a more comprehensive historical picture and also permit Cambodians to come to terms with what happened, to remember and acknowledge the past, and to look to the future. However, alternative mechanisms involving Buddhist ceremonies may be more culturally-relevant and achievable in Cambodia,[35] rather than a formal commission of enquiry as in South Africa or Sierra Leone, and are perhaps more realistic considering the length of time since the crimes were committed.

Much has also been written of the potential institution-building effect an internationally-backed EC will have on the rest of Cambodia's justice system.[36] But in a poor country with limited resources and little legal infrastructure, without the appropriate funding and necessary structural change, not to mention a major shift in judicial practice, Cambodia's court system may not be greatly affected by the Khmer Rouge trials. It is a further challenge for those committed to modernization that the momentum generated by the EC is channelled into long-term developments for Cambodia, but it requires more than simply acknowledging the existence of a UN-supported tribunal in Phnom Penh.

Education is another part of the process of assisting a society to come to terms with its past. Encouragingly, efforts are being made through local groups and non-governmental bodies such as the Centre for Social Development and the Khmer Institute of Democracy to disseminate what information is known and to stimulate public discussion.[37] Similarly, in a recent screening of a documentary produced by

---

33 Linton (2004) (*ibid.*), p.25.

34 Orentlicher (1997), 'International Criminal Law and the Cambodian Killing Fields', 3 *ILSA Journal of International and Comparative Law*, p.705; Klosterman, T. (1998), 'The Feasibility and Propriety of a Truth Commission in Cambodia: Too Little, Too Late?', 15 *Arizona Journal of International and Comparative Law*, p. 833; Ramji (2000), 'Reclaiming Cambodian History: The Case for a Truth Commission', 24 *Fletcher Forum of World Affairs* at p. 137; Linton (2002), 'New Approaches to International Justice in Cambodia and East Timor', 845 *International Review of the Red Cross*, p. 93.

35 For example, the Buddhist tradition of the public 'truth-act' witnessed by senior ecclesiastical figures. see Harris in Ramji and van Schaak (2005) (*ibid.*).

36 Fawthrop and Jarvis (2004) (*ibid.*).

37 See for example, the public discussion panel session held in Phnom Penh, 17 November 2004: www.genocidewatch.org/CambodiaTHEKHMERROUGETRIALS-Aretheyworthit17November2004.htm.

two Dutch film-makers about the experiences of a woman whose father was murdered in the days of Democratic Kampuchea and who 30 years on came face-to-face with the man she accused of playing a part in her father's death,[38] suggestions were made to show the film to a wider audience in the provinces. Such additional initiatives may be helpful for society to come to terms with what happened and to begin the long process towards rebuilding a common national identity, a confident civil society and a truly representative government.

Conclusions

Cambodia does not easily fit the mould of a post-conflict society looking to heal the trauma of atrocities. The situation is compounded by nearly three decades of domestic and international inaction in addressing the crimes committed during Democratic Kampuchea, cementing a damaging culture of impunity. Although there is perhaps an over-ambitious expectation for what the EC's limited prosecutions may achieve, the major compromises and challenges it faces should mask neither the ultimate moral obligation for accountability nor the powerful symbolic effect of the entire process. It is also to be hoped that there will be additional, culturally-sensitive initiatives to assist the process of justice and to bring the possibility of reconciliation nearer.

Although the EC may be a less than perfect mechanism to achieve accountability, if it operates according to the principles upon which it was formed, it has the potential to herald a symbolic new beginning in Cambodia's history, following which a process of education and reflection may lead to the hoped-for reconciliation. If, however, the process is de-railed by undue political influence, absence of procedural fairness, insufficiently- and inappropriately-motivated personnel or lack of funds, the trials of the EC will fail both the Cambodian people and all those who seek accountability for crimes of international concern. Whoever works with the EC will bear a heavy responsibility in rising to these challenges.

---

38 *Deacon of Death: Looking for Justice in Today's Cambodia*, a film by Jan van den Berg and Willem van de Put, premiered in Phnom Penh, 19 July 2005.

Chapter 16

The Prosecution of Genocide –
in Search of a European Perspective

Jan Wouters and Sten Verhoeven

Introduction

Europe has witnessed genocide during the Second World War and, more recently, during the wars in the former Yugoslavia. As a result, the issue of prosecuting genocide is very much alive. Since genocide has rarely been committed on their own territory, quite a number of European States have adopted national legislation permitting the exercise of extraterritorial criminal jurisdiction over this 'crime of crimes', even though this seems to go against the letter of Article VI of the Convention on the Prevention and Punishment of Genocide[1] ('Genocide Convention'), pursuant to which persons charged with genocide 'shall be tried by a competent tribunal of the State in the territory of which the act was committed, or by such international penal tribunal as may have jurisdiction with respect to those Contracting Parties which shall have accepted its jurisdiction'. However, it is nowadays broadly accepted that, under customary international law, States can exercise extraterritorial jurisdiction in this respect.[2]

The present contribution searches for a European perspective with regard to the exercise of extraterritorial criminal jurisdiction over genocide. The first part looks at national practice in this respect. As space does not permit us to examine exhaustively the legislation and case-law of all EU Member States, we have selected seven Member States which represent a main 'legal family' (France, Germany, UK) and/or are interesting because of recent legislation and case-law in this field (Austria, Belgium, Netherlands, Spain). In a second part, measures taken at the level of the European Union itself will be looked at. Although the EU has already been active in this area, it will be argued that there is a need for a framework decision on the prosecution of international crimes in general and genocide in

---

1   Convention on the Prevention and Punishment of Genocide 1948, *UNTS* No. 1021.

2   *The Attorney-General of the Government of Israel v Eichmann Case*, District Court of Jerusalem, Criminal Case No.40/61, Judgment of 15 December 1961, *I.L.R.* 1968, §§ 19–21; American Law Institute, *Restatement (Third) of Foreign Relations Law of the United States*, 1988, § 401.

particular to eliminate the existing loopholes between the national jurisdictions of the Member States.

Extraterritorial Criminal Jurisdiction Regarding Genocide: The Practice in Seven EU Member States

Austria

Austria has criminalized genocide by adopting Article 321 *Strafgesetzbuch*,[3] without determining the jurisdiction over this crime. However, Article 64(6) states that the criminal laws of Austria are also applicable to offences committed in a foreign country irrespective of the law of that country when Austria is under an obligation, including an international one, to prosecute such an offence. Consequently, Austrian courts can exercise universal jurisdiction in the case of war crimes since the Geneva Conventions provide for universal jurisdiction.[4] At first sight, in light of Article VI of the Genocide Convention (Supra), this is not the case for genocide. Nevertheless, the Austrian *Oberste Gerichtshof* has ruled that universal jurisdiction over genocide is possible under certain circumstances.

In the *Dusko Cvjetkovic*[5] case (1994), which concerned a Bosnian Serb accused of war crimes in Kucice, the Supreme Court (Oberste Gerichtshof) ruled that Article VI of the Genocide Convention and Article 321 of the Austrian *Strafgesetzbuch* were badly drafted since – at that time – no international tribunal existed to punish the crime of genocide. Although the accused had to be extradited to the State where he had committed the crime, due to the civil war in Bosnia-Herzegovina there was no functioning judiciary to try him there. Consequently, the Supreme Court held that the duty to extradite ceased and that the object and purpose of the Genocide Convention permitted the exercise of universal jurisdiction. It is noteworthy that the Court did not base its findings on Article 64 *Strafgesetzbuch*, but on Article 65(1), *lit.* 2 which determines that Austrian courts have jurisdiction when a crime is committed abroad under the conditions of double criminality and the impossibility to extradite the alleged perpetrator. Since genocide was criminalized in Bosnia-Herzegovina, charges could be brought against Dusko Cvjetkovic under Austrian criminal law. In the end the accused was found not guilty because of lack of evidence.[6] The question

---

3   Strafgesetzbuch, 23 January 1974, *Bundesgesetzblatt*, 1974/ 60, 29 January 1974.

4   Article 49 Geneva Convention for the amelioration of the condition of the wounded and sick in armed forces in the field, 12 August 1949, *UNTS* No. 970; Article 50 Geneva Convention for the amelioration of the condition of wounded, sick and shipwrecked members of armed forces at sea, 12 August 1949, *UNTS* No. 971; Article 129 Geneva Convention relative to the treatment of prisoners of war, 12 August 1949, *UNTS* No. 972; Article 146 Geneva Convention relative to the protection of civilian persons in time of war, 12 August 1949, *UNTS* No. 973.

5   Beschluss des Obersten Gerichtshofs, OS 99/94-6, 13 July 1994, available through http://www.ris.bka.gv.at/jus.

6   For a more thorough analysis, see A. Marschik (1997), 'European National Approaches to War Crimes', in T.L.H. McCormack and G.J. Simpson (eds), *The Law of War Crimes*: *National and International Approaches*, (Kluwer Law International) pp.79–81.

remains whether Austrian courts have jurisdiction when the requirement of double criminality is not fulfilled; from the decision above one could derive that this is not the case.

Belgium

Belgium has a troubled history in the field of jurisdiction over genocide and other international crimes. It repealed its Law of 16 June 1993 concerning serious violations of international humanitarian law (which provided for unfettered universal jurisdiction for such crimes) by the Law of 5 August 2003.[7] The latter law incorporated the criminalization of genocide in article 136bis *Strafwetboek*[8] and regulated the issue of jurisdiction as part of the *Wetboek van Strafvordering*.[9] The most far-reaching consequence was the elimination of unrestricted universal jurisdiction over war crimes, crimes against humanity and genocide, unless international law obliges Belgium to exercise universal jurisdiction.[10] Instead, the Belgian legislator opted – at least at first sight – for more traditional forms of extraterritorial jurisdiction, namely the active and passive personality principle.[11] Under the new Law every Belgian national or person with main residence in Belgium can be prosecuted if the person allegedly has committed genocide outside Belgium. Furthermore, if the victim of a crime of genocide has Belgian nationality or is a person who legally and habitually resides in Belgium for three years, Belgian courts can exercise jurisdiction, even if the perpetrator does not have Belgian nationality. From this it is clear that the Belgian legislator has not totally abandoned universal jurisdiction, since Belgian courts are competent to try cases of genocide in which the acts did not occur on Belgian territory and involve perpetrators and victims which do not necessarily have to be nationals. However, the initiation of the criminal proceedings is severely limited in the case of jurisdiction based on the passive personality principle: while previously every victim could start criminal proceedings, under the new Law they can only be initiated by the federal prosecutor, who has a wide margin of discretion to refuse to send a case to the investigating magistrate. In particular, he can refuse to forward the case when the complaint is without merits, the allegations cannot be qualified as genocide, crimes against humanity and war crimes, the complaint cannot lead to an admissible prosecution or the concrete circumstances of the case require that the complaint should be heard by a court with international jurisdiction, a court of the place where the crimes have been committed, of whom the perpetrator is a national or of where he can be found under the condition that these courts are independent and impartial. Presently no appeal is possible against the decision of

---

7   Wet betreffende ernstige schendingen van het international humanitair recht, 5 August 2003, *BS* 7 August 2003.

8   Strafwetboek, 8 June 1867, *BS* 9 June 1867.

9   Voorafgaande Titel Wetboek van Strafvordering (VTSV), 17 April 1878, *BS* 25 April 1878.

10   Article 12*bis* VTSV. This is arguably the case for war crimes and torture, but not for genocide since Article VI only requires territorial jurisdiction and customary international law does not provide for mandatory universal jurisdiction.

11   Article 6, 1*bis* and Article 10, 1*bis* VTSV.

the federal prosecutor, although this is bound to change in light of a judgment of the Belgian Constitutional Court.[12]

France

France has penalized genocide by introducing Article 211-1 *Code pénal*[13] and has jurisdiction over it pursuant to the active and passive personality principle. Indeed, Article 113–6 *Code pénal* determines that every crime committed abroad by a French national is punishable in France. Since genocide is categorized as a crime,[14] France will have jurisdiction over genocide pursuant to the active personality principle irrespective of the requirement of double criminality. Furthermore, Article 113–7 states that French criminal law is applicable if a French national or a non-national commits a crime – *in casu* genocide – abroad and the victim has French nationality at the time of the violation. Hence, France has jurisdiction to prosecute acts of genocide committed abroad if the perpetrator and/or the victim have French nationality. French criminal law does, however, restrict the possibility of initiating criminal proceedings based on the active and passive personality principle: in such cases criminal proceedings can only be initiated by the public prosecutor, following a complaint of the victim or his legal successors.[15]

However, this is not the complete picture. According to Article 689 *Code de Procédure pénale*,[16] French courts can prosecute and try offences committed abroad in accordance with the first part of the *Code pénal*, namely active and passive personality principle, or if international conventions to which France is a party, permit the exercise of extraterritorial jurisdiction. The *Code de Procédure pénale* enumerates a number of conventions[17] permitting French Courts to exercise jurisdiction regardless of any link with France if the perpetrator can be found on French territory.[18] Genocide is however not included in the list and therefore cannot be subjected to universal jurisdiction under general criminal law. Despite this, French Courts can exercise universal jurisdiction over genocide in the framework of acts incorporating UN Security Council Resolution 827 creating the International Criminal Tribunal for the Former Yugoslavia[19] and UN Security Council Resolution

---

12 Article 10, 1*bis* VTSV. The Belgian Constitutional Court decided that this provision violated the Constitution, while upholding its effects until 31 March 2006: Arbitragehof, No. 62/2005, 23 March 2005, *BS* 8 April 2005, B.7.6-B.7.8.

13 Code pénal, 22 July 1992, at: http://www.legifrance.gouv.fr/WAspad/ListeCodes.

14 Article 211–1 *juncto* article 132–1 Code pénal.

15 Articles 113–8 Code pénal.

16 Code de Procédure pénale, 31 December 1957, at: http://www.legifrance.gouv.fr/WAspad/ListeCodes.

17 Article 689-2-689-10 Code de Procédure pénale.

18 Articles 689–1 Code de Procédure pénale.

19 Loi No. 95–91, 2 January 1995, *JORF* 3 January 1995.

955 creating the International Criminal Tribunal for Rwanda,[20] as long as the alleged perpetrator can be found on French territory.[21]

Germany

With the adoption of its *Völkerstrafgesetzbuch*[22] in 2002 Germany became one of the leading countries in the field of national prosecution of international crimes. Pursuant to this code German national courts are competent to prosecute and try alleged perpetrators of genocide, crimes against humanity and war crimes without any requirement of territorial nexus with Germany.[23] In other words, Germany has adopted a universal jurisdiction approach *vis-à-vis* these crimes. Furthermore, by eliminating the condition of a territorial nexus, the German legislator invalidated the previous case-law of the German *Bundesgerichtshof*,[24] which required a certain link with Germany in order to initiate proceedings based on universal jurisdiction, a holding which was already weakened by a decision of the *Bundesverfassungsgericht*.[25] Nevertheless, and despite the duty to prosecute international crimes,[26] the public prosecutor (*Staatsanwaltschaft*) can decline to initiate criminal proceedings in cases of alleged acts being committed outside the territorial scope of the *Strafprozeßordnung*[27] or by a non-national in Germany on board of a ship or an airplane, if the accused is not present or is not anticipated to be present on German territory. However, in the case of acts being committed outside the territorial scope of the *Strafprozeßordnung*, the public prosecutor will prosecute if the alleged perpetrator has German nationality and is not prosecuted by an international tribunal or a national tribunal of a State on whose territory the act was committed or whose national was harmed. More particularly, the public prosecutor can dispense with prosecuting crimes of the *Völkerstrafgesetzbuch* if there is no suspicion of a German having committed such crimes, the crimes were not committed against a German, no alleged perpetrator is present in Germany and cannot be anticipated to be present and the offence is being prosecuted before an international tribunal, a national tribunal of a State on whose territory the alleged acts have been committed, whose national is being suspected of the crimes involved or whose national is the victim of such crimes. Moreover, prosecution might not be initiated against a foreigner residing in

---

20 Loi No. 96−432, 22 May 1996, *JORF* 23 May 1996.

21 Article 2 Loi No. 95-1 and Loi No. 96−432; confirmed by Cour de Cassation, Criminal Chamber, 26 March 1996, No. 95−81527 and Cour de Cassation, Criminal Chamber, 6 January 1998, No. 96−82491, rectified by Cour de Cassation, Criminal Chamber, 10 February 1998, No. 96−82491.

22 Völkerstrafgesetzbuch, 26 June 2002, *BGBl*, 2002, 2254.

23 § 1 Völkerstrafgesetzbuch.

24 See Bunnenberg, M. (2001), 'Extraterritoriale Strafrechtsanwendung bei Verbrechen gegen die Menschlichkeit und Völkermord', *AVR*, pp.170−201; Kadelbach, S. (2001), Verfassungsrecht. Strafrecht. Anmerkung', *Juristenzeitung*, pp.975−983.

25 Hoß, C. and Miller, R.A. (2002), 'German Constitutional Court and Bosnian War Crimes: Liberalizing Germany's Genocide Jurisprudence', GYIL, 597-601.

26 § 152(2) Strafprozeßordnung.

27 Strafprozeßordnung, 12 September 1950, *BGBII*, 1950, 455, 512, 629.

Germany and suspected of having committed international crimes abroad, which will be extradited to another State or transferred to an international tribunal if no German national was a victim and if the international tribunal or national courts are willing to prosecute. In any event, the public prosecutor can at any stage of the proceedings decide to withdraw his complaint and to terminate the criminal proceedings.[28]

The Netherlands

The Dutch Law on International Crimes (*Wet Internationale Misdrijven*) of 19 June 2003[29] brings together several previous laws and deals with the jurisdiction of the Dutch Courts over genocide, crimes against humanity and war crimes. The prohibition to commit genocide is laid down in Article 3 of the Law and closely follows the definition of the Genocide Convention and of the Rome Statute on the International Criminal Court. Article 2 regulates the jurisdiction over these crimes. According to Article 2.a Dutch courts have universal jurisdiction over perpetrators of the crimes enumerated in the Law when the alleged perpetrator is present on Dutch territory. In this respect two questions arise. Firstly, do the Dutch Courts have jurisdiction over genocide if the perpetrator is prosecuted or investigations are pending before foreign national tribunals or international tribunals? As such this is not clear, but it can be expected that universal jurisdiction will only be exercised if no other courts have started proceedings against the alleged perpetrator.[30] The preparatory works of the Law indeed bear out that Dutch courts will only prosecute if the alleged perpetrator cannot be extradited to another country on whose territory the acts are committed or whose national is the perpetrator or the victim of the crimes concerned or surrendered to an international tribunal.[31] A second question is at which stage of the procedure the requirement of being present on Dutch territory has to be fulfilled. On this issue, the preparatory works take as a starting point the time the alleged perpetrator can be arrested on Dutch soil[32] in furtherance of the case-law of the *Hoge Raad.*[33] As a result, investigations can only be started from the moment there exist serious reasons to suspect that the alleged perpetrator can be found in the Netherlands.

Article 2.b institutes the passive personality principle over all the crimes contained in the Law, while previously this was only accepted in the case of war crimes. Interestingly, no additional requirements, for instance double criminality, and the presence of the suspect on Dutch territory, have to be fulfilled. This entails that investigations can be initiated previously to the presence of the alleged suspect in the Netherlands. Lastly, Article 2.c lays down the active personality principle,

---

28 § 153f *juncto* § 153c Strafprozeßordnung.

29 Wet Internationale Misdrijven, 19 June 2003, *Staatsblad*, 2003, No. 270.

30 Duyx, P. (2004), De beperkte rechtsmacht van De Wet Internationale Misdrijven, *NCJM-Bulletin*, pp.19–20.

31 Memorie van Toelichting bij de Wet Internationale Misdrijven, Kamerstukken II 2001–2002, 28 337, No. 3, p.18.

32 *Ibid.*, p.38.

33 Hoge Raad, 18 September 2001, 00749/01, CW 2323, 8.5.

which was already accepted under general Dutch criminal law and is also applicable if the perpetrator has obtained Dutch nationality after the committing of the crimes.

It should be pointed out that prosecution in the Netherlands is the monopoly of the public prosecutor, with the possibility of the victim to file a complaint against a decision not to prosecute before the courts, which can subsequently order the furtherance of the criminal proceedings, but can also reject the complaint on the basis of public interest.[34]

Spain

Spain has played a leading role in the prosecution of the crime of genocide. Already in 1985 Article 23 was inserted in the *Ley Orgánica del Poder Judicial*,[35] giving Spanish courts jurisdiction over crimes committed outside Spain by a Spanish national or by foreign nationals when such crimes constitute genocide, terrorism or other crimes which Spain is obliged to prosecute according to an international treaty. While at first instance this article unequivocally provides for an unconditioned universal jurisdiction over genocide, it has been the subject of much judicial interpretation.

The first case in which the scope of this article was discussed was the *Pinochet case*. General Pinochet, the former head of State of Chile, was suspected of torture and genocide against Spanish and Chilean nationals. Consequently, Spain opened investigations asking for his extradition when he was staying in the UK. On 30 October 1998 the *Audiencia Nacional* heard an appeal challenging the jurisdiction of the Spanish courts brought by the public prosecutor. One of the points the court addressed in its decision was whether a national court had jurisdiction under the Genocide Convention in light of the latter's Article VI (supra). However, according to the *Audiencia Nacional*, it would be contrary to the object and purpose of the Genocide Convention to consider Article VI as limiting jurisdiction over genocide, particularly in relation to the gravity of this crime. Furthermore, the fact that the possibility of jurisdiction being exercised by national courts other than in the State where the act was committed was not explicitly provided for in the Convention did not exclude the possibility of a State Party exercising jurisdiction. However, it also held that Article VI of the Genocide Convention laid down the principle of subsidiarity, entailing that Spain cannot exercise jurisdiction if the case is being heard before the courts of the territorial State or an international tribunal.[36]

The *Pinochet case* was not the end of the debate. On 2 December 1999 Nobel Prize Laureate Rigoberta Menchù and others filed a complaint against eight former political and military leaders of Guatemala concerning alleged massacres, accusing them of genocide, torture, terrorism and other crimes. In its decision of 13 December

---

34 Article 12i Wetboek van Strafvordering, 15 January 1921, *Staatsblad*, 1925, No. 343.

35 *Ley Orgánica del Poder Judicial*, 6/1985, 1 July 1985, *BOE* 2 July 1985.

36 Audiencia Nacional, Sala de lo penal, 13 December 2000, Available at: http://www. icrc.org/ihl-nat.nsf/46707c419d6bdfa24125673e00508145/e020bc9287127e7fc1256bc00 033280e?OpenDocument; see also http://www.derechos.net/marga/papers/spain.html for a summary of the proceedings and legal arguments.

2000 the *Audiencia Nacional* dismissed the complaint holding that there was insufficient evidence that the Guatemalan Courts could not dispense with the case. The court reached this decision in two steps. It held first that Article VI of the Genocide Convention imposed a supplementary exercise of universal jurisdiction, giving preference to the court of the territorial State or an international tribunal. Second, since there were no obstacles to start criminal proceedings in Guatemala, the Spanish courts could not claim jurisdiction under the principle of subsidiarity.[37] This decision was partially quashed by the *Tribunal Supremo* in its judgment of 25 February 2003. The court stated that the requirement of subsidiarity was not contained in Article VI of the Genocide Convention and that hence the *Audiencia Nacional* erred in its conclusion. However, the *Tribunal Supremo* added that, if international conventions do not provide for universal jurisdiction, States can only adopt universal jurisdiction taking into account other principles of international law. In particular, the State exercising universal jurisdiction has to point to a certain national interest which would justify its exercise of universal jurisdiction, for instance the presence of the accused on its territory or the Spanish nationality of the victims. Since no accused was present on Spanish territory and no Spanish nationals were the victims of genocide, the Spanish courts could not exercise jurisdiction over the crime of genocide.[38] However, both the decisions of the *Audienca Nacional* and the *Tribunal Supremo* were declared invalid by the *Tribunal Constitucional* in its judgment of 26 September 2005 because the limits created by these tribunals were not in accordance with Article 23 of the *Ley Orgánica del Poder Judicial*: in order to exercise universal jurisdiction a claimant has merely to bring serious and reasonable indications of judicial inactivity by the territorial State.[39]

UK

The UK penalized genocide by the adoption of the Genocide Act of 1969,[40] faithfully incorporating the provisions of the Genocide Convention into its national law. Consequently, the UK only exercised territorial jurisdiction over the crime of genocide. Not surprisingly, this led to a nearly total absence of national cases. The only case was *R. vs. Starkey*,[41] in which the applicants sought the consent of the Attorney General and the Director of Public Prosecutions to institute proceedings against the Prime Minister and the Secretary of State for Defence for conspiring

---

37 Inazumi, M. (2005), *Jurisdiction in Modern International Law: Expansion of National Jurisdiction for Prosecuting Serious Crimes under International Law*, (Intersentia), 89.

38 Some Spanish nationals were however the victim of torture and hence Spanish courts could exercise jurisdiction over this matter. L. Benavides (2003), 'Explicatory Note to the Supreme Court of Spain: Judgment of the Guatemalan Genocide Case', *ILM*, 684.

39 Tribunal Constitucional, Sala Segunda, Sentencia 237/2005, 26 September 2005, available through. http://www.tribunalconstitucional.es/JC.htm.

40 Genocide Act, 1969, at:
http://www.icrc.org/ihl-nat.nsf/0/046f3c072eb70c0ac1256ba500317625?OpenDocument

41 *R. v. Starkey*, Queen's Bench Division, 14 December 1987. Available at: http://www.icrc.org/ihl-nat.nsf/39a82e2ca42b52974125673e00508144/2d8311adee2dc 740c1256ba500363e2e?OpenDocument.

to commit genocide under the Genocide Act 1969 and for conspiracy to murder citizens of the Soviet Union, involving breaches of the Geneva Conventions Act 1957. Neither the Attorney General nor the Director of Public Prosecutions agreed to initiate the prosecution sought. The applicants sought judicial review of these decisions, which the court refused.

The UK's stance changed considerably with the adoption of the International Criminal Court Act[42] in 2001. Section 51 determines that genocide, crimes against humanity and war crimes can be prosecuted if they are committed in the UK and outside the UK, if the alleged perpetrator is a national of the UK, has its residence in the UK or is subject to the UK's service jurisdiction.[43] Furthermore, proceedings can be initiated against a person who commits genocide outside the UK at a time when he is not a UK national, a UK resident or a person subject to its service jurisdiction and who subsequently becomes resident in the UK if the accused is resident in the UK at the time the proceedings are brought and the acts in respect of which the proceedings are brought could be qualified as offences under the law of the UK.[44] Hence, the UK can exercise jurisdiction over acts of genocide committed abroad by a national of the UK or a foreigner who has its residence, or has become a resident, in the UK.

Actual and Potential Role of the EU

The analysis above indicates that a number of EU Member States have enacted legislation, or interpret existing legislation in such a manner as to assume extraterritorial criminal jurisdiction over genocide. Consequently, it can be expected that perpetrators of the crime of genocide will be brought to justice in the future and that criminal proceedings can be expected to follow in Europe. However, the analysis equally shows the existence of considerable disparities between national legislations. Hence, the possibility of safe havens is still there. In this part we will examine the contribution which the EU has hitherto made in combating international crimes and whether it still could take other actions, in particular in order to approximate Member States' legislation.

Existing EU Measures

The EU has always been a staunch supporter of the International Criminal Court (ICC). Recently, it signed an agreement with the ICC regulating the cooperation between the EU as an international organization and the ICC.[45] Furthermore, the EU Council's common positions on the ICC illustrate the emergence of a common

---

42 Available through http://www.opsi.gov.uk.

43 The notions 'UK national', 'UK resident' and 'person subjected to the UK's service jurisdiction' are defined in section 67 of the Act.

44 Section 68 International Criminal Court Act.

45 Agreement between the ICC and the EU, *OJ* 2006, L 115/50.

will within the EU to combat international crimes and impunity worldwide,[46] urging
new Member States, associated countries and EFTA countries to ratify the Rome
Statute.[47] Hence, one could expect the EU to be active within the framework of its
third pillar, justice and home affairs, to encourage its Member States to prosecute
international crimes nationally and applying extraterritorial jurisdictiony thereto.
However, in contrast with other crimes like terrorism the EU has been rather inactive
in this field, focusing its attention on action under the second pillar, i.e., Common
Foreign and Security Policy. Partially, this could be explained by the ambiguity
of Articles 29 and 30 of the EU Treaty,[48] which list a number of crimes, but not
genocide, crimes against humanity and war crimes. It still remains unclear if this
list is exemplary or exhaustive, although the language of the articles and the actual
practice of the EU suggest the former. The European Constitution[49] is clearer on
the issue of EU competence. According to article III–271 only the crimes listed
therein fall within the scope of the EU powers, unless the Council takes a unanimous
decision to expand the list. Since genocide, crimes against humanity and war crimes
do not feature in the list, such a decision would be necessary in order to adopt a
Framework Law on international crimes laying down minimum standards dealing
inter alia with non-territorial jurisdiction.

Despite the relative inactivity of the EU from a third pillar point of view, some
measures which touch upon the issue can be mentioned. First of all, the European
Arrest Warrant Framework Decision, adopted by the Council in 2002,[50] applies to 32
listed crimes and to all other crimes that fall within a specified sentencing threshold.[51]
Article 2(2) determines that the requirement of double criminality should not be
fulfilled in the case of crimes enumerated in the Rome Statute, which facilitates
surrenders to another EU Member State claiming jurisdiction over the alleged
offender. Subsequently, if a Member State exercises extraterritorial jurisdiction over
international crimes and the alleged perpetrator can be found in another Member
State, which cannot claim extraterritorial jurisdiction, the alleged perpetrator will be
handed over to the requesting Member State. This instrument, while not specifically
dealing with extraterritorial jurisdiction, nevertheless can have an important impact
on the prosecution of alleged perpetrators of international crimes. However, the
executing Member State can refuse to hand over the suspect if the offences have
been committed outside the territory of the issuing Member State and the law of
the executing Member State does not allow prosecution for the same offences when
committed outside its territory.[52] Since, as we have seen, extraterritorial jurisdiction
over genocide is quite common in EU Member States, this should not pose too many

---

46 Council Common Position 2003/444/CFSP, 16 June 2003, *OJ* 2003, L 150/67; Council
Common Position 2001/443/CFSP, 11 June 2001, *OJ* 2001, L 155/19 as amended by Council
Common Position 2002/474/CFSP, 20 June 2002, *OJ* 2002, L 164/1.

47 Council Common Position 2003/444/CFSP, 16 June 2003, *OJ* 2003, L 150/67.

48 Treaty on European Union, 7 February 1992, *OJ* 2002, C 325/1 (consolidated version
after the Treaty of Nice came into force).

49 Treaty establishing a Constitution for Europe, 29 October 2004, OJ 2004, C 310/1.

50 Council Framework Decision 2002/584/JHA, 13 June 2002, *OJ* 2002, L 190/1.

51 Articles 2(1) and (2).

52 Article 7b.

problems. Moreover, even if the national legislation of the executing Member State does not permit prosecution, it still can extradite the suspect since refusal is optional and in the case of international crimes it is unlikely that the Member State would tolerate the presence of an alleged perpetrator on its territory without bringing the person to justice in another Member State or a third State.

Furthermore, the Council has adopted a Framework Decision on the mutual recognition of financial penalties,[53] which include financial obligations arising out of criminal proceedings and compensation imposed for the benefit of victims, where the victim may not be a civil party to the proceedings and the court is acting in the exercise of its criminal jurisdiction.[54] The Framework Decision is applicable to a number of crimes, including the crimes over which the ICC has jurisdiction.[55] The competent authorities in the executing State have to recognize a decision which has been transmitted without any further formality being required and take all the necessary measures for its execution, unless the competent authority decides to invoke one of the grounds for non-recognition or non-execution laid down in Article 7, for example if international crimes have been committed outside the territory of the issuing State and the law of the executing State does not allow prosecution for the same offences when committed outside its territory.

It should also be pointed out that a number of EU measures (other than framework decisions) specifically aimed at genocide, crimes against humanity and war crimes have been taken. On 13 June 2002, the Council established the European network of contact points in respect of persons responsible for genocide, crimes against humanity and war crimes,[56] which is now in operation. Although the creation of a network specifically dealing with international crimes has the merit of focusing attention on this issue, it is regrettable that it does not lay down legally binding rules of cooperation. The network merely facilitates regular contacts between professionals specialized in the prosecution of international crimes, but does not even have its own budget. Consequently, its effects are quite limited. Furthermore, on 8 May 2003, the Council adopted a decision on the investigation and prosecution of genocide, crimes against humanity and war crimes.[57] Its goal is to augment the co-operation among national units in the investigation and prosecution of the crimes mentioned. The decision aims at reinforcing the possibilities offered to Member States regarding the investigation and prosecution of alleged perpetrators. It should strengthen the co-operation between national units leading to the enhancement of the ability of law enforcement authorities in different Member States to co-operate effectively in this field. Although the Decision is legally binding upon Member States, its content is almost devoid of any obligation. In particular, two important obligations that had been included in the draft were removed, namely the duty to prosecute and the obligation to provide resources. As a result, the effectiveness of the Decision is quite meagre as was the case with the Decision of 13 June 2002.

---

53 Council Framework Decision 2005/214/JHA, 24 February 2005, *OJ* 2005, L 76/16.
54 Article 1 Framework Decision 2005/214/JHA.
55 Article 5 Framework Decision 2005/214/JHA.
56 Council Decision 2002/494/JHA, 13 June 2002, *OJ* 2002, L 167/1.
57 Council Decision 2003/335/JHA, 8 May 2003, *OJ* 2003, L 118/12.

A Proposed Enhanced European Action in the Field of International Crimes

Until now, the EU has mostly been active in relation to international crimes and the ICC in the framework of its second pillar. However, it is time that this engagement should be translated in actions in the third pillar. The examination of the criminal legislation and case-law of various EU Member States in the first part of this contribution, while demonstrating the will of those States to combat international crimes, has also shown that gaps and loopholes still exist and that the lack of a uniform approach risks to entail safe havens for perpetrators of international crimes and genocide in particular. Consequently, since the EU attaches great importance to the ICC and the fight against impunity over international crimes, it will need to ensure that alleged perpetrators within the EU will be prosecuted if the ICC declines to initiate proceedings based on the complementarity principle and/or the prosecutorial policies of the Prosecutor.

Admittedly, new initiatives have been taken to enhance the fight against impunity and it should be welcomed that genocide, crimes against humanity and war crimes are more and more present in the proposals for future EU measures in criminal matters.[58] What is however needed is the adoption of a framework decision specifically dealing with the prosecution of international crimes. Such a framework decision should lay down minimum standards on jurisdictional rules relating to international crimes seeking to approximate the national legislation of Member States. It should set out minimum standards on the definition of and jurisdiction over genocide, crimes against humanity and war crimes and should address potential restrictions on the exercise of jurisdiction, such as immunities, limitation periods and nexus requirements. Not only would this ensure that treaties are consistently applied throughout the EU and overcome the present hurdles hindering inter-State cooperation in the investigation and prosecution, it would also facilitate the application of the principle of complementarity, so crucial to the success of the ICC. The framework decision would certainly have to deal with extraterritorial jurisdiction over international crimes. A good starting point could be the introduction of the principle *aut dedere, aut judicare*, which would entail that if a Member State refuses to prosecute an alleged perpetrator, it has to extradite or hand over this person to another Member State, third State or international body which will assume jurisdiction. With regard to the nexus requirement, the minimum standard to be adopted could be the condition of habitual residence in a Member State, which can be found in most of the national laws examined in the first part of this contribution, and does not preclude less stringent nexus requirements or the total absence thereof. Lastly, the framework decision should ideally contain provisions

---

58 Initiative of Austria, Finland and Sweden with a view to adopting a Council Framework Decision on the European enforcement order and the transfer of sentenced persons between EU Member States, *OJ* 2005, C 150/1; Initiative of Sweden with a view to adopting a Framework Decision on simplifying the exchange of information and intelligence between law enforcement authorities of EU Member States, in particular as regards serious offences including terrorist acts, *OJ* 2004, C 281/5.

dealing with prosecutorial discretion, limit it, or at least clearly determine on which grounds a refusal of prosecution can be based.

Conclusion

European States and the EU have shown a determined will to bring perpetrators of international crimes to justice. Since Europe has recently been spared of genocide, quite a number of States have assumed extraterritorial jurisdiction in order to try international crimes committed abroad, clearly sending a message to the international community that European States do not want to be safe havens. Unfortunately, due to the differences between the laws of Member States, loopholes continue to exist and it is still possible that no prosecution of alleged perpetrators will take place due to inadequate legislation and/or cooperation. Until now, EU measures have fallen short to remedy this deficiency. Hence, it is time that the EU elaborates a framework decision in this regard, laying down minimum standards for the prosecution of international crimes.

Chapter 17

Reflection on the Separation of Powers: The Law of Genocide and the Symptomatic French Paradox

Caroline Fournet

The French legal position with respect to the crime of genocide is interesting – if not to say rather intriguing and ambiguous – notably due to the fact that legal practice stands in complete opposition to legal theory. Accordingly, this paper focuses both on the French domestic definition of the crime of genocide as well as on the relevant national case law, thus highlighting the dichotomy between theory and practice.

The first part of the chapter deals with the definition of the crime of genocide as embodied in Article 211-1 of the French Penal Code. This theoretical analysis notably focuses on the fact that, although the French definition draws upon the definition enshrined in Article II of the 1948 United Nations Convention on the Prevention and Punishment of the Crime of Genocide,[1] it also significantly departs from it in two important – and positive – aspects.

Paradoxically, the French practice has failed to adequately follow the theory and the crime of genocide has more often than not remained totally and inexplicably absent from prosecutions. The second part of the paper thus explores the practical manifestations of this judicial reluctance towards the crime of genocide and argues that such attitude has no legal or factual justification.

The French Legislator and the Crime of Genocide

France has signed the Genocide Convention on 11 December 1948, only two days after its adoption by the General Assembly of the United Nations on 9 December 1948. France subsequently ratified the Genocide Convention on 14 October 1950, thus showing its attachment to the prevention and punishment of the crime

---

1 Convention on the Prevention and Punishment of the Crime of Genocide, Approved and proposed for signature and ratification or accession by General Assembly resolution 260 A (III) of 9 December 1948, *entry into force* 12 January 1951, in accordance with Article XIII. Hereafter referred to as the Genocide Convention.

of genocide rather early on.[2] And indeed, the Convention entered into force on 12 January 1951. Nonetheless, the crime of genocide only made its 'formal entrance' in French legislation on 1 March 1994 with the entry into force of the New Penal Code, which defines genocide in its Article 211-1:

> Genocide occurs where, in the enforcement of a *concerted plan* aimed at the partial or total destruction of a national, ethnic, racial or religious group, or of *a group determined by any other arbitrary criterion*, one of the following actions are committed or caused to be committed against members of that group:
>
> – wilful attack on life;
> – serious attack on psychic or physical integrity;
> – subjection to living conditions likely to entail the partial or total destruction of that group;
> – measures aimed at preventing births;
> – enforced child transfers.[3]

Although this definition was clearly influenced by the Genocide Convention, two different remarks may be made. First of all, while the conventional definition defines the crime of genocide by the *intent* to destroy a group, the French definition puts the emphasis on the planned and systematic feature of the crime and, to this end, adopts a more objective criterion, that of the existence of *concerted plan*.[4] Second of all, the scope of application of the definition of genocide finds itself significantly enlarged. And indeed, although the Genocide Convention only affords protection to 'national, ethnic, racial or religious' groups as such, the French disposition grants protection to all of these conventionally protected groups as well as to 'group [s] determined by any other arbitrary criterion'. The Genocide Convention has been heavily criticized for its narrow sphere of application and its selective protection of groups and it thus seems that France, by recognizing that genocide could be committed against other groups than the ones expressly listed in the Convention, has adopted a more progressive approach. In this French proactive legislative context, it is therefore intriguing that the concept of genocide has remained absent from prosecutions and the question arises as to whether legal obstacles could have impeded its application in such prosecutions.

The Direct Applicability of the Genocide Convention under French Law

The first legal obstacle which could be invoked regarding the application of the Genocide Convention to acts perpetrated before the entry into force of the French New Penal Code, and the explicit definition of the crime therein, is the applicability of the Convention under French law. Nonetheless, even if the qualification of genocide only entered the French Penal Code in 1994, France had ratified the Convention in

---

2 It can be noted here that, upon ratification, France made no declaration, no reservation and no objection.
3 Emphasis added.
4 'plan concerté'.

1950, and the Convention should have been of immediate application as soon as it had entered into force in January 1951. And indeed, France is a country of monist tradition, where treaties once ratified have a force superior to that of national laws. Thus, at the time of ratification of the Convention, this principle was unequivocally stated in Article 26 of the 1946 Constitution.[5] It was subsequently reiterated in Article 55 of the 1958 French Constitution, which is still in force today.[6]

In other words, the Genocide Convention was directly applicable under French law and, in fact, in his *Commentary of the Genocide Convention*, Robinson expressly cited France as one of the states where 'an international agreement becomes domestic law by ratification'.[7]

The Non-applicability of Statutory Limitations to the Crime of Genocide

The second potential obstacle to the qualification of a crime as genocide under French law before the entry into force of the New Penal Code could be statutory limitations, and it must here be acknowledged that both international law and French law are rather confusing.

At the international level, the legacy of the Genocide Convention on the issue of statutory limitations was one of uncertainty, simply due to the fact that the Convention was totally silent on this particular matter. The first international instrument which solved the question by explicitly prohibiting the application of statutory limitations to the crime of genocide was the 1968 UN Convention on the Non-Applicability of Statutory Limitations to War Crimes and Crimes Against Humanity,[8] which entered into force in 1970. Although this Convention has failed to attract a wide amount of ratification, including the French ratification, it is still submitted here that, as of today, statutory limitations do not apply to the crime of genocide. And indeed, Article 29 of the Statute of the International Criminal Court eliminated all doubts by unequivocally affirming that 'the crimes within the jurisdiction of the Court shall not be subject to any statute of limitations'.[9]

The French position on the matter fails to be totally clear, due to the confusion between crimes against humanity and genocide. Nonetheless, a few elements do demonstrate that, under French law, statutory limitations were not an obstacle to the application of the Genocide Convention.

5 'Les traités diplomatiques régulièrement ratifiés et publiés ont force de loi dans le cas même où ils seraient contraires à des lois françaises, sans qu'il soit besoin pour en assurer l'application d'autres dispositions législatives que celles qui auraient été nécessaires pour assurer leur ratification'. Constitution du 27 octobre 1946.

6 'Les traités ou accords régulièrement ratifiés ou approuvés ont, dès leur publication, une autorité supérieure à celle des lois, sous réserve, pour chaque accord ou traité, de son application par l'autre partie'. Constitution du 4 octobre 1958.

7 Robinson, N. (1960), *The Genocide Convention – A Commentary*, New York: Institute of Jewish Affairs/World Jewish Congress, pp. 34–35.

8 New York, 26 November 1968, *entry into force* 11 November 1970. Article I(b).

9 Rome Statute of the International Criminal Court 17 July 1998. Adopted by the United Nations Diplomatic Conference of Plenipotentiaries on the Establishment of an International Criminal Court on 17 July 1998, UN Doc. A/Conf.183/9, 1998. *Entry into force* 1 July 2002.

First of all, although France did not ratify the 1968 Convention, it must here be noted that, faced with the question whether international treaties established statutory limitations, the French Foreign Affairs Ministry unequivocally held that 'le droit international ignore en général la prescription extinctive. Pour lui, celle-ci ne se présume pas, et à défaut d'une mention explicite, elle ne s'applique pas' ['international law generally ignores extinctive prescription. According to international law, extinctive prescription cannot be presumed and therefore applies only if expressly mentioned'].[10] In other words, the Foreign Affairs Ministry interpreted the silence of the Genocide Convention as a confirmation that the crime of genocide was not subjected to statutory limitations.

Second of all, under French law, the non-applicability of statutory limitations to crimes against humanity is clear and unequivocal. Faced with the urgency emanating from the fact that crimes committed during the Second World War would soon be subjected to statutory limitations,[11] the French legislator unanimously adopted a law recognizing the non-applicability of statutory limitations to crimes against humanity, *and crimes against humanity only.*[12] As the law is silent on this point, the question thus arises as to whether crimes against humanity were here understood as encompassing also the crime of genocide. In light of the *travaux préparatoires*, it appears that the French legislator intended to include the crime of genocide within the notion of crimes against humanity,[13] and the reason why it decided to expressly mention only and exclusively crimes against humanity was that, as explained by M. Edouard Le Bellegon,[14] genocide is only a form of crime against humanity.[15]

Third of all, if it can be noted here that France is not a party to the UN 1968 Convention, the reason for not ratifying it was the conventional recognition of the non-applicability of statutory limitations to war crimes which, under French law, have traditionally been subjected to statutory limitations. Had the UN 1968 Convention only dealt with crimes against humanity and genocide, France would have had no reason not to ratify it.

---

10 15 June 1979, See de Bigault du Granrut. B. (1998), 'le Crime Contre l'humanité', Ecole Cathédrale – Institut de Formation Continue du Barreau de Paris (1998), *Le Crime Contre l'Humanité, mesure de la responsabilité ? Actes du cycle des conférences « Droit, Liberté et Foi », Juin 1997* (CERP) 97. Translation by the author.

11 Under French law, murders were prescribed 20 years after their commission. In other words, after 20 years, no trial could take place.

12 See Law no. 64–1326 of 26 December 1964 and Article 213–5 of the New Penal Code.

13 See Journal officiel, Document de l'Assemblée Nationale, annexes aux procès-verbaux des séances, 2e session ordinaire de 1963–1964; no. 46, 11 mai 1965, Annexe no. 1026, pp. 806–807. Cited in Mertens, p. (1974), *L'imprescriptibilité des crimes de guerre et contre l'humanité* (Editions de l'Université de Bruxelles) 51.

14 Rapporteur au Sénat de la Commission des lois constitutionnelles, de la législation et de l'administration générale.

15 Journal officiel du 18 décembre 1964, Débats parlementaires, Sénat, première session ordinaire de 1954–1965, compte rendu intégral de la séance du 17 décembre 1964, p. 2429. Cited in Mertens (1974), pp. 53–4.

All these elements overwhelmingly show that, since 1964, France recognizes the non-applicability of statutory limitations to genocide. This was confirmed by Article 213–5 of the New Penal Code which states that '[t]he public action relating to the crimes envisaged by this title [genocide and crimes against humanity], as well as the sentences passed, are imprescriptible'.

The Applicability of Retroactive Criminal Norms

A third possible obstacle which could impede the application of the Genocide Convention to acts committed prior the entry into force of the New Penal Code in France is the issue of retroactivity. If, under international law, the principle is that treaties have no retroactive force, this rule nonetheless fails to be absolute and some limitations do apply, notably in the case of genocide and even if the Genocide Convention remains silent on the matter.

For instance, Article 15 of the International Covenant on Civil and Political Rights (ICCPR) which deals with the prohibition of retroactive criminal laws expressly makes an exception to the general principle in the following terms:

1. No one shall be held guilty of any criminal offence on account of any act or omission which did not constitute a criminal offence, under national or international law, at the time when it was committed. Nor shall a heavier penalty be imposed than the one that was applicable at the time when the criminal offence was committed. If, subsequent to the commission of the offence, provision is made by law for the imposition of a lighter penalty, the offender shall benefit thereby.

2. Nothing in this article shall prejudice the trial and punishment of any person for any act or omission which, at the time when it was committed, was criminal according to the general principles of law recognized by the community of nations.

It seems clear the 'general principles of law recognized by the community of nations' do encompass the prohibition of genocide,[16] although it could also be argued that this prohibition stems from international rules of international customary law and is therefore covered by the reference to 'international law' in Article 15(1) rather than by Article 15(2).[17] And, in fact, this reference to 'international law' in Article 15(1) is attributable to proposals by Uruguay *and France*, who argued that it would prevent persons responsible for the commission of international crimes to evade punishment by simply pleading that their offences were not punishable under the domestic law of their state(s).[18] In other words, France expressly showed its attachment to the punishment of international crimes and, in this respect, adopted a proactive approach, in phase with its obligations under international law. In such circumstances, it would be doubtful that France would see any legal obstacle in the application of Article 15

---

16 See Nowak, M. (1993), *UN Covenant on Civil and Political Rights: CCPR Commentary*, (N.P. Engel Publishers) p. 276.

17 See Cassese A. (2006), 'Balancing the Prosecution of Crimes against Humanity and Non-Retroactivity of Criminal Law', 4:2 *JICJ*, 414–5.

18 See E/CN.4/SR.112, 5 ff.; A/2929, 45 (§94).

with respect to the Genocide Convention. As a matter of fact, this would be even more doubtful considering the fact that Article 7 of the European Convention on Human Rights (ECHR) – to which France is a party[19] – reiterates the content of Article 15 of the ICCPR in nearly the exact same terms:

> 1.   No one shall be held guilty of any criminal offence on account of any act or omission which did not constitute a criminal offence under national or international law at the time when it was committed. Nor shall a heavier penalty be imposed than the one that was applicable at the time the criminal offence was committed.
>
> 2.   This Article shall not prejudice the trial and punishment of any person for any act or omission which, at the time when it was committed, was criminal according to the general principles of law recognized by civilized nations.

Far from being a purely theoretical hypothesis, it can be recalled here that the French Cour de cassation itself expressly recognized the applicability of both Article 15(2) of the ICCPR and Article 7(2) of the ECHR to crimes perpetrated during the Second World War.[20]

French Courts and the Crime of Genocide

The memory of the genocide perpetrated during the Second World War took a very long time to emerge in France and the first trial to deal effectively with this genocide was that of Klaus Barbie.[21] For the first time, the Shoah was at the heart of the legal debates. The trial of Barbie was subsequently followed by those of Paul Touvier, active member of the French *Milice*, Maurice Papon, former high civil servant, and Aloïs Brunner.[22] Most surprisingly, all those who stood accused for their participation in the Shoah were not charged with genocide – even though, as we have seen, it could have legally been the case – but with crimes against humanity. If, in theory, one could argue that crimes against humanity and genocide do cover the same reality, genocide being an aggravated form of crimes against humanity, the consequences of this amalgam in practice were far more important, not only regarding the law but also regarding collective memory of the Shoah. The following development thus

---

19   France signed the ECHR on 4 November 1950 and subsequently ratified it on 3 May 1974.

20   *Barbie* case, cass. crim., 6 October 1983.

21   If numerous trials were held in the aftermath of the Second World War, they were based on Article 75 of the French Penal Code, which dealt with the crimes of treason and of intelligence with the enemy.

22   Aloïs Brunner was tried *in abstentia* by the cour d'assises of Paris on 2 March 2001. He was charged with, and found guilty of, crimes against humanity for the following acts committed between 21 July 1944 and 4 August 1944: illegal arrests and confinements of 352 children, 345 of whom were deported; complicity of murders and/or attempted murders against 284 children, all of whom were murdered in Auschwitz-Birkenau and Bergen-Belsen. The youngest, Alain Blumberg, was 15 days old, the oldest was 18 years old. Brunner was sentenced to life imprisonment, although nobody knows whether he is still alive.

analyzes the practice of French courts regarding genocide and their reluctance to apply the Genocide Convention in spite of the fact that, as previously demonstrated, the Convention was applicable in France by French courts as soon as it had entered into force.

The trial of Klaus Barbie was very symptomatic of the reluctance of French courts to apply the Genocide Convention. Klaus Barbie, chief of the Gestapo in Lyon also known as 'the butcher of Lyon', owed this reputation to his fierce and relentless struggle against *Résistance* fighters, but he was also responsible for the deportation of Jews and thus for his active participation in the Shoah.[23] He was nonetheless charged with crimes against humanity and not with genocide.

As the court of appeals of Lyon acknowledged the clear differences between crimes committed against *Résistance* fighters and crimes committed against Jews, it established, and rightly so, two distinct qualifications for these two distinct types of crimes. This is nonetheless where the problems start because the court of appeals qualified crimes against *Résistance* fighters as war crimes and crimes against Jews as crimes against humanity. In practice, this meant that, due to the application of statutory limitations under French law to war crimes, Barbie could only be tried for what the court qualified as crimes against humanity, namely the crimes perpetrated against Jews. In other words, crimes perpetrated against *Résistance* fighters, considered as war crimes, would go unpunished. This partial impunity which would be awarded to Barbie was both illegitimate and unacceptable. And, in fact, the limits of the distinction created by the court of appeals rapidly emerged when the court had to solve the question of the qualification of the crimes perpetrated against Jewish *Résistance* fighters, question which arose with respect to one of Barbie's victims, Professor Gompel. In this particular case, the court explained that:

> Barbie could have thought that he was a Résistance fighter and, therefore, the presumption of innocence must apply here. We must consider, by presumption, that he was a *non-innocent* Jew and that the tortures Gompel had to endure fell within the statutory limitations applicable to war crimes.[24]

---

23 Klaus Barbie had already been tried by French courts *in absentia*. He was tried in 1952 and again in 1954 and sentenced to death for his participation in more than 4,000 killings and in the deportation of more than 7,000 Jews to concentration camps. Barbie managed to evade justice for nearly 40 years, and was supposedly supported by American intelligence officers who sought his assistance in anti-Soviet intelligence. In 1951, he emigrated to Bolivia and, under the name Klaus Altmann, acquired Bolivian citizenship in 1957. After being discovered by Serge and Beate Klarsfeld in 1971, Barbie was extradited to France. His trial lasted from 11 May 1987 to 4 July 1987. He was sentenced to life imprisonment and died in prison on 25 September 1991.

24 Translation by the author. Emphasis added. The original version reads as follows: 'Barbie a pu penser qu'il était résistant, par conséquent la présomption d'innocence qui joue en sa faveur doit jouer là, et l'on doit considérer, par présomption, que c'était un juif non-innocent et que les tortures qu'on a fait subir à ce malheureux Gompel étaient couvertes par la prescription des crimes de guerre.' See Lyon-Caen, A. (1988), 'De Nuremberg au Procès Barbie', in Centre de droit international de l'Institut de Sociologie de l'Université Libre de Bruxelles (Centre Henri Rolin), Fondation Auschwitz-Stichting (Centre d'Etudes et de Documentation) (1988), *Le Procès de Nuremberg – Conséquences et actualisation, Actes du*

In other words, pushing its distinction to the extremes, the court, in order to exclude all *Résistance* fighters from the scope of application of crimes against humanity, defined Jews who were also members of the *Résistance* as 'non-innocent' Jews … a very unfortunate choice of terminology, to say the very least. As, in the eyes of the Court, it could not be ascertained that Barbie knew that they were Jews, the quality of the victims as *Résistance* fighters was found to prevail and the crimes perpetrated against them were thus war crimes subjected to statutory limitations under French law.

Fortunately, faced with this problematic distinction between victims of Nazism – and most probably with the political impossibility to let the crimes committed against *Résistance* fighters go unpunished – the Cour de cassation, on 20 December 1985, put an end to the debate by quashing the decision of the court of appeals. As a result, it seemingly extended the notion of crimes against humanity in order for it to encompass crimes committed against *Résistance* fighters:

> According to Article 6(c) of the Charter of the International Military Tribunal at Nuremberg, appended to the London Charter of 8 August 1945, inhumane acts and persecutions which have been systematically committed in the name of a state practising a policy of ideological supremacy against individuals by reason of their belonging to a racial or religious community as well as against the opponents of this policy, whatever the form of their opposition – whether armed or not – constitute imprescriptible crimes against humanity, and this is the case even if they also qualify as war crimes by virtue of Article 6(b) of the Charter of the International Military Tribunal at Nuremberg.[25]

Legally speaking, this meant that crimes against humanity were defined no longer by the nature and the quality of the victim but by the nature of the acts and the ideological identity of their author. This decision has to be welcomed as the recognition of the commission of crimes against humanity against *Résistance* fighters and as the application of crimes against humanity as defined in the Nuremberg Charter. Nonetheless, by adopting an unduly restrictive approach to the notion of crimes against humanity, the Cour de cassation turned the law of Nuremberg into a law of circumstances. And, in this respect, this decision has two major flaws.

Colloque international, Université Libre de Bruxelles, Bruxelles, le 27 mars 1987 (Editions Bruylant, Editions de l'Université de Bruxelles) 55.

25 Translation by the author. The original version reads as follows: 'Attendu que constituent des crimes imprescriptibles contre l'humanité, au sens de l'article 6 (c) du Statut du Tribunal militaire international de Nuremberg annexé à l'accord de Londres du 8 août 1945, alors même qu'ils seraient également qualifiables de crimes de guerre, selon l'article 6 (b) de ce texte, les actes inhumains et persécutions qui, au nom d'un Etat pratiquant une politique d'hégémonie idéologique, ont été commis de façon systématique, non seulement contre des personnes en raison de leur appartenance à une collectivité raciale ou religieuse, mais aussi contre les adversaires de cette politique quelle que soit la forme de leur opposition – autrement dit forme armée ou forme non-armée'. See Lyon-Caen, A. (1988), p. 56.

The Equalization of the Crimes and of the Victims

The problem with the different decisions in the *Barbie* case lies in the starting point itself. And indeed, if the court of appeals was right in distinguishing between crimes perpetrated against *Résistance* fighters and crimes perpetrated against Jews, it was nonetheless wrong in the qualification of these crimes. Subsequently, in order not to let some crimes go unpunished, the Cour de cassation included crimes perpetrated against *Résistance* fighters within the ambit of crimes against humanity. Far from artificially extending this notion, the Cour merely applied Article 6(c) of the Charter of the Nuremberg Tribunal[26] according to which crimes against humanity are:

> murder, extermination, enslavement, deportation, and other inhumane acts committed against any civilian population, before or during the war, or persecutions on *political*, racial or religious grounds in execution of or in connection with any crime within the jurisdiction of the Tribunal, whether or not in violation of the domestic law of the country where perpetrated.[27]

In other words, right from the beginning of the legal proceedings, crimes against *Résistance* fighters should have been qualified as crimes humanity, by direct application of Article 6(c) of the Nuremberg Charter. On the other hand, French courts should have distinguished between the crimes committed against *Résistance* fighters – crimes against humanity – and crimes perpetrated against Jews, which should have been recognized as genocide. By qualifying all Nazi crimes as crimes against humanity, the Cour de cassation proceeded to an equalization of the crimes and of the victims and thus failed to acknowledge the crucial differences between them. It is indeed a different crime to target political opponents, who had chosen to become opponents, and to target whole families, men, women, children, for the only reason that they were, in the eyes of the perpetrators, Jewish. To them, no choice was ever possible.

The *Barbie* case, which received intense media coverage, could have been a major opportunity for the Cour de cassation to ascertain the specificity of the crime of genocide, and most particularly of the Shoah. By failing to adequately qualify the facts, by proceeding to a merging of all the different victims of Nazism and by ignoring the specificity of each crime and of each victim, the trial of Klaus Barbie was counter-productive. The purpose of this observation is certainly not to establish a hierarchy between different crimes and different victims but merely to establish a distinction: no crime is more serious than another, it is simply different. The Nazis had established a system with a clear hierarchy among the victims and with precise priorities in terms of who to exterminate first. These different *degrees of exterminability* should have been clearly recognized by the French Cour de cassation, by simply applying the law and by qualifying the Shoah as genocide.

---

26 Charter of the International Military Tribunal, Annex to Agreement for the Prosecution and Punishment of Major War Criminals of the European Axis, London, 8 August 1945, 82 UNTS 279. The Nuremberg Tribunal was thus established by a treaty, originally signed by the four major Allies, and thus by France.

27 Emphasis added.

Not only would such a decision clearly have respected the reality of History by acknowledging the differences between the crimes and the victims, it would also have respected international law by recognizing the applicability of the Genocide Convention.

Nuremberg as a Law of Circumstances

With its decision of 20 December 1985, the Cour de cassation made a strict and restrictive reading of Article 6(c) of the Nuremberg Charter, which expressly stated that the International Military Tribunal would try crimes against humanity falling 'within the jurisdiction of the Tribunal'. The Cour de cassation thus interpreted the Nuremberg definition as requiring, for a crime against humanity to be qualified as such, that the crime be committed by a state practising a policy of ideological supremacy or on behalf of such state.[28] In other words, the notion of crimes against humanity found itself unduly enclosed with one particular state policy: Nazism. The consequences of such a finding was that there could be no crime against humanity without Nazism and that, therefore, no subsequent complaint for crimes against humanity could ever be filed, notably as to the crimes committed by the French army during the decolonization process.

The restrictive perspective adopted by the French judges was completely wrong. Instead of referring themselves to the Nuremberg judgment, they referred themselves to the motivations of the drafters of the Charter and made of Nuremberg a law of circumstances, relative to the sole crimes committed by the European Axis Powers during a precise period of time which was now over. In no case should the judges have based their decisions on a time limit, to a given conflict and to specific authors defined by their nationality as neither international law nor domestic law impose such restrictions. This absurd case-law has had terrible consequences in practice as no other crime could be qualified as a crime against humanity, simply because it would necessarily be exterior, in time and circumstances, to the European Axis Powers.[29] Under French Law, it therefore had to be waited for the entry into force of the New Penal Code in 1994 to have the legal possibility of qualifying as one against humanity a crime unrelated with the European Axis Powers. This possibility is however still heavily limited by the fact that the notion of crimes against humanity cannot apply to acts committed between 1945 – the end of the Second World War – and 1994 – date of entry into force of the New Penal Code.

---

28 *Barbie* case: *Fédération Nationale des Déportés et Internés Résistants et Patriotes et Autres v Barbie*, cass. crim., 20 December 1985, in (1986) RGDIP 90, 1024.

29 See notably the *Boudarel* case regarding crimes committed during the Vietnam War. In this case, the Cour de cassation unequivocally held that such crimes did not fall within the category of crimes against humanity punishable in France as, under French law, crimes against humanity only related to 'offences perpetrated on behalf of the Axis European States', cass. crim., 1 April 1993, *Bull. Crim.* p. 143.

The Cour de Cassation subsequently confirmed its decision in both the *Touvier* case[30] and the *Papon* case.[31] In both instances, it indeed found that the authors or accomplices of crimes against humanity were only punishable if they had acted on the account of a European Axis Power, thus again linking crimes against humanity with the crimes committed by the Axis Powers. In these cases, not only did the French judges maintain the qualification of crimes against humanity for crimes perpetrated against Jews, but they also ruled that French participants in the Shoah were accomplices rather than main authors, in complete contradiction with the historical truth. In this respect, both the *Touvier* case and the *Papon* case are very symptomatic of the will of French judges not to link in any fashion crimes perpetrated by Vichy France with genocide.

Had the Cour de cassation applied the qualification of genocide to crimes perpetrated in the context of the Shoah, at least both Touvier and Papon – and through them Vichy France – would have been found guilty of complicity in genocide. If the mere recognition of complicity would still be far beneath the historical truth, at least the policy of Vichy France would have been legally linked with nothing less than a genocidal policy. Not only would this have been more in adequacy with the truth, it would also have been essential in terms of collective memory and of remembrance of the victims.

Conclusion

With the entry into force of the New Penal Code and with the simultaneous express entry into the Code of the crime of genocide, one could have legitimately thought that French judges would have to apply the law of genocide. Again, such hopes were mere illusions. In the *Javor* case, both the court of appeals[32] and the Cour de cassation[33] asserted that there was no jurisdiction with respect to the crime of genocide. The failure of the Genocide Convention to expressly provide for universal jurisdiction here meant that the Genocide Convention could not be relied upon with respect to the crimes perpetrated in Bosnia and Herzegovina. In instances dealing with the genocide perpetrated in Rwanda, the first complaints filed by victims also failed to be successful,[34] and the first interesting case in this respect is the *Munyeshyaka* case. At long last, and after a still ongoing judicial saga,[35] the Cour de cassation found that French courts could have jurisdiction not only over acts of torture or inhuman

---

30 *Touvier* case, cass. crim., 27 November 1992 [1993-II] JCP 21, 977) Touvier was found guilty and condemned to life imprisonment on 20 April 1994, cass. crim., 20 April 1994. He died in prison on 17 July 1996.

31 *Papon* case, cass. crim., 23 January 1997.

32 CA Paris, 24 October 1994, See Stern. B, (1999) 'In re Javor', 'In re Munyeshyaka', *AJIL* 93, p. 527.

33 *Javor*, cass. crim., 26 March 1996, (1996) *Bull Crim*, pp. 132, 379.

34 See Complaint, *Kalinda et al.*, T.G.I. Paris, filed 4 July 1994; Complaint, *Dupaquier et al.*, filed 19 July 1994, Order, 23 February 1995. See Stern, B. (1999) 527, note 15.

35 See notably C.A. Nîmes, 20 March 1996. The length of the procedure – the case is yet to be settled – prompted the condemnation of France by the European Court of Human Rights. See ECHR, 8 June 2004.

treatment as defined in the Torture Convention,[36] but also over acts falling within the jurisdiction of the International Criminal Tribunal for Rwanda,[37] and therefore over the crime of genocide.

The French position with respect to the crime of genocide is thus rather paradoxical. On the one hand, the French legislator has adopted a rather progressive definition of the crime of genocide while, it may here be noted, also taking a proactive approach with respect to genocide denial.[38] On the other hand, French courts have created confusion in many respects, notably by not qualifying the extermination of Jews perpetrated during the Second World War as genocide and by showing clear and obvious reluctance to apply the Genocide Convention to more recent cases of genocide.

Ultimately, the only conclusion that could be drawn is that the French perspective regarding the crime of genocide is a dramatic – and extreme – illustration of Montesquieu's separation of powers – a doctrine to which France is very much attached – between the judiciary, the legislative and the executive. And indeed, not only are French courts in contradiction with the French legislator, they are also in contradiction with the former French President of the Republic who poignantly stated:

> Jews of all ages, all conditions, all origins, who have brought so much to our country, our culture, our civilization, annihilated by the Nazi criminal madness: your children, your families, your compatriots remember you. Your memory, the memory of this 'world which had been', is for France more than sorrow. It is the conscience of a sin. It is a requirement of responsibility.[39]

This 'requirement of responsibility' clearly should encompass judicial recognition and acknowledgement of the crime of genocide, through its unequivocal prosecution and punishment.

---

36 Cass. crim., 6 January 1998; (1998) RGDIP, 3, pp. 825–832.

37 See Law No. 96–432 of 22 May 1996, *Journal Officiel*, 23 May 1996, p. 7695, adapting French legislation to Security Council Resolution 955 creating the ICTR, and which provides for universal jurisdiction over genocide. This new law being procedural, the court of appeal, to which the case was remanded by the Cour de cassation, can retroactively apply it.

38 See Law no. 90-615 du 13 juillet 1990 tendant à réprimer tout acte raciste, antisémite ou xénophobe. See also Law no. 2001–70 du 29 janvier 2001 relative à la reconnaissance du génocide arménien, Journal officiel, 30 January 2001.

39 Translation by the author. The French version reads as follows: 'Juifs de tous âges, de toutes conditions, de toutes origines, qui ont tant apporté à notre pays, à notre culture, à notre civilisation, happés par la folie criminelle des nazis: vos enfants, vos familles, vos compatriotes se souviennent de vous. Votre souvenir, celui de ce "monde qui fut", est pour la France plus qu'une douleur. Il est la conscience d'une faute. Il est une exigence de responsabilité'. Chirac, J. (27 January 2005), 'Discours prononcé lors de l'inauguration de la nouvelle exposition du pavillon d'auschwitz le 27 janvier 2005', *Libération*.

PART V

PREVENTION, ALTERNATIVE JUSTICE SOLUTIONS AND SENTENCING

Chapter 18

The United Nations and the Prevention of Genocide

Juan E. Méndez

As this chapter will underscore, the work of the United Nations on the prevention of armed conflict, the activities and jurisprudence of international courts and tribunals as well as the general development of criminal law are all of importance for the work of the Special Adviser to the United Nations Secretary-General on the Prevention of Genocide.

The Charter of the United Nations and the Convention on the Prevention and Punishment of the Crime of Genocide

I would like to start by recalling some elements of the concept and history of the Charter of the United Nations and the Convention on the Prevention and Punishment of the Crime of Genocide which are relevant for the overall understanding of the current possibilities and limitations of the United Nations to prevent genocide.

The foundation of the United Nations is to a large extent linked to a desire to avert the horrors of the Second World War. The Organization's Charter reveals an awareness of the close connection between respect for human rights and peace. Thus, the Charter provides for the adoption of legally binding measures in cases of threats to the peace, breaches of the peace, and acts of aggression. However, these powers of the Organization are balanced by the principles of national sovereignty and of friendly relations and cooperation among states.

At the end of World War II, pursuant to the London Agreement of 8 August 1945, the Allied Powers also adopted the Charter of the International Military Tribunal. The term 'genocide' itself was used in the Nuremberg indictment of 18 October 1945. By Resolution 95 (1) of 11 December 1946, the General Assembly affirmed the principles of international law recognized by the Charter of the International Military Tribunal and therefore implicitly confirmed that genocide was a crime under international law. Two years later, on 9 December 1948, the General Assembly adopted the Convention on the Prevention and Punishment of the Crime of Genocide in which the parties confirm that genocide is a crime under international law which they undertake to prevent and punish.

The Convention aimed at creating a generic legal term that could cover the destruction of whole populations motivated by racial, national or religious considerations. While the Holocaust served as the most deliberate and thorough example, discussions about the Convention also considered events involving smaller numbers of victims and less systematic approaches, such as the destruction of Carthage, the destruction of religious groups during the wars of Islam and the Crusades and the massacre of the Armenians.[1]

According to the International Court of Justice the Convention primarily confirms pre-existing legal obligations that amount to international *jus cogens*.[2] Thus, preventing genocide is a principle of international law so fundamental that no nation may ignore it. Governments are obliged to take all measures within their power to prevent the commission of the crime of genocide, even before a competent court determines that the Convention actually applies to a case at hand.[3] The Convention, however, focuses more directly on punishment than on prevention – although, clearly, the punishment of the crime of genocide is meant to have a general preventive effect. In addition, some of the acts referred to in Article 3 of the Convention have a preventive dimension, such as the prosecution of conspiracy or attempts of public incitement to commit genocide. Another preventive element can be found in Article 8, which provides for the possibility of any contracting party to call upon the competent organs of the United Nations to take action on the prevention or repression of acts of genocide. Apart from the scholarly debate on the relevance of this provision, it has never been invoked. More recently, the Security Council has considered that significant and widespread human rights violations may be qualified as a threat to international peace and security[4] and can provide it with a basis to act, without necessarily qualifying the situation as genocide. The Council has even asked the Secretary-General to forward it information regarding serious violations of international law, including international humanitarian law and human rights violations.

Notwithstanding the existing legal obligation to prevent genocide, numerous cases of massive violations of human rights and humanitarian law occurred since the adoption of the 1948 Convention without triggering action as described in Article 8 of its text and without even eliciting action by Member States. In hindsight, the United Nations, Member States and NGOs have concluded that many of these situations could have been anticipated and prevented.

---

1   Lemkin, R. (1947), 'Genocide as a Crime under International Law', 41:1 *American Journal of International Law*, pp.145–151.

2   *Reservations to the Convention on the Prevention and Punishment of the Crime of Genocide*, Advisory Opinion, ICJ Reports 1951, pp.15–69.

3   *Case Concerning the Application of the Convention on the Prevention and Punishment of the Crime of Genocide* (*Bosnia and Herzegovina v Yugoslavia (Serbia and Montenegro)*) (Request for the indication of provisional measures), ICJ Reports (1993, p.2), para. 46.

4   S/1993/794 (Somalia), S/1994/929 (Rwanda).

The Mandate of the Special Adviser to the Secretary-General on the Prevention of Genocide

The source of my mandate[5] is Security Council Resolution (1366 (2001), which the Council approved in an effort to acknowledge the lessons from the failure to prevent such tragedies as the genocide in Rwanda and the massacre in Srebrenica.[6] Important guidance on the interpretation of this mandate derives from its background and history. On the one hand, the creation of the position of Special Adviser on the Prevention of Genocide is part of the Action Plan presented by the Secretary-General on the 10th anniversary of the Rwanda Genocide to the Commission on Human Rights, on 7 April 2004. On the other hand, the mandate has to be seen in the wider context of UN efforts to create a culture of prevention[7] and previous discussions regarding the prevention of massive violations of human rights and humanitarian law.[8]

The International Commission on Intervention and State Sovereignty strongly believed that the responsibility to protect implies an accompanying responsibility to prevent. The Commission established that what is lacking is not the basic data, but its analysis and translation into policy prescriptions, and the will to do something about it.[9] The Secretary-General's High-level Panel on Threats, Challenges and Change endorsed the notion that there is a collective international responsibility to protect, to be exercised by the Security Council including the authorization of military intervention as a last resort, in the events of genocide and other large-scale killing, ethnic cleansing or serious violations of international humanitarian law.[10] The Panel also recommended deterring parties to a conflict from committing crimes against humanity, war crimes or genocide by the Security Council referring cases to the International Criminal Court at an early stage.[11]

The current debate on the reform of the United Nations reflects many concepts and ideas for a comprehensive approach that includes the prevention, mitigation and removal of threats to international peace and security. Member States appear to agree that the protection of populations from genocide, war crimes and crimes against humanity lies primarily with individual governments. This responsibility to protect should entail the prevention of such crimes. At the same time, there is a growing consensus that the international community must use diplomatic, humanitarian and other peaceful means to help protect populations at risk while also recognizing its shared responsibility to take collective action, in a timely and decisive manner

---

5   See Notes on Contributors (*The Editors*).

6   UN doc. S/Res/1366 (2001) of 30 August 2001, preamble para. 18.

7   See 'An Agenda for Peace,' UN doc. A/47/277, paras. 15, 18, 20, 23; Report of the Secretary-General on the work of the organization, UN doc. A/54/1.

8   Revised and updated report on the question of the prevention and punishment of the crime of genocide prepared by Mr B. Whitaker, UN-doc. E/CN.4/Sub.2/1985/6 of 2 July 1985.

9   *The Responsibility to Protect*, Report of the International Commission on Intervention and State Sovereignty (2001), p.19 et seq.

10 *A more secure world: Our shared responsibility*, Report of the Secretary-General's High-level Panel on Threats, Challenges and Change (2004), para. 203.

11 See fn. 5, para. 90.

through the Security Council, should peaceful means fail. This inclusion of these commitments into the final outcome document of the High-level Plenary Meeting of the General Assembly from 14 to 16 September 2005 could be important in the context of the implementation of the United Nations Action Plan to Prevent Genocide. At the same time, I consider that the current debate on the concept of the so-called 'responsibility to protect' must not obscure the existing international legal obligation to prevent genocide.

My office cannot be regarded at present as a universal early-warning and early-action mechanism for the prevention of genocide worldwide, but rather an effort to improve the United Nations' response to situations of potential massive violations of human rights and humanitarian law with an ethnic, racial, religious or national character. This is an effort that requires strong support from Member States, NGOs, academia and others.

The purpose of the Special Adviser is not to determine whether genocide has occurred or is occurring, but to propose steps to prevent it. I am approaching my mandate pragmatically. The last paragraph of the outline of my mandate states clearly that 'the Special Adviser would not make a determination on whether genocide within the meaning of the Convention had occurred'. I prefer to see this limitation, not as a reflection of political sensitivities, but as a practical one deriving from the preventive character of my mandate. My role is to provide early warning before all the elements that constitute the definition of genocide under the Convention are present and to suggest appropriate action. Too often the debate over whether genocide is occurring has become more important than taking action to reverse the situation and prevent further violations.

The mandate of the Special Adviser on the Prevention of Genocide involves gathering information, providing early warning and presenting appropriate recommendations to prevent a situation from degenerating into genocide. The functions of the Adviser were outlined to the Council as follows:[12] 1) Collecting existing information, in particular from within the UN system, on massive and serious violations of human rights and international humanitarian law of ethnic and racial origin that, if not prevented or halted, might lead to genocide; 2) Acting as an early-warning mechanism to the Secretary-General, and, through him to the Security Council, by bringing to the latter's attention potential situations that could result in genocide; 3) Making recommendations to the Security Council through the Secretary-General, on actions to prevent or halt genocide; and 4) Liaising with the UN system on activities for the prevention of genocide and working to enhance the UN capacity to analyse and manage information relating to genocide and related crimes.

Early-warning and Early-Action to Prevent Genocide

Early warning requires indicators. Numerous governmental agencies, NGOs and academic institutions provide indicators and methodology for the early-warning of

---

12 Letter dated 12 July 2004 from the Secretary-General addressed to the President of the Security Council, UN doc. S/2004/567 of 13 July 2004.

massive violations of human rights and humanitarian law. Interestingly, all models, when applied, seem to identify more or less the same list of five countries most at risk and about 10 countries with a potential risk of massive violence based on national, ethnic, racial or religious grounds. The use of quantitative indicators is broadly based on the assumption that certain models could be defined that would allow automatic detection of critical developments in particular countries. The use of quantitative early warning methods using causal factors requires ongoing analysis and evaluation of a critical amount of information. It also demands the development of a tracking system for such information. The impact of certain events on the prevalence of the causal factors in a particular country requires thorough analysis based on the genocide literature. Very often, indicators of genocide are not clarified in a risk analysis that rather reviews the general socio-political situation. In other cases, the models simply track all raw information on genocide and items related to past and present ethnic, national, racial and religious violence without offering any analysis. Most of the internal UN mechanisms rely on the analysis and expertise of staff on the ground and in HQ to evaluate a situation based on a case-by-case basis.

Given its limited resources, my office acts as a focal point for early-warning information coming from sources inside and outside the UN system. According to my mandate to advise the Secretary-General and the Security Council of situations of massive violations, I take up country situations presented to me on a case-by-case basis. In doing so, the starting point is the legal definition of the crime of genocide and other punishable acts according to the Convention of 1948.[13] Accordingly, information needs to point towards the existence of a national, ethnic, racial or religious group at risk. Violations of human rights or humanitarian law, which may become massive or serious, have to take place. Additional factors derive from the developing international case-law on genocide and the findings of academic research. An important criterion is a history of acts of genocide in the country in question. Countries matching most criteria in these categories will be closely followed by my office. Additional precipitating or external factors can serve to determine those countries in which immediate involvement is necessary. One precipitating factor to look for is the prevalence of expressions of hate speech directed at certain populations at risk, especially if they are uttered in the context of an actual or potential outbreak of violence.

Prevention requires both early warning and early action. From a methodological point of view, early warning should be clearly distinguished from early action, even though, politically, it could already be a form of early action in itself. In addition, I believe that early warning should always be accompanied by practical proposals and recommendations that enable the international community to act in a timely fashion.

So far, my office has provided advice on the situation in Darfur, Sudan, the DRC and Côte d'Ivoire. We have also been following a number of other situations of concern. Upon request of the Secretary-General, we undertook a joint mission with the High Commissioner for Human Rights to Darfur and provided recommendations

---

13 Arts II, III, Convention on the Prevention and Punishment of the Crime of Genocide, GA Res. 260 A (III) of 9 December 1948.

to the Security Council on the protection of civilians and the prevention of future violations of human rights and humanitarian law. In addition, we have provided various UN offices with guidance on issues related to the prevention of genocide, such as guidelines on hate speech and public incitement to violence for the Department of Public Information (DPI) and peacekeeping missions.

Both in the short and long term, the prevention of genocide seems predicated on acting comprehensively in four interrelated areas: the protection of populations at risk against serious or massive violations of human rights or humanitarian law, establishing accountability for violations of human rights and humanitarian law, humanitarian relief or access to basic economic, social and cultural rights, and steps to address underlying causes of conflict through peace agreements and transitional processes.

The protection of populations at risk will sometimes require deployment of international forces, both military and police forces. Occasionally, the only way to prevent a humanitarian catastrophe will be to order such deployment regardless of the consent of the local authorities. We must be ready to take that ultimate step, but we must also act with a sense of responsibility not to make matters worse; recent examples of non-consensual use of force do not give us any sense of comfort that such actions will always help and never hurt the innocent. For the most part, however, it is possible to deploy international protective forces with the consent of the government involved, and if that possibility is available it will always be preferable.

Accountability in the form of punishment for genocide, crimes against humanity and war crimes is crucial to prevention of similar acts in the future. The sense of impunity for the crimes already committed breeds insecurity among the populations at risk and creates an incentive for repetition among the perpetrators. Breaking the cycle of impunity is greatly aided by the existence of an institution like the permanent International Criminal Court. However, we must realize that it will be important to press the domestic judicial authorities to assume their responsibilities, and for civil society to contribute efforts towards a comprehensive set of policy prescriptions that will meet everybody's expectations of justice and do so with respect for international standards of fair trial and due process.

Humanitarian relief and access to basic economic, social and cultural rights is important to prevent loss of life from continuing after the initial killings have ceased, and also to avoid placing populations at risk under conditions of life designed to bring about their extinction. In addition, by their very presence international civilian monitors and relief workers can provide a basic measure of protection to the population they serve.

Finally, it is important to pursue the resolution of conflicts that can deteriorate into genocide. Peace will be the ultimate prevention of genocide, but in order to have that effect it must be a lasting peace, one that tries to avoid winners and losers and that is more than a mere cessation of hostilities. Most important, it must be a peace that addresses the danger of spoilers in the peace process, while not rewarding them with impunity. The resolution must address open wounds in societies that could erupt in future conflict down the road. In other words, what we must strive for is peace with justice.

Chapter 19

Criminal Justice in the Aftermath of the 1994 Rwanda Genocide

Shivon Byamukama and John A. Kapranos Huntley

Introduction

The aftermath of genocide affects all sections of Rwandan society and all areas of the country. Not only was a particular section of the community decimated, but also a significant proportion of the population was implicated, to varying degrees in the perpetration of the genocide.

It is simplistic to conceive the genocide as one catastrophic event. It is a period within a series of events in a troubled history. It is also a myriad of concomitant events that contrived to destroy a society. Children were left without parents; wives without husbands, fathers without daughters. Property was stolen or destroyed and homes razed. Rape, mutilation and torture were commonplace.

Little was done following previous atrocities to prosecute offenders, both perpetrators and instigators. The Gacaca process is in part an attempt to end that culture of impunity.[1] Genocide ultimately comprises acts committed by one person against another. The numbers awaiting trial and the potential numbers of accused reflect how extensive the culture of impunity was.[2]

Reconstruction also requires reconciliation. To heal the wounds, a process was needed that would offer both the prospect of ending impunity and of reconciliation. The ordinary criminal law process could not deal with the scale of the problem.[3] Some alternative form of litigation and dispute resolution, rooted in a common heritage that could fulfil both these aims had to be established. The Rwandan authorities turned to traditional methods of dispute resolution – the Gacaca process. Traditionally, a civil process, over 12,000 Gacaca courts have been established with jurisdiction over 'offences that amount to the crime of Genocide and any other crimes against humanity' perpetrated during the genocide.[4] The first hearings before

---

1 Preamble to the Organic Law No 16/2004 of 19/6/2004 Establishing the Organisation, Competence and Functioning of Gacaca Courts charged with the Prosecution and trying the Perpetrators of the crime of Genocide and other crimes against humanity committed between October 1st 1990 and December 31st 1994 (hereafter *Organic Law*, 2004).

2 Below, 237.

3 Below, 237.

4 Articles 3, 5 and 6, *Organic Law 2004*.

Gacaca courts took place on 10 March 2005.[5] The scale of the task is monumental and estimates that the process could be completed by 2007 seem optimistic.[6]

This chapter examines the effectiveness of Gacaca as an efficient and humane method of disposing of the huge backlog of prosecutions and as a 'participative'[7] and restorative justice device to assist Rwandan society to coalesce and escape its past.

The Legal Background

Whereas it might be trite law that domestic tribunals do have jurisdiction – indeed an obligation to try violations of international humanitarian law, the Rwandan genocide is no different from other similar criminal phenomena in demanding the creation of a specific tribunal.[8] The International Criminal Tribunal for Rwanda[9] (ICTR) was established by the UN Security Council[10] in the immediate aftermath of the Genocide. The competence of the ICTR is expressly limited to the prosecution of 'serious violations of international humanitarian law committed in … Rwanda and [by] Rwandan citizens … in … neighbouring States between 1 January 1994 and 31 December 1994 …'.[11] Although the tribunal has concurrent jurisdiction with national courts, it has primacy over national courts of all States.[12] The effect is that serious violations fall within the jurisdiction of the ICTR, but other violations, subject to the Tribunal's primacy and power of deferment, are for national courts.

There is therefore a close relationship between ICTR and domestic Rwandan jurisdiction. The Organic Law of 2004 closely follows the drafting of the ICTR Statute.[13] Although there is no definition of, or case law on the compass of the term 'serious violation', the Organic Law reserves such potential offences to the

---

5   *Newsletter 2005 III*, Avocats Sans Frontieres (hereafter ASF Newsletter) http://www. asf.be/EN/ENnews/Newsletter_2005_III_EN.htm.

6   *Newsletter 2005 II*, 'Zoom 5'.

7   *Ibid.*

8   Article VI of the UN Convention on the Prevention and Punishment of Genocide, adopted by Resolution 260 (III) A of the UN General Assembly, 9 December 1948, Entry into force 12 January 1951.

9   http://69.94.11.53/default.htm. The ICTR sits in Arusha, Tanzania.

10   S/RES/955 (1994) 8 November 1994, available at: http://69.94.11.53/ENGLISH/ Resolutions/955e.htm.

11   See notably Statute of the ICTR, Article 1, http://69.94.11.53/ENGLISH/basic docs/ statute.html. The territorial and temporal jurisdiction of the Tribunal is defined in similar terms in Article 7 of the Statute.

12   *Ibid.* Article 8 (1) and (2) respectively. The tribunal may formally request a national to defer to the Tribunal's competence at any time in the proceedings: *ibid.* See Cassese, A. (2003), *International Criminal Law*, (New York, Oxford University Press) p. 349.

13   'In tune with the ICTR statute and with international law, Rwanda has removed the death penalty and automatically shifted persons under the death penalty to life imprisonment' *New Times*, Rwanda's Daily English Newspaper, www.newtimes.co.rw 'Parliament Scraps Death Penalty' by Felly Kimenyi, 11 June 2007.

criminal courts of Rwanda.[14] Similarly, both the Gacaca and arguably the ICTR process aim at reconciliation.[15] Yet the Gacaca court differs from the ICTR and the national criminal courts in ways that are neither trite nor immediately obvious. Its traditional jurisdiction – in more recent times at least – had been entirely civil and this is reflected in its processes and even the fact that for the least serious offences the 'penalty' might be reparation to the victim. It is also a jurisdiction based upon the confession of the accused: a feature that emphasizes a vitally important aspect of the Gacaca experiment – the need to achieve reconciliation.[16]

The ICTR's emerging jurisprudence is therefore important in evaluating Gacaca. For example, the ICTR's decision in *Rutaganda* put beyond doubt that the Tutsi, as a self-identifying and identifiable relatively stable and permanent group, can be treated as a protected group under the Genocide convention,[17] although they do not fall readily into the four groups specified in the definition of genocide in Article 2 of the ICTR Statute.[18]

The Gacaca Process in Traditional Rwandan Culture

The conflict in Rwanda is essentially one of identity. There is much that unites Rwandans. They share a common language (Kinyarwanda)[19] and culture, customs and names.[20] Rwandans belong, however loosely and regardless of whether they are Hutu, Tutsi or Twa, to one of 18 clans.[21] Neither clans nor the three major groupings, Hutu, Tutsi and Twa predominate or inhabit exclusive geographic areas.

---

14 'Seriousness' of the offence is determined by the categorisation of the offence as seen in both Articles 51 and 73 of Organic law 16/2004, see below 240.

15 The UN Security Council Resolution, specifically states that, in setting up the ICTR the prosecution of such offences 'would enable this aim to be achieved and would contribute to the process of national reconciliation and to the restoration and maintenance of peace'. Footnote 11, above.

16 Gacaca accused who have not made a confession in accordance with the Ordinance do not benefit from reduced penalties.

17 'The Chamber notes that for the purpose of applying the Genocide Convention, members of the group is in essence, a subjective rather than an objective concept. The victim is perceived by the perpetrator as belonging to a group slated for destruction. In the same instances, the victim may perceive himself/herself as belonging to the said group.' *Prosecutor v Rutaganda* (ICTR-96-3) Trial Chamber 1, 6 December 1999, para. 56, available at: http://69.94.11.53/ENGLISH/cases/Rutaganda/judgement/2.htm. See also comments in *Prosecutor v Akayesu*, ICTR-96-4-T, Trial Chamber 1, 12 September 1998, paras. 168–173, 494–524, available at: http://69.94.11.53/ENGLISH/cases/Akayesu/judgement/akay001.htm

18 This provision reproduces *verbatim* the language of Articles 2 and 3 of the Genocide Convention 1948.

19 A branch of the Niger–Congo linguistic sub-family.

20 See generally Magnarella, P.J. (2000), *Justice in Africa: Rwanda's Genocide, its Courts, and the UN Criminal Tribunal*, (Aldershot: Ashgate), 2 hereafter Magnarella (2000).

21 In pre-colonial Rwanda, the primary identity was with the clan, which links by descent. Sellstrom suggests that a person who had migrated to a region where he had no family ties would join an established clan for both social and economic reasons: Sellstrom, T.

Yet there is even more that divides them. That any Rwandan has strong personal identification with one of the three groupings, Hutu, Tutsi or Twa is undeniable.[22] An explanation for a Rwandan's strong personal identification with one of the three groupings lies, at least in part in the caste, or class system based on economic power that, although relatively fluid[23] resulted in a political and economic system where the Tutsi held power.[24] These political and economic differences were discernible in the pre-colonial administration, most particularly and controversially in the feudal relationships of *ubuhake* and *ubukonde*.[25] The ultimate expression of the Hutu/Tutsi divide was the hereditary Tutsi monarchy that survived into the 1950s. Yet, despite this 'segregated' structure, social order and cohesion appears to have been maintained through a triple chieftaincy in which Tutsi and Hutu were involved.[26] This was equally true of the settlement of disputes.

The Hutu/Tutsi divide became institutionally entrenched when during 1933–34 the Belgians conducted a census and introduced an identity card system that indicated the Tutsi, Hutu, and Twa 'ethnicity' of each individual.[27] Ownership of cows was the main criterion used to determine to which group an individual belonged.[28] The census determined that 85 per cent of the population were Hutu, 14 per cent Tutsi and 1 per cent Twa.[29] The identity cards issued on the basis of that census firmly attached a sub-national identity to all Rwandans. These identity cards in the 1994 genocide had the unfortunate role of identifying who had a right to life and who did not.

---

and Wohlgemuth, L. (1996), 'International Response to Conflict and Genocide, Lessons from the Rwandan Experience, Historical Perspective', *Journal of Humanitarian Assistance*, Study 1: Historical Perspective: Some Explanatory Facts, Steering committee of the Joint Evaluation of Emergency Assistance to Rwanda, 24 and http://www.reliefweb.int/library/nordic/book1/pb020.html (hereafter Sellstrom (1996), quoting Newbury, D. (1980), 'The Clans of Rwanda: [An] Historical Hypothesis', 50:4 *Africa: Journal of the International African Institute*, p. 390.

22 It has been asserted that these identities held a different meaning in pre-colonial Africa: Semujanga, J. (2003), *Origins of Rwandan Genocide* (New York: Humanity Books), p. 88 hereafter Semujanga (2003); Shyaka, A. (2005), *The Rwandan Conflict, Origin, Development, Exit Strategies, by the National Unity and Reconciliation Commission* (Kigali: Select Graph Publishers) 9 hereafter Shyaka (2005).

23 A Hutu who became wealthy or a chief became a Tutsi through a process of *Kwihutura* (cleansing oneself of Hutuness); a Tutsi could become Hutu if he lost his cattle. Shyaka (2005), 11.

24 Shyaka (2005), p. 9; Semujanga (2003), p. 137.

25 Portier, J. (2002), *Re-imagining Rwanda, Conflict, Survival and Disinformation in the Late 20th Century*, Cambridge: Cambridge University Press, p. 13 hereafter Pottier (2002).

26 Semujanga, (2003), p. 137.

27 Sellstrom (1996), p. 27.

28 Those with more than ten cows and all their descendants in the male line were Tutsi, those with less than ten cows were Hutu, and those recognized as Twa at the time of the census remained Twa: Lee Ann Fujii, 'Origins of Power and Identity in Rwanda' – Annual Conference of the International Studies Association, 20–24 February 2001, Chicago, Illinois.

29 Magnarella (2000), p.11. Shyaka (2005) p. 12 disputes these figures as 'not on the basis of adequately collected and periodically updated numerical data, but rather a repetition of the representation of the colonial view …'.

The Origins of Gacaca

Gacaca (literally 'grass' in Kinyarwanda) refers to a resting or relaxing lawn in the Rwandan homestead where family members or neighbours meet to exchange views on issues directly affecting them.[30] Historically, it refers to informal, participative and customary mediation for the settlement of disputes, apparently unaffected by the Hutu, Tutsi and Twa divide. Two features particularly ensured inclusion and acceptability. Adjudication was one of debate and discussion by the community as a whole; and an assembly of judges (*infura* or *inyangamugayo*) accepted by the community by virtue of age, wisdom, experience and social standing would hear a case and pass sentence according to the gravity of the offence.[31] The usual penalty was reparation[32] to the injured party and all members of the offender's clan shared the responsibility for making reparation. If both parties agreed to the terms of reparation, they would share a drink as a symbolic gesture of agreement.[33] Within this highly structured society, reliance on Gacaca for the settlement of disputes was universally recognized and respected.

Gacaca under Colonial Administration

During the colonial period[34] Gacaca played an uneasy role as an aspect of customary law, within a codified civil law structure based on the Belgian model. Both the Germans and Belgians relied on the monarchy to administer their colony and this included Gacaca; but such reliance exacerbated divisions.[35] The Belgians' reliance on forced labour and inhuman punishment in their drive for profit similarly increased Hutu/Tutsi tensions. The colonizers, preoccupied by nineteenth century anthropological attitudes to race[36] favoured the Tutsi over the Hutu, and inevitably replaced Hutu chiefs with Tutsi.[37] Even admission to schools was strictly reserved for the Tutsi,[38] inevitably increasing Hutu/Tutsi tension. 'Sixty years of such prejudicial

---

30 Morrill, C.F. (2004), 'Reconciliation and the Gacaca: The Perceptions and Peace Building Potential of Rwanda Youth Detainees', *Online Journal of Peace and Conflict Resolution*, http://www.trinstitute.org/ojpcr/6_1morrill.pdf hereafter Morrill (2004).

31 *Ibid.*

32 Imprisonment was unknown as a penalty in pre-colonial Rwanda.

33 Morrill (2004), p. 3.

34 Following the Anglo-German treaty of 1890, Germany was given the present day Rwanda, Burundi and Tanzania as colonies. The League of Nations in 1924 mandated Rwanda and Burundi to Belgium: Gasana, E. (1999), *Comprehending and Mastering African Conflicts: The search for sustainable Peace and Good Governance* (London: Zed Books) p. 146.

35 Magnarella (2000), p. 10.

36 *Ibid.*

37 Sellstrom (1996), p. 27.

38 Magnarella (2000), p. 142. Education later became available to the Hutu (for education in mines and as tutors).

fabrications ended up inflating the Tutsi cultural ego inordinately and crushing Hutu feelings until they coalesced into an aggressively resentful inferiority complex.'[39]

Gacaca survived the colonial interlude, although after 1924 it was confined to civil and commercial jurisdiction. Criminal cases were the responsibility of the colonial courts.[40] Gacaca judges were now appointed from a legally qualified pool by the colonial government.[41]

Gacaca and Post-colonial Rwanda: Background to the Genocide[42]

Independence Day dawned in Rwanda with a majority nursing a sense of grievance and a minority whose rights and safety were precarious. Having altered their policy of discrimination to favour the Hutu, the Belgians withdrew support for the *mwami* (king), discarded their policy of indirect rule and quickly brought Rwanda to independence. The revolutionary transition from Tutsi-dominated monarchy to Hutu-led Republic in November 1959–September 1961 impacted fundamentally on subsequent ethnic divisions.[43]

Economic and demographic factors also exacerbated the post-colonial Hutu/Tutsi divide. One of the most densely populated countries in Africa, Rwanda had a population density approaching 300 persons per s km^2 just before the genocide.[44] With only 46% agricultural land, every square kilometre supports more than 400 people.[45] Land shortages and disputes arising from straightforward population pressure rather than from a complex political economy[46] were undoubtedly a factor.[47] This was exacerbated by the collapse of commodity prices during the late 1980s

---

39 Magnarella (2000), p. 10. This perhaps also resonated with the colonial masters who had their own Walloon-Flemish divisions and who may have intensified divisions among the Rwandans that reflected their own.

40 Morrill (2004), p. 3.

41 *Ibid.*

42 One of the most accurate summaries of the historical background to the genocide is to be found in the judgment of the First Chamber of the ICTR in *Akayesu*, op.cit, paras. 78–139.

43 Sellstrom (1996), p. 29. 'The political struggle in Rwanda was really never a quest for equality; the issue was who would dominate the ethnically bipolar state.' Magnarella (2000), 12.

44 Rwanda, a land locked country of about 26,388 km^2 is one of the smallest countries in Africa. By 1993, one year before the genocide, Rwanda's population was 7.7m: Magniarella (2000), 2. In the 2002 census, it had increased to 8.1m.

45 Prunier, G. (1995), *The Rwanda Crisis 1959–1994: History of a Genocide*, Kampala: Fountain Publishers (hereafter Prunier (1995)) p. 2.

46 Portier (2002), p. 10.

47 'The decision to kill was of course made by the politicians for political reasons. But at least part of the reason it was carried out so thoroughly by the ordinary ranks and file peasants... was the feeling that there were too many people on too little land, and that with a few less, there would be more for survivors.' *Prunier* (1995), 4. See also Magnarella (2000), p. 24.

and early 1990s.[48] Unemployment, poverty, and land shortages caused unrest among people now desperate for solutions.[49]

A Hutu mass revolt toppled the monarchy in 1959 and resulted in bloody ethnic clashes.[50] In 1960, the colonial administration replaced Tutsi chiefs with Hutus. Full independence made the position of the Tutsi even more precarious. The 1960 general election was followed immediately by hostile campaigns against the Tutsi. By 1963, thousands of Tutsi had been massacred and about 130,000 fled to neighbouring countries.[51] Persecution of the Tutsi recurred in 1973 and 1990–1993. Invasion by the Rwanda Patriotic Front (RPF) led to immediate massacre and torture of Tutsi living in Rwanda.[52] The pattern of impunity accepted throughout latter colonial and post-colonial Rwanda, coupled with a culture of obedience facilitated encouragement to participate in the genocide. Political leaders in fear of losing power could manipulate citizens to kill a portion of the population that they were mandated to protect. In the words of one authority:

> The recent history of Rwanda is punctuated by countless examples of bloodshed and violence ... the scale and method by which [it] was perpetrated suggest that it can only be regarded as an extreme example of pathological behaviour, as the blinding reaction of people traumatized by a deep and lasting sense of inferiority.[53]

On the eve of the genocide, in such a polarized environment, Gacaca seemed almost an irrelevance. In a culture of violence and impunity, where rights were violated without redress, turning to such customary legal structures for relief seemed illusory.

Gacaca and the Aftermath

Gacaca is a common participative thread that seems to have survived the vicissitudes of Rwanda's recent past. Arguably the scale of the genocide was such that, if justice were to be transparent and timely, the normal criminal law process would not readily cope. In its current manifestation the Gacaca thread has been spun differently. It is now essentially a criminal court structure; it is has been superimposed on existing

---

48 Magnarella (2000), p. 25.

49 'It is not rare, even today, to hear Rwandans argue that a war is necessary to wipe out an excess of population to bring numbers into line with the available resources.' *Magnarella* (2000), p. 24.

50 Approximately two thousand Tutsi were killed and thousands more fled to neighbouring countries. It is believed that over 25,000 refugees set up camps in Uganda: Melvern, L. (2004), *Conspiracy to Murder* (New York: Zed Books) hereafter Melvern (2004).

51 The World Council of Churches estimated deaths between 10,000–14,000 people: Melvern (2004) p. 9.

52 Melvern (2004), p. 15. In Gisenyi province alone, at least 348 people were killed and 550 houses burned in 48 hours. At least 248 people were accused and arrested, but released in less than one month.

53 Lemarchand, R. (1970), *Rwanda and Burundi*, (London: Praeger) p. 44.

adjudicative structures;[54] it has the power to imprison. Yet much survives: it is participative; the judges are still the *Inyangamugayo*; the process is still one of debate; the remedies can still be restorative and focused on the victim. Although the current Gacaca jurisdiction is based on offences that amount to genocide and crimes against humanity, its preoccupation is the multitude of individual crimes perpetrated by persons against persons and their property during the period of the genocide. It is therefore an *ad hoc* jurisdiction that is limited both in time and range. They have not replaced the criminal courts,[55] but for several reasons they have become Rwanda's unique response to the events of 1994.

The Scale of the Problem

The genocide led to the death of approximately one million people and three million people fled into exile. It is estimated that 800,000 persons will have to account for their actions.[56] Of these, the Public Prosecutor has put forward the names of 100,000 for trial in the ordinary courts for category 1 crimes.[57] Approximately 135,000 people are in detention accused of genocide related crimes and the number is increasing steadily. The number of prisoners suspected of genocide is overwhelming and congestion in prisons is serious and inevitable.[58] Rwanda has had to balance releasing potentially dangerous prisoners against detaining persons presumed innocent for long periods

---

54 It is nevertheless a jurisdiction apart – see Stainier, C. et al. (2004), *Organisation, compétence et fonctionnement des Juridictions Gacaca chargées des poursuites et du jugement des infractions constitutives du crime de génocide et d'autres crimes contre l'humanité commis entre le 1er Octobre 1990 et le 31 décembre 1994* (Brussels: Avocats sans Frontiéres) hereafter Stainier (2004).

55 Since 1996 the ordinary criminal courts have dealt with many such cases, but despite encouragement and support they could not be expected to deal with the backlog within a reasonable time. See Archive of decisions on the ASF web site, http://www.asf.be/ AssisesRwanda2/fr/frStart.htm. The ordinary courts had only tried 7,193 persons between 1997–2002 see Drumbl, A. (2000), 'Sclerosis: Retributive Justice and the Rwanda Genocide', *Punishment and Society: International Journal of Penology*, p. 291 Also see footnote 56.

56 Estimate of the National Service for Gacaca Courts, reported in ASF Newsletter, Zoom, 4. Earlier estimates suggested lower figures of 'between 500,000 and 600,000 genocide suspects'. Augustin Nkusi, director, legal department, National Service of Gacaca Jurisdictions quoted in Arusha, Tanzania, *Rwanda Genocide suspects to swell to over 500,000*, 03/09/2003, 1.

57 *ASF Newsletter* and June 2005. http://www.asf.be/EN/ENnews/Newsletter_2005_III_ EN.htm. The Pilot phase estimated that about 10% or crimes committed fell within category 1: *ibid*. Between 15 January 2005 and 30 June 2006, 59,171 accused persons were categorised in accordance with article 51 of Organic law 16/2004. 6,817 (11.5%) were in Category 1, 36,426 (61.6%) in Category 2 and 15,928 (26.9%) were in Category 3. Gacaca courts will inevitably deal with majority of the case load. www.inkiko-gacaca.gov.rw.

58 Gitarama prison for example, which had an initial capacity of 2070 prisoners, was now accommodating 7,000 prisoners.

before trial; and mass amnesties against overcoming the culture of impunity.[59] There is therefore an element of expediency and *realpolitik*.[60]

The institutions upholding the law was a corrupt and distorted system of justice that left little to 'rebuild'.[61] According to Schabas: 'Prior to the 1994 genocide, it comprised about 700 judges and magistrates, of whom fewer than 50 had any formal legal training. Of these, the best elements had perished during the genocide, often at the hands of their own erstwhile colleagues.'[62]

The economic burden of the aftermath is severe. Even the FRW 5 billion (approximately £526 million) spent annually to feed prisoners strains the already weak economy. The effect of a detainee's absence on the economic – and social – welfare of his family and community is severe.

Finally, the ICTR deals with small numbers of category 1 offenders. How Rwanda deals with the remainder will be a major determining influence on whether or not that society will achieve long-term peace and stability. 'Gacaca was an innovation created out of necessity. We have tens of thousands of people in prison awaiting trial, which we know the classical justice system will not be able to handle in the reasonable space of time.'[63]

The New Gacaca Jurisdiction

Organic law No 16/2004 establishing the organization, competence and functioning of Gacaca courts[64] introduced a new Gacaca system that deals exclusively with genocide crimes committed between October 1990 and December 1994.[65] The Gacaca courts operate at three levels, Cell Sector and Sector Appeal.[66] This is a truly

---

59 *ASF Newsletter* and June 2005. http://www.asf.be/EN/ENnews/Newsletter_2005_III_EN.htm

60 Morrill (2004), p. 3.

61 Schabas, W. (2005), 'The Rwandan Courts in Quest of Accountability: Genocide Trials and Gacaca Courts', 3 *Journal of the International Criminal Justice*, pp. 879, 883.

62 'There were only about 20 lawyers with genuine legal education in the country when I visited Rwanda in November 1994 as part of the international response to Minister Nkubito's appeal': *ibid.*

63 President Paul Kagame in a BBC interview on the eve of the official launch of the Gacaca courts. http://www.gov.rw/government/president/interviews/2001/gacaca.html.

64 Original and authoritative texts and commentaries are almost entirely in French and English versions are not always reliable. The most comprehensive and authoritative commentary is the *Manuel Explicatif sur la Loi Organique portant Creation des Jurisdictions Gacaca*, published by the Gacaca Jurisdictions Department of the Supreme Court of Rwanda and available at http://www.asf.be/FR/FRnews/manuel_gacaca.pdf (hereinafter *Manuel Explicatif*).

65 Article 1 of Organic Law No 16/2004 Establishing the Organization, Competence and Functioning of Gacaca Courts.

66 Gacaca courts of the Cell are responsible for collecting of information, categorisation of offences and prosecution of offences in category 3 (offences against property). The Sector Court is responsible for prosecuting offences against person not belonging to category 1. Sector Appeal is responsible for appeals against sentence. See Articles 33–38 Organic law 16/2004.

massive operation comprising 12,103 Gacaca courts.[67] Each level of court reflects the three levels of civil administration in Rwanda. Each level of jurisdiction is based on a three-category classification of offences that indicates the seriousness of the offence and the appropriate penalty. The initial enquiry into the Genocide files is carried out by the Cell jurisdictions based on local knowledge and information.

Although a pilot scheme began in 2002 following the first enactment of the Organic Law in 2001,[68] the new framework under Organic Law No. 16/2004 is currently governing the Gacaca courts. The accused are placed on a list in one of the three categories.[69] Category 1 comprises planners and ideologues of the genocide who are prosecuted in the ordinary courts.[70] Those accused of category 3 offences[71] are tried in the Cell courts and, if convicted, must make reparation to the victim.[72] There are around 9,000 Gacaca courts at cell level, dealing with category 3 accused. Those accused of category 2 offences[73] are tried in the Sector courts.[74] There are 1545 Gacaca sector courts and 1545 Sector Courts of Appeal.

Facing Up to the Truth

Cell jurisdictions, being closest to locus of the offence are entrusted with the fact-finding function. Establishing the truth is the beginning of reconciliation, but detailed confessions are an important part of the Gacaca process for two reasons: only the perpetrators know the details of what actually happened:[75] and confessions are essential to the sentencing process written into the legislation.[76] Confession may

---

67 *ASF Newsletter* (2005), http://www.asf.be/EN/ENnews/Newsletter_2004_VII_EN.htm. For a more analytical survey of the Gacaca jurisdictions from a human rights perspective, see now generally Stainier (2004).

68 Organic Law No, p. 40/2000 of 26/01/2001, Setting up Gacaca Jurisdictions and Organising Prosecutions for Offences constituting the crime of genocide or crimes against humanity committed between 1 October 1990 and 31 December 1994. 751 Gacaca courts began their investigations under this law.

69 Article 51 of Organic law No. 16/2004.

70 Organic Law No. 16/2004, Article 51. Category 1 deals with persons whose criminal participation places them in the position of planners, organisers and supervisors of the genocide.

71 *Ibid.*

72 *Ibid.*

73 Category 2 covers other persons who committed serious acts whether or not they resulted in death, and their accomplices.

74 These cases have now gone to trial, investigations into the files having been carried out during the trial phase. Priority is being given to files of those who have confessed. ASF Newsletter, June 2005, http://www.asf.be/EN/ENnews/Newsletter_2005_III_EN.htm

75 Potential witnesses were killed during the genocide. Those who survived the genocide were in hiding, so might not be able to give first-hand information. Those who actually knew what occurred either took part in the killings some of whom are in custody or sympathized with those who did. Gacaca is therefore facing a problem of 'conspiracy of silence' which inevitably slows the process.

76 Article 54 of Organic Law No. 16/2004. It is in effect a form of plea-bargaining.

significantly reduce the penalty to which the accused is exposed.[77] For a category 2 offender a 25–30 year prison term is reduced to between 12 and 15 years and, depending on when the accused confesses,[78] between 7 and 12 years. The key factor in all cases is that the accused must fully denounce his accomplices.[79]

This procedure speeds up the process and makes the Gacaca courts' work more manageable. The process is however the most controversial aspect of Gacaca. *Confessions* can be, on their own notoriously unreliable evidence and the potential for abuse is well known.[80] It is also true that many detainees confess purely for pragmatic reasons, like gaining a sentence reduction, or for other ends, showing a lack of remorse that does little to reconcile survivors.[81] Truth also comes at a cost. Protection of potential witnesses is difficult with few resources available. Those convicted through the Gacaca process are restored in the community to live with the already traumatized survivors. Furthermore, there is an element of mistrust, however circumscribed of the process itself.[82]

Reconciliation and Restorative Justice

Gacaca as a form of restorative justice aims to restore victims, offenders and the community to a harmony based on a mutual sense that justice has been done.[83] Reconciliation between the victim and the offender is achieved through the social

---

77 Article 55 of Organic Law No. 16/2004 stipulates: 'Genocide perpetrators coming under the first category who have had recourse to the procedure of confession ... before their names appear on the list drawn by the Gacaca courts, shall enjoy commutation of their penalties'. Article 73 defines reduction of sentences for those who confess.

78 That is, before the name is placed on the list. Article 73 provides that for those in category 2 who had recourse to the confession and guilty plea procedure sentence is reduced by 1–15 years, half the sentence served in custody and the other in community service. Article 78 provides for persons who were between the ages of 14 and 18 at the time of the commission of the crime.

79 Under Article 54, the party has to give a detailed description of the offence in question, how and where it was committed, the damage caused, where the body was buried or thrown and all the accomplices to the crime.

80 See generally Stainier (2004).

81 'Neither the Government, nor the Church which was among those leading the call for reconciliation have fostered large scale national initiatives to encourage those guilty of genocide to ask for forgiveness from the victims', African Rights (2000), *Confession to Genocide: Responses to Rwanda's Genocide Law* (Kigali: A Publication of African Rights), p. 96.

82 In mid-April, 7,500 people had already fled the country, some voicing fears of false accusations in Gacaca courts. ASF *Newsletter*, June (2005) http://www.asf.be/EN/ENnews/ Newsletter_2004_VII_EN.htm. See also *Research Report on Gacaca courts: Gacaca and Reconciliation*; Kibuye case study, with the assistance of SWIS Agency for Development and reconciliation (SDC) May 2004, p. 7; see also www.penalreform.org/download/ Gacaca/ Rapport%20Kibuye%20II_EN.pdf

83 Braithwaite, J. (2003), 'Restorative Justice and a Better Future', *Restorative Justice: Critical Issues*, (London: Sage Publications), pp. 54, 56

rituals of remorse, apology and forgiveness and reparation.[84] It offers offenders the opportunity to humanize the relationship with their victims, accept responsibility for their actions, express remorse and ask for forgiveness. Offenders are given the opportunity to understand the harm they have caused victims and the community and to develop plans for making appropriate restitution. It also empowers victims to participate effectively in defining the offender's obligations. Victims express their anger and anguish through dialogue with the offender, and actively contributing to forgiveness and rehabilitation. Offenders also engage in direct dialogue with victims to explain their actions, through direct expression of remorse and by restoring losses and making good harm. As the African saying goes, when solving disputes, you do not cut with a knife, but sew with a needle.

A defining claim of restorative justice is that it redistributes power and disperses decision-making to a wider and more heterogeneous community. The self-managing community, including victims and offenders would themselves define justice and realize greater safety and security.[85] The community elects the non-professional 'judges'. Gacaca, being locally driven, people centred and people owned evokes the pre-colonial *ubumwe bw' Abanyarwanda* (unity of Rwandans) and stresses confession of crimes and seeking forgiveness. It attempts to bridge the uneasy gap between the accused and the victim though restorative justice.

The structure of the Gacaca courts, notably of the Cell jurisdictions where the entire community takes part and the courts' procedure is intended to reflect restorative justice. The hearings are not those adopted in criminal courts; the debate is on the facts attributed to the accused based not only on his testimony and that of witnesses, but also on the contributions of others taking part. The ultimate decision and the sentencing are in the hands of the *Inyangamugayo*.[86] In addition, convicted persons help in the re-building of the very community they partook in destroying. Under Gacaca jurisdiction, convicted persons serve half their sentence in custody and the other half in community service.[87]

If the Gacaca process is to be restorative in the fullest sense, there should be provision for the rehabilitation of the victims, including those subjected to psychological torture, but there is no provision for counselling, neither of the victims nor the accused. The issue of medical care is not tackled, yet it is no secret that many

---

84 Zehr, H. and Mike, H. (2003), 'Fundamental Concepts of Restorative Justice', *Restorative Justice – Critical Issues*, (London: Sage Publications) hereafter Zehr (2003), p. 44.

85 Braithwaite (2003), p. 56.

86 Like lay magistrates in England, the Gacaca 'judiciary' is cheaper and non-professional – not an insignificant factor for the Rwandan economy. The scale of the aftermath also means that training a temporary judiciary of adequate proportions is impossible. Yet training for the Gacaca judiciary is equally vital – on which see *Manuel* and see, generally *ASF Newsletter*, http://www.asf.be/EN/ENnews/. Note the support provided by Avocats sans Frontiéres in training and legal advice.

87 Articles 69 and 70 of Organic Law No 40/2000 of 26th/01/2001 setting up Gacaca Jurisdiction, and Articles 15 and 26 of Organic Law No8/96 of (30 August 1996).

people contracted HIV and AIDS as a result of rape.[88] The economic means to do so simply do not exist.

Justice Delayed is Justice Denied

This is as true for the victims as it is for the accused. The backlog of cases results in such overcrowding in prisons that human rights are compromised. Gitarama prison for example has capacity for 2,070 inmates, but holds about 7,000.[89] Nyamabuye commune detains 339, of whom twelve are aged below 12.[90] The Gacaca process is intended to deal quickly with cases and through commuted sentences served in part in community service to reduce prison congestion, allowing offenders to help rebuild their communities and provide for their families. The genocide took place in 1994, but persons accused of serious crimes are still in detention without trial. More than 36,000 prisoners were released,[91] many of whom had already been in custody longer than any sentence under the Gacaca laws. Although this is a positive step towards justice and reconciliation[92] that goes deeper than justice and reconciliation, and it also will also improve the general conditions of society,[93] it is a fine line between reconciliation and removing the culture of impunity. Meanwhile, the victims of the genocide wait patiently for justice for them, their families and those they have lost.

Removing the Culture of Impunity

When gross human rights violation occur, either as a result of international or internal conflict, the existing laws and legal institutions or their successors always have a vital role to play in the post conflict reconstruction. Rwanda has experienced a number of genocides that went unpunished.[94]

88 According to General Assembly Resolution 40/34 of November 1995, available at http://www.asc41.com/un5.htm victims should receive necessary assistance through the government and voluntary means and the state should provide remedies to such victims including restitution and compensation.

89 'In March of (1995), 7,000 prisoners were living in the prison of Gitarama which is in our diocese of Kabgayi. That prison was built for a few hundred prisoners. It means that four people were living in one square meter! Naturally, the death toll was very high; as an average, 158 persons were dying each month!' http://www.ofm.org/3/news/assasin5.html.

90 *Ibid.*

91 http://www.news.bbc.co.uk

92 *The New Times* (3 August 2005), (Rwanda's National English Newspaper) http://www.newtimes.co.rw/

93 'I was told that my father was incarcerated when I was only one year old, now I am eleven, I had to forego education to assist my mother take care of my dad. Now that he is free, I will go to school.' *Ibid.*

94 'In Rwanda, the Consultative Mission was advised that speaking of the Genocide of 1994 was a misnomer. Killings that targeted people along ethnic lines had occurred in 1959, 1962, 1963, 1964, 1967, and 1973; there had been organized killings in 1990, 1991, 1992, 1993. When it happened again in 1994 the term "genocide" began to be used.' Prof. Ebrima Sall (17–22 May 2002) Rwanda: Report on Consultative Mission, Nordic Africa Institute, 4 www.upeace.org/documents/news/Rwanda_Report.pdf.

Breaking this culture of impunity is a priority for Gacaca.[95] This is not simply retributive justice or, worse, the spoils of the victor. In Rwanda there were no victors; and the horror was on such a scale that it is beyond retribution. Yet the need to break the culture of impunity is urgent, even if tempered by reconciliation and even if it is not enough on its own.[96]

Conclusion

In African traditional systems, the individual's rights and duties exist within her/his group. The individual and the group are complementary. In traditional Gacaca, conflicts in the community were approached holistically, which facilitated reconciliation. The offender's responsibility to repair his wrong was extended to his family and clan causing blame and guilt to be associated and shared with the primary offender. Gacaca is a strategy for conflict management through restorative justice, while serving its role of ensuring cohesion in the society. The experiment with Gacaca in Rwanda is a major attempt to achieve reconciliation in the most difficult of circumstances, both social and economic. It generates, as we have shown, conflicts and fine balances that will unfold over the next few years. It is the purpose of this research to observe, track and evaluate these events, especially during the currently critical phase in the Gacaca process. The international community looked away more than once in Rwanda. It must never do so again.

---

95 'When a populace sees high rates of rape and murder, and crimes going unpunished, the arguments of those advocating political solutions, the rule of law, and non-violent measures of fighting for human rights are severely undermined.' *Ibid.*, Preamble, Organic Law No. 16/2004.

96 Gacaca is the main tool for reconciliation, but in addition there are Ingando (solidarity) camps for inmates, for students (before university) and for demobilized soldiers. A National Community for Unity and Reconciliation (NURC) has been created; the genocide museum in Kigali has been inaugurated and there is a projected community for the prevention and fight against genocide.

Chapter 20

The Normative Context of Sentencing for Genocide

Ralph Henham

Introduction

This chapter draws attention to some fundamental conceptual and practical difficulties revealed by the sentencing of genocide cases before the ICTY and the ICTR.[1] There are several reasons for focusing on the treatment of genocide before the *ad hoc* tribunals. The first, most obviously, is that since the offence of genocide criminalizes the most heinous behaviour known to humankind, it seems axiomatic that the rationales and principles governing its punishment should be free from obfuscation. Secondly, the fledgling ICC's emphasis on indicting the leaders and principal instigators of those responsible for grave breaches of international criminal law[2] makes it all the more important that the definitions of harm necessary to satisfy the substantive offence requirements of international crimes, and the principled allocation of responsibility for those crimes, are matters which are adequately addressed and clarified. Thirdly, the ICC is likely to draw heavily on the sentencing jurisprudence of the *ad hoc* tribunals in the early stages of its development, thereby intensifying the need for clarification of rationale and principle.[3] Finally, the sentencing of genocide illustrates graphically the dilemma faced by Trial Chambers in trying to ensure that the rationales used to justify sentencing decisions are capable of satisfying both global and local demands for justice.

---

1   Respectively, the United Nations International Criminal Tribunals for the Former Yugoslavia and Rwanda, The ICTY was established by United Nations Security Council Resolution 827 of 25 May 1993, UN Doc.S/RES/827. The ICTR was established by United Nations Security Council Resolution 955 of 8 November 1994, UN Doc. S/RES/955. The approaches of national/hybrid tribunals, special courts and those of national courts exercising universal jurisdiction are not considered in this chapter.

2   This strategy is compatible with the policy adopted with respect to prosecutions in the ICTY/ICTR by the United Nations Security Council President on 23 July 2002 (S/PRST/2002/21).

3   As with the *ad hoc* tribunals, the sentencing provisions in the Statute and the Rules allow ICC Trial Chambers virtually unfettered discretion to take into account whatever they regard as necessary in order to arrive at the correct sentence.

This chapter describes how the interplay between substantive and procedural norms in trials before the ICTY and ICTR reflects and exposes tensions which go to the root of the difficulties experienced in the sentencing of genocide cases. In order to illustrate these problems more effectively the chapter focuses on the procedural expedient of pleading guilty in cases involving genocide.[4] Adopting this perspective also facilitates the exploration of broader arguments concerning the legitimacy of what takes place in international sentencing in terms of its engagement with the demands for justice of the 'international community'[5] and post-conflict societies.[6]

It is my contention that the resolution of the substantive and procedural difficulties faced in sentencing genocide cases can only be advanced if we begin[7] by analysing the normative context for sentencing in genocide cases. Ultimately, it needs to be recognized that the substantive and procedural norms of international trial institutions are informed by ideologies which may represent competing claims for moral legitimacy. The extent of this depends on the plurality of moral claims and the degree to which competing groups are able to exert power to assert what they perceive as morally legitimate claims.[8]

Systemic Weaknesses

It is important to recognize that the sentencing of cases involving genocide in the *ad hoc* tribunals and the development of principles relating to the use of plea agreements in such cases is governed by procedural norms that are universally applicable to all offences within the jurisdiction of these courts. This is highly significant because many of the problems that have been identified in the sentencing practices of the *ad*

---

4   For earlier analyses, see Combs, N.A. 'Copping a Plea to Genocide: The Plea Bargaining of International Crimes', 151 *University of Pennsylvania Law Review*, p. 1; Jorgensen, N.H.B (2002), 'The Genocide Acquittal in the *Sikirica* Case Before the International Criminal Tribunal for the Former Yugoslavia and the Coming of Age of the Guilty Plea' (2002), 15 *Leiden Journal of International Law*, p. 389. For detailed examination of the use of guilty pleas in this context, see Symposium on the Guilty Plea, Part I: Theoretical Background (2004), 2 *Journal of International Criminal Justice*, p. 1018.

5   It is worth making the point that, whilst politics and power shape and determine the will of the 'international community', its actions provide symbolic affirmation of the universally accepted moral principles embodied in international humanitarian law.

6   For writings taking a broader contextual approach see, in particular, Alvarez, J.E. (1999), 'Crimes of States/Crimes of Hate: Lessons from Rwanda', 24 *Yale Journal of International Law*, p. 365; Amann, D.M. (2002), 'Group Mentality, Expressivism, and Genocide', 2 *International Criminal Law Review*, p. 93.

7   Issues of moral and sociological significance are addressed elsewhere, see Henham, R. 'Theorising Law and Legitimacy in International Criminal Justice' (forthcoming, *International Journal of Law in Context*).

8   For detailed analysis of the practice of plea bargaining in the ICTY, see Henham, R. and Drumbl, M. (2005), 'Plea Bargaining at the International Criminal Tribunal for the Former Yugoslavia' ,16 *Criminal Law Forum*, p. 49.

hoc tribunals are generic.[9] They are both a function of the procedural norms provided to facilitate the punishment of those convicted of crimes within the tribunal's jurisdiction and a consequence of the ideological framework within which these procedural norms operate. These systemic difficulties are concerned with:

- Problems of assessing gravity
- Problems of reflecting harm and culpability
- The emphasis on individualization
- How to weigh mitigating and aggravating factors
- How to gauge the relative severity of the penalty
- The absence of any sentencing guidance
- How to relate aims and effectiveness.

Particularly significant is the fact that retributive and deterrent justifications for punishment have continue to predominate in international criminal trials. These rationales have influenced the design of the procedural norms which govern sentencing and exerted a correspondingly disproportionate influence over their interpretation and implementation.

A key aspect of this is that the judiciary of the *ad hoc* tribunals have used their largely unfettered sentencing powers to individualize particular sentences whilst the overarching influence of the retributive dynamic has continued to influence the context in which sentencing decisions are reached. Consequently, the rationale of retributivism provides a paradigm within which discretionary decisions about the relationship between substantive and procedural norms, such as those concerning the appropriateness of plea agreements, are made.

The international judiciary have been able to reconcile the objectives of individualized and retributive punishment through symbolism and rhetoric.[10] The context for decision-making, as elaborated in ICTY judgements such as *Kupreskic*[11] and *Furundzija*,[12] makes it clear that for the sentence to reflect the inherent gravity of the crime requires consideration and assessment of the seriousness of the offence and the conduct of the accused. The balance between the two limbs of this approach is achieved through the exercise by judges of their wide discretionary powers to individualize each sentence within the context of the retributive dynamic that

---

9   See, Beresford, S. (2002) 'Unshackling the Paper Tiger: The Sentencing Practices of the ad hoc International Criminal Tribunals for the Former Yugoslavia and Rwanda' 1, *International Criminal Law Review*, p. 33; Henham, R. (2003) 'Some Issues for Sentencing in the International Criminal Court', 52 *International & Comparative Law Quarterly*, p. 81; Dana, S. (2004), 'Revisiting the Blaskic Sentence: Some Reflections on the Sentencing Jurisprudence of the ICTY', 4 *International Criminal Law Review*, p. 321.

10   Henham, R. (2007), 'Developing Contextualised Rationales for Sentencing in International Criminal Trials: A Plea for Empirical Research', 5 *Journal of the International Criminal Justice*, p. 757.

11   *Prosecutor v Kupreskic* et al. (Case No. IT-95-16), Appeals Chamber, Judgement, 23 October 2001, paras. 443–444.

12   *Prosecutor v Furundzija* (Case No. IT-95-17/1), Appeals Chamber, Judgement, 21 July 2000, para. 249.

influences how the provisions of the relevant foundation documents are interpreted. Since this normative framework does not even adumbrate, let alone discuss, particular punishment rationales or how they might relate in sentencing to specific crimes such as genocide, the dynamic of retributive justice, and the predominant liberal political ideology which underpins this penal philosophy, continues to prevail.[13] This desire for retribution is symbolically rationalized and equated by the Trial Chambers of the *ad hoc* tribunals with the achievement of their fundamental humanitarian mission; namely, that the essential virtues of humanity are coextensive with those of the 'international community' and its pluralistic demands for justice, and that it is their role to give them effect.[14]

Notwithstanding, the morality of retribution as a penal justification is further questionable without any concomitant requirement for consistency, or any rational framework to determine how the severity of punishment should relate to the harm sustained by the offending behaviour. At this point it is instructive to consider briefly the theoretical arguments involved in the normative assessment of gravity. It is clearly far too simplistic merely to draw a distinction between the gravity of the offence and the culpability of the offender because this overlooks two crucial issues. The first is that it ignores the consequences of making a distinction between the determination of gravity for the purposes of establishing criminal liability and its determination for sentencing purposes. The second problem is that the determination of gravity involves the application of objective and subjective tests which vary in their relevance and emphasis according to whether they relate to offence gravity, offender culpability or both.[15] Carcano[16] draws a distinction between determining

---

13 Support for the view that the context of the *ad hoc* tribunals is vindication and western exculpation derives from their primacy over national jurisdictions, subordination of the tribunals' jurisdictions through case selection, the provision of limited resources and other Security Council pressure, see Bassiounni, M.C. and Manakas, P. (1996), *The Law of the International Criminal Tribunal of the Former Yugoslavia* (Irvington-on-Hudson, NY: Transnational Publishers), pp. 228–231.

14 The associated desire for revenge or vengeance being regarded as a negation of such principles; see *Prosecutor v Delalic* et al. (Case No. IT-96-21-T), Judgement, 16 November 1998, para. 1231 (the 'Celebici' case). The position was clarified by the Appeals Chamber of the ICTY in *Aleksovski*: 'This [retribution] is not to be understood as fulfilling a desire for revenge but as duly expressing the outrage of the international community at these crimes ... Accordingly, a sentence of the International Tribunal should make plain the condemnation of the international community of the behaviour in question and show that the international community was not ready to tolerate serious violations of international humanitarian law and human rights.' See, *Prosecutor v Aleksovski* (Case No. IT-95-14/1-A), Judgement, 20 March 2000, para. 185.

15 For instance, potentially aggravating factors in sentencing, such as premeditation, motive, the vulnerability of victims and the use of gratuitous violence, or mitigating factors, such as provocation, duress, intoxication.

16 Carcano, A. (2002), 'Sentencing and the Gravity of the Offence in International Criminal Law', 51 *International and Comparative Law Quarterly*, pp. 583, 609. In *Prosecutor v Blaskic* (Case No. IT-95-14-T), Judgement, 3 March 2000, the Trial Chamber proposed a mixed objective/ subjective method for assessing crime seriousness whereby legal characterization of the crime would be determined by its intrinsic seriousness, with subjective considerations

the gravity of an offence *in abstracto* and *in concreto*, suggesting that the former is based on an assessment of the objective/subjective requirements imposed by the substantive offence definition, whilst the latter depends on the degree of harm done and the degree of culpability of the offender. According to Carcano, the ICTR has adopted a broad approach, taking into account both gravity *in abstracto* and *in concreto*. The ICTY, on the other hand, has been more circumspect, adopting a more *in abstracto* approach by inferring gravity largely from its analysis of the circumstances of the case.

Unfortunately, Carcano's distinction between *in abstracto* and *in concreto* gravity fails to provide a meaningful paradigm for identifying what should be the appropriate punishment for international crimes because it fails to take full account of the critical distinction drawn between the concept of gravity as required for the purposes of satisfying substantive offence definitions and its significance as a factor for determining sentence severity. Arguably, Carcano fails to acknowledge that objective and subjective conditions for fixing criminal and penal liability fulfil different purposes so that they cannot be taken to serve rational objectives beyond those identified as relevant to the instant case. For example, whilst the subjective principle may serve as a minimum condition for fixing criminal liability[17] and may also act to fix the boundaries of responsibility for sentencing purposes in determining the relevance and effect of aggravating and mitigating factors, it does not establish a principled basis for comparison between cases of varying severity.

In short, Carcano's paradigm does not address what western desert theorists have referred to as the problems of cardinal and ordinal proportionality in the context of punishment.[18] The latter is significant because the philosophy of just deserts is strongly reflected in the sentencing model prevalent in international criminal trials. Unfortunately, an unresolved weakness in deserts theory is its inability to distinguish convincingly between different degrees of responsibility, or quantify harm.[19] Therefore, whilst deserts theory recognizes that sentencing policy must consider the extent to which deserved punishment is applied in individual cases, it fails to provide

---

relating to the individual circumstances of the case being reserved for sentencing. Sentence levels would depend on a determination of the appropriate balance between objective and subjective seriousness factors, although the weight to be accorded to the latter would not (except in exceptional circumstances) be permitted to override the former (see Carcano, *ibid*, for arguments supporting this approach). However, the later Appeal Chamber decision in *Furundzija (Prosecutor v Furundzija* (Case No. IT-95-17/1-A), Appeals Judgement, 21 July 2000) did not refer to *Blaskic*, preferring instead an approach which retained greater flexibility for individual decision makers to determine the appropriate relationship between individual factors and the relative gravity of crimes against humanity and war crimes for sentencing purposes.

17 This may be in combination or separately from objective considerations.

18 See von Hirsch, A. (1976), *Doing Justice* (New York: Hill and Wang) Chapter 8.

19 See Ashworth, A. (1983), *Sentencing and Penal Policy* (London: Weidenfeld & Nicolson) pp. 173–181; Ashworth, A. (1989), 'Criminal Justice and Deserved Sentences', *Crim LR*, pp. 340, 346.

a rational framework for scaling punishments or ranking them in terms of offence seriousness.[20]

The criteria for comparison Carcano[21] utilizes in order to discriminate between international crimes in terms of their gravity fail to address these difficulties. Carcano uses the example of genocide, arguing that it is possible to measure the degree of disrespect for the rule of law as indicative of the criminal relevance of a given offence. He appears to suggest that the identification of a subjective element in an offence definition such as genocide[22] provides a useful *in abstracto* preliminary assessment of gravity against which to measure the accused's culpability *in concreto*. But this does not really take us very far, and certainly not beyond the circumstances of the individual case. Knowing that the perceived wickedness of an individual accused increases exponentially the greater the level of disregard shown for the values embodied in the criminal law does not provide us with a rationale (let alone a moral principle) that will help us to determine the relative seriousness of offences generally, nor a paradigm for deciding how punishments should be related to them in terms of their severity.

Secondly, in suggesting certain criteria for comparison, Carcano ignores the relative demands for justice of different communities and different perceptions of the legitimacy of international sentence outcomes in post-conflict societies. To suggest that it should be possible to 'verify the extent to which the values protected by a legal provision have been infringed' and that a system of international criminal law exists to protect the values of 'a *given* community',[23] or that we should take into account the 'disapproval of the community in which a given criminal system is based' simply begs the question. Not only do these criteria fail to address the question of how moral relativity and pluralism produce differing interpretations of what constitutes justice,

---

20 As Bohlander suggests in his extensive commentary on *Tadic*, a consideration of sentencing factors beyond the realms of the facts of the particular case come into play where the same conduct can be charged differently. Bohlander uses the distinction between the offence of murder as a war crime and a crime against humanity to illustrate his point. In the latter case the mens rea requirement is higher since the criminal act must be committed in the knowledge that it is part of a widespread campaign of murder. This would be reflected in the more lenient sentence for a person convicted of murder as a war crime, since that individual would not have had such knowledge. However, the distinction is important in terms of the source of the sentencing factors taken into account. In effect, because knowledge of the widespread character of the murder campaign forms part of the offence description for murder as a crime against humanity, Bohlander suggests that this becomes a general sentencing factor for murder as a war crime; one that acts to aggravate the offence charged and elevate it to a higher plane of seriousness for the purpose of determining sentence. He concludes: 'And in this way, when it comes to sentencing, especially without a sentencing scale, one may of course take all the typified elements of one type of offence and use them as general sentencing factors for others requiring some element of the former, thereby equalising the abstract distinction of criminal repugnance'; Bohlander, M. (2000), 'Prosecutor v Dusko Tadic: Waiting to Exhale' 11 *Criminal Law Forum*, pp. 217, 246.

21 *Supra*, note 16, p. 592.

22 Namely, that it must be proved that the offender had the intention of destroying the whole or part of a group on discriminatory grounds.

23 *Supra*, note 16, p. 593 (emphasis added).

they suggest no methodological imperatives for understanding or comparison in any meaningful way. Carcano's paradigm is tautological because it rests on the flawed assumption that the recursive affirmation of existing international trial ideology and its processual norms through sentencing is compatible with fulfilling the aspirations and values it identifies as necessary to protect.

As suggested, sentencers in international criminal trials have a great deal of freedom to individualize the penalty through their consideration of the particular circumstances of a case and the form and degree of participation in the crime on the part of the accused. However, the unstructured use of discretion in a situation where the parameters set for determining the relative seriousness of offences in international criminal law are unclear inevitably produces obfuscation and inconsistency in sentencing. Regrettably, the present conceptualization of individualization and its potential engagement with the demands for justice of victims and victim communities is further inhibited by the retributive dynamic prevalent in international trial ideology discussed earlier.

Additionally, the concept of individualization is constrained in its practical application by legalistic criteria. Although international sentencers have wide discretionary powers which could be used to develop sentencing principles that promote consequentialist objectives, the individualization of sentences as currently practised fails to engage with such purposes and focuses instead on issues of individual criminal responsibility and its clarification within the retributive paradigm.

More generally, confusion persists in the sentencing decisions of the *ad hoc* tribunals regarding the interpretation of 'individualisation' as a sentencing concept. Zappala[24] in particular appears to elevate 'individualization' for crimes under international law to the level of a due process right on the basis that it is instrumental in defining the limits of individual criminal responsibility for acts committed during the course of armed conflicts, although falling short of recognizing an allied right to rehabilitation on the part of the convicted person. In any event, the precise ambit of the 'individualization' concept and its relationship to rehabilitation as a possible sentencing objective for the *ad hoc* tribunals remains conjectural. It is difficult to see how individualization as a philosophical approach to the resolution of the conflicting demands of sentencing can be conceptualized as an enforceable legal right in international sentence decision-making. This would only be possible should the rationale(s) for sentencing international crimes accommodate such an approach. As things stand, the predominant ideological framework of retributivism and deterrence for international sentencing suggests a particularly narrow interpretation of individualization confined to delineating the parameters of individual responsibility for international crimes; certainly not one that engages constructively with the wider social context of sentencing outcomes. Thus, the attribution of rights status to individualization within a normative framework informed by retributive ideology does not imply any recognition that the broader demands for justice of victim communities are being addressed through sentencing.

---

24 Zappala, S. (2003), *Human Rights in International Criminal Proceedings*, (Oxford: Oxford University Press), p. 204.

In summary, the preceding analysis illustrates the inherent dangers of failing to provide mechanisms to regulate effectively the largely unfettered discretionary sentencing powers available to Trial Chambers in the ICTY and ICTR. In effect, this paucity of sentencing guidelines is a reflection of the failure on the part of successive Preparatory Commissions to settle questions relating to the relative gravity of international crimes and, consequently, the issue of cardinal proportionality for the punishment of such crimes. The result for both tribunals has been that judicial discretion has been employed to rationalize the question of offence gravity on a case by case basis rather than through the principled application of universally agreed norms embodied in their respective foundation instruments.[25] In consequence, the concept of individualization, so enthusiastically endorsed by judges, is circumscribed by the pervading ideology which underpins the substantive and procedural framework for trial and sentence in international criminal trials. This retributive and deterrent ideology not only militates against the development of sentencing guidance which embraces a more broadly conceived and constructive conceptualization of individualization, it crucially hinders that objective by facilitating the use of procedural devices such as plea bargains that reduce the possibilities for principled intervention on the part of the judiciary.

Rationalizing Practice

The use of plea agreements, the possibility of sentence discounts in return for guilty pleas and other forms of charge and sentence bargaining[26] in international criminal trials is not unique to cases where defendants are charged with counts which include genocide. As I have suggested, the generic and systemic weaknesses which affect the functioning of substantive and procedural norms in international criminal trials impact on all kinds of cases, including those involving genocide. Accordingly, the general principles which influence the use of procedural devices such as plea agreements and sentence discounts have been considered in cases across the full range of international crimes triable before the *ad hoc* tribunals.[27]

---

25 Research by Meernik suggests that judges in the ICTY sentence those convicted of genocide to the longest sentences, those convicted of crimes against humanity receive lesser sentences and those found guilty of war crimes receive the lightest sentences; see, Meernik, J. (2003), 'Victor's Justice or the Law? Judging and Punishing at the International Criminal Tribunal for the Former Yugoslavia', 47 *Journal of Conflict Resolution*, p. 140.

26 In the case of the ICTY/ICTR there is no possibility of a 'plea bargain' in the sense of a guaranteed (possibly graduated) discount resulting from a change of plea depending on the stage at which it is entered. Such a course would be entirely at the discretion of the Trial Chamber judges.

27 See, in particular; ICTY – *Prosecutor v Erdemovic* (Case No. IT-96-22), Trial Chamber, Sentencing Judgement, 5 March 1998 (plea agreement); *Prosecutor v Todorovic* (Case No. IT-95-9/1), Trial Chamber, Sentencing Judgement, 31 July 2001 (plea agreement); *Prosecutor v Banovic* (Case No. IT-02-65/1-S), Trial Chamber, Sentencing Judgement, 28 October 2003 (plea agreement); *Prosecutor v Dragan Nikolic* (Case No. IT-94-2-S), Trial Chamber, Sentencing Judgement, 18 December 2003; Sentencing Appeal Judgement, 4 February 2005 (plea agreement); *Prosecutor v Cesic* (Case No. IT-95-10/1-S), Trial Chamber, Judgement,

Notwithstanding, it is important to distinguish the different circumstances and contexts in which guilty pleas for cases involving genocide have been accepted before the ICTY and ICTR. In both tribunals there have, of course, been cases resulting in convictions on genocide charges where no guilty plea or plea agreement was involved.[28] There have also been cases where convictions for genocide have followed a guilty plea,[29] and other cases with indictments including genocide which have produced convictions on lesser counts following a guilty plea.[30]

The ICTY Trial Chamber in *Plavsic*[31] concluded that the accused's guilty plea and acknowledgement of responsibility should carry significant weight in mitigation

---

11 March 2004 (guilty plea/no plea agreement); *Prosecutor v Jokic* (Case No. IT-01-42/1-S), Trial Chamber, Sentencing Judgement, 18 March 2004 (plea agreement); *Prosecutor v Deronjic* (Case No. IT-02-61-S), Trial Chamber, Sentencing Judgement, 30 March 2004; *Prosecutor v Mrda* (Case No. IT-02-59-S), Trial Chamber, Sentencing Judgement, 31 March 2004 (plea agreement); *Prosecutor v Babic* (Case No. IT-03-72-S), Trial Chamber, Sentencing Judgement, 29 June 2004 (plea agreement).

28 For example; ICTY – *Prosecutor v Krstic* (Case No. IT-98-33-A). Appeals Chamber, Judgement, 19 April 2004: ICTR – *Prosecutor v Akayesu* (Case No. ICTR-96-4), Trial Chamber, Judgement, 2 September 1998, Sentence, 2 October 1998; *Prosecutor v Kayishema* (Case No. ICTR-95-1), Trial Chamber Judgement and Sentence, 21 May 1999; *Ruzindana* (Case Nos 1: ICTR-95-1; 2: ICTR-96-10), Trial Chamber, Judgement and Sentence, 21 May 1999; *Prosecutor v Rutaganda* (Case No. ICTR-96-3) Trial Chamber, Judgement and Sentence, 6 December 1999; *Prosecutor v Musema* (Case No. ICTR-96-13-A), Trial Chamber, Judgement and Sentence, 27 January 2000; *Prosecutor v Niyitegeka* (Case No. ICTR-96-14-T), Trial Chamber, Judgement and Sentence, 16 May 2003; *Prosecutor v Ntakirutimana* (Case No 1: ICTR-96-10; 2: ICTR-96-17), Trial Chamber, Judgement and Sentence, 21 February 2003; *Prosecutor v Semanza* (Case No. ICTR-97-20-T), Judgement and Sentence, 15 May 2003. Note that these issues have also been debated in cases where defendants were acquitted of charges involving genocide, See, for example; ICTY – *Prosecutor v Jelisic* (Case No. IT-95-10), Trial Chamber, Judgement, 14 December 1999 (guilty plea/no plea agreement).

29 See, in particular; ICTR – *Prosecutor v Kambanda* (Case No. ICTR 97-23-S) Trial Chamber, Judgement and Sentence, 4 September 1998 (plea agreement); *Prosecutor v Serushago* (Case No. ICTR 98-39-S), Trial Chamber, Sentence, 5 February 1999 (plea agreement); *Prosecutor v Ruggiu* (Case No. ICTR 97-32-I), Trial Chamber, 1 June 2000 (plea agreement).

30 For example; ICTY – *Prosecutor v Sikirica* et al. (Case No. IT-95-8-S), Trial Chamber, Sentencing Judgement, 13 November 2001 (plea agreement); *Prosecutor v Plavsic* (Case No. IT-00-30 and 40/1-S), Trial Chamber, Judgement, 27 February 2003 (plea agreement); *Prosecutor v Momir Nikolic* (Case No. IT-02-60/1-S), Trial Chamber, Sentencing Judgement, 2 December 2003 (plea agreement); *Prosecutor v Obrenovic* (Case No. IT-02-60/2-2), Trial Chamber, Sentencing Judgement, 10 December 2003 (plea agreement); ICTR – *Prosecutor v Rutaganira* (Case No. ICTR-95-1C), Judgement and Sentence, 14 March 2006.

31 *Ibid.*, para. 81. The guilty plea was entered pursuant to Rule 62 *bis*, ICTY Rules of Procedure and Evidence which states that:

If an accused pleads guilty in accordance with Rule 62 (vi), or requests to change his or her plea to guilty and the Trial Chamber is satisfied that:
(i)   the guilty plea has been made voluntarily;
(ii) the guilty plea is informed;
(iii) the guilty plea is not equivocal; and

as a 'positive impact on the reconciliatory process.' It therefore accepted that the guilty plea and other expressions of remorse contributed towards establishing the 'truth' of what took place. However, this raises the important issue of whether such a procedural mechanism operating in the context of a (predominantly) adversarial trial paradigm is best placed to determine 'truth,'[32] and indeed, raises questions about the context in which this particular version of 'truth' is being produced, and for whom.

This observation highlights the paradox for sentencing in international criminal trials; how to produce sentencing outcomes which can engage with victims and victim communities whilst concurrently satisfying retributive demands for punishment. It might be argued that it is impossible to envisage an international trial paradigm that could reconcile the aspirations of both positions, or that this can only be achieved through some accommodation with non-judicial means. Alternatively, a fundamental reconceptualization of the trial paradigm may be necessary to promote a principled engagement of retributive and restorative themes.[33]

These difficulties were illustrated by the outcome in *Pavlic* itself. Despite acknowledging that it would give significant weight to the accused's plea of guilty, expressions of remorse and their positive impact on reconciliation, the Trial Chamber was eventually swayed by the heinous nature of what had taken place and its effects. The prosecution was criticized for giving insufficient weight to (*inter alia*) the accused's guilty plea and her post-conflict conduct, yet there was a distinct lack of clarity in the Trial Chamber's determination of exactly what the effect of the mitigation (described as 'very significant') should be on the sentence. Such an outcome tends to support Zappala's assertion,[34] based on the Appeal Chamber's unwillingness to entertain a sentence discount in *Kambanda*, that it may not be appropriate to allow plea-bargaining and plea agreements for crimes of extreme gravity.[35]

(iv)   there is a sufficient factual basis for the crime and the accused's participation in it, either on the basis of independent indicia or on lack of any material disagreement between the parties about the facts of the case,

the Trial Chamber may enter a finding of guilt and instruct the Registrar to set a date for the sentencing hearing.

32 Zappala *supra*, note 24, p. 89, makes the important point that the determination of 'truth' where a guilty plea is entered is neither judicial nor pedagogical, and, therefore, appears to contradict the mission of international criminal courts to take account of victims' interests. But see, Article 65, para. 4 of the ICC Statute which, in relation to proceedings on an admission of guilt, permits the Trial Chamber to call for additional factual evidence in the interests of justice (especially victims) and remit the case for ordinary trial where it considers the admission of guilt as not having been made.

33 Findlay, M. and Henham, R. (2005), *Transforming International Criminal Justice: Retributive and Restorative Justice in the Trial Process* (Cullompton: Willan Publishing).

34 *Supra*, note 24, p. 89.

35 Zappala's reasons for supporting the practice are not totally convincing. He appears to advocate the pragmatic use of guilty plea discounts and plea agreements, on the basis of their advantages to the Prosecutor in shortening investigations, and that it may be in the public interest to shorten the trials of minor participants on the basis of cost. It should be noted that

Not only are there are difficulties in drawing the appropriate distinctions between the assessment of gravity for the purposes of establishing substantive offences and the assessment of seriousness for sentencing purposes, it is also clear that the balance between offence seriousness and the acceptability of procedural devices such as plea agreements based on expediency has yet to be drawn. However, the apparent absence of any willingness on the part of the international tribunals to preclude such practices, or lay down comprehensive guidelines for sentencing practice, indicates their tacit acceptance as institutional procedural mechanisms.

Further justifications for the increased and continued use of plea agreements by the ICTY were provided more recently in the related cases of *Obrenovic*[36] and *Momir Nikolic*.[37] The latter contained a principled discussion of the issues wherein the Trial Chamber addressed many of the arguments for and against the use of plea agreements for serious violations of international humanitarian law.[38] Passing reference was made to the varying reasons for their widespread adoption in common law jurisdictions and the importance of juridical context and culture in determining the emphasis that might be given to specific justifications, such as the level of consideration accorded to victims, the public interest and the administration of justice. However, the rationalizations offered for the explicit institutionalization of plea agreements in the ICTY remain unconvincing, and indeed illustrate the paradoxical nature of the ideological justification for international penalty.

The Trial Chamber in *Momir Nikolic* was at pains to stress the dual conception implicit in the trial ideology of the ICTY; that of putting an end to impunity for those who perpetrate gross breaches of international humanitarian law, on the one hand, and contributing to peace and reconciliation, on the other.[39] It employed this latter ideology to distinguish its mandate from national criminal justice systems, arguing that the principled use of plea agreements actually made a constructive contribution

---

in many jurisdictions sentence discounts for guilty pleas are generally forbidden for cases of first degree murder.

36 *Supra*, note 30.

37 *Supra*, note 30. The ICTY Trial Chamber in *Dragan Nikolic* (*supra*, note 27, paras. 57–73) referred to its decision in *Momir Nikolic* for detailed discussion on the appropriateness of plea agreements in cases involving serious violations of international humanitarian law. The former case is important in a number of respects, not least for its reaffirmation of the principled use of plea agreements and, additionally, for its admission and consideration of comparative research evidence on sentencing law and practice commissioned from the Max Planck Institute for Foreign and International Criminal Law in Freiburg, Germany; Sieber, U. (2003), *The Punishment of Serious Crimes: A comparative analysis of sentencing law and practice*, Vol. 1 Expert Report; Vol. 2 Country Reports, Max Planck Institute for Foreign and International Criminal Law: Freiburg im Breisgau, Germany. For additional comment see; Henham, R. (2005), 'Plea bargaining and the legitimacy of international trial justice: some observations on the Dragan Nikolic sentencing judgement of the ICTY', 5 *International Criminal Law Review*, p. 601.

38 *Ibid.*, para. 43 *et seq.*

39 *Ibid.*, paras. 58–62. The Appeals Chamber recently confirmed the Trial Chamber's earlier interpretation of this (and other) principles, particularly relating to the timing and credit for a guilty plea; *Prosecutor v Momir Nikolic* (Case No. IT-02-60/1-A), Judgement on Sentencing Appeal, 8 March 2006.

towards full accountability, thereby distancing itself (implicitly) from the remarks of Judge Cassese in *Erdemovic*,[40] supporting their use for (*inter alia*) reasons of bureaucratic and administrative expediency. In so doing, the Trial Chamber stressed the argument that guilty pleas can often make a significant contribution to peace and reconciliation,[41] particularly when coupled with sincere expressions of remorse. Procedural safeguards should ensure that the interests of 'justice' were not compromised.

Nevertheless, I would argue that there is an inherent philosophical contradiction in the argument advanced in support of the restorative capability of plea agreements in international criminal trials. Firstly, the ICTY cannot effectively divorce itself from the administrative efficiency argument. Essentially, what the Trial Chamber in *Momir Nikolic* tries to argue is that the trial ideology of the ICTY forces a reconceptualization of plea agreements. We are asked to suspend belief in those rationales and implications that do not sustain the ICTY's professed search for 'truth' (such as, control of process; suppression of evidence; exclusion from participation; denial of process; erosion of rights; absence of public accountability) in return for a vision of plea agreements as procedural mechanisms that underpin the ideological commitment of international penality to the constructive ideals of reconciliation and reconstruction. Without denying that this may be one effect, such a conception of plea agreements conveniently ignores the substantive reasons for their increased use in common law jurisdictions in recent years, and introduces a rationale for their continued expansion which attempts to redefine the underlying purpose of plea agreements as procedural devices.

Finally, a specific criticism which illustrates the distorting effect of plea agreements and their capacity for downgrading the 'truth' in terms of how the trial marks the seriousness of what has taken place through punishment concerns the factual basis underlying the conduct charged. This difficulty was particularly evident in *Momir Nikolic*[42] where the defendant was originally charged with numerous crimes, including genocide. Following an amended plea agreement the defendant eventually pleaded guilty to the lesser charge of persecutions (a crime against humanity), and all remaining counts on the indictment against him were dropped. In considering Rule 62 *bis* of the ICTY's Rules of Evidence and Procedure,[43] the Trial Chamber observed that it was satisfied that the factual basis upon which the charge of persecutions was based reflected the totality of the defendant's criminal conduct.[44] Whilst the sufficiency of the factual basis for the crime eventually charged, and the accused's participation in it, is not in doubt, the application of this rule ignores

---

40 *Prosecutor v Erdemovic* (Case No. IT-96-22), Appeals Judgement, 7 October 1997, para. 8.

41 *Supra*, note 27, para. 72. This was a significant finding in the judgement itself; para. 145.

42 See also the powerful dissenting judgement of Presiding Judge Wolfgang Schomberg in *Deronjic* (*supra*, note 27) regarding proportionality and the compromising effect of plea agreements; Dissenting Opinion of Judge Wolfgang Schomburg, especially paras. 8, 10, 14(a)(b), and 20.

43 *Supra*, note 31.

44 *Supra*, note 27, para. 51.

the fundamental capacity of plea and other forms of negotiation for manipulating evidential 'truth' to suit processual goals. Not only does the plea deny the possibility of testing the evidence in open court, the acceptance of a charge as reflecting the totality of the accused's criminal conduct effectively denies the court the opportunity to give full expression to the totality of that criminality through the imposition of a penal sanction which adequately reflects the seriousness of the crime(s) and the culpability of the offender. In effect, the effectiveness of international penality in terms of its undoubted capacity for symbolic public expression and denunciation of past breaches of international criminal law is seriously compromised if the totality of the punishment is not seen to be proportionate to the totality of the defendant's criminal conduct.

The increasing readiness of the ICTY to embrace the rationale for utilizing plea agreements in cases involving genocide may be contrasted with their more cautious acceptance by the Trial Chambers of the ICTR.[45] Notwithstanding that indictments for genocide predominate in ICTR trials, the rationalization and adoption of plea agreements in genocide trials has been more circumscribed, with plea agreements featuring in cases such as *Kambanda*, *Serushago* and *Ruggiu*.[46] Despite maintaining that his guilty plea indicated 'remorse, repentance and acceptance of responsibility', the Appeals Chamber in *Kambanda*[47] rejected the accused's contention that the Trial Chamber had incorrectly failed to give effect to the principle that a mitigating factor once accepted automatically carries with it a sentence discount. On the other hand, the decisions in *Serushago* and *Ruggiu* were both notable for the mitigating weight given by the Trial Chamber in each case to their substantial and continuing cooperation with the authorities, in addition to expressions of remorse, contrition and repentance. Whilst it is impossible to gauge the relative weight attached to such mitigation, or draw meaningful comparisons between them, in all three cases the ICTR was at pains to stress the administrative benefits accruing from guilty pleas, and hinted at their positive benefits in terms of promoting reconciliation in Rwanda.[48]

---

45 For recent analysis of ICTR jurisprudence; see, Meernik, J. (2004), 'Proving and Punishing Genocide at the International Criminal Tribunal for Rwanda', 4 *International Criminal Law Review*, p. 65.

46 *Supra*, note 29; See Combs *supra*, note 4, for analysis of these cases in the context of plea bargaining.

47 *Prosecutor v Kambanda* (Case No. ICTR-97-23), Appeals Chamber Judgement, 19 October 2000.

48 However, Combs, *supra*, notes 4, 151, suggests that, although sentencing concessions undermine reconciliation, their elimination is not viable because it would result in a substantial reduction in guilty pleas.

Conclusion

Such opinions have been generally endorsed by commentators such as Combs,[49] Jorgensen[50] and Meernik.[51] Whether or not the encouragement of guilty pleas through sentence discounts contributes to reconciliation because guilty pleas constitute an acknowledgement of the truth of what actually happened is clearly a moot point when the incentives for pleading guilty are significant, especially where crimes of the magnitude of genocide are involved. Even if such a confession of guilt is true, it is arguable that the need to promote understanding and tolerance in post-conflict states is better served through the cathartic experience of a trial, or some alternative process such as a truth and reconciliation commission.

Whether truth contributes to justice depends on the capacity of the truth-finding body to deliver justice. I have argued here, and elsewhere,[52] that the legitimacy of the truth available in international criminal tribunals is conditioned by ideology and its effects on normative practice. As Jorgensen suggests,[53] there is a need for clarity and consistency in international sentencing, but I would argue that 'pragmatism' surely cannot be utilized as a moral justification which should inform penality at any level. 'Pragmatism', as the unprincipled exercise of free will, is implicitly self-serving and will always aim to satisfy other ideological and practical objectives. Although the exercise of free will may be deemed by certain utilitarian measures to be intrinsically good, and bring undoubted benefits, my objection to the elevation of pragmatism to the status of a philosophical justification for punishment lies is the fact that it eschews any clearly defined purpose for restricting the free will of others, except that of assessing the value of actions in terms of their practical benefits.

Furthermore, promoting the notion of 'pragmatism' as an ideological imperative merely serves to endorse existing forms of hegemony and social control, since it does not espouse any rationale for action beyond that which favours ends over means. I would suggest that those ends as presently constituted in the international tribunals are systemic and driven by a retributive dynamic that clouds the meaning and potential for trial justice to deliver a meaningful form of 'truth' for victims and victim communities in post-conflict societies.[54]

---

49 *Supra*, note 4.

50 *Supra*, note 4.

51 *Supra*, note 45.

52 Henham, R. (2005), *Punishment and Process in International Criminal Trials*, (Aldershot: Ashgate).

53 *Supra*, note 4, p. 407.

54 *Supra*, note 10.

Chapter 21

Genocide, Reconciliation and Sentencing in the Jurisprudence of the ICTY

Shahram Dana[1]

Introduction

This chapter is a reduced version of the author's paper presented at the International Conference on the Crime of Genocide at Nottingham Trent University.[1] The organizers' invitation suggested 'the role of sentencing in preventing genocide' as the subject of the author's address. A number of factors presented challenges to such an inquiry. The most significant is lack or insufficiency of empirical data linking punishment to the prevention of genocide; not far behind is the absence of consistent and certain enforcement necessary for such an assessment. The ensuing research into a variety of literary and legal sources revealed a recurring theme: the possible contribution of sentencing, and arguably the role of criminal justice in general, in preventing genocide is somewhat dwarfed by the greater pertinence of other mechanisms, outside the criminal justice process, which bare closer proximity to the goal of preventing mass atrocities.[2] The criminal trial process, not to mention sentencing which constitutes a limited phase within that process, occupies a diminutive space in the spectrum of initiatives and efforts that are available to our leaders, from initiatives in the early pre-crisis phase prior to the onset of violence to enterprises that seek to heal the wounds of society in a post-conflict setting.[3]

---

1 My sincere appreciation to Ralph Henham and Paul Behrens for inviting me to participate in this well-organized conference, bringing together a number of outstanding scholars and practitioners from whom I had the privilege to learn. I am grateful to Professors André Klip and Menno Kamminga for their willingness to offer thought provoking reactions.

2 Due to the word limit, some of the substance and references of the original conference contribution could not be reproduced in this chapter.

2 On the limited role of sentencing in crime prevention in the domestic context *see* A. Ashworth (2005), *Sentencing and Criminal Justice* (Cambridge: Cambridge University Press).

3 For a discussion on objections to employing criminal law as the mainstay response to mass atrocities *see* M. Osiel (2000), 'Why Prosecute? Critics of Punishment for Mass

Admittedly, it is not customary for an author to marginalize the topic of his paper in the opening paragraph. The aim here is not to suggest that the issue of sentencing lacks relevance in this discussion. In the context of 'seeing justice done', the punishment and sentence are what the public at large will be most familiar with; they are, in a sense, the 'external affairs officers' of international criminal justice and thus linked to the achievement of its goals, including prevention of crimes such as genocide. The point in acknowledging the limits of what can be achieve through law and legal mechanisms is two fold. First, post-harm measures, of which the international criminal justice process is one of them, can never be a substitute for the failure of international leaders to take all necessary measures to prevent mass atrocities, be they legally classified as genocide or not.[4] The moral authority of international prosecutions cannot be allowed to serve as an escape route for world leaders in the face of legitimate questions regarding their failed leadership.[5] Second, the creation of international forums for prosecution of crimes does not, obviously, alleviate us of our obligation to 'police' ominous situations and to respond decisively when confronted with warning signals. Nations must equally and genuinely commit to early action to prevent mass atrocities. Otherwise, we run the risk that international criminal courts result in little more than monumental memorials for the dead.

In addressing the challenges facing international judges in their task of fixing a penalty for the crime of genocide, this presentation will begin with some issues of general concern to international sentencing and then proceed to illustrate them with some specific examples using the crime of genocide. The discussion will not be limited to cases involving convictions for genocide. Instead, a broader approach will be taken to include situations where evidence supports the charge of genocide but, for one reason or another, the genocide charged was either dropped from the original indictment or never charged in the first place. The study focuses on the application of reconciliation ideology to reduce the penalty in such cases and theorizes that the current trend has unwittingly rewarded those most culpable for the crime of genocide.

Lack of Identity in International Criminal Justice

When imposing the ICTY's first sentence, international judges acknowledged that '[n]either the Statute nor the Report of the Secretary-General nor the Rules elaborate

---

Atrocity', 22 *HRQ*, p. 118.

4   Sadly, even today, we witness the same failures re-occurring. Although the UN Security Council has referred the situation in Darfur to the International Criminal Court (ICC), it has failed to take any serious and effective measures to halt the violence which is now spreading into Chad, threatening to collapse that country into a failed state. *See*, Stephanie Hancock, 'Rebels and robbers rampage in eastern Chad', BBC News, eastern Chad, 20 April 2006, available at http://news.bbc.co.uk/2/hi/africa/4925978.stm.

5   *See generally*, Romeo Dallaire, Kishan Manocha and Nishan Degnarain (2005), 'The Major Powers on Trial', 3 *Journal of International Criminal Justice*, p. 861; J. Kamatali (2003), 'The Challenge of Linking International Criminal Justice and National Reconciliation: the Case of the ICTR', 16 *Leiden J. Int'l L.*, p. 115.

on the objectives sought by imposing such a sentence.'[6] In developing the objective and purpose of international sentencing, they extrapolated from the preamble of Security Council Resolution 827 (1993) establishing the ICTY. Their implicit assumption was that the conditions required to trigger the Security Council's powers under Chapter VII of the UN Charter would suffice for developing a normative framework for international sentencing.[7]

Early judgements identified deterrence and retribution as the two primary purposes of sentencing in international criminal justice.[8] Some trial chambers added two more principles to create 'four parameters' for international sentencing: retribution, deterrence, rehabilitation, and protection of society.[9] However, it is fair to say that rehabilitation was never highly significant[10] and did not act as a meaningful 'parameter' to limit the sentence, as made apparent in the Trial Chamber's judgement of General Blaškić.[11] Despite acknowledging 'rehabilitation' as one of the parameters guiding its determination of Blaškić's sentence and despite its own factual findings strongly indicating the possibility of rehabilitation in his individual case, the Trial Chamber nevertheless decided to not give these factors any weight and certainly its 45 year sentence leaves little trace of rehabilitation considerations, especially since Blaškić was 40 years old when he was sentenced.[12] Such a sentence suggests that the Tribunal, early on, was eager to send a strong signal of deterrence and that this predominated its sentencing considerations, even to the extent, some would argue, of trial chambers distributing exemplary sentences or exemplary justice and placing that foremost in their considerations.[13] Taking caution that this practice did not go too

6 *Prosecutor v Erdemović, Sentencing Judgement*, Case No. IT-96-22-T, 29 November 1996, para. 57 (hereafter *Erdemović Sentencing Judgement*).

7 While there is some overlap between the justification for international prosecutions and the rationale of international sentencing, they cannot be assumed to be identical. Unfortunately, this distinction and its relevance to international sentencing cannot be pursued in the short context of this contribution.

8 *See, Prosecutor v Tadić, Sentencing Judgement*, Case No. IT-94-1-T*bis*-R117, 11 November 1999, paras. 7–9 (*stating* that 'retribution and deterrence serving as the primary purposes of sentence') and *Prosecutor v Furundžija, Judgement*, Case No. IT-95-17/1-T, 10 December 1998, para. 288. For more resent cases *see Prosecutor v Deronjić, Sentencing Judgement*, Case No. IT-02-61-S, 30 March 2004, para. 142 (hereafter '*Deronjić Sentencing Judgement*') (*concluding* that the '[f]undamental principles taken into consideration when imposing a sentence are deterrence and retribution'); For cases from the ICTR *see Prosecutor v Rutaganda, Judgement and Sentence*, Case No. ICTR-96-3-T, 6 December 1999; *Prosecutor v Serushago, Sentence*, Case No. ICTR-98-39-S, 5 February 1999.

9 *E.g., Prosecutor v Blaškić, Judgement*, Case No. IT-95-14-T, 3 March 2000, para. 761 (hereafter '*Blaškić Trial Judgement*').

10 *Erdemović Sentencing Judgement*, para. 66.

11 *Blaškić Trial Judgement*, paras 780–82.

12 For a critique of the Trial Chamber's sentencing analysis in the *Blaškić* case *see*, S. Dana (2004), 'Revisiting the Blaškić Sentence: Some Reflections on the Sentencing Jurisprudence of the ICTY', 4 *International Criminal Law Review*, p. 321.

13 *See*, J.C. Nemitz (2004), 'The Law of Sentencing in International Criminal Law: The Purpose of Sentencing and the Applicable Method for the Determination of the Sentence', 4 *Yearbook (2001) of International Humanitarian Law* 87, 93-93 (*suggesting* that the ICTY

far, the Appeals Chamber stated that 'this factor [deterrence] must not be accorded undue prominence in the overall assessment of the sentences'.[14]

Interestingly, the Tribunal has likewise explicitly pronounced that rehabilitation should not be given undue weight,[15] confirming what was already implicit in the early sentencing practice. Some have characterized this process of seemingly sea-sawing between various principles as '*ex post facto*' justification, although the International Tribunal is probably deserving of a less cynical assessment. It may also be viewed as a natural process whereby an relatively unprecedented justice system finds its footing. In any event, it appears as though the Tribunal was not yet ready to commit itself to one particular ideological approach.

The above-mentioned 'four parameters' – deterrence, retribution, rehabilitation, and protection of society – mirror the rationalizations for sentencing found at the national level. In addition to these objectives, international judges have advanced other considerations which influence sentencing in the international context, such as national reconciliation, preserving history, combating impunity, and maintaining peace. The notion of 'reconciliation' is typically elaborated in sentencing judgements resulting from plea bargaining.[16] The concept is used to both justify the practice of plea bargaining as well as to rationalize mitigation of the sentence.[17] While 'reconciliation' is a laudable aspiration, its viability as a legal factor in sentencing is ambiguous. From fundamental conceptual development to practical applications, ICTY trial chambers have struggled to harmoniously, effectively and consistently integrate this concept into their sentencing practice. This will be discussed in further detail below.

In recent years, the sentencing jurisprudence has continued to further elaborate on the justifications for punishment in the international context. For example, a steady stream of cases have addressed the notion of 'positive deterrence' or 'general affirmative prevention', acknowledging thereby the educational function of international punishment. For example, in the *Dragan Nikolić* case, the Trial Chamber stated:

> One of the main purposes of a sentence imposed by an international tribunal is to influence the legal awareness of the accused, the surviving victims, their relatives, the witnesses and

---

sentence of Jelisić was exemplary punishment); *see also, Prosecutor v Jelisić, Judgement,* Case No. IT-95-10-T, 14 December 1999, para. 116 (*holding* that 'Trial Chamber must pronounce an exemplary penalty both from the viewpoint of punishment and deterrence') (hereafter '*Jelisić Trial Judgement*').

14 *Prosecutor v Tadić, Judgement in Sentencing Appeals,* Case No. IT-94-1-A and IT-94-1-A*bis*, 26 January 2000, para. 48.

15 *See, Prosecutor v Delalić* et al*., Judgement,* Case No. IT-96-21-A, 20 February 2001, para. 806 (*stating* that 'although rehabilitation ... should be considered as a relevant factor, it is not one which should be given undue weight') (hereafter '*Čelebići Appeals Judgement*'); *see also, Deronjić Sentencing Judgement,* para. 143.

16 *E.g., Prosecutor v Plavšić, Sentencing Judgement,* Case No. IT-00-39&40/1-S, 27 February 2003 (hereafter '*Plavšić Sentencing Judgement*').

17 *E.g., Prosecutor v Momir Nikolić, Sentencing Judgement,* Case No. IT-02-60/1-S, 2 December 2003.

the general public in order to reassure them that the legal system is implemented and enforced. Additionally, the process of sentencing is intended to convey the message that globally accepted laws and rules have to be obeyed by everybody. ... This fundamental rule fosters the internalisation of these laws and rules in the minds of legislators and the general public.[18]

The inculcation of the 'message that globally accepted laws and rules have to be obeyed by everybody' is particularly needed in the context of international law, especially international humanitarian law. Unfortunately, the norms and values protected by international law usually do not carry the same compulsion for obedience as national laws in the minds of the relevant actors. In the context of war, the need for inculcation of the moral awareness of values underlying international humanitarian law is most needed considering the 'culture of inverse morality', as described by some authors,[19] where an individual's inner sense of morality and repulsion towards such gruesome crimes is overridden by peer pressure from immediate comrades and superiors. Consequently, killing, rape, and terrorizing civilians becomes an accepted part of the warfare itself.

In sum, the ICTY jurisprudence not only identifies rationales for international sentencing based upon fundamental criminal law justifications found in domestic criminal justice systems (e.g. deterrence, retribution, rehabilitation) but also develops a sentencing philosophy particular to international prosecutions (e.g. national reconciliation, combating impunity, preserving a historical record). In addition, these and other objectives, ambitions, and hopes have been placed upon international criminal justice by other participants in the field such as diplomats, academics, and human rights activists, including for example, to eradicate a culture of impunity, to end on-going armed conflict,[20] to delegitimize nationalist regimes and racist ideologies; to support the process of transitional justice, to provide a historical record of the atrocities to prevent revisionism,[21] to contribute to national reconciliation in post-conflict societies[22] while also meeting the demands of victim

---

18 *Prosecutor v Dragan Nikolić, Sentencing Judgement*, Case No. IT-94-2-S, 18 December 2003, para. 139; *see also, Deronjić Sentencing Judgement*, para. 149.

19 P. Akhavan (2001) 'Beyond Impunity: Can International Criminal Justice Prevent Future Atrocities'? 95 *American Journal of International Law* 7.

20 *See*, UN Security Council Resolution 827 (1993), Preamble, S/RES/827 (1993), 25 May 1993; UN Security Council Resolution 995 (1994), Preamble, S/RES/995 (1994), 8 November 1994; R. Teitel (2005), 'The Law and Politics of Contemporary Transitional Justice', 38 *Cornell Int'l L. J.* pp. 837, 857.

21 J. Bush (1993), 'Nuremberg: The Modern Law of War and Its Limitations', 93 *Columbia L. Rev.* 2022, 2070 (*reviewing* T. Taylor (1992), *The Anatomy of the Nuremberg Trials: A Personal Memoir*). The ICTY apparently recognizes that this function should not dominate the proceedings and is not first and foremost among the objectives of international criminal prosecution. It likewise acknowledges that the criminal justice process is not ideally suited to this function. *Deronjić Sentencing Judgement*, para. 135 (*noting* that the 'Tribunal is not the final arbiter of historical facts. That is for historians.').

22 *See*, Teitel (2005), *supra* note 21, at 857. For arguments on how the ICTR approach to jurisprudential issues regarding genocide can undermine Rwandan reconciliation *see*, Kamatali (2003), *supra* note 5, pp. 121–124.

communities,[23] to demonstrate that culpability is individual[24] so as to end cycles of violent revenge against between entire groups,[25] to provide a solid foundation for lasting peace,[26] to provide a forum for considering restitution and reparations, to enforce international law,[27] to strengthen legal awareness about international humanitarian law and international criminal law,[28] to protect the rights of the accused,[29] and to set a benchmark standard for fair trial and due process.[30]

This growing list of aspirations associated with international prosecutions has complicated the task of international judges. The failure to prioritize the various objectives, and to distinguish the primary rationale underlying international sentencing from secondary objectives, has precipitated an identity crisis in international punishment. Generally speaking, international criminal justice lacks a clear identity and nowhere does its problems arising from these competing personalities manifest themselves more dramatically then in the process of sentencing. Consistency in international sentencing philosophy appears to be absent.[31] Consequently, from case to case, different rationales have been emphasized which has in turn affected the severity of the punishment. This undermines the principle of equal treatment. The problem can be illustrated through the notion of reconciliation as a mitigating factor in sentencing.

Practice and Sentencing Jurisprudence on Genocide and Reconciliation

Early ICTY Practice: Erdemović, Jelišic and Sikirica Cases

It is worth while to review the early practice of the Tribunal in relation to both reconciliation and genocide. The ICTY's first sentencing opportunity came unexpectedly when Dražen Erdemović pled guilty.[32] Given that sentencing matters arise, if at all, at the end stages of the criminal justice process, it was unforeseen

---

23 *See*, T. Farer (2000), 'Restraining the Barbarians: Can International Criminal Law Help?', 22 *HRQ*, pp. 90, 91; J. Pejic (1998), 'Creating a Permanent International Criminal Court: The Obstacles to Independence and Effectiveness', 29 *Columbia Human Rights L. Rev.*, pp. 291, 292.

24 *See*, Teitel (2005), *supra* note 21, at p. 857; Pejic (1998), *supra* note 24, at p. 292.

25 *See*, Farer (2000), *supra* note 24, at p. 91.

26 *See*, Teitel (2005), *supra* note 21, at p. 857.

27 *See*, UN Security Council Resolutions 827 (1993) and 995 (1994), *supra* note 21; *see also,* Farer (2000), *supra* note 24, at p. 91; Pejic (1998), *supra* note 24, at p. 292.

28 *See*, Pejic (1998), *supra* note 24, at p. 294; Farer (2000), *supra* note 24, at p. 91.

29 *See*, Pejic (1998), *supra* note 24, at p. 294.

30 *Id.*

31 A 'positive justice' approach to *nulla poena sine lege* can further consistency in international sentencing. For an advancement of a theory on this subject under international law *see*, S. Dana (forthcoming 2007), *Nulla Poena Sine Lege in International Law and International Criminal Justice.*

32 'Croat pleds guilty to war crimes in Bosnia', CNN News Service, 31 May 1996, available at http://www.corpuschristischoolno.com/WORLD/Bosnia/updates/9605/31/guilty. war.criminal/index.html (last visited 12 May 2006).

that one of the ICTY's earliest decisions would call upon the judges to interpret its sentencing provisions. Academics, legal officers, and judicial law clerks had been focusing on questions of jurisdiction, applicability of treaties regulating international verse internal armed conflicts, and substantive elements of crimes. [33] Little analysis had been done on the articles of the Statute and Rules of Procedure and Evidence pertaining to sentencing or on the underlying philosophy behind international punishment. Accordingly, in this first sentencing judgement, the notion of reconciliation appears to have hardly any influence on Erdemović's sentence. In fact, the Trial Chamber employs the term only twice and then only in a very abstract manner.[34] No meaningful attempt is made to integrate the concept into the rationalization of the specific sentence imposed on Erdemović.

Regarding the crime of genocide, the interesting point to bear in mind regarding the Tribunal's early practice is the Prosecutor's unwillingness to engage in plea bargaining in relation to the charge of genocide. For example, in the *Jelišic* case, although the accused eventually pled guilty to 15 counts of crimes against humanity and 16 counts of war crimes, the Prosecutor nevertheless proceeded to trial on the charge of genocide against Goran Jelišić. Believing that the evidence against the accused, who once declared himself to be 'the Serbian Adolf', fully indicated genocidal intent, the Prosecutor was unwilling to dismiss the charge of genocide against Jelišić despite his admission to a total of 31 other crimes.[35] In the *Sikirica* case,[36] only the most senior ranking of the three defendants, Duško Sikirica, was charged with genocide. Pursuant to a Defense motion in accordance with Rule 98*bis* after the close of the Prosecution's case-in-chief, the Trial Chamber dismissed the charges of genocide against Sikirica. Subsequently, one of Sikirica's co-defendants changed his plea and pled guilty to persecutions as a crimes against humanity. Like falling dominos, the remaining defendants soon approached the Prosecutor seeking a plea bargain. Sikirica also agreed to pled guilty to persecutions as a crimes against humanity. The Prosecutor accepted his plea offer, but made very clear that it would not have accepted his plea while the charges of genocide were still pending against him.[37] As in the *Jelisić* case, the Prosecutor again signals its unwillingness to compromise to plea bargains by way of charge reduction when the accused's criminal responsibility encompasses the crime of genocide.

In sum, the ICTY's early jurisprudence and practice seems to indicate that reconciliation was not a central issue in sentencing and that the Prosecution was

---

33 For an early commentary on the ICTY Statute *see*, V. Morris and M. Scharf (1995), *An Insider's Guide to the International Criminal Tribunal for the former Yugoslavia: A Documentary History and Analysis* (New York: Transnational Publishers).

34 *Erdemović Sentencing Judgement*, para. 58. In comparison, in the *Plavšić* case, the concept of reconciliation appears no less than 27 times in the sentencing judgement.

35 *Jelisić Trial Judgement*, para. 102.

36 For a commentary on this case see W. Schabas (2005), *Commentary* in: A. Klip and G. Sluiter (eds), Annotated Leading Cases of International Criminal Tribunals, Vol. VIII, p. 1078 (Antwerp: Intersentia).

37 *Prosecutor v Sikirica, Došen and Kolundžija, Sentencing Judgement*, Case No. IT-95-8-S, 13 November 2001, para. 24.

unwilling to bargain away the charge of genocide. The *Plavšić* case[38] reversed the trajectory on both matters.[39] It was the first time the Prosecutor willingly dropped the charges of genocide against an accused in return for her guilty plea. Moreover, it marked the coming of age of 'reconciliation' as it proved an influential force in mitigating Biljana Plavšić's sentence.

ICTY Practice Takes a New Turn: The Plavšić Case and the Deronjić Case

The *Plavšić* case and *Deronjić* case illustrate the increasing willingness of the ICTY Prosecutor to negotiate the crime of genocide in two different contexts. In the *Plavšić* case, the Prosecutor willingly dismissed the charge of genocide against the accused in turn for her guilty plea to one count of persecutions as a crime against humanity.[40] The *Deronjić* case involves a compromise on genocide in a manner that is less transparent: allegation preemption. Although Deronjić was not charged with genocide, there is ample credible evidence to support the charge.

In the *Plavšić* case, the indictment charged the accused with genocide and complicity in genocide.[41] Subsequently, the Prosecutor agreed to dismiss with prejudice the charge of genocide and complicity in genocide, as well as all remaining counts of indictment, in exchange for Plavšić's agreement to pled guilty to the crime of persecutions as a crime against humanity.[42] It will be interesting to ponder whether these concessions by the Prosecutor could possibly tie its hand in future cases, for example, in prosecuting Radovan Karadžić when, and if, he is apprehended and handed over to the Tribunal. The indictment against Plavšić alleged that she was 'a member of the three-member Presidency of the Serbian republic' with Karadžić as the 'elected President of the Presidency' and that together, along with others, they constituted the 'the Supreme Command of the armed forces of the Serbian republic [of Bosnia and Herzegovina]'.[43] How far now can the Prosecutor push the case of genocide against Karadžić, having dropped the genocide and complicity in genocide charges against Plavšić? Will it be accepted that Karadzić is criminally responsible for genocide and the policies from the leadership that allowed this crime to occur while another member of the Presidency had charges of complicity in genocide

---

38 *Prosecutor v Plavšić, Sentencing Judgement*, Case No. IT-00-39&40/1-S, 27 February 2003 (hereafter '*Plavšić Sentencing Judgement*').

39 For further critique of the *Plavšić Sentencing Judgement see* S. Dana (forthcoming) *Turning Point in International Criminal Prosecutions* in A. Klip and G. Sluiter (eds), Annotated Leading Cases of International Criminal Tribunals, Vol. XI, (Antwerp: Intersentia).

40 Local reactions appear to perceive Plavšić's guilty plea as a failure to fully account for the atrocities. *See*, M. Saponja-Hadzic (2003), 'Hague Deals Reduce Impact', Institute of War and Peace Reporting (IWPR), 24 July 2003, http://www.iwpr.net/?p=tri&s=f&o=164725&apc_state=henitri2003.

41 *Prosecutor v Plavšić, Indictment,* Case No. IT-00-40-I, 3 April 2000 (hereafter '*Plavšić Indictment*'), Count 1 (Genocide) and Count 2 (Complicity in Genocide).

42 *Prosecutor v Krajinik & Plavsic, Plea Agreement*, Case No. IT-00-39&40-PT, 30 September 2002 (filed *ex parte* confidential and under seal). This document is available and on file with the author.

43 *Plavšić Indictment*, paras. 4–5.

against her dropped?[44] Will the outcome be accepted as 'truth', presumably so vital for the reconciliation process?

The reasons for dismissing the charges of genocide against Plavšić are not accounted for and this lack of transparency may itself undermine the goal of reconciliation. The observer is left to infer that it must have been the result of a deal with the Prosecution. Thus, not only is reconciliation apparently compromised but so to is the goal of truth-finding and establishing a historical record to prevent revisionism. There may very well be principled grounds justifying the dropping of genocide charges but, recalling the euphemism 'justice must not only be done, but seen to be done', those reasons are not apparent to the observer.

Whereas the discussion concerning the dropping of charges of genocide is notably absent, a lengthy discussion of Plavšić's purported contribution to reconciliation is ever present and appears to have an appreciable impact on reducing Plavšić's penalty. If presented as a 'short story', Plavšić's case is quite perplexing: Based on the initial evidence, she was charged with genocide. She came to court. She negotiated with the Prosecutor. She confessed that she was wrong. The genocide charges were dropped. She pled guilty to other crimes and publicly stated that 'yes, atrocities occurred' and that she, in part, was responsible. She was sentenced to 11 years and sent to a prison in Sweden. The question begs: how is it that someone who was initially charged with genocide ends up receiving 11 years?

In the case of Miroslav Deronjić, the concern arises whether prosecution of genocide was compromised as the result of a watered-down presentation of the accused's criminal responsibility, prompting one judge to open his dissenting opinion with '*da mihi factum, dabo tibi jus*'.[45] The dissenting judge's principle concern was that the facts presented to the court in the final plea agreement were so trimmed down, so calculated in its presentation, that it raised serious concerns about whether it presented the truth about the atrocities. The dissenting judge wrote 'the series of indictments, including the Second Amended Indictment, arbitrarily present facts, selected from the context of a larger criminal plan and, for unknown reasons, limited to one day and to the village of Glogova only'. With only an abridged presentation of the facts relevant to the accused's criminal responsibility, international judges are put in a precarious position in their duty to achieve justice in sentencing. It also undermines the goal of reconciliation[46] which is seen not only as part of the Tribunal's mandate, but has also been relied on to justify the practice of plea bargaining. Moreover, although there was only one voice in dissent, the majority also appeared to have the same concerns as they went to great lengths to repeatedly

---

44 It is interesting to further consider these questions in light of the jurisprudence on aiding and abetting in the *Krstić* case *see*, *Prosecutor v Krstić*, *Judgement*, Case No. IT-98-33-A, 19 April 2004 (hereafter '*Krstić Appeals Judgement*'). Even assuming that Plavšić personally lacked the *mens rea* necessary for the crime of genocide (i.e. intent to destroy the group as such), she arguably could still have been convicted for aiding and abetting in the commission of genocide because the 'aiding and abetting' mode of criminal responsibility does not require the intent to destroy.

45 Literally, 'give me [all] the facts and I will give you justice'.

46 The Tribunal's jurisprudence acknowledges the importance of 'full disclosure' to the achievement of reconciliation. *See, Plavšić Sentencing Judgement*, para. 77.

emphasise that the accused is being punished only for his conduct on that one day and that the principle of *ne bis in idem* is accordingly limited. The dissenting judge further questioned why the accused had not been indicted 'as a co-perpetrator in the joint criminal enterprise leading to the horrific massacre at Srebrenica in 1995'. In this judge's opinion, there was sufficient grounds to so indict Deronjić, based on his own confession. At minimum, he could have been held criminally responsible for aiding and abetting in the crime of genocide as General Krstić was for his role in the Srebrenica genocide.[47]

Although the Prosecution was unwilling to charge Deronjić with the crime of genocide, it had no problem characterizing his conduct as 'ethnic cleansing':

> [t]he crime for which Miroslav Deronjić is to be sentenced is precisely the type of crime about which the Security Council expressed its grave alarm in Resolution 808. The events in Glogova on the 9th of May 1992 are a classical case of ethnic cleansing, and precisely the reason why the Security Council established this Tribunal. The attack on Glogova was not an isolated or random event, but a critical element in a larger scheme to divide Bosnia and Herzegovina and create Serb-ethnic territories.[48]

However, 'ethnic cleansing' as such is not listed as a crime under the Statute of ICTY, nor is there a settled juridical definition of 'ethnic cleansing'. Thus, lacking legal effect, the question arises why does the Prosecutor rely on this characterization when presenting the accused's criminal conduct before the trial chamber? It could be perceived as 'damage control' by the Prosecution in the eyes of the public after having compromised on holding the accused fully accountable. Is it seeking to appease victim communities in those regions affected Deronjić's crimes?

When you combine Deronjić's admissions of his criminal conduct with the Prosecutor's assessment (that this is a 'classical case of ethnic cleansing'), it is not difficult to share in the dissenting judge's concerns. What is the reason for the Prosecution's limited presentation – or to borrow the words of the dissenting judge, 'clinically clean compilation of selected facts'?[49] There is not sufficient transparency in the process to say. Perhaps there was insufficient evidence to establish the requisite *mens rea* of 'intent to destroy', although this would not have been necessary for criminal liability as an aider and abettor to the crime of genocide.[50] Unfortunately, an equally plausible explanation is that the limited accounting of Deronjić's crimes resulted from a special deal offered by the Prosecution. While there may be compelling reasons for offering such a deal,[51] these reasons remain obscured. Even if we can accept that in order to 'break the circle of silence' certain limited concessions must be made to an accused, such matters should be openly disclosed by the Prosecutor to the Trial Chamber.

---

47 *See, Krstić Appeals Judgement*, *supra* note 45.

48 *Deronjić Sentencing Judgement*, para. 179.

49 *Deronjić Sentencing Judgement*, *Schomberg Dissent*, para. 9.

50 *See, Krstić Appeals Judgement*, *supra* note 40.

51 Such as breaking the circle of silence among the leadership or providing limited concessions to low-level perpetrators in order to secure convictions against more culpable perpetrators.

This lack of transparency creates a number of significant problems. First, it has the potential to create the undesirable perception among the public, in particular among the communities broken by the conflict, that justice has been inexplicably compromised and that an individual has not been adequately held accountable. Second, the aim of contributing towards reconciliation is undermined. As experts before the Tribunal have testified, full accountability and disclosure are critical to the achievement of reconciliation.[52] Unexplained compromises on issues of such importance generates suspicion and damaging speculation that the International Tribunal is biased in favor of one party to the conflict or has no real interest in justice or reconciliation but is simply there to appease the guilty conscience of an international community that failed to take measures within its powers to prevent the atrocities. Third, it places judges in a difficult position of having to determine an appropriate punishment on the basis of an incomplete record that does not sufficiently reflect the individual's culpability. A sanction that appears unjust because it is too lenient can in turn hamper the achievement of not only reconciliation, but also other goals such as justice, adequate deterrence, and just retribution. Finally, the desire of preserving an accurate historical record of the atrocities is likewise jeopardized by partial accounting that obscures the individual's involvement or the gravity of the crimes. This is not to suggest that reconciliation or preserving a historical record are the most important considerations in the operation of a criminal court. Rather, the point is to recall that, because the Tribunal itself considers these aims as part of its mandate, it should avoid a practice that would undermine them.

Moreover, serious deficiencies in the presentation of an accused's criminal conduct and related atrocities, whether resulting from charge reduction or allegation preemption, undermine the ICTY's justification for plea bargaining which seeks to link this common law practice to the objectives of international prosecution and the mandate of the International Tribunals:

> The Trial Chamber finds that, in contrast to national legal systems where the reasons for mitigating a punishment on the basis of a guilty plea are of a more pragmatic nature, the rationale behind the mitigating effect of a guilty plea in this Tribunal is much broader, including the fact that the accused contributes to establishing the truth about the conflict in the former Yugoslavia and contributes to reconciliation in the affected communities. The Trial Chamber recalls that the Tribunal has the task to contribute to the "restoration and maintenance of peace" and to ensure that serious violations of international humanitarian law are "halted and effectively redressed".[53]

The Trial Chamber's confidence in the contribution of a guilty plea to the objectives of 'establishing the truth' and 'contributing to reconciliation' hinges precariously on the veracity and completeness of the admissions underlying the guilty plea. The Trial Chamber's unabated endorsement of guilty pleas here would lead one to conclude that all guilty pleas naturally aid the process of truth-finding

---

52 *Plavšić Sentencing Judgement*, para. 77.
53 *Deronjić Sentencing Judgement*, para. 236.

and reconciliation without qualification.[54] In reality, it is not the guilty plea itself that can make a meaningful contribution to the process of international justice, but instead a number of other factors, such as the quality of the statements underlying the plea, the degree of frankness in the accused's disclosure and his willingness to tell the truth about his own conduct, accept responsibility, and provide, to the fullest of his knowledge, information concerning the conduct of his peers and superiors, his willingness to give evidence in trials against them and fully cooperate with the Prosecution and the International Tribunal.

Considerations for Improving International Sentencing Practice

In light of the foregoing, it is suggested that international prosecutors adopt a reverent approach towards charging the crime of genocide and that international judges follow a cautious approach towards the influence of reconciliation ideology in the determination of a penalty. In light of limitations on the length of this presentation, only a few words will be said about the former and the focus of the remainder of this presentation will be on the latter.

While charge reduction in the process of obtaining a criminal's admission to certain crimes is a common feature of some national systems, careful reflection must be exercised on whether this is an appropriate practice in relation to the crime of genocide in international criminal justice. The accusation of genocide cannot be compared to charges of ordinary crimes in the domestic context. Using the crime of genocide as a bargaining chip can have a demoralizing effect on post-conflict communities and the process of reconciliation. Moreover, if it is accepted that developing a historical record is within the mandate of international criminal courts, then charging the crime of genocide and subsequently dismissing it can greatly undermine confidence in the judgements as historical records, especially because the current practice of the ICTY lacks transparency regarding the reasons for the removal of charges or allegations.

As for reconciliation, as noted above, the concept was not a significant factor in the ICTY's early sentencing practice. However, since the Plavšić Sentencing Judgment, it has received frequent consideration by trial chambers. In the Plavšić case, it exerted a significant influence in mitigating her punishment resulting in a very lenient sentence, a criticism that many commentators have regarding ICTY sentences in general.[55] As it has done with other factors such as deterrence and rehabilitation, the Appeals Chamber should likewise encourage a cautious approach towards awarding significant sentencing discounts on the basis of 'contribution towards reconciliation'. Caution here is justified both morally and pragmatically.

At this stage, the ICTY's jurisprudence appears to suggest that the benefits of mitigation on the basis of 'contribution toward reconciliation' is disproportionately

---

54 *Cf.*, Ralph Henham (2005), 'Plea Bargaining and the Legitimacy of International Trial Justice: Some Observations on the Dragan Nikolic Sentencing Judgement of the ICTY', 5 *International Criminal Law Review*, p. 601.

55 M. Bagaric and J. Morss (2006), 'International Sentencing Law: In Search of a Justification and Coherent Framework', 6 *International Criminal Law Review*, p. 191.

bestowed upon perpetrators who held high ranking or leadership positions, like for example Plavšić. Both the Defense and the Prosecution emphasized the significance of Plavšić's superior position in the Bosnian Serb leadership in relation to contributing to reconciliation.[56] The arguments effectively turned on its head the consequence of superior position, which had thus far been a significant aggravating factor. The Plavšić Trial Chamber appears to accept this line of reasoning linking the mitigating weight it affords to reconciliation to the accused's leadership position.[57] The perverse effect of this ruling is that the leaders who are most culpable for the atrocities are now placed in the best position to receive mitigation of their sentence under the label of 'reconciliation'. The suggestion that the ICTY gives greater weight to 'reconciliation' as a mitigating factor when sentencing high-level perpetrators than it does when dealing with punishment of low-level perpetrators is bolstered by the sentences imposed on Mirsolav Bralo[58] and Dragan Nikolić.[59]

The case against Bralo was initially one of war crimes. The charge of persecutions as a crime against humanity was added subsequently as a direct result of information Bralo himself provided to the Prosecution. Bralo did not oppose the Prosecution's amendment to the indictment which added persecutions as a crime against humanity as a new charge. Moreover, he did not challenge any of the other charges and pled guilty to the full indictment against him. Bralo's full acceptance of his criminal responsibility was considered as a strong indicator of his genuine remorse and desire to make amends for his crimes. In fact, Bralo was the first indictee from the Ahmići municipality to acknowledge and take responsibility for the atrocities in that region. The manner of a war criminal's acceptance of criminal responsibility is critical to any hopes of reconciliation.[60] Bralo and Plavšić provide contrasting examples. Whereas Bralo accepted full responsibility for his conduct, even beyond crimes alleged in his initial indictment, Plavšić maneuvered a careful plea bargain and was the beneficiary of a reduction in charges (significantly the dropping of genocide charges), accepting responsibility for only a portion of the crimes against her.

Both Plavšić and Bralo, as well as Dragan Nikolić, pled guilty to persecutions as a crime against humanity. In each case, the trial chamber accepted that the accused had made a contribution towards reconciliation. Indeed, Bralo's contribution to reconciliation can be described as 'direct' reconciliatory acts, including apologies to victims, assisting in locating and exhuming bodies, and volunteering for de-mining operations. However, Bralo and Nikolić, comparatively lower level perpetrators, did not receive as much mitigation for their contribution towards reconciliation as the

---

56 Transcript, *Plavšić* Sentencing Hearing, p. 649; *Plavšić Sentencing Judgement*, para. 70.

57 *Plavšić Sentencing Judgement*, para. 70.

58 *Prosecutor v Bralo, Sentencing Judgement*, IT-95-17-S, 7 December 2005.

59 I do not intend to suggest that a camp commander, such as Dragan Nikolić, is *per se* a low level perpetrator; only that in relation to Plavšić, he held a lower position in the political structure of the Bosnian Serb leadership and had a lesser role in the overall context of the conflict.

60 Dana, *Turning Point, supra* note 40.

senior figure Plavšić appears to have received.[61] Given that the former two received imprisonment terms of 20 and 23 years respectively, while Plavšić received only 11 years, it is difficult to rebut the suggestion that the ICTY disproportionately awards more penalty reduction for reconciliation to high level perpetrators.

The relatively lenient sentence imposed on Plavšić compared to the more severe penalty visited upon Bralo and Nikolić is even more difficult to defend if one considers that both Bralo and Nikolić cooperated with the Prosecution. The ICTY sentencing jurisprudence considers 'cooperation with the Prosecution' as a significant mitigating factor. While this factor is wholly absent in the *Plavšić* case, both Bralo and Nikolić were found to have provided cooperation with the Prosecutor. Moreover, cooperation with the International Prosecutor may itself be considered as a form of 'contribution towards reconciliation' and deliberate non-cooperation may undermine the accused's purported efforts towards reconciliation to the extent of rendering it as an insignificant factor.[62]

The troubling possibility that high-level perpetrators receive more favorable sentencing discounts when reconciliation is mitigating factor is not limited to the approach of the trial chambers. The ICTY Prosecutor, perhaps unwittingly, appears to support this approach as suggested by both its argumentation and sentencing recommendation. The Prosecutor took the position that Plavšić's contribution to reconciliation as a result of her 'expression of remorse is noteworthy *since it is offered from a person who formerly held a leadership position*, and that it "merits judicial consideration"'.[63] Thus, the Prosecutor links the mitigating value of an accused contribution to reconciliation to her superior position.

Moreover, the Prosecutor's sentencing recommendations further reinforce the suggestion that it offers greater concessions to high-ranking perpetrators when reconciliation is a factor. In the *Plavšić* case, the Prosecutor recommended a sentence of 25 years and stated at the sentencing hearing that had Plavšić not pled guilty it would have sought life imprisonment. Thus, Plavšić's guilty plea, expression of remorse, contribution towards reconciliation, *inter alia*, had the effect of reducing the appropriate punishment in the eyes of the Prosecutor from life imprisonment to 25 years. If Plavšić had been sentenced to 25 years, she most likely would have been

---

61 This proposition is necessarily qualified because the *Plavšić* Trial Chamber does not state what the penalty would have been in the absence of this mitigation factor. The general sentencing practice of ICTY trial chambers does not include the practice of making explicit what the penalty would have been in the absence of mitigating factors. One exception, among others, is the *Bralo* Trial Chamber which clarified that, in the absence of mitigating factors, the accused would have been sentenced to 25 years. The reduction of the penalty by 5 years, however, encompasses consideration of all mitigating factors. *Bralo Sentencing Judgement*, para. 95.

62 For further analysis *see*, Dana, *Turning Point*, *supra* note 40. The sincerity of Plavšić's remorse, and consequently the vitality of her contribution towards reconciliation, appear to have been damaged by an interview she gave while serving her sentence. *See*, Transcription of interview with Biljana Plavšić on Banja Luka ATV, 11 March 2005 available at http://www.atvbl.com/home.php?id=billjanaintervju. An unofficial English translation by the ICTY Outreach Office in Sarajevo is available on file with the author.

63 *Plavšić Sentencing Judgement*, para. 70 (emphasis added).

released after serving a little more than 16.5 years, pursuant to the ICTY practice of granting early release after two-thirds of the sentence has been enforced. In the end, however, the Trial Chamber went below the Prosecutor's recommendation, sentencing her to only 11 years.

In the *Bralo* case, the Prosecution also recommended a sentence of 25 years' imprisonment. Significantly however, in contrast to the *Plavšić* case, the Prosecution clarified at the sentencing hearing that they were in fact seeking a 'mandatory minimum' of 25 years.[64] Given the Tribunal's practice of enforcing only two-third of the sentence, the Prosecution's position would require an absolute sentence of 37.5 years. In light of the fact that reconciliation was a mitigating factor in both cases and that only in Bralo's case was cooperation with the Prosecution found it be a mitigation factor, it is quite puzzling why the Prosecution would seek a heavier penalty against Bralo.

Conclusion

This presentation began with an attempt to put into context the 'role of sentencing in preventing genocide'. It was acknowledged that, in relation to other mechanisms available, the institution of punishment plays a relatively modest role in preventing genocide. Nevertheless, inept sentencing policies can undermine the aims of international criminal justice. Accordingly, the presentation sought to address some of the challenges facing international judges when determining a penalty for international crimes such as genocide. It is hoped that some of the recommendations may help bridge the gap between the proffered justifications for international sentences and the aspired goals of international prosecutions. The focus has been on sentences resulting from plea bargains, especially where the crime of genocide has been bargained away either explicitly by removal of charges of genocide or implicitly by removal of factual allegations that may support the charge of genocide. In this context, the impact of reconciliation ideology in international sentencing has been addressed.

The trial chambers' current approach of reducing the sentence due to finding reconciliation as a mitigating factor unwittingly favors high-ranking perpetrators. In other words, the 'big fish' appear to be receiving greater reduction in their punishment than the 'small fry' when weighing the impact of reconciliation as a mitigating factor. In the eyes of the public, the principle of equality before the law is compromised. Moreover, this approach arguably fails to proportionately reflect the culpability of high-ranking officials in the perpetration of the atrocities.

Regarding the usage of reconciliation ideology as a factor mitigating punishment, the paper advocates a cautious approach. In the past, the Appeal Chamber has called for caution in relation to the influence of other ideological factors on the determination of a sentence, such as deterrence or rehabilitation. It held that consideration for deterrence or rehabilitation should not unduly influence the penalty imposed. In light

---

64 *Bralo Sentencing Judgement*, para. 90.

of the current trend in the jurisprudence on reconciliation, it would be timely for the Appeal Chamber to make a similar ruling on reconciliation.

Index